WATER LAW

SECOND EDITION

ROBIN KUNDIS CRAIG
Robert A. Schroeder Distinguished Professor
University of Kansas School of Law

ROBERT W. ADLER
Dean Emeritus and Distinguished Professor Emeritus
S.J. Quinney College of Law, University of Utah

NOAH D. HALL
Professor of Law
Wayne State University Law School

CONCEPTS AND INSIGHTS SERIES®

FOUNDATION PRESS

860 Blue Gentian Road, Suite 350
Eagan, MN 55121
1-877-888-1330

Published in the United States of America

ISBN: 978-1-68561-114-9

This book is dedicated to all those who learn and study water law, the students who will shape future law and policy to reflect evolving values and challenges regarding our most important natural resource.

ACKNOWLEDGMENTS

We would like to thank the last several years of our Water Law students at the University of Utah S.J. Quinney College of Law, the Wayne State University School of Law, and the USC Gould School of Law who have very much helped to shape how the three of us think about and teach Water Law, and who provided us with their own insights into water law during class discussions. Professor Hall would especially like to thank his former research assistants for their contributions, Sabra Bushey (Wayne Law, '17) and Emily Petrovski (Wayne Law, '24).

SUMMARY OF CONTENTS

TABLE OF CONTENTS

WATER LAW

SECOND EDITION

Chapter 1

INTRODUCTION TO WATER LAW

Water law governs the right to use fresh water, including both surface water—the water in lakes, rivers, and streams—and groundwater. (Coastal states might also use water law to regulate withdrawals of ocean water, such as for cooling water at power plants, but that is a far less important aspect of water law.) In most respects, water law is a form of property law, but the rules governing property rights in water differ greatly from the rules governing ownership of land. Moreover, some aspects of water law incorporate principles of tort law as well. In particular, it is rare to speak of water "ownership." Because water is usually a flowing resource, water rights are characterized as ***usufructuary rights***—that is, as a right to use rather than title ownership.

However, water law also has aspects of public law. Water sustains human life and is an important in-place environmental resource, and thus it has crucial value to the public. As a result, water law is characterized by tension between private use rights and public ownership, management, and protection. Water law in the United States has evolved over time to acknowledge the changing human uses for, and valuation of, water resources. More recently, international human rights law has influenced water law to address inequities in access to adequate supplies of safe water for human use. The evolution of water rights, and the forces that influence that evolution, are the subjects of this book.

This chapter first provides an overview of the three sections that comprise this book. It then surveys critical background information on aquatic systems, hydrology, water use, water quality and ecosystem health, climate change, and the human right to water.

A. Overview of This Book

Part I of this book explores the evolution and current state of private rights to the use of water, beginning with ***surface water*** use and withdrawals. Chapter 2 examines the ***doctrine of riparian rights***, a common-law doctrine that functions as the basis of water rights in most eastern states. However, a ***hydrological divide***, running roughly along the 100th Meridian (see Figure 1–1), divides the United States into two basic precipitation regimes: the humid East, where rainfall historically has been sufficient to support agriculture without irrigation; and the arid West, in most portions of which irrigation has been necessary for agriculture. These meteorological and ecological differences are reflected in state water law. As Chapter 3 explains, western states largely rejected eastern riparianism in favor of the ***doctrine of prior appropriation*** for water rights in surface water.

Figure 1–1: The United States Hydrologic Divide

Image courtesy of the South Dakota Department of Environmental and Natural Resources

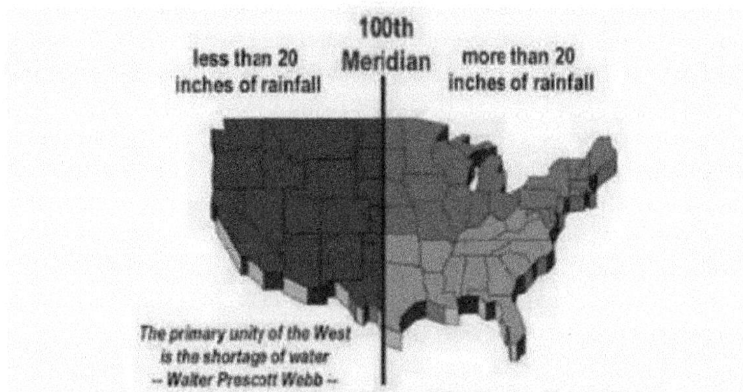

The evolution of private ***groundwater rights*** is detailed in Chapter 4. States have used at least five different legal doctrines to govern private rights in groundwater, and many states have changed groundwater doctrines over time as the deficiencies of particular doctrines became increasingly apparent and as pressures to integrate surface water and groundwater law mounted.

States have also developed the structure and processes of water law. Chapter 5 examines how states have created and implemented statutory water codes, administrative permitting schemes, and water planning to replace the pure common law of water rights. These statutes, permitting regimes, and plans generally provide states with better tools to understand and control the use of both groundwater and surface water within their borders. However, they can also provide states with the means to change certain substantive aspects of the common law.

Following this exploration of private water rights, Part II moves to consider the public rights and interests in water that make the field of water law unique. Chapter 6 looks at the federal government's paramount interest in protecting ***navigation*** and explores both the many doctrines that serve that goal and the federal government's authority to regulate water uses. Chapter 7 examines the ***public trust doctrine***, under which states protect the general public's rights to use water for a variety of purposes, such as commerce, fishing, and recreation. The federal government holds water rights in trust for Indian tribes and federal lands, known as ***federal reserved***

water rights, and international water treaties impose legal obligations on the federal government, all of which are the subjects of Chapter 8. Finally, Chapter 9 covers ***interstate water management***, exploring the doctrines and policies that allocate waters shared between and among states.

The final section of the book explores the intersections of traditional water law and modern energy and environmental policies and laws. Chapter 10 looks at the links between water use and energy policy, known as the ***water-energy nexus***, suggesting that the United States needs to better coordinate water and energy law. Environmental protections have wrought considerable changes in how fresh water is managed in the United States, from water quality standards and pollutant discharge requirements under the ***Clean Water Act*** (Chapter 11), to protections for aquatic species under the ***Endangered Species Act*** (Chapter 12), and finally to increased attention to systemwide, watershed-level protection and restoration of aquatic ecosystems (Chapter 13). However, the increased legal attention to the *public* values inherent in waterways, watersheds, and aquatic ecosystems has also created numerous tensions and conflicts with private rights, leading to the complex realm of water rights ***constitutional takings*** cases explored in Chapter 14.

In order to study the development of water law, however, it is necessary to first understand some fundamentals of how water works in nature, how humans use water, and what pressures humans are putting on the country's water resources. This chapter thus begins by introducing the basis of hydrology and the water cycle. It then provides an overview of how humans use water and affect both water quality and the health of aquatic ecosystems, in the United States and globally. It also addresses the ways in which climate change is altering the availability, timing, and quality of water resources in the United States, resulting in the newest and potentially most significant challenge to the evolution of water law. The chapter concludes with one of the newest developments in water law, the relatively new recognition of a human right to water.

B. The Aquatic Cycle and Basic Concepts of Hydrology

The ***water cycle*** describes the interconnected movement of all water on Earth. The major transfers of water occur between water in the atmosphere, surface water, and groundwater. As water vapor in the air condensates and falls as precipitation, water is widely distributed. Precipitation that collects in mountains can reach surface water by traveling through streamflow or as surface or snowmelt runoff. Water that infiltrates the ground will either become stored as groundwater or be absorbed by plants, or in some cases seep into surface water from springs. (For a detailed examination of the hydrologic cycle as it relates to groundwater, see Chapter 4.) When groundwater is discharged into nearby waterbodies, heat triggers the evaporation process that reincorporates water into the atmosphere. Similarly, water absorbed by plants is released and also reenters the atmosphere through transpiration.[1] Although some water moves through this cycle relatively quickly, much of the globe's water is stored for longer periods of time in glaciers and polar icecaps and in deep or geologically isolated aquifers.

In the absence of this interconnectedness, the movement of water would not be possible. However, the close nexus between each hydrological process makes the entire water cycle responsive to slight changes in any one process. Both natural forces and human activities can cause these changes. The United Nations Educational, Scientific and Cultural Organization (UNESCO) has linked several human activities to changes in runoff, infiltration, and evaporation:

- Deforestation increases runoff and disturbs groundwater recharge
- Hydroelectric dams divert water from downstream rivers and lakes
- Agricultural activities reduce the water-holding capacity of soil, which leads to greater runoff
- Urbanization and the expansion of paved surface areas reduce infiltration
- The large surface areas of reservoirs accelerate the evaporation process[2]

Moreover, the impact on the water cycle is compounded by human activities that must constantly change in response to fluctuations in water availability and demand compound impacts on the hydrological cycle. When there is adequate precipitation, agricultural areas rely less on irrigation systems, resulting in lower groundwater pumping rates. However, these rates can increase suddenly in times of drought. Additionally, human-controlled reservoir releases increase and decrease the flow of water in response to highs and lows in water demand. When water demand constantly shifts, it "may cause high flows and low flows to differ considerably

---

1 U.S. Geological Survey, *Summary of the Water Cycle*, https://www.usgs.gov/special-topics/water-science-school/science/water-cycle.

2 UNITED NATIONS EDUCATIONAL, SCIENTIFIC AND CULTURAL ORGANIZATION (UNESCO), THE UNITED NATIONS WORLD WATER DEVELOPMENT REPORT 4: MANAGING WATER UNDER UNCERTAINTY AND RISK, Vol. 1 (2012).

in magnitude and timing compared to natural flows."[3] Changes in the earth's climate also affect the hydrologic cycle, as will be explored in more detail in Section E of this chapter. As a result, the natural equilibrium of the water cycle is in a constant state of flux.

C. Water Use in the United States and Globally

We use water in every aspect of our economy and lives. Nonconsumptive water uses, such as navigation and boating, fishing, recreation, and ecosystem health, create demand to keep water in natural watercourses. Consumptive water uses are often described by sector (domestic, agricultural, energy, and industrial) and create pressure to withdraw and divert water from its natural watercourse. To better understand the legal pressure on water, we must start with information on current water uses. The following government reports examine the ways in which water is put to use, along with the effects of limited access to water resources on human welfare, security, and broader domestic and global issues.

The U.S. Department of the Interior's report, "Estimated Use of Water in the United States in 2015,"[4] outlines how demographics, new manufacturing and cooling-system technologies, economic trends, legal decisions, and climatic fluctuations impact water supplies and their uses.

Between 2010 and 2015, population in the United States increased 4 percent, or approximately 12 million people, from 313 million people in 2010 to 325 million people in 2015. Such great population growth puts additional pressure on existing public utilities and increases demand on sometimes already limited water supplies. In response to these pressures, communities have sought additional water sources or implemented water-conservation measures.

The Department of the Interior's report estimated total water withdrawals in the United States for 2015 for eight categories of use: public supply, domestic, irrigation, livestock, aquaculture, industrial, mining, and thermoelectric-power generation. Until about 1965, withdrawals of water for agricultural use were the largest industrial category of withdrawals, but since then withdrawals for thermoelectric power has been the largest category of water withdrawal, followed by irrigation and public supply. However, agriculture remains the largest *consumer* of water, underscoring an important distinction in water law between *water withdrawals* and

---

[3] Thomas C. Winter, et al., *U.S. Geological Survey, Circular 1139, Groundwater and Surface Water: A Single Resource* 69 (1998).

[4] Cheryl A. Dieter, et al., *U.S. Dep't of the Interior, Circular 1441, Estimated Use of Water in the United States in 2015* (2018).

consumptive use. Power plants, for example, need to withdraw a lot of water for cooling, but many of them also return most of that water to the stream in the form of *return flow*, which then can be used again downstream. The 2015 estimates put total withdrawals at the lowest level since before 1970, following the same overall trend of decreasing total withdrawals observed from 2005 to 2010.

Figure 1-2: Trends in Water Use, 1950—2015

Graphic courtesy of the U.S. Geological Survey

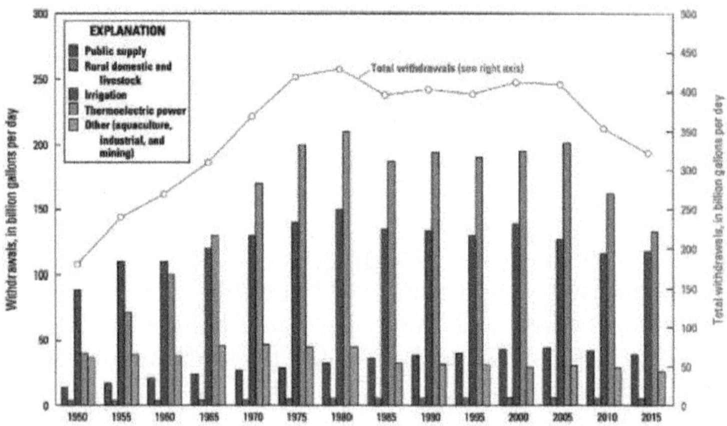

Public supply refers to water withdrawn by public and private water suppliers that provide water to at least 25 people or have a minimum of 15 connections. An estimated 283 million people—about 87 percent of the total U.S. population—rely on public water supplies for their household use. Unsurprisingly, states with the largest populations (California, Texas, New York, and Florida) withdraw the largest amounts of water for public supply. About 61% of the water withdrawn for public supply in 2015 came from surface sources, such as lakes and streams; the remainder came from groundwater. Of the total public-supply water, most is delivered to customers for domestic, commercial, and industrial needs. Part of the total, often unbilled, is used for public services, such as pools, parks, firefighting, water and wastewater treatment, and municipal buildings.

Irrigation water use includes water that is applied by an irrigation system to plants in agricultural and horticultural operations. As of 2015, total irrigation withdrawals were about 118,000 million gallons per day, or 132 million acre-feet per year, in the United States. (An ***acre-foot*** is a measure of water quantity often used for agricultural irrigation water. It is the amount of water that can cover one acre of land to a depth of one foot. One acre-foot of water equals 325,851 gallons.)

Industrial water use includes water used for such purposes as fabricating, processing, washing, diluting, cooling, or transporting a product; incorporating water into a product; or for sanitation needs within the manufacturing facility. Industrial water withdrawals accounted for about 5 percent of total withdrawals in 2015.

Water for thermoelectric power is used in generating electricity with steam-driven turbine generators and for power plant cooling. Thermoelectric-power withdrawals accounted for 41 percent of the United States' total water use in 2015.

Reports produced by the Office of the Director of National Intelligence[5] and the United Nations Educational, Scientific and Cultural Organization (UNESCO)[6] similarly discuss the effects of increased global water demand on human welfare, security, and other domestic and global issues. The reports estimate that by 2050, global water demand will increase by 20–50 percent. Population growth, lifestyle changes, socio-economic development, and agricultural practices are identified as some key factors that will lead to this increased demand for fresh water.

In many parts of the world, populations already face water insecurity—defined as the availability of an acceptable quantity and quality of water for health, livelihoods, ecosystems, and production. As of 2020, about 2.1 billion people worldwide lack access to safe drinking water or reliable water service.

Anthropogenic degradation of landscapes and waterscapes as well as climate change are affecting the quantity, quality, and timing of water supplies. Poor governance and resource management, development practices, and agriculture are also likely to diminish the quantity and quality of water supplies in many parts of the world. Many industrial and infrastructure development practices, including overuse of groundwater, surface water diversions, large dams, unregulated mining and extractive industries, and urban development without adequate sanitation, erode water security by reducing soil capacity to store water, thereby decreasing groundwater recharge, and increasing evaporation, erosion, and pollution.

---

[5] The United States Office of the Director of National Intelligence, *The Future of Water: Water Insecurity Threatening Global Economic Growth, Political Stability*, NIC-2021-02489 (2021).

[6] The United Nations Educational, Scientific and Cultural Organization, *The United Nations World Water Development Report 2023: Partnerships and Cooperation for Water*, Paris: UNESCO (2023).

Declining water security almost always equates to a decrease in individual livelihoods, health, and overall wellbeing. Reduced water security during the next 20 years is also likely to harm businesses, industries, and the overall economic wellbeing of many countries. Water is essential for creating and maintaining jobs, with at least half of the global workforce employed in water and natural-resource dependent industries, including agriculture, forestry, fisheries, energy, manufacturing, recycling, construction, and transportation. Moreover, declining water security is likely to exacerbate existing social grievances and divisions, potentially triggering or worsening conflict between societal groups and industry sectors and increasing the risk of political instability. Given the intensification of water security risks and a more competitive geopolitical landscape, cooperation in combination with good water governance and management is likely to be more difficult to achieve in the years ahead.

D. Water Quality and Aquatic Ecosystem Health

Rivers, lakes, wetlands and other water bodies in the United States have been seriously degraded as a result of chemical pollution, physical alterations to aquatic ecosystems, habitat loss and degradation, invasive species, and other factors. According to a 2004 Environmental Protection Agency (EPA) report, there are 38,886 impaired water bodies throughout the country, and a total of 64,581 causes of impairment.[7] Leading sources of impairment were pathogens, mercury, sediment, other metals, nutrients, oxygen depletion, pH, temperature, habitat alteration, polychlorinated biphenyls (PCBs), turbidity, pesticides, and salinity.

This widespread contamination of surface waters can have impacts on human health. An average of 17 disease outbreaks per year from contaminated drinking water were reported in the United States between 1991 and 2002, resulting from inadequately treated water and distribution system contamination, and experts believe that many water-borne disease outbreaks are undetected or unreported. Those outbreaks caused almost a half-million reported illnesses, and 73 reported deaths. Further, fish advisories have become common because of bioaccumulation of contaminants such as mercury, PCBs, chlordane, dioxins, and DDT in fish species. These toxins accumulate in fat tissue, allowing higher-level predators to acquire body concentrations of contaminants that exceed the concentration of those same contaminants in the ambient water.

In addition, the EPA has concluded that 42 percent of the nation's streams are in poor biological condition, 25 percent in fair

---

[7] Robert W. Adler, *Freshwater: Sustaining Use by Protecting Ecosystems*, Chapter 14 *in* AGENDA FOR A SUSTAINABLE AMERICA (John C. Dernbach, ed. 2009).

condition, and only 28 percent in good biological condition (with 5 percent not assessed). The most significant causes of impairment were nutrients, riparian disturbance, streambed sediments, and loss or alteration of in-stream fish habitat and riparian vegetation.

Some progress has been made in protecting critical wetland resources in the United States, although these gains should be interpreted with caution. After decades of steady losses in the acreage of wetlands identified by the U.S. Fish and Wildlife Service (FWS) in the National Wetlands Inventory program, FWS recently reported the first ever national "net gain" in wetlands acreage of nearly 200,000 acres of wetlands between 1998 and 2004. However, net wetland acreage does not necessarily translate into wetlands functions and values. Most wetland gains from 1998 to 2004 reflected artificial freshwater ponds created as mitigation for the loss of natural wetlands of different kinds. In addition to this net shift in the percentage of wetlands of different types, the report notes that open ponds typically do not provide the same range of wetland values and functions as the kinds of wetlands they replaced.

E. Climate Change and Water Resources in the United States

As previously addressed in Part C, there is a limited supply of water resources, continually strained by increases in water demand and consumption. Part D demonstrated that these resources are further strained by pollution and other human impairment of freshwater and aquatic resources. Although water availability is largely affected by direct human influence, it is also affected by climate change. Climate change will alter the global hydrologic cycle as well as regional water supplies and quality. Uncertainty about the scope and extent of such impacts creates another challenge for modern water law.

A brief review of how climate change will affect regional water supplies demonstrates the pressures and challenges that the United States will face. Climate change is expected to lead to reductions in water supply in most regions in the United States, particularly the Southwest, Mountain West, and Southeast. Scientists predict significant loss of snowpack in the western mountains, a critically important source of natural water storage for California and other western states. As sea levels rise, salt water will intrude into surface freshwater supplies and aquifers along the Pacific, Atlantic, and Gulf coasts. Even the Great Lakes region, which has over 90 percent of the available surface freshwater in the United States, will experience water supply impacts from climate change. Groundwater supplies are also vulnerable to climate change, as evapotranspiration losses (the loss of water to the air through evaporation and plant transpiration) will drastically reduce aquifer recharge and storage. Expected increases in water demand resulting from higher temperatures will compound the loss of water supplies, unless new conservation and allocation policies are widely applied. As if those predictions were not dire enough, they take no account of the additional water demand in the energy sector that will accompany vigorous efforts to reduce carbon emissions, unless such energy demands are displaced through efficiency measures and are met with solar and other non-hydro renewable resources (see Chapter 10).

The warming of the Earth is evident in average global air and ocean temperatures. Polar snow and ice are melting, and the average sea level around the globe is rising. Not only is the Earth becoming warmer, but it is warming faster than at any time during the 20th century. Global mean surface temperatures increased by 1.33°F (0.74°C) over the period between 1906 and 2005. However, during the past fifty years, the rate of global warming has nearly doubled. Eleven of the last twelve years rank among the twelve warmest years on record since 1850.

The scientific consensus is that the increase in global average temperatures since the mid-20th century was caused by anthropogenic releases of greenhouse gases. Thus, it is quite probable that the changes to the global climate system during the 21st century will be larger than those observed during the 20th century. Over the next two decades, average global warming is forecast to be about 0.4°F (0.2°C) per decade. During the 21st century, the best estimates are that average global temperatures will increase by 3.2° to 7.2°F (1.8° to 4.0°C), with more intense warming occurring in most of North America and especially in the Arctic. Some regions, such as the southwestern United States, will see greater temperature increases than the North American average.

Similarly, climatologists anticipate increased temporal and regional variability in precipitation. The incidence of both floods and droughts will increase. One effect of the rising temperatures expected over the next century is that the atmosphere's capacity to hold moisture will go up. For every 1.8°F (1°C) increase in temperature, the water-holding capacity of the atmosphere increases 7 percent. Increased moisture in the atmosphere will lead to more intense precipitation events—even when the annual total amount of precipitation is slightly reduced.

The southwestern United States will become even more arid during the 21st century as the subtropical dry zone expands poleward. Over the next century, temperatures in the American West are expected to increase by 3.6° to 9°F (2° to 5°C). In addition to the generally hotter climate, the western and southwestern United

States will be particularly affected by reduced snowpack in the mountains. The loss of snowpack will reduce the availability of water for California and the other Colorado River basin states (Arizona, Colorado, Nevada, New Mexico, Utah, and Wyoming). Under warmer climate conditions, such as those expected during the next century, precipitation will be more likely to fall as rain than snow. This trend is already observable, as the volume of snowpack has been dropping over much of the American West since 1925 and especially since 1950.

The eastern and southeastern United States will become warmer and more humid over the next century. Depending on location within the region, temperatures are expected to increase anywhere from 2.0° to 5.6°F (1.1° to 3.1°C) by mid-century. Precipitation is also expected to increase (by between 5 percent and 8 percent), but, at the same time, increasing evapotranspiration will pull much of the new moisture into the air. In addition, the southeastern United States will experience a greater clustering of storms over the next century.

The future changes in temperature and precipitation portend several challenges related to agriculture. Soils will become drier if the higher temperature projections are correct. Evapotranspiration would then increase, creating demand for more extensive crop irrigation and further aggravating water shortages already affecting the southeast. These and other changes in climate conditions will require increased use of fertilizers and pesticides, which would further contaminate runoff. The precise impact from climate change on agricultural yields is unclear. In general, however, agriculture in the lower Mississippi Valley and the Gulf Coast regions is more likely to be negatively affected by climate change, while agriculture in the northern Atlantic Coastal Plain is more likely to be positively affected.

Many activities and climate trends will affect water quality. Urban development, coastal processes, and mining activities will lead to increased contamination. In addition, population is expected to increase significantly in the southeast over the next century, exacerbating stresses on water resources. In addition, the southeast is particularly vulnerable to climate change in its coastal regions. Rising sea levels and more intense storms pose significant threats to the heavily populated coasts, which often depend on coastal aquifers that are becoming increasing vulnerable to salt water intrusion.

The Great Lakes, the largest freshwater resource in North America, will also be impacted by climate change. Most climate models predict that Great Lakes' water levels will drop during the next century to below historic lows. Lake levels in Lake Michigan and

Lake Huron may drop by as much as 4.5 feet (1.38 meters) as a result of changing precipitation and increased air temperature/evapotranspiration.[8]

Temperature is expected to increase significantly within the Great Lakes region—anywhere from 3.6°F (2°C) to 7.2°F (4°C) by the end of the century—with more warming in the western part of the region than in the eastern part. Precipitation may increase in the Midwest, though there will be considerable variation across the region. The northwest may be somewhat drier, but some models predict precipitation increases in the rest of the region.

Drastic reductions in ice cover may also result from air and lake temperature increases—by 2090 most of Lake Erie is projected to be ice-free 96 percent of the time during the winter. The loss of ice cover will lead to increased evaporation losses for the Great Lakes. In addition, winters with less ice will result in more coastal erosion and property damage.

Lower lake levels and rising temperatures (both in the air and water) will significantly impact fisheries, wildlife, wetlands, shoreline habitat, and water quality in the Great Lakes region. The impacts are not only an environmental concern, but also impose a huge economic cost. Tourism and shipping are critically important to the region, and both industries are extremely vulnerable to climate change impacts on water resources.

In addition, the increased variability in timing, intensity, and duration of precipitation under global warming conditions is expected to increase the frequency of droughts and floods in the Great Lakes region and upper Midwest. These changes will lead to significant impacts to agriculture and livestock. Even where precipitation increases, any gains could be wiped out by greater evaporation, leading to drier soils.

Coastal areas throughout the country will face additional challenges. Rising sea levels are caused by thermal expansion of the oceans and increased melting of glaciers and the Greenland and Antarctic ice sheets. Water expands as it warms, and the oceans are getting warmer. The oceans are absorbing more than 80 percent of the heat that is added to the climate system. Further, rising air temperatures will cause glaciers and icecaps to melt faster.

---

[8] A newer study by the National Oceanic and Atmospheric Administration's Great Lakes Environmental Research Laboratory offers more moderate predictions regarding the impact of climate change on Great Lakes water levels as a result of improvements in climate impact modeling. *See* Brent M. Lofgren, Timothy S. Huntera & Jessica Wilbargerb, *Effects of Using Air Temperature as a Proxy for Potential Evapotranspiration in Climate Change Scenarios of Great Lakes Basin Hydrology*, 37 J. GREAT LAKES RESEARCH 744 (2011).

Mean sea levels have risen approximately 5 to 9 inches (12 to 22 centimeters) since the 1890s. The Intergovernmental Panel on Climate Change (IPCC) has predicted that global mean sea levels will rise by 7 to 23 inches (18 to 59 centimeters) by 2100. A more recent study indicates that the IPCC projections might be conservative and that global sea levels could rise as much as 31 to 79 inches (80 to 200 centimeters) by 2100. Rising sea levels will have a myriad of adverse effects, including property damage, destruction of wetlands, and salinization of fresh water resources, among others.

Climate change will also affect groundwater resources nationwide. Groundwater contributes flow to many rivers and streams and is an important source of drinking and irrigation water. Climate change is expected to reduce aquifer recharge and water levels, especially in shallow aquifers. In aquifers where stream-aquifer interactions dominate, aquifer levels are assumed to be directly proportional to precipitation, absent evapotranspiration. However, the higher temperatures and droughts expected over the next century will result in increased evapotranspiration, likely taxing aquifers even further. Aquifers will also suffer from the trend of heavier precipitation events, because more water will go to runoff before it can percolate into aquifers. Thus, even in a future where overall precipitation increases, aquifer levels may decrease as a result of the increased intensity of precipitation events.

Water resources in many regions of the United States are already stressed, and climate change will only exacerbate these problems. The potential for increased demand as a result of higher temperatures comes from all types of water use. Domestic use, especially for outdoor purposes (such as yard and garden irrigation) is expected to increase with warming temperatures. Industrial use may increase as well. Water is used for cooling in many electricity generating systems. An increase in water temperature would decrease the cooling efficiency of the water and require more water to be used. Similarly, demand for water will increase to compensate for inconsistent precipitation in many areas. The most significant water demand problems relate to irrigation. Irrigation accounts for 39 percent of all U.S. water withdrawals and 81 percent of consumptive water uses. It appears that irrigation needs will increase substantially in regions where future drying is expected.

Climate change scholars and commentators separate legal responses to climate change into two categories: climate change mitigation and climate change adaptation. Although there is some overlap with respect to particular actions taken, from a policy and legal perspective, climate change mitigation seeks to reduce greenhouse gas emissions and eventually the overall greenhouse gas concentrations in the atmosphere, while climate change adaptation seeks to respond to climate change impacts and their effects on human society. Climate change mitigation has been, until recently, the primary focus of international efforts to address climate change. However, the consensus of the world's scientists, as represented in the IPCC's reports and other publications, is that climate change impacts are now occurring in measurable way.

As a result, although the reduction of greenhouse gases through legal devices and public initiatives remains critical, climate change can no longer be addressed through mitigation alone. Rather, mitigation should be pursued in conjunction with climate change adaptation in order to more comprehensively and effectively address climate change. As the above discussion suggest, water law is rightly a key focus of many climate change adaptation efforts, and adapting the historically grounded tenets of U.S. water law and policy to climate change is probably the greatest challenge facing this area of governance in the 21st century. Therefore, as you explore the basic doctrines and rules of water law and policy in this book's remaining chapters, you might want to think about how they help or impede climate change adaptation—and how they could be improved.

F. The Emerging Human Right to Water

The most fundamental human need is water. As water stress and cost increase and vulnerable populations become more impoverished, millions of people in the United States (and billions of people globally) are struggling to meet their basic water needs. As a result, some states (often through ballot initiatives) are recognizing and establishing the human right to water in their laws and constitutions.[9]

The opinion for the combined *Boler v. Earley* and *Mays v. Snyder* is one of the first federal decisions to consider due process rights involving safe drinking water.[10] Plaintiffs in *Boler* and *Mays* were residents of Flint affected by the unsafe city water. In 2014, state officials switched the City of Flint's water supply from Lake Huron water to the Flint River without proper corrosion control treatment, disregarding expert reports and regulatory advice. This marked the beginning of significant problems with the safety and quality of Flint's water supply that the state denied for nearly two years.

---

[9] In 2012, California became the first state to enact "human right to water" legislation, providing that "every human being has the right to safe, clean, affordable, and accessible water adequate for human consumption, cooking, and sanitary purposes." Cal. Water Code § 106.3. In 2021, New York voters approved an amendment to the state Constitution's Bill of Rights providing that: "Each person shall have the right to clean air and water, and to a healthful environment." N.Y. Const., Art 1, § 19.

[10] 865 F.3d 391 (6th Cir. 2017).

The plaintiffs in the two lawsuits (which were consolidated for appeal) asserted claims pursuant to 42 U.S.C. § 1983 against various public officials for violations of numerous constitutional rights, including, most notably violation of substantive due process through an invasion of the fundamental right to bodily integrity. Finding that the claims were preempted by the federal Safe Drinking Water Act (SDWA), the district court dismissed the Plaintiffs' claims for lack of subject matter jurisdiction. The SDWA establishes standards for national drinking water and requires treatment to reduce concentrations of certain contaminants in order to protect human health.[11]

On appeal, the U.S. Court of Appeals for the Sixth Circuit reversed the district court's judgment, holding that the SDWA was not a substitute for protecting constitutional rights that may have been violated in Flint. The Sixth Circuit reasoned that the text and legislative history of the SDWA do not suggest that Congress intended for SDWA's remedial scheme to preclude § 1983 suits enforcing constitutional rights. It found that the contours of the rights and protections provided by SDWA diverge so much from those that the Constitution protects that it was impossible to infer congressional intent in the SDWA to foreclose § 1983 claims.[12]

In a subsequent decision, *Guertin v. Michigan*, the Sixth Circuit held that the actions of state officials involved in the Flint water crisis "shocked the conscience" and may violate citizens' right to bodily integrity as guaranteed by the Due Process Clause of the Constitution's Fourteenth Amendment.[13] The court concluded: "In providing a tainted life-necessity and falsely assuring the public about its potability, government officials stripped the very essence of personhood from those who consumed the water."[14]

---

[11] 42 U.S.C. § 300f et seq.

[12] *Boler*, 865 F.3d at 401–409.

[13] 912 F. 3d 907 (6th Cir. 2019).

[14] *Id.* at 935.

Chapter 2

RIPARIAN LAW

Riparian law is the common-law system of private, surface water rights utilized in states east of the 100th Meridian. Moreover, while the western states have adopted prior appropriation to replace riparianism with respect to rights to withdraw and consume surface water, most western states continue to apply some aspects of riparian rights, especially those rights directly related to riparian land ownership.

Under riparian common law, an owner of land abutting a waterbody is a riparian and has certain rights, including: (1) the right to the continued existence of the waterbody in largely the same quantity and quality; and (2) the right to make reasonable use of the water, subject to the equal rights of other riparians on the same waterbody. Thus, any given waterbody functions as a common resource for the riparians who own property bordering it.

However, the riparians do not own the water itself; instead, they possess a right to use the water for certain purposes—termed a *usufructuary* right. This usufructuary right is not absolute and is held subject to the usufructuary rights of other riparians. When riparian uses interfere with each other, courts resolve the dispute equitably by applying numerous factors regarding the nature of the waterbody and the conflicting uses. As a result, riparian rights are always inherently uncertain, and existing uses may, under common law, still have to yield to the rights of other riparians who want to make new uses of the waterway.

A. Defining Riparian Property and Riparian Rights

1. The Importance of a Water Boundary

Under common-law riparianism, only riparian landowners have rights to take and use surface water from lakes, streams, and rivers. (A note on terminology—landowners who are adjacent to lakes rather than flowing rivers and streams are technically referred to as "littoral" owners, but the legal rules are the same and both are generally called by courts "riparian rights.") As such, qualifying as a riparian landowner is a critically important step in exercising surface water rights in common-law riparian jurisdictions.

The exact definition of riparian ownership varies by state. Many states require that a riparian owner's property have a water boundary that extends beyond dry land—say, to the low-water mark of a river. Other states, however, do not require that property ownership extend to underneath the water for the land to be considered a riparian, so long as there are no intervening property owners between the water and the tract of land in question.

There are many policy and practical rationales that support the underlying premise of riparianism. Limiting water use to riparians reduces the pressure and demand on a waterbody, which typically maintains a sustainable level of withdrawals from the water supply. Moreover, proximity to a waterbody makes riparians more efficient water users, because they avoid the considerable waste and expense involved in moving water any significant distance. Riparian landowners also tend to have a more holistic and long-term interest in the sustainable use of the water body, because their riparian interests include aesthetic appreciation, recreational use, and enhancement of property values. Further, the riparian system is less burdensome administratively, because water rights are based on established real property law, eliminating the need for an independent system to establish water rights.

The riparian system also has some fundamental drawbacks. Riparian lands may not be well situated for a given water use, and the common law makes it very difficult to use water on non-riparian lands. Similarly, water may be more valuable to non-riparian users, and riparianism is an obstacle to marketing of water rights without attached land. Giving water use rights only to riparian landowners also raises questions of fundamental justice and equity. If water is a public good, or perhaps a human right, should access and use be restricted to those persons wealthy or fortunate enough to own waterfront property?

2. Riparian Rights in Artificial Waterways

Riparian rights attach to natural waterways, and courts are reluctant to extend riparian rights to properties abutting artificial waterways. *Alderson v. Fatlan* reflects this distinction.[1]

In *Alderson*, the plaintiffs, Robert and Wanda Alderson, were landowners who alleged that they had surface rights to a water-filled quarry used for recreation because they owned a portion of the underlying quarry bed. The defendants, Leo Fatlan who owned the quarry bed and four other adjacent landowners, installed a fence that blocked the Aldersons' access to the surface waters, except for where water was directly above their property. The Aldersons filed suit seeking: (1) a declaration that they had a right to the reasonable use and enjoyment of the surface waters of the entire lake; and (2) an injunction to prevent the defendants from taking any action that

---

1 Alderson v. Fatlan, 898 N.E.2d 595 (Ill. 2008).

would deprive the plaintiffs of their access to all the surface waters of the lake. The Aldersons argued that ownership of a portion of the lake bed is sufficient to establish a right to use the entire lake.

The trial court granted summary judgment to the Aldersons pursuant to *Beacham v. Lake Zurich Property Owners Ass'n*,[2] wherein the Illinois Supreme Court had held that the owner of a portion of a natural lake bed obtains rights to the surface waters of the entire lake, subject to the reasonable use of other owners of the lake bed. On appeal, in *Alderson*, however, the Illinois Supreme Court reversed and concluded that *Beacham* applies only to natural water bodies, not to artificial water bodies such as the filled quarry at issue.

The *Alderson* court explained that the general rule is that riparian rights do not extend to artificial waters because it would be inequitable to grant a property owner rights to a water body artificially made by someone else's labor solely because the property abuts the water. The court explained, however, that riparian rights can extend to artificial bodies of water pursuant to the "artificial-becomes-natural" rule. Pursuant to this rule, an artificial water body may eventually come to be considered a natural one if it exhibits the characteristics of a natural body of water. This analysis, in turn, rests on three factors. Specifically, if a water body: (1) is permanent; (2) is created under circumstances that indicate an intent that it shall become permanent; and (3) has been used consistently with such an intention for a considerable period, then the water body is regarded as "natural," even if it was artificially created.

The *Alderson* court stressed that, in addition to these three factors, the main consideration in determining whether a water body satisfies the "artificial-becomes-natural" rule is whether the party invoking the rule has relied upon use of the artificial body of water without dispute for a lengthy period of time. The court concluded that the Aldersons could not meet this requirement because their use had been disputed for years. Thus, the Aldersons were entitled to use only the portion of the lake above their own property and were not entitled to riparian rights that would permit them to use the entire man-made lake.

3. Division and Boundaries of Submerged Land

Unlike the surface waters of riparian waters that are shared equally among riparians, the submerged lands underneath *non-navigable* waters are owned by individual riparians—that is, riparian property lines extend underwater. (The submerged lands

2 Beacham v. Lake Zurich Property Owners Ass'n, 526 N.E.2d 154 (Ill. 1988).

beneath *navigable* waterways, in contrast, are generally owned by the relevant state, a doctrine that we will explore in Chapter 6.)

Waterbodies are rarely regular. As a result, states and their courts have developed a variety of methods for dividing up non-navigable streambeds and lakebeds. Ownership of streambeds is typically determined through a two-step process: (1) a surveyor identifies the midline thread, or median, running through the middle of the stream; and then (2) the boundaries of the riparian owners' properties are extended from the property boundary where the upland property hits the stream to the midline, joining that midline at a right angle (see Figure 2–1).

Figure 2–1: Ownership of Stream Beds

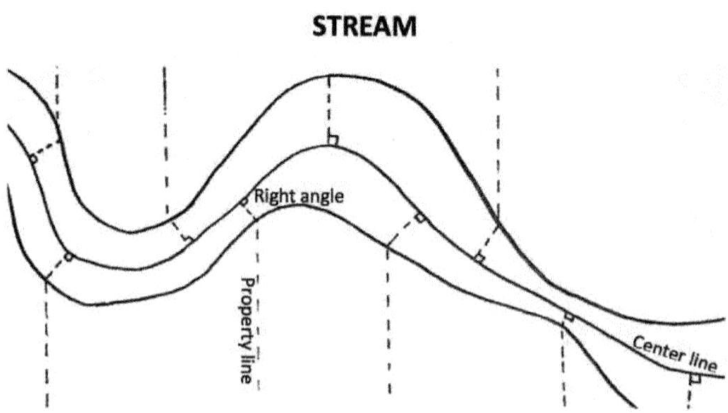

Ownership of lakebeds, on the other hand, depends on whether the shape of the lake bed is circular, oblong, or irregular. If the lake is circular, first a center line is established that splits the lake in half. Then, the littoral property's boundaries along the shoreline establish the base of a triangle, which creates a pie-shaped lakebed property division among riparian landowners (see Figure 2–2). If the lake is oblong, the property lines will be drawn more like for streams: First, the midline of the lake is determined, and then lines extend from the respective properties perpendicularly to the median (see Figure 2–3). If the lake's shape is so irregular that neither of these methods are possible, the lake bed is divided in proportion to the shoreline owned (see Figure 2–4).

Figure 2–2: Ownership of Beds of a Circular Lake

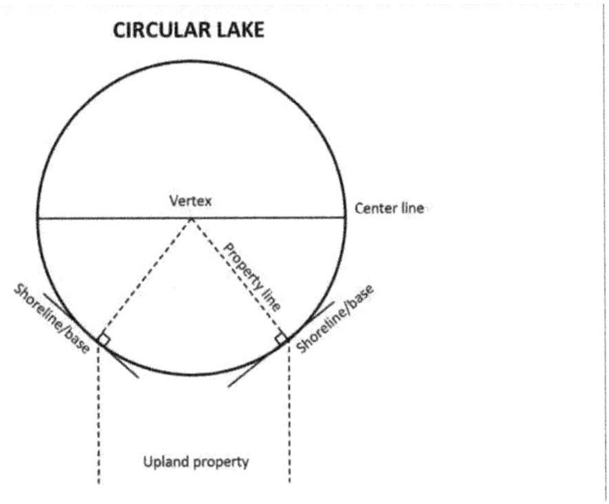

Figure 2–3: Ownership of Beds of an Oblong Lake

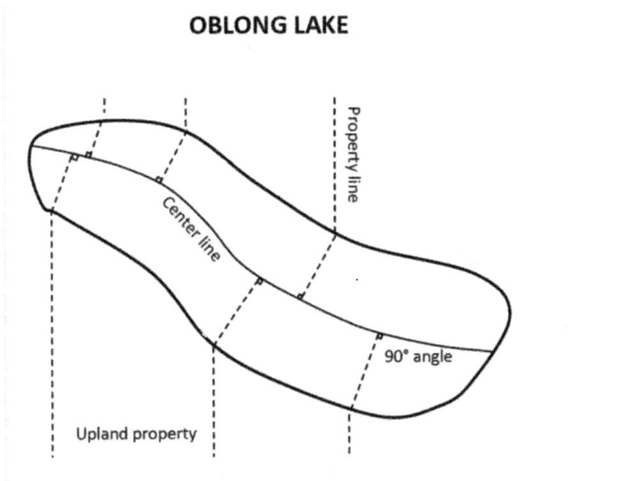

Figure 2–4: Bed Ownership in an Irregular Lake

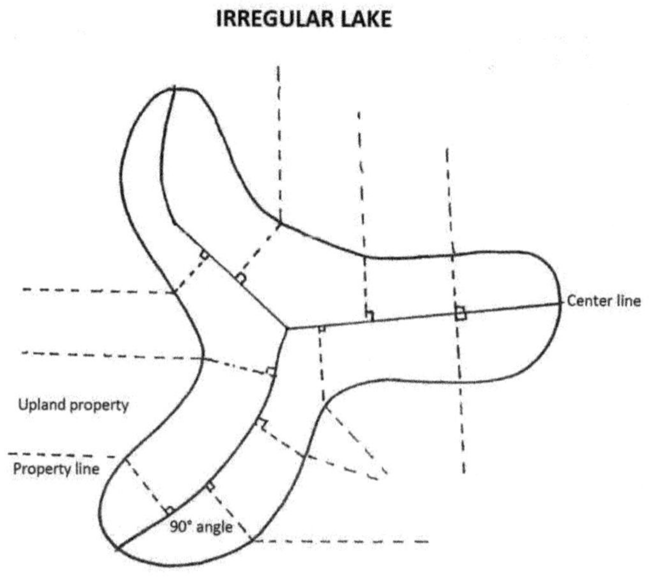

Streambed ownership of non-navigable water bodies is one of the riparian property rights that generally applies throughout the United States, regardless of whether a state uses riparian water rights or prior appropriation. Moreover, the ownership of submerged land can be important with respect to several other riparian property rights that also tend to exist regardless of whether the state uses riparianism or prior appropriation law for actual water rights. These other riparian property rights include the right to construct docks and wharves (the right to "wharf out," discussed below) and control over streambed mining for sand, gravel, petroleum, or natural gas. These land ownership-based rights, however, are often subject to state regulation, which is sometimes extensive.

4. Conveyances of Riparian Rights

Riparian rights are appurtenant to riparian land, and usually cannot be severed and sold separately to non-riparians. Riparians may, however, grant easements that allow non-riparians to enjoy some riparian rights, such as access to water. The easement does not create a new riparian; instead, it gives the grantee a legally recognizable right that is enforceable against the grantor. Courts generally are protective of riparians and place the burden of proving the existence of an easement upon the party asserting its existence.

Further, courts will determine the scope of the non-riparian owners' rights as a question of fact, examining the language of the easement and the surrounding circumstances at the time of the grant, just as they interpret easements that do not involve access to water. Finally, the use of the easement must not unreasonably interfere with the rights of the other actual riparians on the waterbody.

Little v. Kin involved a dispute regarding such an easement.[3] In *Little*, a dispute arose between riparian property owners, the plaintiffs, and neighboring non-riparian "backlot" owners, the defendants, regarding the scope of the non-riparian owners' right to enjoy Pine Lake. Three riparian owners had the exclusive use of a 33-foot shoreline, and the backlot owners held a non-exclusive permanent easement over the remaining shoreline for access to and use of riparian rights to the Lake. The defendants were landowners of two separate backlots: one of the backlots was owned by Thomas and Darle Trivan, and the other was owned by Steven and Rosalyn Kin. The original landowners of the plaintiffs' property granted the easement to the defendants. The plaintiffs, Robert and Barbara Little, bought one of the three riparian lots with knowledge of this easement. The previous owners of the Kins' property approached the Littles about building a dock on their easement, to which the Littles consented.

The Littles, however, brought this case to prevent the defendants from using the dock, which would obstruct their own riparian uses of the lake. Specifically, the Littles sought: (1) an injunction to remove the dock and prevent any further docks from being constructed; and (2) a declaration of the defendants' rights under the easement. The Littles alleged that non-riparian lot owners may not maintain a dock on another's riparian land because a riparian landowner may not transfer his or her rights. The defendants counterclaimed that the Littles intentionally placed thorny bushes and landscape timbers on the easement, which interfered with the Kins' use and enjoyment of their easement rights.

The Michigan Supreme Court in *Little* explained that the scope of a non-riparian lot owner's rights under an easement over riparian land must be examined in light of the intent of the grantors, which should be determined from the language and surrounding circumstances. In addition, the court must ensure that the easement will not unreasonably interfere with the rights of adjacent riparians. The *Little* court held the trial court erred in concluding that the easement granted to the defendants cannot include the right to build or maintain a dock and that the easement was only for access to the water. The trial court also erred in concluding that the plaintiffs

[3] Little v. Kin, 644 N.W.2d 375 (Mich. App. 2002).

could landscape without consideration of the defendants' use of the easement. The Michigan Supreme Court remanded the case so that the trial court could consider the easement's language and circumstances at the time of the grant to determine whether the Lins' easement rights include the right to build a dock. If the easement did include the right to construct a dock, then the Michigan Supreme Court instructed the trial court to consider whether this dock would unreasonably interfere with the plaintiffs' use and enjoyment of their property.

The *Little* court thus allowed for the legal possibility that riparian owners can convey many of their riparian rights, such as the right to build a dock. The modern trend in riparian jurisdictions is to allow conveyance of all riparian rights, but courts generally require that: (1) such conveyances are clear; and (2) such conveyances do not unreasonably multiply the number of people using the waterbody. The second point can be a bit tricky to apply. For example, suppose a riparian landowner conveys "half my right to wharf out and half my right to take and use water" to a non-riparian. Does this conveyance allow for the building of two docks and the withdrawal of twice as much water? As you puzzle over that question, you should begin to understand why conveyances of riparian rights can breed significant litigation.

5. Rights Regarding Diffuse Flow and Runoff

Diffuse flow is rainwater or snowmelt that is not absorbed by the ground but instead runs downhill across the land when it rains or during spring snowmelt. In regions with water scarcity, diffuse flow can be a valuable asset. In wetter regions, diffuse flow can, by contrast, be a significant liability, causing significant property damage from flooding, erosion, and, if the flows are strong enough, sheer physical impact. Disputes arise between landowners when an uphill landowner attempts to channel this water away from his or her property and damages a downhill neighbor as a result. There are three main legal doctrines that govern property owners' rights regarding and liability for diffuse flow: common enemy, civil law, and reasonable use.

Keys v. Romley provides an overview of these three doctrines.[4] The plaintiffs, Wesley and Ruth Keys, owned property abutting property owned by Gus and Engra Lusebrink. The Lusebrinks leased their property to the defendant, Edward Romley. Romley constructed an ice rink on the property surrounded by asphalt, and he graded and leveled the property as part of this construction. Romley also installed downspouts along the ice rink that sent water onto the Keys'

---

[4] Keys v. Romley, 412 P.2d 529 (Cal. 1966).

property. The diversion of water from the Lusebrinks' property flooded and eroded the Keys' property.

The trial court determined that Romley had artificially discharged surface water onto the Keys' property in a greater and different manner than what had occurred prior to the ice rink's construction. It granted the Keys damages and issued an injunction restraining Romley from causing further damage to the Keys' property. On appeal, the Superior Court upheld the injunction against Romley and granted the Keys over $4,000 in property damage. On further appeal, the California Supreme Court had to determine which doctrine California should adopt for diffuse flows before it could evaluate whether Romley was liable to the Keys for the property damage resulting from the altered flow of water, leading it to consider the three main U.S. doctrines regarding diffuse flow.

First, the *common enemy doctrine* derives from the conception of diffuse runoff as the "common enemy" of all. It provides that, as an incident to the use of his or her own property, each landowner has an unqualified right to fend off surface waters in any way that he or she sees fit, without being required to take into account the consequences to other landowners, who have the identical right to protect themselves as best they can.

The second doctrine is the *civil law rule*, which recognizes a servitude for natural drainage as between adjoining lands so that the lower owner must accept the surface water that drains onto his land. However, the upper owner has no right to alter the natural system of drainage so as to increase the lower owner's burden and hence can be liable for any damage that occurs as a result of any such increase.

The final doctrine, the *rule of reasonable use*, is essentially an ordinary negligence test for liability. Specifically, this rule employs a balancing test to determine the rights of the parties with respect to the disposition of diffuse waters through an assessment of all the relevant factors.

The *Keys* court concluded that the civil law rule was the prevailing doctrine and again upheld it as the rule in California. It reversed and remanded the case to be decided in accordance with that doctrine. However, the pervasive modern trend has been for courts to adopt the rule of reasonable use or just to evaluate property owners' redirection of diffuse water in terms of ordinary negligence.

B. The Riparian Right to Take and Use Fresh Water

1. The Natural Flow Rule and the Transition to Reasonable Use

Courts in England and America resolved early disputes between riparians using the natural flow doctrine. Under this system, each riparian owner was entitled to have the waterbody preserved in its natural state, not noticeably diminished in quantity or impaired in quality. Uses of the water that altered the water level or water quality could be enjoined.

During the Industrial Revolution, streams and rivers became increasingly valuable as sources of power through water mills. Building water mills, however, often involved the construction of a dam and an alteration in the water's natural flow. As a result, and often in the name of economic progress, courts moved further and further away from pure natural flow doctrine, instead opting to balance the reasonableness of various uses, or create exceptions to pure natural flow doctrine to accommodate these often-desirable new developments that caused greater impact to the waterway.

Nevertheless, the concept of protecting natural flow as a riparian right continued into the 20th century as courts began transitioning to a more modern view of reasonable use. *Harris v. Brooks* illustrates this evolution.[5] One of the appellants in *Harris*, Theo Mashburn, conducted a commercial boating and fishing business on leased riparian property. Mashburn and the lessors, Ed Harris, Jesse Harris, Alice Lynch and Dora Balkin, collectively filed a complaint to enjoin the appellees, John Brooks and John Brooks, Jr., from pumping water from the lake to irrigate their crops. Brookses, like Mashburn, also leased their property from another riparian, Ector Johnson. Mashburn and his lessors alleged that the Brookses had reduced the water level of the lake to such an extent that the lake had become unsuitable for fishing and recreation, violating the natural flow doctrine in violation of Mashburn's leased riparian rights. The chancellor denied injunctive relief, and Mashburn and his lessors appealed.

On appeal, the Arkansas Supreme Court in *Harris* began its analysis by stating that the dispute could be resolved by using either the natural flow doctrine or the reasonable use rule. It explained that the reasonable use rule provides each riparian owner an equal right to make a reasonable use of waters in the waterbody to which his or her property is riparian, subject to the equal rights of all other

---

5 Harris v. Brooks, 283 S.W.2d 129 (Ark. 1955).

riparian owners to make reasonable use of the same water body. The reasonable use rule, according to the *Harris* court, is much more flexible and can promote economic development. The court acknowledged that in some cases both theories could work together concurrently, but in the event of a conflict the reasonable use rule should control in Arkansas.

The *Harris* court then provided four general principles to guide lower courts in applying the reasonable use rule:

> (a) The right to use water for strictly domestic purposes—such as for household use—is superior to many other uses of water—such as for fishing, recreation and irrigation.
>
> (b) Other than the use mentioned above, all other lawful uses of water are equal. Some of the lawful uses of water recognized by this state are: fishing, swimming, recreation, and irrigation.
>
> (c) When one lawful of water is destroyed by another lawful use the latter must yield, or it may be enjoined.
>
> (d) When one lawful use of water interferes with or detracts from another lawful use, then a question arises as to whether, under all the facts and circumstances of that particular case, the interfering use shall be declared unreasonable and as such enjoined, or whether a reasonable and equitable adjustment should be made, having due regard to the reasonable rights of each.[6]

The *Harris* court applied these principles to the facts of the case to conclude that it should enjoin the Brookses from withdrawing water beyond the undisturbed, natural water level. The court stated, however, that it selected this depth not because of the natural flow doctrine but because this depth was the "reasonable" level for the lake. As a result, if the Brookses withdrew so much water for irrigation that they lowered the lake level, those withdrawals would be an "unreasonable use."

One aspect of the reasonable use rule is important, even under the *Harris* principles. Unless the plaintiff riparian is using the water for domestic use (the privileged use), *both* the plaintiff's and the defendant's water uses are subject to evaluation under the reasonable use test. Thus, it is perfectly possible for a court to conclude that the *plaintiff* is the unreasonable user, or that *both* uses

---

[6] *Id.* at 134.

are unreasonable. Common-law reasonable use litigation in riparian states, therefore, can be a bit unpredictable.

2. Legal Development of the Reasonable Use Factors

Courts have long struggled with the complex task of defining analytic criteria for the reasonable use doctrine. Nevertheless, the idea that disputes between two or more riparians should be settled by analyzing the reasonableness of the competing uses and then attempting to find an equitable solution has remained the guiding principle. *Red River Roller Mills v. Wright* demonstrates an early court embracing the reasonable use doctrine.[7]

The plaintiff in *Red River Roller Mills* sought to restrain that defendant from depositing byproducts from its saw-mill into the Red or Otter Tail River because those by-products clogged the plaintiff's flour mill. The defendant claimed that there was no other alternative than to allow these byproducts to float downstream and alleged that this form of disposal was common practice at the time. The lower court found that the defendant's use of the river was reasonable because there was no apparent alternative way for the defendant to operate his saw-mill. On appeal, the Minnesota Supreme Court had to determine whether the defendant's behavior was in fact "reasonable."

The Minnesota Supreme Court listed several factors that it considered in its analysis to determine whether the use was reasonable:

- The subject-matter of the use;
- The occasion and manner of its application;
- The object, extent, necessity, and duration of the use;
- The nature and size of the stream;
- The kind of business to which it is subservient;
- The importance and necessity of the use claimed by one party, and the extent of the injury to the other party;
- The state of improvement of the country in regard to mills and machinery, and the use of water as a propelling power;
- The general and established usages of the country in similar cases; and
- All the other and ever-varying circumstances of each particular case bearing upon the question of the fitness

---

[7] Red River Roller Mills v. Wright, 15 N.W. 167 (Minn. 1883).

> and propriety of the use of the water under consideration.[8]

The court also stated that when an upstream riparian owner interferes with a downstream riparian owner's reasonable use of the water body, "either by the interruption, diversion, obstruction, or pollution of the water," the burden of proof is upon the upstream riparian to demonstrate that his or her use is reasonable and necessary. The *Red River Roller Mills* court concluded that because the defendant did not demonstrate that this was an ideal location for the saw-mill, nor that this was where the saw-mill needed to be located, the defendant's behavior was not reasonable.

3. The Restatement (Second) of Torts § 850

In 1979, the drafters of the Restatement (Second) of Torts wrote a series of provisions related to water law, Sections 850–858, in a conscious attempt to "reform" eastern water law, including the reasonable use doctrine. Nevertheless, few states have adopted the Restatement approach. Missouri is one of these states, and the Missouri Court of Appeals' decision in *Ripka v. Wansing* introduces the Restatement (Second) of Torts § 850 as an analytical framework for resolving riparian disputes.[9]

The plaintiffs in *Ripka* sought an injunction to prevent the defendants from pumping water for irrigation from Sugar Creek. Both parties owned tracts of land along the creek that they used for agriculture. The creek flowed across land owned by plaintiffs, then across two tracts of land owned by defendants, and then across plaintiffs' second tract. The defendants used the water to irrigate crops on their land adjoining the creek. The plaintiffs operated a cattle business, and they alleged that the defendants' irrigation caused a drop in water levels that impacted their business.

The *Ripka* court analyzed the issue by outlining the Restatement's factors to determine whether a riparian's use of water is reasonable:

(a) The purpose of the use,

(b) The suitability of the use to the watercourse or lake,

(c) The economic value of the use,

(d) The social value of the use,

(e) The extent and amount of the harm it causes,

---

8 *Id.* at 169.

9 Ripka v. Wansing, 589 S.W.2d 333 (Mo. App. 1979) (*en banc*).

(f) The practicality of avoiding the harm by adjusting the use or method of use of one proprietor or the other,

(g) The practicality of adjusting the quantity of water used by each proprietor,

(h) The protection of existing values of water uses, land, investments and enterprises, and

(i) The justice of requiring the user causing harm to bear the loss.[10]

Applying these factors, the court concluded that the defendants' use of the water from the creek to irrigate their crops was a reasonable use. The court emphasized that there was no evidence that the plaintiffs were actually harmed by the defendants' withdrawals, nor was there evidence that the use had a noticeable effect on the water flowing downstream. In fact, there was evidence that there had always been sufficient water for the plaintiffs' cattle.

Essentially, going back to the *Harris* factors, the plaintiffs had failed to prove any interference with their own water use whatsoever. As a practical matter, and regardless of what principles and factors a particular court relies on, courts in riparian jurisdictions will generally not label a water use "unreasonable" until there is a real (or extremely imminent) conflict between riparian users. Thus, for example, if only one riparian along a river is withdrawing water, that riparian can withdraw relatively large amounts of water without becoming unreasonable. However, if nine other riparians along the river begin to use water, interference becomes much more likely and the original riparian's large withdrawals will more likely be deemed unreasonable.

This example also demonstrates one of the reasons why common-law riparian rights are inherently uncertain and variable, because they are subject to the whims of some riparians who begin using water long after other riparians have become dependent on their earlier withdrawals. This uncertainty of right was one of the problems with riparianism that the drafters of the Restatement (2nd) of Torts tried to "fix," by insisting that courts consider "the protection of existing values of water uses, land, investments and enterprises"—*i.e.*, who was using the water first. Again, however, few riparian jurisdictions have adopted the Restatement's approach.

4. Accommodating Public Water Suppliers Under Riparian Law

Most water users (residential and commercial) that reside within a major town or city depend on a public utility or municipal

---

[10] *Id.* at 335.

water company to provide their water. These utilities and companies pump water from streams and reservoirs and provide it to their customers.

Nevertheless, fitting municipalities into the riparian system presents several challenges. First, cities need a lot of water, which can place large demands on limited local supplies and can lead to the need to obtain water from other watersheds or from groundwater (see Chapter 4). Most riparian jurisdictions employ a watershed limitation, requiring that riparian water users keep the water within the watershed of origin. Cities' attempts to obtain surface water from other watersheds, therefore, violate this restriction. Second, the overwhelming majority of actual water users in cities are not themselves riparian owners. Because municipal water is not used on riparian land, the use would be barred as per se unreasonable under traditional riparian doctrine. Third, even if the off-tract use issue is ignored, there is no easy way to classify the reasonableness of each of the many uses that municipal customers make of water.

To cope with these issues, courts and legislatures have had to modify the application of riparian law to public water suppliers. First, the law evolved so that it treats the municipality, and not the individual customers, as the riparian. The municipality must own, or purchase, riparian land in order to become a riparian; the city's location next to a river is still generally not good enough. Second, to obtain the water that municipalities need, cities regularly employ the power of eminent domain to condemn the water rights of riparians. Municipalities receive the power of eminent domain from the state through "home rule" or state legislation. Because supplying water for the needs of a city's population is almost always considered a public use, riparians can do little to prevent a condemnation of their water rights and are often forced to focus any such disputes with condemning cities on ensuring that the city pays adequate—"just"—compensation (see Chapter 14). When courts prevent cities from condemning water rights, it is usually because either: (1) the city is trying to condemn water rights for use by a single customer and thus not using its power for the public generally; or (2) the city is attempting to service customers outside of the municipal boundaries.[11]

Adams v. Greenwich Water Co. demonstrates this conflict between the necessity of water for a municipality's public supply and traditional riparianism concepts.[12] The plaintiffs were riparian owners along the Mianus River in Connecticut who brought suit to enjoin the Greenwich Water Company from diverting water from the

---

[11] *E.g.*, Burger v. City of Beatrice, 147 N.W.2d 784 (Neb. 1967).

[12] Adams v. Greenwich Water Co., 83 A.2d 177 (Conn. 1951).

river through the construction of a reservoir. Greenwich Water filed a cross-complaint seeking a declaratory judgment regarding whether it had the right to condemn the water rights for the benefit of local citizens to be used as public supply. The plaintiffs used the water for recreational use and benefitted from increased property values of their waterfront homes.

The Connecticut Supreme Court stated that when "a legislature endows a public utility company with the power to take by eminent domain such property as is necessary to fulfill its corporate purposes without restriction, the determination of what is necessary to be taken lies in the discretion of the company. The courts will interfere with the exercise of that discretion only in cases of bad faith or unreasonable conduct."[13] Thus, the *Adams* court concluded that it was "necessary for the defendant to acquire water rights for the construction of a reservoir in the Mianus River in order to continue to furnish an adequate supply of water to its customers."[14] The plaintiffs also challenged Greenwich Water's withdrawal because most of the public supply would be benefitting out-of-state residents in New York, rather than residents of Connecticut. The *Adams* court disagreed, however, stating that "if a taking of property by eminent domain is for a public use within the state authorizing it, such a taking is not to be prevented because it will also serve a public use in another jurisdiction."[15]

The court remanded the case to determine what a reasonable time would be to allow Greenwich Water to acquire the water rights of the plaintiffs. Notably, the court rejected Greenwich Water's asserted "emergency" exception, emphasizing again that cities need to use their condemnation authorities to obtain necessary riparian water rights.

C. Riparian Rights Beyond Consumptive Use

In addition to the right of consumptive water use in accordance with the reasonable use doctrine, riparians also possess the rights to: (1) wharf out and build piers into deeper water; (2) access the water; (3) use the entire surface of the water for navigation and recreation; (4) gain or lose land through accretion and reliction; (5) have and maintain an unobstructed view of the water (in some states); and (6) have water of a certain quality. These additional rights must be exercised subject to the principles of reasonable use and often are subject to additional state-law restrictions. However, riparian landowners throughout the United States generally retain these

---

13 *Id.* at 213–214.

14 *Id.* at 214.

15 *Id.* at 215.

property rights, even if they live in prior appropriation states—one reason that even western water lawyers need to understand riparianism.

1. The Right to Wharf Out

Riparian property ownership includes the right to build piers and wharf out to deeper water, subject to the authority of regulatory agencies and the reasonable use doctrine. In *Borsellino v. Wisconsin Department of Natural Resources*, the Wisconsin Court of Appeals examined some of the ways that states can limit that right.[16]

The plaintiff, Lewis Borsellino, disputed the Wisconsin Department of Natural Resources' (DNR's) grant of a permit to his neighbors, Samuel and Marilyn Bonanno, to build a pier. Borsellino claimed that the permit violated a town pier placement ordinance, Wisconsin's public trust doctrine (see Chapter 7), and the reasonable use doctrine.

Borsellino's lot was located on the lakeshore, and the Bonannos and Ralph and Eileen Rothstein owned property upland from Borsellino. The Bonannos also owned a strip of land on the shore of the lake between Borsellino's lot and another adjacent lot owned by John and Susan Ciciora. The Bonannos and Rothsteins built a 78-foot long pier into the lake stretching out from the Bonannos' access strip, and the pier existed there without dispute for decades.

Borsellino filed a complaint with DNR regarding the pier because of its potential interference with his use of the lake. An administrative law judge (ALJ) ordered the Bonannos to remove the pier because it exceeded the reasonable use of public waters and extended into Borsellino's riparian zone (the area of submerged lands subject to Borsellino's exclusive use). The Bonannos applied to DNR for a permit to construct a new pier in the water adjacent to the access lot that would be 96 feet long. Both Borsellino and the Cicioras objected to the proposal and argued that the pier would interfere with their riparian rights and create excessive congestion. The ALJ granted the permit, concluding that it would neither impair navigation nor be detrimental to the public interest. The circuit court affirmed the ALJ's decision, and Borsellino appealed.

On appeal, the Wisconsin Court of Appeals had to decide whether DNR erred in granting the permit for the 96-foot pier, which, when built, would violate a provision of the Wisconsin Code that requires docks to be placed at least 12.5 feet from the property boundary. The court acknowledged that although the Bonannos could not comply with this provision because of the narrowness of their

---

[16] Borsellino v. Wisconsin Dept. of Natural Resources, 606 N.W.2d 255 (Wis. App. 1999).

access strip, a different subsection of the code provided an alternative. Relying on this alternative, the court directed the Bonannos to place their pier within their twelve-foot space to best maximize maneuvering room on each side. Because the Bonannos could not move their pier any further, the burden as a result was placed on their neighbors to move their piers, "far enough to the side regardless of shoreline proportions to afford the necessary clearance."[17] The court also upheld the ALJ's decision to limit the Bonannos to only one boat slip and his conclusion that the ecology of the lake would not be impacted and hence that the permitted dock would not violate the public trust doctrine.

Most states now have permitting requirements for private docks. The permitting authority—the DNR in Wisconsin—usually tries to ensure that dock builders are not interfering with their neighbors, intruding on their neighbors' property or riparian zones, overburdening the waterbody (such as with huge structures that give multiple non-riparians access to the water), or interfering with navigation or other public uses. The permitting authority generally also has to be conscious of environmental impacts, whether through the permitting statute itself or the state's more general environmental impact analysis requirements, or both.

2. The Right to Access the Water

Riparians possess the right to access the water for a variety of further uses, such as recreation, boating, or fishing. Pursuant to this right, riparians can seek to enjoin, or receive compensation for, any activity or action that frustrates or impedes their access to the water.

In New York, *627 Smith St. Corp. v. Bureau of Waste Disposal of Department of Sanitation of City of New York* involved a dispute regarding this right.[18] The plaintiffs owned a property that adjoined and fronted the Gowanus Canal, and the City of New York owned and operated a waste disposal plant across the Canal. The City placed waste and refuse on barges that were towed by a tugboat on the canal for final disposal. The plaintiffs alleged that the City's barges and tugboats destroyed their bulkhead and other structures fronting the Canal, eliminating their ability to access the Canal. They brought suit alleging a de facto appropriation or inverse condemnation of their riparian rights.

The New York Appellate Division stated that a finding of de facto appropriation or inverse condemnation requires a showing that the government had intruded onto an owner's property and

---

[17] *Id.* at 260.

[18] 627 Smith St. Corp. v. Bureau of Waste Disposal of Dept. of Sanitation of City of N.Y., 289 A.D.2d 472 (N.Y. App. Div. 2001).

interfered with his or her property rights to such a degree that the conduct amounts to a constitutional taking, which requires the government to compensate the property owner (see Chapter 14). The court explained that a riparian's right to access water is included in the bundle of rights a riparian landowner possesses, and thus if the government interferes with this right, the government must compensate the riparian's loss of access to water. Therefore, because the City had impeded the plaintiffs' right to access the water when it destroyed the bulkhead and waterfront structures, the *627 Smith St. Corp.* court found the City responsible for damages. The court concluded that the calculation of damages would be determined by the difference between the sales of similar properties with and without riparian rights.

3. The Right to Use the Entire Surface of the Waterbody for Boating, Fishing, and Recreation

If a property is considered riparian, its owner possesses, under the majority common-law rule, the right to use the entire surface of the natural waterbody to which it is riparian, regardless of the amount of the bottomlands the riparian owns or the size of the riparian tract. As discussed in *Alderson, supra*, these rights do not apply to owners adjacent to an artificial body of water.

In Minnesota, *Johnson v. Seifert* involved a plaintiff who sought to enjoin the defendants from constructing and maintaining a fence through and across two lakes and from taking water from one of the lakes for irrigation.[19] The plaintiff owned relatively little of the waterfront compared to the defendants, and the defendants placed a fence along the section between their properties and the plaintiff's property and through the bodies of both lakes to prevent the plaintiff from having free access to the main body of either lake.

The issue before the Minnesota Supreme Court was whether the owner of a tract abutting on a lake has a right to make use of the lake over its entire surface, irrespective of whether the lake is navigable and irrespective of the ownership of the lakebed. The Minnesota Supreme Court concluded that the plaintiff may use the entire surface of the lake. In reaching this conclusion, the *Johnson* court stated that an abutting owner on a non-navigable lake has the right to use the entire surface of the lake for all suitable and reasonable purposes in common with all other riparian owners, so long as the use is reasonable and does not unduly interfere with the exercise of similar rights on the part of other abutting owners, regardless of ownership of a lake bed.

---

[19] Johnson v. Seifert, 100 N.W.2d 689 (Minn. 1960).

The *Johnson* court followed the majority rule for a riparian landowner's right of use. However, a very few courts have used the minority rule instead, holding that riparian landowners can use only that part of the water in a non-navigable waterbody that lies over the submerged lands that the riparian owns. The minority rule is difficult to enforce and contradicts the expectations of most people who buy riparian land—two reasons why it is the very limited minority rule.

As Chapters 6 and 7 will explore in more detail, navigable waterbodies are public waterbodies. Thus, riparians who own property on the shore of a navigable waterbody have the right to use the entire waterbody, but—unlike in non-navigable water bodies—they share this right with every member of the public who can find legal access to the water.

4. The Doctrines of Accretion, Reliction, and Avulsion

Waterbodies are not static. Streams and rivers change course, and lakes can change shape and water levels. Changes in the shape and location of a waterbody can affect riparian property owners in different ways, depending on the speed and conspicuousness of the change. The ***doctrine of accretion*** covers gradual, natural changes to the shore or bank caused by accretion, erosion and reliction. Accretion is the almost imperceptible addition of land to a shore or bank through the buildup of sand or silt. Erosion is the gradual wearing away of a shore or bank caused by the waterbody. Reliction is the gradual uncovering of land as water gradually recedes or the land rises. Accretion, erosion and reliction are treated legally in the same way: the boundaries between riparians on the new or lost land follow the change in the waterbody.

As a result, if a riparian property is bounded by a stream and, over the years, the stream gradually deposits silt on the riparian's bank, the stream remains the boundary and the "new" land created by accretion belongs to the riparian. Conversely, if the riparian is located on the eroding side of the stream, the riparian loses real property. The premises behind the doctrine of accretion are that: (1) landowners both assume that the waterbody remains their boundary and actually want it to remain so, because continued adjacency to water is valuable; and (2) keeping track of gradual boundary changes is administratively and legally difficult.

In contrast, the doctrine of avulsion applies to more sudden and perceptible changes in a waterbody that cause land to be covered or uncovered. For example, rivers often jump their banks during a flood event and then flow in new channels after the flood recedes, a very obvious change in the waterbody. In most jurisdictions, avulsive changes leave property boundaries in the same place as before the change to the waterbody. As a result, some property owners cease to be riparians after an avulsive change. Determining whether a change is accretive or avulsive is a question of fact to be determined by the trial court.

While riparian landowners are more or less stuck with *natural* changes in waterbodies, causing unwanted accretion or erosion to another's land is actionable as a tort.[20] Usually, a riparian cannot deliberately increase the size of his or her own property through artificial accretion or reliction.[21] However, a riparian usually receives the benefit of artificial accretion or erosion resulting from a third party's activities,[22] but not from artificially induced avulsions.[23]

The Washington Court of Appeals addressed some of these rules in *Strom v. Sheldon*.[24] The plaintiffs and defendants in *Strom* were neighboring landowners. The border between their properties was the center of the "Whiskey Slough." The defendants' predecessor in title dredged the Slough to widen it, and as a result a significant portion of the waterbody was shifted onto the defendants' property. The defendants used the enlarged Slough to moor barges and trollers. The plaintiffs purchased the property unaware of the previous modifications. Eventually, however, the defendants asserted title to the entire slough and refused to move their barges from the plaintiffs' half. The plaintiffs brought suit to quiet title to the portion of land running from the original boundary to the present thread and sought an injunction to prevent the defendants from interfering with the plaintiffs' use of their half of the slough.

The Washington Court of Appeals was faced with the question of whether an owner of a parcel that extends to the thread of a non-navigable stream may artificially shift the course of the stream onto his property and then claim the protection of avulsion, so that the adjacent riparian landowner is deprived of access to the watercourse. The *Strom* court held the avulsion rule was not applicable in this case, applying the accretion-reliction rule instead. The court concluded the boundary between the plaintiffs' and defendants' properties remained the thread of the Whiskey Slough and had shifted with the change in the Slough's location.

The *Strom* court emphasized that the determinant criterion as to which rules applies is not whether the waterbody change is

---

[20] *See, e.g.,* Montijo-Reyes v. United States, 436 F.3d 19 (1st Cir. 2006) (holding such private changes actionable).

[21] *E.g.,* Alexander Hamilton Life Ins. Co. v. Virgin Islands, 757 F.2d 534 (3rd Cir. 1985); Brundage v. Knox, 117 N.E. 117 (Ill. 1917).

[22] *See, e.g.,* Williamson v. Crawford, 310 N.W.2d 419 (Mich. App. 1981).

[23] *E.g.,* Peterman v. State, 521 N.W.2d 499 (Mich. 1994).

[24] Strom v. Sheldon, 527 P.2d 1382 (Wash. App. 1975).

artificial or natural, but rather the speed of the change. However, equity and policy considerations were also at play in the case: Courts generally do *not* want to fashion legal rules that empower riparians to alter waterbodies in ways that hurt their fellow riparians. These considerations often help to explain the actual results in accretion/avulsion litigation when the change to the waterbody is not obviously one or the other.

5. The Right to an Unobstructed View

Florida, Mississippi, Georgia and New Jersey are part of a small group of states that recognize, to varying degrees, a riparian right to an unobstructed view of the water. These states recognize that a view of the water makes property more valuable and that blocking the view decreases the value of the property.

Lee County v. Kiesel involved riparian landowners in Florida seeking to preserve this riparian right.[25] The plaintiffs, Edward and Lorraine Kiesel, were riparians who challenged Lee County's construction of a bridge adjacent to their home because the bridge obstructed about 80 percent of their waterfront view. As a result of the construction, the Kiesels' home lost over $300,000.00 in value, and the Kiesels brought an inverse condemnation action against the County. The *Kiesel* court found that the County's construction of the bridge substantially and materially blocked the Kiesels' riparian right of view. It explained that, in Florida, riparians have a right to an unobstructed view of the water, which constitutes a property right. Thus, the government may not take or destroy this property right without paying just compensation to the owners (see Chapter 14).

6. Right to Water of a Certain Quality

Courts in riparian jurisdictions can apply the general riparian rules and principles to disputes arising over water pollution. Riparians are entitled to the reasonable use of water flowing by their property in a natural stream and likewise have the right to create a reasonable amount of pollution. Determining whether a riparian is unreasonably polluting the water is an issue that courts address using the same factors as when analyzing an unreasonable use of the water, with the added considerations of the federal Clean Water Act[26] and state water quality requirements. We will explore this aspect of riparian rights more thoroughly in Chapters 11 and 13.

---

[25] Lee County v. Kiesel, 705 So.2d 1013 (Fla. App. 1998).

[26] 33 U.S.C. §§ 1251–1388.

Chapter 3

DEALING WITH WESTERN WATER REALITIES: THE CREATION AND ADOPTION OF PRIOR APPROPRIATION

A. Introduction

As the United States expanded westward through colonization and conquest, and as new territories and later states were admitted into the Union in the 19th and early 20th centuries, settlers faced very different hydrological, meteorological and geographic conditions, as well as patterns of land ownership and management, than those that dominated in the East, where the U.S. versions of the riparian rights doctrine evolved. Those different western conditions would suggest a very new system of water law.

The West is a very large and diverse region, with hydrological conditions ranging from the very wet and lush Pacific Northwest to the arid Southwest. Nevertheless, as discussed in more detail in Chapter 1, the West[1] is generally more arid and sources of surface water are more dispersed than in the East. In addition, because the majority of the region's precipitation comes in the form of winter snowfall and spring runoff, water supplies often are more variable in flow from season to season and from year to year, requiring artificial storage to make water available when it is most needed, particularly throughout the hot, dry growing season in much of the region. Moreover, in the rugged topography of the West, with deep canyons and tall mountains, significant physical barriers often separate sources of water and desired places of human water use. As the Colorado Supreme Court noted in the seminal case of *Coffin v. Left Hand Ditch Co.*:

> The climate is dry, and the soil, when moistened only by the usual rainfall, is arid and unproductive; except in a few favored sections, artificial irrigation for agriculture is an absolute necessity. Water in the various streams thus acquires a value unknown in moister climates. Instead of being a mere incident to the soil, it rises, when

---

1 Commentators identify the 100th Meridian as a reasonable dividing line between the humid east and the arid west. *See, e.g.*, WALLACE STEGNER, BEYOND THE HUNDREDTH MERIDIAN: JOHN WESLEY POWELL AND THE SECOND OPENING OF THE WEST (1954). Although this division is reasonable, any clear delineation is necessarily imprecise and somewhat arbitrary.

> appropriated, to the dignity of a distinct and usufructory estate, or right of property. . . . Houses have been built, and permanent improvements made; the soil has been cultivated, and thousands of acres have been rendered immensely valuable, with the understanding that appropriations of water would be protected. Deny the doctrine of priority or superiority of right by priority of appropriation, and a great part of the value of all of this property is at once destroyed.[2]

The West is also very large geographically, and white settlers often needed to use water at locations far away from the most reliable, plentiful or convenient sources of supply. Moreover, at the time of settlement, large portions of the region were—and in most places in the West still are—in public ownership, generally federal public lands. Particularly in the early years of settlement, miners and others did not own the land on which they wanted to put water to use. In an early case arising out of the California gold rush, the California Supreme Court wrote:

> Courts are bound to take notice of the political and social conditions of the country, which they judicially rule. In this State the larger part of the territory consists of mineral lands, nearly the whole of which are the property of the public. . . . Among the [attributes of the system governing mining on those lands] the most important are the rights of miners to be protected in the possession of their selected localities, and the rights of those who, by prior appropriation, have taken the waters from their natural beds, and by costly artificial works have conducted them for miles over mountains and ravines, to supply the necessity of gold diggers, and without which the most important interests of the mineral region would remain without development.[3]

All those factors, in various ways, suggested to white western settlers that attributes of the system of riparian rights applicable in the eastern states might be less appropriate in the West. Restricting the right to use water to riparian landowners, for example, would exclude large swaths of arable land and other economically valuable uses from water rights. It could also grant valuable water monopolies to a small group of landowners. The strict version of riparian rights, in which water could not be substantially diminished in quantity or quality, which was viable in regions where spring and summer rainfall were sufficient to water crops, could discourage or prevent

---

[2] 6 Colo. 443, 446 (1882).

[3] Irwin v. Phillips, 5 Cal. 140, 146–47 (1918).

the irrigation essential to growing food and other crops in an arid region. It could also impede or prevent significant diversion of water to lands and uses distant from the source, or storage of water when runoff was available for times when it was not. Finally, scarcity rather than surplus was the stark reality in the West. The lack of certainty inherent in riparian law, in which new riparian users might constantly shift the balance in what uses were considered "reasonable," with no guaranteed protection of or preference to existing users, might discourage investment in the infrastructure necessary to put water to use in arid regions.

The prior appropriation doctrine, sometimes known as "western" water law after the states in which it evolved, operates in ways designed to address some of riparianism's limitations relative to western circumstances. This chapter begins with a description of the basic concepts of prior appropriation law that set it apart from riparian rights, and for each concept, it provides an explanation of how or why the doctrine addresses one of those limitations. It then describes the legal elements necessary to perfect an appropriative water right and the factors that govern the priority system. Next, this chapter provides historical overviews of the evolution of the prior appropriation system in different parts of the West, and the three major variations on the doctrine (the Colorado doctrine, California doctrine and Oregon doctrine), including the extent to which they preserve aspects of the riparian rights system of water law. Throughout, this chapter provides insights into the practical aspects of prior appropriation law and what factors should be considered when making investments and other important decisions affected by the doctrine and its application.

One important note before turning to those issues, however, is to emphasize that the details of prior appropriation law vary from state to state, both in the substantive aspects of the doctrine and in administration and management. The following discussion, therefore, conveys only the most fundamental aspects of prior appropriation law. State-specific research and analysis is needed for details and additional variations.

B. The Basic Concepts of Prior Appropriation

1. Divergence from Riparian Rights

Two related concepts of prior appropriation law most notably distinguish the doctrine from riparian rights and illustrate the fundamental and intentional departure from pre-existing U.S. water law to address the conditions in which western settlers found themselves trying to develop an economy and a society. First, riparian land ownership (or littoral land ownership in the case of lakes) is irrelevant to the right to use water under prior appropriation.[4] In other words, riparian land ownership is not necessary to confer, and in fact does not confer, the right to use water. In the wetter eastern states, the riparian land ownership requirement does not restrict development by many landowners, or on a large percentage of the land. Streams and other water sources are relatively plentiful, as is rainfall even for those parcels with no riparian access. By contrast, limiting the right to use water to riparian properties in an arid or semi-arid region in which surface water sources are spaced very far apart, and where rainfall is limited and unreliable, would leave vast areas of land unusable for many economically desirable purposes. In addition, in arid regions restricting water use rights to riparian owners would confer monopoly power that would either restrict economic opportunities to a small percentage of the population or allow them to charge extortionist prices to allow others to develop and use nonriparian properties. Decoupling the right to use water from riparian ownership, therefore, was more egalitarian economically and opened a larger portion of land in the West to development.

Second, under prior appropriation, the place of water use is irrelevant. Traditional riparian law allowed water use only on the riparian parcel, although most riparian states have softened that limitation to varying degrees, or eliminated it (see Chapter 2). That limitation, designed to restrict or eliminate the degree to which stream flows were reduced and water was diverted from its source watershed, was considered an inefficient luxury in a drier region where alternative sources of water are sparse or unreliable. In prior appropriation states, water can be used wherever it can be put to beneficial use (a concept described in more detail below). This aspect of prior appropriation is also more egalitarian and is designed to maximize the utility of scarce water resources.

Of course, use of water from a surface source but at a distant location still requires access, and these two new principles of western water law did not abandon the law of trespass. However, if a water user obtains the necessary surface access through contract, easement, prescriptive rights, or otherwise, water law no longer prohibits off-parcel use. Many western states ultimately addressed this issue by granting broad rights of eminent domain to governmental and quasi-governmental water institutions, which developed as a means of pooling resources to build the storage and

---

[4] As discussed in Chapter 2, some of the property rights conferred by and governed by the riparian rights doctrine, such as riparian land ownership and the right to access water bodies and to exclude others, remain even in prior appropriation states. This chapter focuses only on the right to use water for consumptive and other purposes.

diversion structures necessary to take advantage of distant and dispersed water use.

If land ownership and place of use were no longer the fundamental principles for establishing water rights, what replaced them? Most fundamentally, the prior appropriation system was designed to provide incentives, in the form of increased certainty of legal rights, for the investment in labor and other resources necessary to put water to beneficial use, in ways that optimized the utility of a scarce resource. Two concepts developed to define water rights in ways designed to accomplish those goals, both of which are suggested by the name of the doctrine: (1) *priority* of rights based on the timing of the appropriation, which gave rise to the concept of "first in time, first in right;" and (2) *appropriation* of water to be put to a beneficial use, which suggested the "use it or lose it" principle of prior appropriation law.

2. First in Time, First in Right

In prior appropriation law, the concept of "first in time, first in right" (in Latin, *qui prior est tempore, potior est jure*) defines the relative rights of competing appropriators in times of shortage. Under this system, those who hold more "senior" water rights—i.e., who began using water from a particular source earliest—are entitled to their full water right before "junior" right-holders receive any water at all. For example, at the height of the California drought in 2015, only people who had water rights on the Merced River dating to before 1858 could take water from that river; everyone with more junior rights was curtailed. Seniors also have the right to prevent juniors (through judicial or other processes that vary from state to state, a process generally known as "calling the river") from diverting and using water in ways that interfere with senior water rights. This is an unusually powerful and relatively absolute legal right, given the extent to which it can shut down or substantially impair another party's water use and accompanying economic activity.

Of course, ironically, adoption of the "first in time" principle by white western settlers largely ignored longstanding water use by Native American Tribes. As the Washington Supreme Court noted in 2021, "Native Americans have been making beneficial use of the waters in the Yakima River Basin for centuries . . . ."[5] As a result, early prior appropriation law failed to recognize those pre-existing uses as valid water rights or as constraining use by white settlers. The U.S. Supreme Court partially addressed this omission, as discussed in Chapter 8, by acknowledging "reserved" water rights that the federal government implicitly held for use by Native

[5] Matter of Rights to Use of Surface Waters of Yakima River Drainage Basin, 198 Wash.2d 687, 714 (2021).

Americans on reservations (but probably more accurately viewed as water rights that the Tribes reserved to themselves when they granted the federal government land). That federal law doctrine, however, does not eliminate the implicit "appropriation" of indigenous Native American water rights under the new system of law.

One of the very few limits on seniority rights is the "futile call doctrine," in which a junior can avoid a curtailment of its water right if they can show that the withheld water would not be available to the senior anyway. In a classic example of a futile call, the junior is located upstream of the senior and hydrological or other physical factors (such as evaporation or infiltration into permeable soils) would prevent any water from reaching the senior regardless of whether the junior appropriator uses that water. Other limits on the seniority doctrine, discussed further below, arise when the junior user can demonstrate that the senior is "wasting" water or has abandoned or forfeited all or part of its water right through nonuse.

Prior appropriation law provides further incentives for investments in water infrastructure through the "relation back" doctrine. At common law, this doctrine fixed the priority date at the time when a user initiates the first steps necessary to perfect a water right, rather than the date at which water is first put to beneficial use. Under modern permit systems (see Chapter 5), this first step is the permit application. The relation back doctrine recognizes that it often takes time to construct and begin to operate the structures like canals and pumps that are necessary to divert water and put it to use. It recognizes further that some water use schemes require phased investment—for example, where farm acreage is brought under cultivation over time rather than all at once. In both cases, the priority date relates back to the date of initial construction (or permit application), so long as the full development was part of a common plan and so long as the party exercises due diligence in completing the plan in a reasonable and timely way.

Several factors explain why early western water users deemed a strict priority system necessary and appropriate. In the eastern states, water was sufficiently plentiful relative to demand that the "reasonable use" principle sufficed to allocate water among competing users. Most economic activities could continue, even if at a somewhat less profitable level, and even if reasonable use doctrine required some curtailment during times of drought or other shortage. In many parts of the West, by contrast, water was so scarce, and needs often so essential, that a clearer system of prioritization was desirable. In essence, the doctrine means that earlier uses should be maintained fully rather than "sharing" water in ways that might appear equitable in theory but result in the failure of *everyone*'s crops or other activities for lack of sufficient water.

The priority system necessarily favored earlier users over newcomers, and unlike riparian rights under the reasonable use doctrine, allows for no judicial or other balancing of economic or social value.[6] From an efficiency perspective, it made little sense for water users to make the necessary investments and to rely on water rights essential to developing and conducting related economic activities (farming, ranching, mining, community development), only to have those rights and the activities that depend on them substantially diminish in value over time. Users developed businesses and other activities that required certain amounts of water, often at specific times of year and in particular locations. Greater certainty of water rights was needed, especially where significant amounts of capital and labor were necessary to construct and operate the storage, diversion, and conveyance systems to put water to use for mining, irrigation, and other purposes.

There are two potentially perverse consequences of this emphasis on priority. First, so long as later junior users understand that they might not get any water in drier years, nothing in common-law prior appropriation prohibits them from piling up water rights in streams and rivers for exercise during the wettest years. Unlike the riparian reasonable use doctrine, therefore, prior appropriation incentivized the full appropriation of all available water, drying up streams and rivers and essentially ignoring the consequences to fish and other aquatic life, as well as other non-consumptive uses such as public recreation. Many western states have since tried to provide mechanisms that allow water to be left in the streams and rivers, many of which are discussed in Chapters 11, 12 and 13. Still, over-appropriation remains a problem for many of the West's waterways.

Second, the priority system has increasingly come under attack for "locking in" early uses even if they are no longer the most valuable use of water. In theory, even if a junior can put water to a more valuable use than a senior (whether measured by economic or other factors, such as in-stream environmental benefits), the senior has the right to curtail the more economically efficient or beneficial use. Stated differently, some question whether "first in utility" rather than "first in time" should be the principle that dictates who is "first in right." Nevertheless, the reality remains that, in most western states, the most senior water rights allocate a substantial portion of the state's water (often ~80%) to agriculture.

---

[6] Some states, however, have statutory or other preferences for some uses, such as domestic water use. *See* Robert E. Beck, *Use Preferences for Water*, 76 N.D. L. REV. 753 (2000).

One response to this critique of prior appropriation doctrine is that appropriative rights are alienable—that is, they can be sold to other would-be users like any other kind of property, either separately or as part of a larger real estate sale. Therefore, as is true for other property, water rights sales can be used to allocate the resource most efficiently. Someone whose use is more valuable than an existing use can, subject to restrictions described in more detail below, purchase a senior appropriative right. Obviously, the more senior the existing right, the more valuable it is and the higher the price will be.

From a practical perspective, however, various legal restrictions limit the degree to which "water marketing" can actually re-allocate water from old, senior uses. Under the regulatory versions of prior appropriation discussed in Chapter 5, the responsible state official usually must determine that a transfer will not harm the public interest—for example, by dewatering an important fishery. Likewise, any sale is subject to the rule that the transfer cannot injure any other water rights holders, even those with junior rights. For example, a junior may rely on return flow from a senior irrigator to satisfy his or her right. If the senior sells his or her right to someone in a different drainage, that change may cause unacceptable harm to the junior user. Likewise, water rights cannot be sold in ways that "enlarge" the existing right. Both problems are illustrated by *Barron v. Idaho Department of Water Resources*,[7] in which the Idaho Supreme Court upheld a decision by the Idaho Department of Water Resources to deny a water transfer where it would allow more total water to be used and where it would harm other users who relied on the transferred flows.

Litigation and other expenses associated with attempted water transfers can also impose hefty transaction costs that may inhibit the "market" in water. Despite these limitations, however, water transfers have occurred with increasing frequency in the West—for example to allow reallocation from agricultural to urban use, or from less valuable to more valuable crops.[8] Recently, some parties have begun to purchase water rights in large quantities for purposes of investment in large portfolios or water futures. Like other investment funds, these ventures assume that the value of scarce water will increase over time.

---

7 18 P.3d 219 (Idaho 2001).

8 *See* Jedediah Brewer, Robert Glennon, Alan Ker & Gary Libecap, *Transferring Water in the American West: **1987–2005***, 40 U. MICH. J. L. REFORM 2021 (2007).

3. Use It or Lose It

Prior appropriation doctrine also tries to make water use more efficient through the "use it or lose it" principle. This aspect of prior appropriation law is designed to make sure that water is put to beneficial use rather than being held for speculation or in other ways that improperly prevent other people from using the water. States effectuate the "use it or lose it" concept, at least in theory, through either the common law doctrine of abandonment or statutory forfeiture, or both, depending on the state. States also vary in the evidentiary burden of proof necessary to establish abandonment. Both doctrines provide that if a water right holder does not use the water for the intended beneficial use for a prescribed period of time, the water reverts to the state or the public (whichever state law deems to be the actual "owner" of water in the state), allowing other would-be users to appropriate it. However, a right holder can only abandon or forfeit a water right if the water is actually available. For example, if a drought is so severe that juniors are curtailed from use, they cannot forfeit or abandon their water because of nonuse.

Abandonment is a common law doctrine that allows plaintiffs, usually junior appropriators, to assert that a senior appropriator has abandoned all or part of that senior right as a result of nonuse. Abandonment requires clear and convincing evidence of intent to abandon, plus an actual relinquishment or surrender of the right. The intent requirement is a question of fact. Especially with the heightened "clear and convincing evidence" burden of persuasion, "mere nonuse" is usually not sufficient to prove intent to abandon. Long periods of actual nonuse, however, can create a rebuttable presumption of abandonment. States created challenging standards of proof for abandonment to ensure water rights are not easily lost, given their extreme importance to landowners and other users in an arid region. However, they achieved that goal so well that abandonment claims rarely work, or are even pursued—even by state regulators.[9]

Forfeiture is a statutory analog to abandonment, adopted by most western state legislatures because of the uncertainty and difficulty inherent in abandonment doctrine. Indeed, many states have replaced the common law doctrine entirely with statutory forfeiture. Statutory forfeiture provisions are more objective and more easily proven because they eliminate the intent requirement. Rather, if some or all of the water defined in a water right is not put to beneficial use continuously for a prescribed statutory period (often seven years), it is subject to automatic forfeiture. Several factors,

---

[9] For a relatively rare case in which water rights have been lost through nonuse, *see* State ex rel. Reynolds v. South Springs Co., 452 P.2d 478 (N.M. 1969).

however, also have limited the utility of statutory forfeiture. Long periods of nonuse can still be difficult to prove, particularly in remote regions or where the actual use is not subject to rigorous reporting or obvious physical manifestations. Some forfeiture provisions require action by a state official or agency, and such officials and agencies are often reluctant to terminate citizens' valuable water rights. Moreover, a user can defeat forfeiture simply by using the water in one year, thus re-setting the seven-year (or other) statutory forfeiture clock.

C. The Elements of Prior Appropriation

Although the basic concepts outlined above characterize the prior appropriation doctrine and the nature of appropriative rights generally, would-be appropriators have to meet a set of specific elements in order to perfect an appropriative water right. Those elements vary somewhat from state to state, but they define the more precise rules and requirements that govern the establishment, relative value, and implementation and enforcement of the prior appropriation system of water law.

Four basic elements are necessary to establish an appropriative water right: (1) diversion or other form of notice; (2) of unappropriated water; (3) from a source subject to appropriation; (4) for beneficial use.[10] Those legal elements have evolved over time as the administration of the prior appropriation system has become more sophisticated and as both law and technology have improved in relevant ways. However, the basic concepts explaining each element have remained more stable.

1. Diversion or Other Notice

In the early years of prior appropriation, physical diversion of water was required to establish a water right. This physical diversion requirement served multiple purposes. In an era in which only off-stream uses were considered "beneficial," a physical diversion of water from the stream was a clear indication that water had been put to such use. Moreover, when physical measurements of the amount of use were relatively unsophisticated, and when public records of actual water use were similarly primitive, the *size* of a diversion structure served as a reasonable surrogate measure of the amount of water a user was appropriating. Of course, that concept provided a somewhat perverse incentive to build a larger diversion structure than was strictly necessary to fulfill a particular use, meaning that the size of the water right might be artificially inflated.

---

[10] *See* CHARLES J. MEYERS, A HISTORICAL AND FUNCTIONAL ANALYSIS OF THE APPROPRIATION SYSTEM 4 (1971).

Most fundamentally, however, physical diversion served as a form of notice to other users, and a form of proof from an institutional perspective, that a particular party was putting water from a particular source to beneficial use at a particular place. Given the priority system, newcomers needed some way to know who was already diverting water from a stream, and in what amounts, before deciding whether to invest in an activity requiring a new appropriation. When there were no clear institutional records, or where those records might be hundreds of miles away in a state or territorial capital, a physical diversion served both as notice to those new arrivals and as a form of tangible proof by which an existing appropriator could document their priority.

Over time, two factors led to the erosion of the physical diversion requirement and its elimination in many states. First, as will be discussed in Chapter 5, administration of the prior appropriation system evolved from the quasi-legal customs developed by early settlers in the mining camps and other areas, to a common law legal system that required proof in individual cases, to a more formal administrative system with recording requirements in government offices. As the system became more formal and records more accurate, those records replaced the physical diversion requirement as a form of notice and proof of prior appropriations. Indeed, to the extent that the size of the diversion served as an imperfect approximation of the size of an appropriative right, a formal record that specified the exact amount of water diverted from a particular location and at specified times both limited the existing appropriator and gave more precise notice of both the fact and the size of water use to new appropriators and the state.

Second, as the concept of "beneficial use" evolved to recognize the legitimacy of obtaining appropriative rights for instream uses such as fish and wildlife support or recreational flows, the diversion requirement made no sense. Certain environmental or other non-consumptive water uses do require diversions—for example, to provide water for wetland restoration. Simply leaving water in situ to support instream uses, however, requires no diversion. For example, in *In re Adjudication of the Existing Rights to the Use of All the Water*,[11] the Montana Supreme Court held that a physical diversion is not required "where no diversion is necessary to put the water to a beneficial use."[12]

---

[11] 55 P.3d 396 (Mont. 2002).

[12] *Id.* at 406.

2. Unappropriated Water

The concept that unappropriated water must be available to support a new right to appropriate seems so fundamental that one might think it need not even be stated. If a party takes all of the steps otherwise necessary to support and appropriative right, but if all of the available water has been accounted for by more senior appropriations, then the newcomer will have a paper right but no "wet water" to put to actual beneficial use. On more careful consideration, however, the issue is not as obvious as it appears.

First, as discussed in Chapter 1, in many streams and stream systems, the water supply is highly variable from year to year. Thus, the available water in many or even most years may have been allocated to prior appropriators, but in particularly wet years some water may be "available for appropriation." Because prior appropriation policy seeks to maximize the use of a scarce resource, that water remains available to appropriate even if it is only available physically during wet years.

Second, existing users may or may not use all of their appropriations in any given year, depending on weather and other conditions. For example, if stored soil moisture or precipitation is high in a given year, or if temperature (and resulting evapotranspiration) is unusually low, irrigators may not need to apply their full appropriation to successfully grow crops in that year. Under the abandonment and forfeiture doctrines, failure to use all of the appropriated water in any single year does not result in a loss of the water right, again making that water available for use in those years by other potential appropriators.

Third, in most systems, multiple appropriators can re-use the same actual water because of return flows. In irrigation, for example, a certain percentage of water applied to the land runs off of or seeps into the stream rather than being taken up by the crops, evaporated, or otherwise "consumed." Once returned to the stream, the water is again available for appropriation. Although models can predict how much water is likely to return to the stream under various conditions, those models are based on variable assumptions, and return flows can be variable from year to year. For example, in *Central Platte Natural Resources District v. Wyoming*,[13] the Nebraska Supreme Court needed to choose between two competing methods of modeling the percentage of existing water rights that were actually being used in order to determine whether additional water was available for appropriation. Similarly, in states that acknowledge the hydrological connection between surface water and groundwater, additional water

[13] 513 N.W. 2d 847 (Neb. 1994).

may be available to appropriate from adjacent aquifers, even if it is not readily available from the stream itself.

Finally, as explained above, because of the "relation back" doctrine, some appropriations may remain conditional until fully perfected, but the priority date for a subsequently perfected appropriation may predate a new appropriation, even if the latter appropriation is put to beneficial use first. Thus, until all pending appropriation claims are perfected or lost as a result of a lack of due diligence or other steps necessary to perfect the right, the amount of water available for appropriation may remain uncertain.

One theme common to all of the above uncertainties is *risk*. A new potential appropriator in search of additional water available to appropriate from a system has an economic incentive to evaluate all of the above factors carefully before deciding whether to invest in the infrastructure needed to divert water and put it to beneficial use, as well as the underlying economic activities the water will support. Water may be available for appropriation in the sense that some portion of the appropriative right will be available for actual use ("wet water") some of the time. However, whether the economic investment necessary to put the water to beneficial use is justified relative to the economic or other utility of the use is a business decision informed by available information about the percentage of time that sufficient water will be available. Making that business decision requires sufficient historical data on the hydrology of the system, coupled with expert analysis—based on predictive modeling and other factors—regarding the probability that water will be available, and in what amounts, over time. Changing hydrology because of climate change further complicates this analysis. Water lawyers can play a key role in counseling their clients about the relative risks and rewards of a particular investment decision, in addition to doing the legal work necessary to apply for and perfect a water right.

From a policy perspective, each state needs to consider how it will decide whether water is "available" for appropriation, in terms of the scientific and technical methods that it uses and of the state's overall goals for its water and the aquatic ecosystems it supports. Traditionally, prior appropriation doctrine sought to maximize the utility of water in a fairly narrow economic sense—i.e., maximizing human development through homes, farms, and industry. That goal suggests that any unused water should be made available for appropriation by subsequent applicants even if it is available only in some years or at certain times of the year and that water is "wasted" if it simply remains in the stream. A more conservative approach, however, is more likely to leave water in the system for environmental sustainability (see Chapters 11, 12, and 13) and is more likely to avoid intensive disputes and "calls on the river" during times of shortage.

3. Sources Subject to Appropriation

An issue related to water availability is the source of water subject to appropriation, or the places from which an appropriator can lawfully divert water. It is important to understand the consequences of this classification: If a water source is subject to appropriation, people taking water from that source must comply with the legal requirements to establish a water right. If a source is *not* subject to appropriation, however, people can use water from that source without fulfilling the requirements for an appropriative right. Classically, all surface water sources confined by a bed and banks—e.g., creeks, streams, lakes—were subject to appropriation, but diffuse surface runoff was not. Groundwater is a tad more complicated (see Chapter 4), but many states distinguished between "underground streams" and more diffuse forms of groundwater.

Of course, in the real world, these legal categories make little sense. From the perspective of the "water cycle" discussed in Chapter 1, all water in the natural world is connected to some degree, and diversion of any water from one place in a connected system is likely to change the amount or place of water available to other users. For example, water diverted upstream will reduce the amount available for appropriation downstream, but the same may be true for water pumped from an adjacent aquifer with a sufficient hydrological connection that groundwater pumping reduces the water in the stream (see Chapter 4). The same may be true for water taken from springs, wetlands or surface seeps that might eventually reach or recharge the stream if not used first, or for surface runoff from precipitation. In *Martiny v. Wells*,[14] for example, the court held that spring water that would have reached the stream but for defendants' diversion was "tributary water" subject to the appropriation requirements. Most western states have similarly been evolving this "subject to appropriation" element to better reflect the hydrological connections among water sources, as evidenced by their increasing conjunctive management of surface water and groundwater.

Nevertheless, legal discontinuities regarding hydrologically connected water sources remain, and this tendency warrants particularly close attention to the details of a specific state's law. Key issues include what water is considered "surface water" for purposes of a state's prior appropriation system and what water is subject to separate regulation as groundwater, and under what principles. Although most, but not all, prior appropriation states also use prior

---

[14] 419 P.2d 470 (Idaho 1966).

appropriation principles to govern groundwater withdrawals and to resolve disputes among competing groundwater users, courts or administrators may need to determine whether a withdrawal from one source will adversely affect users in the other. If there is an impact, further decisions include whether the respective diversion is permissible and, if so, where it fits within the priority system if they are allowed. We revisit these issues in more detail in Chapter 13.

This issue is complicated further by the legal status of water as public or private property. In general, most states provide by constitutional provision or otherwise that water is the property of the state, or that the state holds it in trust for the people at large.[15] Some beneficial uses, however, allow appropriators to confine water in discreet containers (for example, in large storage tanks or in plastic water bottles), and this water then becomes private property, with all of the usual attributes of chattel property. However, most of the time under the prior appropriation doctrine, private parties obtain only a usufructuary property interest in water, that is, the right to put water to beneficial use as opposed to absolute ownership. Water in streams and other sources that cross property boundaries are "subject to appropriation" for that purpose. Some kinds of water, however, such as precipitation runoff that simply ponds on private land, is considered sufficiently bound to that private property that the landowner can make use of it or reduce it to private ownership independent of the appropriation system.

States vary considerably in what water sources remain subject to appropriation. For example, the Utah Supreme Court ruled that seepage water is available for subsequent reuse by the appropriator unless that water returns to the natural stream channel and has been appropriated by another user.[16] Such reliance is not generally recognized, however, for water that seeps onto a neighboring owner's land without returning to the stream channel[17] or for so-called "developed water" imported from one watershed to another, and on which an appropriator could not have relied in the natural system.[18] Utah's legislature recently allowed residents to capture a limited amount of rainwater without meeting the requirements for an appropriative right, but Colorado views rainfall as already part of the prior appropriation system.

---

[15] *See, e.g.*, COLO. CONST. art VXI, § 5 (declaring water to be the "property of the public"); MONT. CONST. art. IX, § 3 (identifying water as the "property of the state for the use of its people").

[16] Estate of Steed v. New Escalante Irrigation Dist., 846 P.2d 1223 (Utah 1992).

[17] *See, e.g.*, Bower v. Big Horn Canal Co., 307 P.2d 593 (Wyo. 1957).

[18] *See, e.g.*, Stevens v. Oakdale Irrigation Dist., 90 P.2d 58 (Cal. 1939).

4. Beneficial Use

The last and perhaps most fundamental element of prior appropriation is beneficial use, which is referred to as the "basis, measure, and limit of an appropriative right."[19] The word "basis" refers to the fact that "beneficial" uses are the uses of water that society wants to promote—that are worth granting to a private person a usufructuary right in a public resource. "Measure" indicates that a user gets the amount of water necessary for that beneficial use—power plants and irrigators have different needs—but irrigators growing alfalfa also have different needs than irrigators growing artichokes. Likewise, "limit" indicates that only as much water as can be used beneficially, without undue waste, is included in the right, with the goal of maximizing the amount of water available for appropriation for other uses and thus optimizing overall utility and value of the resource.

The breadth of what is considered "beneficial" has evolved over time and varies from state to state. Conceptually, why should the state limit what is deemed a beneficial use rather than leaving that determination to the market, as is true for most natural resources? The classic explanation is that the beneficial use requirement ensures that water is used in ways that are deemed constructive to ensure the viability of human communities and economies in an arid region. An alternative and perhaps more cogent explanation is that, aside from the infrastructure necessary to divert water, the resource itself is most often free, in contrast to other public natural resources such as timber, hard rock minerals, or fossil fuels, for which the government usually charges rents or royalties. Whether or not the different treatment of water reflects sound policy, it means that the market forces that usually incentivize users to maximize value are not in play.

The first logical question regarding the beneficial use element is, what is considered "beneficial"? In the early years of prior appropriation doctrine, the only uses considered beneficial were for basic life support (domestic water for drinking, bathing, and home gardens, including municipal water supply) and traditional economic activities such as irrigation, mining, and industrial use. Those uses invariably required diversion from the stream and use outside the confines of the water source. More recently, states have broadened the doctrine to allow governmental or private parties to obtain appropriative rights for instream uses such as fish and wildlife support or recreation. For example, Montana recognizes instream

---

[19] *E.g.*, UTAH CODE ANN. § 73–1–3.

water rights for fish, wildlife and recreation, and requires a physical diversion for those uses only when necessary to support them.[20]

The second, often more challenging, question is how to quantify the amount of water that goes with a particular beneficial use. As discussed above, in the early years of prior appropriation law, the size of the diversion structure was used to quantify the size of the right, in part under the assumption that users would use the full amount of water they could divert to maximize use, and in part because it was a simple, determinative means of assigning a quantitative measure and limit on a water right.

That method, however, did not quantify how much water was *actually* put to beneficial use (the measure of the right). Nor did it ascertain how much water was *necessary* to fulfill that beneficial use (the limit of the right), or stated differently, whether water was being wasted by being used less efficiently than possible to meet the identified beneficial use. If the goal of prior appropriation doctrine is to promote the maximum utility of such a limited resource, the system should provide incentives for efficiency rather than waste. For example, it takes a lot more water to irrigate any crop through flood irrigation than through pipes and sprinklers, and drip irrigation requires even less water. In theory, therefore, beneficial use requirements and their corollary prohibitions on waste could allow state regulators to require all farmers to install drip irrigation systems (as the government of Israel did, for example, as part of its water conservation policies). In practice, however, incentives for efficiency are weak and infrequently and inconsistently enforced, leading some commentators to question the effectiveness of the anti-waste policy of prior appropriation law.[21] Moreover, the "use it or lose it" tenet of prior appropriation doctrine, discussed above, arguably cuts in exactly the opposite direction by encouraging appropriators to use every drop of water to ensure that the associated right is not abandoned or forfeited, despite the typically weak enforcement of those doctrines.

The failure of the beneficial use doctrine to police inefficiency in water use rigorously is highlighted by a somewhat tepid "reasonable use" and "customary practice" standard articulated by the California Supreme Court in *Tulare Irrigation District v. Lindsay-Strathmore Irrigation District*,[22] which is applied in many prior appropriation states. In one portion of the opinion, the court constrained the concept of beneficial use in an extreme case by holding that use of irrigation

[20] In re Adjudication of the Existing Rights to the Use of All the Water, 55 P.3d 396 (Mont. 2002).

[21] *See* Janet C. Neumann, *Beneficial Use, Waste and Forfeiture: The Inefficient Search for Efficiency in Western Water Use*, 28 ENVTL. L. 919 (1998).

[22] 45 P.2d 972 (Cal. 1935).

water to drown gophers during the winter did not constitute a legally recognized beneficial use.[23] In the context of appropriation for the beneficial use of irrigation, the court indicated that the "measure" of the water right was "the amount of water . . . diverted for beneficial purposes, plus a reasonable conveyance loss, subject to the limitation that the amount be not more than is reasonably necessary, under reasonable methods of diversion, to supply the area of land theretofore served by his ditch."[24]

The fact that conveyance losses are included in the water right reflects the fact that it is impossible to divert water from a stream and use it for irrigation, and many other purposes, with 100% efficiency. Some of the conveyance water evaporates, seeps into groundwater, or is taken up by natural plants rather than irrigated crops. As discussed above, some of the conveyance water or water that is applied to crops but not actually used becomes "return flow" available for use by a downstream appropriator. Of course, a lined canal or a closed pipe will convey water more efficiently, that is, with less conveyance loss, than an unlined ditch through porous soils. In specifying the degree of efficiency with which water must be diverted and used, the *Tulare* Court clarified:

> In so far as the diversion exceeds the amount reasonably necessary for beneficial purposes, it is contrary to the policy of the law and is a taking without right and confers no title, no matter for how long continued. In determining what is a reasonable quantity for beneficial uses, it is the policy of the state to require within reasonable limits the highest and greatest duty from the waters of the state. However, an appropriator cannot be compelled to divert according to the most scientific method known. He is entitled to make a reasonable use of water according to the general custom of the locality, so long as custom does not involve unnecessary waste.[25]

Thus, although the "reasonably necessary" standard appears to impose a duty to divert and convey water efficiently, the "custom in the locality" clarification eliminates any incentive for improved efficiency so long as all irrigators in the region continue to use existing, inefficient practices.

Other states use a somewhat more rigorous concept of "water duty," in which a state administrative official determines how much water is necessary for a particular purpose. For example, for a new proposed water right to irrigate x acres of a particular crop at a

---

23 *Id.* at 1007.

24 *Id.* at 997, 1009–1010.

25 *Id.* at 997.

designated location, the state will take into account the locate climate, hydrology, soils, and the amount of water typically needed to grow that crop in identifying water demand, and that determination is subject to review similar to other administrative agency decisions.[26] Arguably, this is a more rational, scientific and accurate system to ascertain the actual amount of water needed for particular uses. This ensures the most efficient use of scarce water and leaves as much as possible in stream for other users and for ecosystem support without compromising the beneficial uses associated with appropriate water rights. As discussed more fully in Chapter 5, however, this practice fundamentally shifted the relationship between private parties and the government in water rights determinations. In the traditional system of prior appropriation, users would divert whatever quantities they believed were necessary and appropriate for a given beneficial use, and that usage was subject to later judicial review in the context of stream adjudications or claims brought by adverse users. In the administrative water duty variation of prior appropriation, a government agency determines in advance how much water is needed for a particular beneficial use, and an opportunity for judicial review is available if the applicant questions that quantification.

Whether or not it is enforced rigorously, it is important to distinguish the anti-waste doctrine from the related doctrines of abandonment and forfeiture discussed above. All three principles are designed to ensure that as much water as possible is put to beneficial use and can result in a partial or complete loss of an appropriative water right. However, unlike the doctrines of abandonment and forfeiture, which support a claim that a right holder has not been using some or all of the right at all, in the doctrine of waste an adverse user asserts that another party has been using water inefficiently, and therefore not beneficially.

D. The Three Main Variations on Prior Appropriation Doctrine

As part of the process of adopting a legal system that was generally consistent with the Anglo-American law to which western migrants were accustomed, and on which their commerce and property rights depended, all of the western territories and states in the west adopted "the common law of England" as the background body of applicable law. Absent specific change by constitution, statute, or judicial action, that body of law included riparian rights. Therefore, the states that subsequently adopted the prior appropriation doctrine had to take affirmative steps to do so, via

[26] *See, e.g.*, State Dep't of Ecology v. Grimes, 852 P.3d 1044 (Wash. 1993) (reviewing water duty finding by the Washington State Department of Ecology).

judicial decision, statute, constitutional provisions, or a combination of those methods over time.

Replacing riparian rights with prior appropriation, however, suggested challenging questions about the relationship between those two doctrines of law. Would the state or territory recognize *any* existing riparian rights at the time it adopted prior appropriation? Were those riparian rights extinguished, in which case did that legal change constitute a "taking" of private property rights for purposes of the Due Process and Just Compensation provisions of the Fifth and Fourteenth Amendments to the U.S. Constitution (see Chapter 14)? Or did any riparian rights that had vested by the time of the change remain valid, and if so, what was the relationship between two very different kinds of water rights when a conflict emerged between the two?

Different states addressed these thorny questions in different ways that fall into three distinct categories, known by reference to the first state that adopted the doctrine in that form.[27] Those are the "Colorado Doctrine," the "California Doctrine," and the "Oregon Doctrine."

1. The Colorado Doctrine

Despite their adoption of the common law generally, and supposedly of riparian rights along with it, six states in the intermountain West, led by Colorado, rejected the validity of riparian rights altogether in favor of a pure system of prior appropriation.[28] Notably, those states did retain those aspects of prior appropriation governing ownership of streambeds and stream access (see Chapter 2).[29] In the context of off stream water use, however, prior appropriation became the exclusive means of obtaining a usufructuary water right.

The legitimacy of Colorado's complete rejection of riparian rights was perhaps questionable, given the expectations of new property owners at the time that common law principles would be honored as well as early territorial laws that appeared to recognize riparian

---

[27] Although the federal courts did not definitively rule on the degree to which water law in the west was a matter of state as opposed to federal law, it confirmed that position in California Oregon Power Co. v. Beaver Portland Cement, 295 U.S. 142 (1935), which held that the federal government severed water from land when it issued federal land patents to western settlers, leaving that water subject to state allocation. It also clarified that states were free to decide, as a matter of policy, whether to adopt prior appropriation, riparian rights, or some combination of the two.

[28] The other states that adopted this variation include Arizona, Idaho, Montana, Nevada, New Mexico, Utah and Wyoming, although Montana and Nevada did so after initially appearing to recognize riparian rights.

[29] *See* People v. Emmert, 597 P.2d 1095 (Colo. 1979).

rights.[30] However, at statehood, Colorado clearly adopted prior appropriation in its founding constitution, as did most other western states.[31] Article XVII, § 5 of the Colorado Constitution provides that the "water of every natural stream, not heretofore appropriated . . . is declared to be the property of the public, and the same is dedicated to the use of the State, subject to appropriation." Article XVI, § 6 provides: "The right to appropriate the waters of any natural stream shall never be denied. Priority of appropriation shall give the better right as between those using water for the same purpose." In *Left Hand Ditch Co. v. Coffin*, the Colorado Supreme Court squarely rejected the proposition that riparian rights were *ever* the law in that state, or in the pre-existing territory:

> We conclude, then, that the common law doctrine giving the riparian owner a right to the flow of water in its natural channel upon and over his lands, even though he makes no beneficial use thereof, is inapplicable to Colorado. Imperative necessity, unknown to the countries which gave it birth, compels the recognition of another doctrine in conflict therewith. And we hold that, in the absence of express statutes to the contrary, the first appropriator of water from a natural stream for a beneficial purpose has, with the qualifications contained in the constitution, a prior right thereto, to the extent of such appropriation.[32]

Adoption of prior appropriation as the solitary means of obtaining usufructuary water rights had two distinct advantages from a legal perspective. First, by holding that riparian rights *never* existed in the territory or state, the Colorado Supreme Court (and other states to follow) avoided any claim that, in adopting the prior appropriation system, the state had unlawfully taken established riparian property rights without due process or just compensation. Second, this approach avoided conflicts between two competing and potentially inconsistent systems of water rights, as would become the case in so-called "dual system" states under the California and Oregon doctrines.

2. The California Doctrine

As discussed at the beginning of this chapter, in the early case of *Irwin v. Phillips* the California Supreme Court recognized the applicability and legal validity of prior appropriation in the context of a dispute between two miners, neither of which owned riparian property. Just two years later, however, the California court *also*

---

[30] *See* Coffin v. Left Hand Ditch, *supra*, 6 Colo. 443, 450–51 (citing Colo. Session Laws 1861, p.67, § 1 and Colo. Session Laws 1862, p. 48, § 13).

[31] *See, e.g.*, IDAHO CONST. art. XV, § 3.

[32] 6 Colo. at 447.

recognized riparian rights in a conflict between an appropriator and a riparian landowner.[33] Conflicts between riparian landowners and prior appropriators led to protracted legal and political battles in California. In the seminal case of *Lux v. Haggin*,[34] a highly divided California Supreme Court confirmed that pre-existing riparian rights remained valid and trumped later-perfected appropriative rights. On the other hand, later California cases held that an appropriative right that predated riparian land ownership (i.e., the date that the riparian property passed from government ownership to private ownership, usually through a land patent) would maintain its priority, thereby reducing the value and significance of the riparian right.

The co-existence of riparian rights and appropriative rights is inherently problematic. As explained in Chapter 2, riparian rights are defined in a far less determinative manner than fixed appropriative rights, because the amount of water use allowed by the "right" is not defined precisely and can change over time as the balance between competing uses shifts under "reasonable use" principles. By contrast, appropriators are assigned fixed quantities of water according to specific designated priority dates. Thus, an appropriator may invest in a new water diversion in reliance on existing use, but the new right might later be curtailed through a new water use by a riparian landowner whose title pre-dated the new appropriation, thus adding uncertainty to a system designed to promote more predictability. California later modified this uneasy relationship between riparian rights and prior appropriation. First, the legislature provided that new water rights could be established only through the prior appropriation system. Later, the State adopted a constitutional amendment[35] providing that riparian rights were abrogated to the extent that they allowed wasteful or unreasonable uses.

3. The Oregon Doctrine

The Oregon Doctrine is the final variation on the theme, but one that prevails in a large number of states.[36] Those states, like California, initially recognized riparian rights, but later they made prior appropriation the exclusive means for obtaining water rights, either by statute or constitutional amendment. Riparian rights that had actually been exercised at the time of the conversion continued to be valid, but only to the extent of beneficial use, thus in a sense

---

[33] Crandall v. Woods, 8 Cal. 136 (1857).

[34] 10 P. 674 (Cal. 1886).

[35] CAL. CONST. art. X, § 2.

[36] In addition to Oregon, this includes Washington, Kansas, Nebraska, Oklahoma, Texas, North Dakota, South Dakota and Alaska.

converting them into a hybrid riparian and appropriative water right. Unexercised (inchoate) riparian rights, on the other hand, were cut off.

One key issue in both California and Oregon Doctrine states is the degree to which changes that curtailed riparian rights constituted a taking of property without just compensation. Although the Oklahoma Supreme Court has suggested that the Oklahoma Legislature's attempt to cut off riparian rights did constitute a taking,[37] other courts have held to the contrary.[38] Takings issues in water law are addressed in more detail in Chapter 14, but timing is important here, because the U.S. Supreme Court did not recognize the concept of a "regulatory taking" until 1922.

---

[37] Franco-American Charolaise, Ltd. v. Oklahoma Water Resources Control Board, 855 P.2d 568 (Okla. 1990).

[38] *E.g.*, In re Hood River, 227 P. 1065 (Or. 1924), *appeal dismissed*, 273 U.S. 647 (1926).

Chapter 4

ALLOCATING GROUNDWATER: THE FIVE GROUNDWATER DOCTRINES USED IN THE UNITED STATES

A. Introduction

1. A Brief Primer on Hydrogeology (Groundwater Hydrology)

Groundwater law has evolved in the United States in response to improved science, which helped to demystify the location and movement of groundwater for courts. This improving science also includes information about groundwater quantity and quality, the degree to which groundwater and surface water are connected, and the extent to which withdrawals from one source might affect—and be affected by—the other. Thus, although hydrogeology is a complex science and is fraught with considerable sources of uncertainty, a basic understanding of the science is useful to understand related legal principles. Indeed, an understanding of the sources of uncertainty about groundwater and its interactions with surface water provides insights into some of the basic concepts in various groundwater doctrines.

Figure 4–1: Groundwater Zones
Graphic courtesy of the U.S. Geological Survey

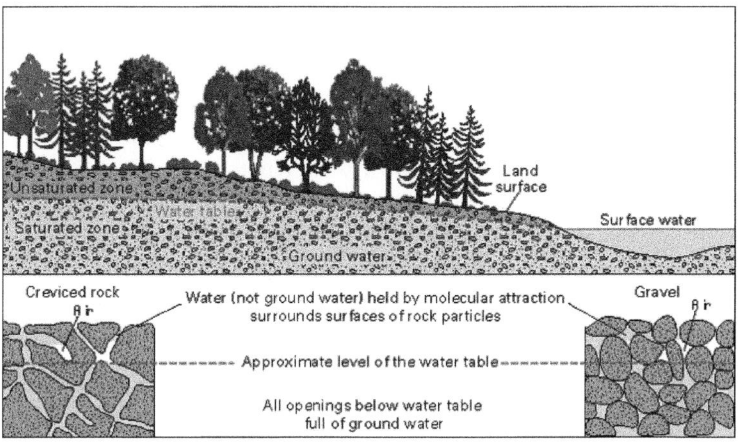

First, although the legal definition of groundwater varies from state to state, from a modern scientific perspective groundwater is simply all water found beneath the surface of the earth. Beyond this simple and intuitive concept, however, groundwater is divided into two major categories (see Figure 4–1). The ***saturated zone*** of groundwater consists of the area in which water fills all available spaces in the soil or other subsurface material (pores, fractures, etc.). The ***unsaturated zone*** above it, also known as the ***vadose zone***, is the region in which those spaces are filled by a mixture of water and air. The boundary between these two zones is the ***water table***. In any location, however, this water table varies depending on precipitation, groundwater pumping, and other factors. The depth to the water table can dictate the cost and feasibility of extracting groundwater from wells.

The saturated zone is also divided into discrete areas known as ***aquifers***, which are areas that are saturated with water but that also have sufficient permeability that people can extract water through wells. Aquifers can vary considerably based on the composition of the substrate material (soil, rock, gravel, clay, etc.), which affects both how much water can be stored in the aquifer and how much groundwater movement can occur. Some aquifers are sufficiently defined geologically that they receive names and can be viewed legally as identifiable sources of water like a stream or lake. The U.S. Geological Survey has identified approximately 66 "principal" aquifers of this nature in the United States based on their size and national significance,[1] but there are many others on a more regional or local scale.

Some aquifers are ***confined*** because relatively impermeable layers of material (such as low porosity rock or clay) above or around the aquifer restrict or prevent groundwater movement, while others are ***unconfined***, allowing freer movement of water in and out of the aquifer (see Figure 4–2). Confined aquifers with high water pressure are known as ***artesian*** and are particularly valuable because water rises to the surface naturally in a well without the cost and energy consumption of pumping. Thus, aquifers are defined spatially in both vertical and horizontal dimensions, and multiple aquifers often exist at different depths at any given point beneath the ground.

---

1 *See* U.S. Geological Survey, *USGS Groundwater Information, Aquifer Basics*, http://water.usgs.gov/ogw/aquiferbasics/alphabetical.html.

Figure 4–2: Unconfined and Confined Aquifers
Graphic courtesy of the U.S. Geological Survey

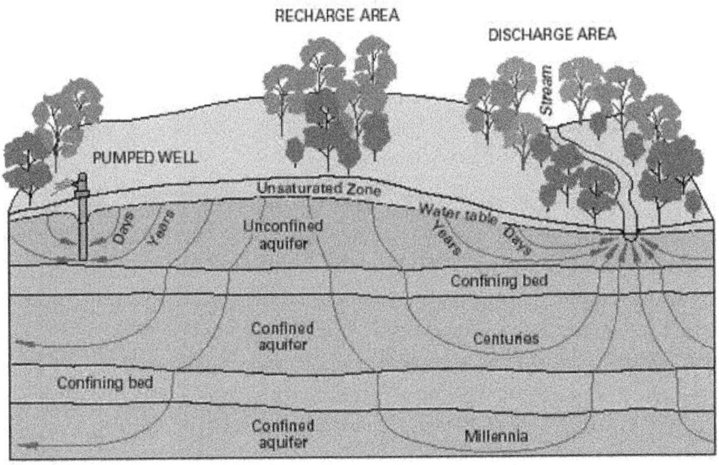

It is a mistake to think of groundwater as separate and distinct from surface water. First, all groundwater ultimately is connected to the global water cycle described in Chapter 1, recharged by precipitation and acting as a potential recharge source for streams and other surface waters (see Figures 4–1 and 4–2). Where groundwater is relatively distant from surface water, it can be pumped with no discernible effect on surface waters. However, in aquifers that are closer to streams both laterally and in depth, there is often a close connection between the two water sources. In these circumstances, vigorous pumping of groundwater can deplete surface water sources. Where the water table is above or adjacent to the lower level of a water body, groundwater may recharge the stream. Where the water table is beneath the surface water level, the opposite may be true. As a result, groundwater pumping can affect surface water supplies and surface water extraction can affect groundwater levels.

2. From Groundwater Science to Groundwater Law

As a source of water for human use, groundwater can provide several significant advantages over surface water, depending on location and other factors. In many parts of the country, groundwater reserves are very large, at least compared to available surface water supplies. Especially in the West, groundwater may be closer to most users than surface water supplies. Moreover, users can often access groundwater with relatively small infrastructure (a well and a pump), compared to the large dams and diversion structures required for many sources of surface water. Groundwater users avoid the evaporation and seepage losses that occur during surface water storage and conveyance, especially in hot, arid regions. Groundwater supplies generally vary less from season to season and year to year, although as discussed below they are not immune from overuse. Finally, absent significant interference with connected surface waters, groundwater can be extracted and used without the kind of harm to surface water ecosystems that occurs as a result of large-scale surface water withdrawals.

On the other hand, groundwater use also poses several challenges that create legal issues. For some individual landowners, the infrastructure costs for well drilling and pumping can be significant, especially when competition between neighboring users requires deeper and deeper wells. Such competition and excessive pumping can result not only in increasing costs, but also aquifer depletion, saltwater intrusion in coastal areas, land subsidence, and other problems. In some regions, groundwater has water quality problems as a result either of heavy natural salt or mineral content (high total dissolved solids (TDS)) or because of groundwater pollution from industrial, agricultural, or other chemical use and disposal. Moreover, the hydrological connections between surface water and groundwater mean that extraction from one source might affect the other for legal as well as physical purposes.

Based on the discussion of the water cycle in Chapter 1, a logical approach might be to address all issues of water rights through a single, integrated body of water law governing both surface water and groundwater. That is not, however, what most states did. Nevertheless, there are ways in which the bodies of law governing surface water and groundwater intersect, but they do so to varying degrees and in different ways in different states.

The reasons for this artificial separation of surface water and groundwater law are largely historical but at least partially explained by physical differences between the two water sources. Historically, water law evolved in a period during which the physical connections between surface water and groundwater were poorly understood at best. In fact, groundwater hydrology was so poorly understood that one court was prompted to write that groundwater movement is "so secret, occult, and concealed that an attempt to administer any set of legal rules . . . would be involved in hopeless uncertainty, and would, therefore, be practically impossible."[2] Therefore, efforts to determine the impacts of one user's groundwater pumping on another user for purposes of either the natural flow or reasonable use variations of the riparian rights doctrine would likely

---

[2] Houston & Texas Central Ry. Co. v. East, 81 S.W. 279, 281 (Tex. 1904).

have been futile. Likewise, efforts to quantify groundwater allocations by priority under the prior appropriation doctrine were difficult before governments and courts had the knowledge and methodologies to measure and quantify the impacts of groundwater pumping on other users or on the overall water supply.

We now have a much better understanding of the connections and interactions between groundwater and surface water. In most states, the traditional separation of surface water and groundwater law remains, but both courts and legislatures are more willing to connect the two in various ways, as described more specifically at the end of this chapter. However, the interconnections between surface water and groundwater also provide opportunities for more flexible solutions to water management as well as the potential for conflicts. For example, through a system known as ***conjunctive management***, excess water can be stored in aquifers during wet years when surface supplies suffice and then withdrawn during drought years. Similarly, water users may trade their surface water rights for new groundwater rights to reduce conflicts among surface water users, to improve surface water quality, and to leave more water instream for aquatic ecosystem restoration and protection.

However, as groundwater use increases—especially with the aid of more powerful pumps and deeper wells and in response to increasing population or other pressures—aquifers can become depleted. Even though aquifers sometimes hold very large reserves of fresh water, they are subject to depletion like any other resource, especially when their recharge rates are very slow. Aquifer depletion leads to conflicts among groundwater users and sometimes between groundwater and surface water users. Any groundwater pumping, but particularly large-scale extraction with powerful mechanical pumps, lowers the water table in a cone-shaped depression radiating in a circle away from the well, with the level of impact diminishing with increasing distance from the well. For example, assume one user has an established well, Well B. A second user then drills Well A nearby. If Well A lowers the water table below the level of Well B, it will limit or prevent operation of that well, causing a legal conflict between the two well users (see Figure 4–3). The owner of Well B may need to bear the expense of drilling a deeper well, incur higher pumping costs, or both. The law needs to allocate that risk either by retaining it with B, by shifting it to A (requiring or allowing A to reduce or eliminate the cost by replacing the lost water), or by preventing A from drilling the new well altogether (or requiring A to move the well to a more distant location to reduce or minimize well interference).

Figure 4–3: Cones of Depression and Well Interference
Graphic courtesy of the U.S. Geological Survey

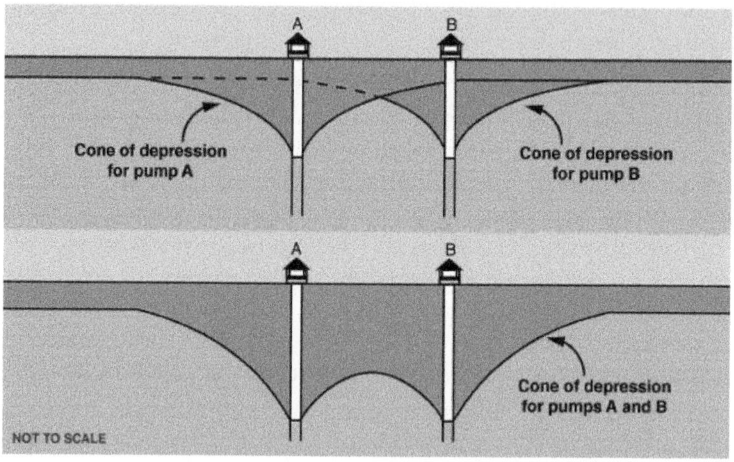

Over a broader area, groundwater pumping at levels that exceed the rate of aquifer recharge via precipitation and infiltration will "mine" the aquifer, causing the water table to drop over time. Major examples in the United States include significant declines in the Great Plains (sometimes called the Ogallala) Aquifer in the Central Plains region and in the Edwards Aquifer in Texas. In fact, recent satellite imagery documents significant groundwater depletion around the world, particularly in areas where population growth and water demand exceed natural recharge rates.[3] Excess groundwater pumping can also cause subsidence (sinking) of neighboring land.[4] Groundwater law, therefore, must address both short-term and localized conflicts among individual users and long-term impacts that may affect entire regional economies.

B. Common-Law Groundwater Doctrines

As is true for surface water, individual states are free to develop their own legal rules governing groundwater use and allocation. This freedom resulted in *five* (rather than only two, as was the case for surface water) basic doctrinal approaches to groundwater law among the states: (1) rule of capture; (2) American reasonable use; (3) correlative rights; (4) the Restatement (2d) of Torts; and (5) prior

---

[3] Alexandra S. Richey et al., *Quantifying Renewable Groundwater Stress with GRACE* [Gravity Recovery and Climate Experiment satellite mission], 57:7 WATER RESOURCES RESEARCH 5217–5238 (2015).

[4] *See* U.S. Geological Survey, *Land Subsidence*, https://www.usgs.gov/special-topics/water-science-school/science/land-subsidence.

appropriation. Prior appropriation and the rule of capture are fairly distinct, but some states complicate groundwater law further by blending aspects of the other three doctrines, all of which are based on shared rights.

The differences between the U.S. groundwater doctrines can be confusing and sometimes subtle. It is helpful to evaluate them as a series of sequential modifications to the absolute nature of the rule of capture, although it would be highly misleading to suggest a clear linear progression from doctrine to doctrine.

1. Rule of Capture

The rule of capture is the oldest, and arguably most absolute, U.S. groundwater doctrine, but only persists in a handful of states—in particular, Texas and Maine.[5] It originated in the 19th century English case of *Acton v. Blundell*,[6] in which the court ruled that any harm caused by one groundwater pumper (in *Acton*, a coal mine) on another property (in that case, a cotton mill) was *damnum absque injuria*, or loss without legal harm, and therefore gave rise to no legal cause of action. Given the almost complete scientific uncertainty about groundwater at the time, competing groundwater users had no clear way to know what portion of the water came from beneath their land or was drawn from beneath other properties, or what the impact of that pumping might be on neighboring landowners. Another rationale given for the doctrine is that it allows landowners to develop their property fully, thus promoting economic development. The doctrine does not limit the place of use, however, meaning that the landowner may use groundwater taken from beneath his or her land anywhere and for any purpose, subject only to the narrow limits discussed below.

One way to conceptualize the rule of capture is by virtue of similar doctrines in property law, including rules regarding capture of wildlife.[7] Game animals are not subject to human ownership while in the wild (*ferae naturae*), even within the boundaries of owned real property. Once lawfully hunted or captured, however, individual animals can be reduced to private ownership. Likewise, under the rule of capture, one does not "own" groundwater in an aquifer, even an aquifer underlying one's property. Once a well owner lawfully pumps out the water, however, bringing it within their physical control, that water becomes the personal property of the owner.

---

5 *See, e.g.*, Sipriano v. Great Spring Waters of America, Inc., 1 S.W.3d 75 (Tex. 1999) (reaffirming applicability of the rule of capture in Texas absent legislative action).

6 152 Eng. Rep. 1223 (Ex. Ch.), 12 Mees. & W. 324 (1843).

7 *See* Pierson v. Post, 3 Cai. R. 175 (N.Y. 1805) (applying rule of capture to wild animals).

A second way to conceptualize the rule of capture is as a doctrine of tort non-liability. A landowner who withdraws groundwater from beneath the surface of their land cannot be held liable to adjacent landowners for the injuries those withdrawals cause. However, there are exceptions to the doctrine of non-liability for malicious pumping for the sole purpose of causing harm, for the wanton and willful waste of water,[8] or for negligence that proximately causes subsidence of another's land.[9] Thus, like all of the groundwater doctrines, the rule of capture has both a property component and a tort component.

In those few states that retain rule of capture, courts justify its retention on grounds of economic development and the stability of property rights, *i.e.*, pumpers made investments in reliance on the concept of absolute ownership of groundwater drawn from beneath one's property, and courts should not disrupt those expectations absent legislative intervention. Nevertheless, the rule of capture has been abandoned—or was never adopted—in most U.S. jurisdictions. Improved understanding of groundwater hydrology eliminated its fundamental rationale, and courts also cite its potential for harm to third parties (or reciprocal harm among them) as a reason to adopt a different rule.

In addition, the rule of capture incentivizes overuse of groundwater. The concept that a private property owner can pump groundwater virtually without limit, and with little fear of liability for resulting harm, provided little incentive for conservation and careful stewardship of the resource, contrary to virtually every other doctrine of water law. The fact that each landowner could pump more water so long as they drilled a deeper well or installed a more powerful pump could cause a pumping war that didn't necessarily benefit either party. Over time, therefore, U.S. jurisdictions developed doctrines of groundwater law that borrowed from relevant principles of riparian rights or prior appropriation, which supported states' preferred policy goals.

2. American Reasonable Use

The American reasonable use groundwater doctrine reflects the most modest shift from the rule of capture. Like the rule of capture, it allows a landowner to pump an unlimited amount of water, but only so long as the landowner puts that water to "reasonable use" on the overlying tract of land. So long as the landowner uses the water on-tract, the landowner is liable only for unreasonable use. However,

---

[8] *See* City of Corpus Christi v. City of Pleasanton, 276 S.W.2d 798 (Tex. 1955).

[9] *See* Friendswood Dev. Co. v. Smith-Southwest Indus., Inc., 576 S.W.2d 21 (Tex. 1978); *see also* Bingham v. City of Roosevelt Corp., 235 P.3d 370 (Utah 2010) (suggesting possible liability for negligent pumping of groundwater in state with prior appropriation groundwater doctrine).

where a landowner uses groundwater off-tract—for example, by selling it to others for use at other locations—they risk more liability because such off-tract use may not interfere with groundwater use by neighboring property owners.[10] Thus, one way to conceptualize the American reasonable use doctrine is that it restricts the rule of capture to on-tract use, with liability for interfering with neighboring users when the water is exported off site.

Importantly, the term "reasonable use" under the American reasonable use rule does not mean the same thing as "reasonable use" in riparian rights law. In groundwater law, on-tract uses typically are viewed as *per se* reasonable so long as they are not overtly wasteful or harmful to others. The concept does not incorporate the same balancing of interests as is true under the reasonable use variation of riparian rights, and it does typically not scrutinize the nature and purpose of the onsite use. Some courts, however, have distinguished between groundwater uses that are directly beneficial to economic activity and those that are merely "incidental" to land uses and that are therefore subject to higher scrutiny when harmful to neighbors.[11] Others have articulated a preference for "natural," or domestic, uses over artificial groundwater uses.[12]

The American reasonable use rule is not a completely coherent improvement over the rule of capture. To the extent that the rule of capture was deemed insufficient because it didn't respond to harm to other groundwater users or other property interests, the American reasonable use rule responds differently to harm based on place of use, which is not a logical distinction. As between two on-tract pumpers, the American reasonable use rule retains the basic elements of rule of capture, leaving in place a "race to the bottom of the well." However, to the extent that the American reasonable use rule maintained the rule of capture's focus on economic development, it clearly favored onsite development, and in a conflict between an on-tract and an off-tract user, the on-tract owner is likely to prevail. To that extent, the doctrine might be viewed as an early example of area of origin protection (in this context aquifer of origin), with roots in the original riparian prohibition against use outside of a watershed.

---

10 *See* Meeker v. City of East Orange, 74 A. 379 (N.J. 1909).

11 *Compare* Finley v. Teeter Stone, Inc., 248 A.2d 106 (Md. App. 1968) (finding groundwater pumping to dewater a quarry pit reasonable and not subject to liability for subsidence on neighboring land) *with* Henderson v. Wade Sand & Gravel Co., 388 So.2d 900 (Ala. 1980) (holding that pumping from quarry was "incidental" and therefore subject to liability if it interfered with neighbor's beneficial on-tract use of groundwater).

12 *See* Michigan Citizens for Water Conservation v. Nestle Waters North America Inc., 709 N.W.2d 174 (Mich. App. 2005).

Although it is sometimes difficult to determine whether a state has retained the pure American reasonable use doctrine, most "reasonable use" states have modified their groundwater law via either the doctrine of correlative rights or Restatement (2d) of Torts concepts, both of which impose additional constraints on groundwater use to reflect more balance between competing property rights and interests. Even some states that purport to follow the American reasonable use rule have modified the doctrine in disputes between on-tract users to conduct the kind of balancing analysis that is more characteristic of the correlative rights doctrine described next.

3. Correlative Rights

According to most commentators, the doctrine of correlative rights originated in California but spread quickly to other states that were searching for legal rules to soften the harsh implications of the rule of capture. The roots of that terminology can be somewhat confusing, however, because some courts in American reasonable use states use the term "correlative rights" in a more general way.[13] In addition, it may seem ironic that California was first to import more components of riparian rights into its groundwater doctrine[14] than its eastern cousins, but recall that California was the first "dual system" state, and at the time it was still struggling to reconcile the balancing aspects of riparianism with the more determinative nature of prior appropriation.

In the seminal case of *Katz v. Walkinshaw,* the California Supreme Court considered a dispute between plaintiffs whose pumping of groundwater for on-tract domestic and irrigation use was interfered with by defendant's pumping for use on a distant tract of land. The court rejected the argument that California had adopted the rule of capture when it embraced the common law of England at statehood—the same argument that justified the early recognition of riparian rights—despite the vastly different geographic and hydrological conditions of the region. Instead, using reasoning similar to that in *Irwin v. Phillips* in the context of the prior appropriation doctrine for surface water (see Chapter 3), the California Supreme Court adopted the new rule of correlative rights based on the conditions in arid parts of the state and the absolute need for groundwater for irrigation in regions where stream flow was insufficient.[15] Other states around the country, however, also would

---

[13] *See* Meeker, 74 A. at 380 (using the term "correlative rights" while applying the American reasonable use doctrine). *But see* Woodsum v. Pemberton Twp., 412 A.2d 1064 (N.J. App. 1980) (concluding seven decades later that the *Meeker* court in fact intended to adopt correlative rights).

[14] Katz v. Walkinshaw, 74 P. 766 (Cal. 1903).

[15] *Id.* at 771–72.

find the idea of correlative rights superior to both the rule of capture and the doctrine of American reasonable use even in less arid conditions, because of the potential for groundwater pumping to adversely affect neighboring wells or land condition even if overall supplies are sufficient regionally.[16]

The correlative rights doctrine differs from both rule of capture and American reasonable use because, in conflicts between competing on-tract users, it engages in the same kind of reasonable use analysis as the reasonable use version of riparian rights. Moreover, in times of shortage, the doctrine requires equitable sharing between on-tract users. As such, the doctrine might be considered the groundwater equivalent of riparian rights. The correlative rights doctrine also employs a somewhat different version of local use protection than American reasonable use, identifying a *preference* for on-tract use in the case of shortages, thus borrowing more from the water allocation (or usufructuary property) model of water rights characteristic of prior appropriation rather than the tort-based doctrine of harm employed in the American reasonable use doctrine first developed in eastern states.

Nevertheless, water law scholars classify very few states as "pure" correlative rights doctrine states. Moreover, as of 2015 California itself replaced its common-law groundwater doctrine with a comprehensive statutory regime for groundwater management.

4. Restatement (Second) of Torts

The drafters of the Restatement (Second) of Torts, as Chapter 2 mentioned, tried to "modernize" riparian rights law, and they tried to do the same for groundwater law. Moreover, as is true for riparian rights, a relatively small number of states have adopted the Restatement (Second) of Torts provisions to resolve groundwater use conflicts.

The Restatement assumes ownership of pumped groundwater from one's overlying land as a matter of property law, and thus it retains a presumption against liability for pumping groundwater. However, the Restatement (Second) also provides three exceptions to this presumption that take it far beyond the rule of capture. Specifically, the Restatement (Second) allows a landowner/groundwater pumper to be liable to others if: (1) the pumping causes "unreasonable harm" to a neighbor by lowering the water table or reducing artesian pressure; (2) the withdrawal exceeds the landowner's "reasonable share" of groundwater storage or annual supply; or (3) the withdrawal has a "direct and substantial effects" on a nearby stream or lake and "unreasonably causes harm" to a lawful

16 Woodsum v. Pemberton Township, 412 A.2d 1064 (N.J. Super. 1980).

user of that water.[17] Thus, the Restatement (Second) blends elements of reasonable use and correlative rights and recognizes that groundwater and surface water are connected.

In evaluating the comparative reasonableness of competing uses, the Restatement relies on the same factors as it applied to reasonable use balancing in the riparian rights context, which we discussed in Chapter 2.[18] Those factors include the purpose of the use; the suitability of the use to the place; the economic value of the use; the social value of the use; the extent and amount of harm caused; the practicality of avoiding harm by adjusting the means of use or the use itself; the practicality of adjusting the amount of use by each landowner; protection of existing uses, land value, and investments; and the "justice of requiring the user causing harm to bear the loss."[19] These factors provide more flexibility to courts in resolving disputes among competing users, but as a result less certainty for users because of the wide range and inherent subjectivity of many of the factors the court will consider.

Compared to rule of capture, American reasonable use, and correlative rights, the Restatement (Second) approach maintains its focus on the basic right of landowners to extract and use groundwater pumped from beneath their lands to promote the beneficial use of property and economic development. The four doctrines differ, however, in the legal standards for imposition of liability for harm caused by the exercise of those rights and in the implications for which party bears the risk, or the cost, of loss resulting from interfering uses, with a sequential trend toward increased liability. In the rule of capture, liability is found only for malicious harm or willful and wanton excess of use, regardless of the purpose or place of use. As a result, the party harmed by the competing use almost always bears the cost of that harm. The American reasonable use doctrine imposes liability for on-tract use if it is not a "reasonable use" and eliminates the absolute priority for on-tract uses. Thus, the harmed party typically bears the costs of interference where the use is on-tract, but not for off-tract uses. The correlative rights doctrine imposes essentially the same result for off-tract uses, but it also borrows from riparian rights the concept of equitable sharing among competing on-tract users. The Restatement (Second) approach essentially promotes the same balancing between competing groundwater users as it does for riparian rights, resulting in no presumption about which party will bear the costs of harm.

---

[17] Restatement (2d) of Torts, § 858.

[18] *Id.* §§ 850–850A.

[19] *Id.* § 850A.

5. Prior Appropriation

Not surprisingly, the majority of western states that adopted prior appropriation for surface water did so for groundwater as well, either as part of an integrated system but more commonly in a separately administered way. Arizona and California are the two prominent exceptions. Also not surprisingly, the same basic rules apply to prior appropriation in the groundwater context. Seniority is determined based on the order in which water from a given aquifer is extracted and put to beneficial use. Beneficial use is the basis, the measure, and the limit of the right, as is true for surface water. The "use it or lose it" and waste doctrines apply to groundwater as well as to surface water.

Applying the priority system in the groundwater context, however, poses somewhat different challenges than for surface water. In a surface water system, a senior user can "call the river" when insufficient water is available at the designated point of withdrawal because of withdrawals by upstream juniors. In the groundwater context, the same may be true if pumping by a junior affirmatively interferes with the groundwater right of a senior. Does that rule, however, allow a senior with a shallow well to tie up an entire aquifer when a deeper well would allow use by new or junior appropriators? Giving such control to shallow-well seniors would contradict prior appropriation's policy of maximizing beneficial use of the resource. One obvious solution is for a junior or potential new appropriator to pay the costs for the senior to improve an existing well, thus protecting the senior's status while allowing additional groundwater development and use.

Perhaps a more challenging scenario occurs when an existing aquifer is being "mined"—i.e., where existing withdrawals, or existing plus proposed new withdrawals, deplete the aquifer at levels that exceed the rate of recharge, causing the water table to lower over time. As discussed in the introduction, that kind of groundwater depletion is becoming more and more common around the country, but particularly in areas from the western portion of the Great Plains westward, where groundwater use for irrigation is very high given the lack of available surface water or precipitation. Absent adequate controls, these problems are likely to increase in both frequency and magnitude in areas in which demand for groundwater use is rising while precipitation and recharge may be declining as a result of climate change.

A prior appropriation state can adopt different policies about groundwater mining to address this issue. The most conservative approach, from the perspective of protecting the resource for future use, is to prohibit any groundwater mining at all.[20] This approach involves calculating or estimating the recharge rate of the aquifer, limiting approval of appropriative rights to those levels, and implementing the resulting priority system in the same way as in a stream system that has been fully appropriated. Many states have been reluctant to take such a limiting approach, however, preferring to allow limited amounts of groundwater depletion to accommodate new development. The more groundwater mining is allowed, however, the more likely it becomes that use by a junior will interfere with use by a senior, or that all groundwater use in the affected region will become impaired because of declining water levels or water quality problems. Thus, the degree to which the "first in time" aspect of prior appropriation doctrine is implemented to limit pumping by a junior depends on what choices the state makes about groundwater mining and protection of seniors. Given those policy considerations, many western states have adopted groundwater statutes, a trend that has migrated to eastern states as well.

C. Managing Groundwater-Surface Water Interactions

As discussed in the introduction, surface water and groundwater are interrelated. In some areas, those connections suggest little discernible impact resulting from withdrawals from one source or the other, or impacts that may occur over very long periods of time. Where the groundwater and surface water are closely connected, however, with a relatively short time lag before withdrawal from one source affects the other, there is potential that such interactions will create legal conflicts.

It makes little sense to administer the prior appropriation system within a stream system in order of seniority when a more junior groundwater pumper can reduce the water available to more senior users. Likewise, it makes little sense to administer a system of equitable sharing of shortages pursuant to the reasonable use principles of riparian rights—either judicially or through an administrative permit system—if a groundwater user adjacent to the stream can reduce the surface water available to riparian users without limitation. The systems of water law in most states have been slow to respond to these challenges, but an increasing number of states have done so through judicial or administrative actions.

For example, in the seminal case on interactions between groundwater and surface water in a prior appropriation state,[21] the

---

[20] *See, e.g.*, Baker v. Ore-Ida Foods, Inc., 513 P.2d 627 (Idaho 1973) (holding that Idaho statute prohibited groundwater mining).

[21] City of Albuquerque v. Reynolds, 379 P.2d 73 (N.M. 1962).

New Mexico Supreme Court upheld the State Engineer's authority to deny applications for groundwater pumping from aquifers that provided base flow to the fully appropriated Rio Grande River because the new groundwater rights would impair the rights of existing surface water appropriators. However, the court also approved the State Engineer's authority to issue such permits if the applicant curtailed its surface water uses to mitigate impacts to surface water users, an arrangement that suggested the broader programs of conjunctive management of surface water and groundwater discussed below.

Other western states followed suit to integrate their surface water and groundwater management. Just a few years after the *City of Albuquerque* case in New Mexico, in *Fellhauer v. People,*[22] the Colorado Supreme Court similarly recognized the detrimental impact of groundwater pumping on surface water users because of the lack of similar regulation of groundwater. As described in a more recent case,[23] in the wake of that decision the Colorado Legislature enacted legislation seeking "to integrate the appropriation, use and administration of underground water tributary to a stream with the use of surface water, in such a way as to maximize the beneficial use of all of the waters of the state."[24] The new statute required a determination of what constituted "tributary groundwater," that is, groundwater with a sufficiently close connection to a nearby surface water to require the two to be managed conjunctively.

The *Kobobel* case in Colorado, brought as a takings challenge to the state's authority to restrict groundwater pumping, also reinforced the usufructuary nature of groundwater pumping rights in Colorado's prior appropriation system:

> In accordance with Colorado's doctrine of prior appropriation, the well owners neither hold title to the water in their decreed wells, nor is their right to use the water unfettered. What the well owners possess is a legally vested priority date that entitles them to pump a certain amount of tributary groundwater from their wells for beneficial use, subject to the rights of senior water rights holders and the amount of available water.[25]

Thus, for purposes of allocating the limited resource, tributary groundwater holds exactly the same legal status in Colorado as surface water under the prior appropriation system. The heightened

---

[22] Fellhauer v. People, 447 P.2d 986 (Colo. 1968).

[23] Kobobel v. State, 249 P.3d 1127 (Colo. 2011).

[24] *Id.* at 1135 (*quoting* Ch. 373, Sec. 1, § 148–21–2(1), 1969 Colo. Sess. Laws 1200 (codified at § 37–92–102(1)(a), C.R.S. (2010))).

[25] *Id.* at 1137.

challenge is in determining when sufficient interference occurs to curtail groundwater pumping to protect senior surface water users (or vice versa). Although other prior appropriation states implement this basic concept in different ways, they all recognize the need to manage the resource conjunctively to protect senior water users and to ensure fair and efficient administration of the priority system.[26]

Even though these interactions between groundwater and surface water pose problems when there are conflicts between users of the two different water sources, particularly when they are governed by separate legal regimes, that relationship can also induce states to develop programs of "conjunctive management" of surface water and groundwater. In the most frequent application, states may choose to allow larger withdrawals from aquifers during drought periods when surface water supplies are low and to recharge the aquifer (or to allow it to recharge) during wet years when surface water supplies are sufficient to do so.[27] In essence, those programs use aquifers as underground storage reservoirs in ways that may cause less environmental disruption of surface water ecosystems than dams and surface water reservoirs and that avoid high infrastructure construction and operating costs, evaporation, and other problems inherent in reservoir storage.

Some riparian states have also recognized and addressed the interactions between groundwater and surface water and have grappled with the appropriate means of reconciling the two bodies of law. Given the variability in groundwater doctrines, the manner in which those disputes might be resolved necessarily varies as well, and in part the issue depends on whether the court applies the applicable groundwater doctrine in the state, the applicable version of riparian rights, some combination of the two, or other principles entirely. For example, in an absolute rule of capture state, in theory an aggrieved riparian user might have no claim whatsoever for harm. In an American reasonable use jurisdiction, a similarly harmed party may have a greater chance of prevailing if the groundwater is pumped and transported offsite. If the water is used onsite, however, they might only obtain relief if the use is not "reasonable" within the limited meaning of that doctrine, that is, only if the used is wasteful and causes harm because of that waste.

---

[26] *See, e.g.*, Clear Spring Foods, Inc. v. Spackman, 252 P.3d 71 (Idaho 2011) (upholding curtailment of junior groundwater right to protect senior surface water user).

[27] *See, e.g.*, UTAH STATE WATER PLAN, CONJUNCTIVE MANAGEMENT OF SURFACE AND GROUND WATER IN UTAH (July 2005); JOSH HAZARD & DAVID SNIVELY, UNIVERSITY OF MONTANA DEPT. OF GEOGRAPHY, CONJUNCTIVE MANAGEMENT OF SURFACE AND GROUND WATER RESOURCES IN THE WESTERN UNITED STATES (2011).

Both the correlative rights and the Restatement (Second) groundwater doctrines are more likely to generate an analysis in which competing groundwater and surface water uses, including the riparian right to enjoy unimpaired stream conditions, are evaluated under an equitable balancing test. *Michigan Citizens for Water Conservation v. Nestle Waters North America Inc.*, for example, involved a dispute between riparian landowners and a large commercial groundwater pumping operation for bottled water. The Michigan Court of Appeals adopted a "reasonable use balancing test . . . as the law applicable to disputes between riparian and groundwater users."[28] Although different states might articulate and apply such a balancing test in varying ways, the Michigan court sought to ensure "fair participation" in use of available water by the maximum number of users, to protect only "reasonable uses" of water, and to redress only "unreasonable harms."[29] Although such a test is inherently somewhat subjective and leaves users with less certainty than is the case under more absolute doctrines, it stays close to the underlying doctrine of riparian rights in its focus on balancing interests among competing users, while recognizing the interconnection between groundwater and surface water use and potential for one use to harm the other.

[28] 709 N.W.2d 174, 201–02 (Mich. App. 2005), *rev'd in part on other grounds*, 737 N.W.2d 447 (Mich. 2007).

[29] *Id.* at 202–03.

Chapter 5

MOVING FROM THE COMMON LAW TO PERMITS

A. Introduction

Chapters 2, 3, and 4 provided an overview of the common law governing water rights. All of these common-law systems can work well enough when water supplies exceed demand. However, when people start competing for water, relying on common-law approaches to create and enforce water rights can create a lot of uncertainty for both the state water managers and individual water rights claimants. Consider, for example, all of the common-law water rights regimes that are based on sharing a particular water resource—reasonable use-based riparian rights for surface water (Chapter 2) and the two reasonable use rules and correlative rights doctrine for groundwater (Chapter 4). If you were entitled to water based on one of these regimes, would you be confident regarding the amount of water you were entitled to take into the future? What if there's a drought? What if residential or commercial subdivisions double or triple the number of landowners who also have rights to water from the same river or aquifer?

Common-law prior appropriation creates different kinds of certainty problems, usually centered on issues of proof. If someone upstream starts interfering with your right, how do you prove that your right is senior? How do you prove how much water you're actually entitled to and where you're entitled to use that water? If you are the state water official (or a court) in a state with common-law prior appropriation, how do you sort out these competing claims among water users?

In addition, certain common-law schemes for water rights, especially common-law prior appropriation for both surface water and groundwater and the English rule of capture for groundwater, also allow or even encourage overuse of the water resource—over-appropriation of streams and rivers and mining of groundwater. Under these legal regimes, how can the state keep water in the system for, say, fish (in rivers and streams) or extended future use (in aquifers)?

Wyoming historians have detailed some of the chaos that preceded the adoption of a water permit system in that state, providing a good overview of why state legislatures might consider permit systems to be an improvement:

> In Wyoming's early years, all that was required to reach out and appropriate the water you saw in a stream was to post a sign on a nearby tree, saying "I hereby claim this water and here's how much of it I claim." Later, the Territorial Legislature decided it might be good to get some record of those claims, so people had to go file them in the county courthouse. That could mean someplace 50 or 150 miles or more away—not often a handy place for someone else to go check before they wanted to get water out of that same stream.
>
> . . . In one case, someone claimed from one stream more water than actually flowed in the entire state of Wyoming, and proposed to divert that water with a ditch two feet wide and six inches deep. When people started arguing over conflicting claims, and some fights moved from the creek-bank into court, the territorial courts (whose judges didn't know much about water) often wound up allocating water by the amount stated on paper in the claim, or perhaps by the size of the ditch.
>
> No matter that that meant more water per acre for one irrigator than for his neighbor just downstream. Wyoming Territory was rife with excess water claims, covering much more water than people were using or could use—generating conflict, wasting time, money and energy, and providing ample opportunity for speculators.
>
> The final straw was the famous drought-plus-hard-winter of 1886–1887 that busted Wyoming's open-range stock industry. The stockmen who survived financially decided it might be a good idea to secure their claims to watering holes, and grow some hay in summer to tide the herds over the winter.
>
> Some started to think about irrigated agriculture as a new endeavor that might be a little more stable than their industry. Stockman and businessman Francis E. Warren had already, along with Joseph Carey, started an irrigation venture, the Wyoming Development Company, at the site that is now Wheatland. . . . Now they wanted a water-law system that would confirm their own water claims and build a basis for new irrigation development.[1]

All of the uncertainty issues under the common law become much easier to handle—and require far less litigation—when states

[1] Anne MacKinnon, Wyoming State Historical Society, *Order out of Chaos: Elwood Mead and Wyoming's Water Law*, https://www.wyohistory.org/encyclopedia/order-out-chaos-elwood-mead-and-wyomings-water-law (as viewed May 23, 2024).

define water rights through administrative permit systems. Water permits clearly define for individual users what their water rights are and, generally, how those water rights interact with the rights of other water users. Permit systems also create a public record (originally paper but increasingly electronic) of who has what rights to which water resource. These records both provide notice to future water users of pre-existing rights and allow state water managers to keep track of water resource use, allowing for a more comprehensive understanding of what's happening with the state's waters. Records of water use can also form the starting point for state water resources planning, helping the state to meet its future demands for water.

However, while administrative permit systems have clear benefits, they also create new procedural and substantive legal issues. This chapter examines what can happen when states convert their common-law water systems into permit systems. It begins with the issue of how states treat previously created and exercised common-law water rights when their legislatures create new permit systems. It then briefly compares the prevalence of water permitting in the West, where states adopted permit systems early and nearly universally, to the much later adoption of permit systems in riparian states, a process that is still ongoing. This chapter finishes by exploring two sets of issues that permit systems create: substantive changes in a state's water law created during the adoption of a water code; and procedural issues arising from administrative law requirements.

B. Changing to a Permit System: What Happens to the Already-Existing Common-Law Rights?

By the time most states got around to creating permit systems, people within that state or its predecessor colony or territory already had been creating and exercising water rights under the common law. Thus, state legislatures faced the issue of what to do about those pre-existing rights: Should they be destroyed, or would the state continue to recognize them as valid under the new permit system?

State legislatures universally chose to continue to recognize common-law water rights,[2] at least if they had been exercised by the time the permit system was created. (NOTE: Although common-law riparian surface water rights are part of the rights attached to riparian land and continue to exist even if the landowner does not use any water, eastern states have been less enthusiastic about preserving *unexercised* riparian rights.) As you might imagine, part of the reason is political: Members of the state legislature are

---

[2] *E.g.*, WASH. REV. CODE § 90.03.010 ("Nothing contained in this chapter shall be construed to lessen, enlarge, or modify the existing rights of any riparian owner, or any existing right acquired by appropriation, or otherwise.").

unlikely to remain popular if they just up and destroy water rights that citizens of the state have been relying on for decades. However, part of the reason is legal: Because water rights are considered property under state law, state legislatures cannot destroy them constitutionally without paying just compensation, under both the U.S. Constitution and state constitutions. We'll look at constitutional takings of water rights more thoroughly in Chapter 14; for now, just be aware that destroying all previously created water rights statewide would be a very expensive way for a state legislature to create a permit system.

The result of continuing to recognize common-law water rights, however, is that all state enactments of water permit systems start with a little bit of chaos, because there has to be some way of incorporating those older common-law rights into the new system. One of the administrative problems with common-law water rights is that they usually don't require any paperwork or state registration, so there is no official record that they exist or how big they are. Thus, while water permits give the state comprehensive records of all the new water rights created *after* the state legislature adopts a permit system, at that moment of creation, state water officials may have only the vaguest of notions of how many common-law water rights are being claimed by what users for which waterways and aquifers within the state and for how much water.

If you are the state official charged with rationally managing the state's water resources, this lack of information about who's doing what with the state's water can be a significant problem, especially as state populations grow. Moreover, individuals with common-law water rights might still have considerable uncertainty regarding exactly what their water rights are—or whether the new permit holders are actually interfering with those rights. To resolve these lingering uncertainties surrounding common-law water rights, individual states have tended to take one of two paths: general stream adjudications or permit conversion.

1. General Stream Adjudications

Western states tend to rely on the cumbersome process of ***general stream adjudications*** to sort out common-law prior appropriation rights for surface water and, increasingly, for groundwater as well. In a stream adjudication, the state or (sometimes) an individual water claimant uses special processes (defined in the state water law statutes or water code) to join all of the people who claim a right to water from a particular water resource or system into a single court proceeding. The judge then evaluates the validity, quantity, and priority of all of the prior appropriative rights for that resource or system. (If you remember your Civil Procedure, general stream adjudications are essentially the water law version of interpleader—everyone with a claim to the same river or linked water resources is joined in the same legal proceeding, where they and the court hash out everyone's relative rights to the water.) Assuming that the proceeding meets the due process requirements of notice and an opportunity to participate, all claimants existing at the time of the proceeding are bound by the court's final determination of water rights (subject to the normal appeals processes, of course).

All 18 western states have enacted statutes that allow for general stream adjudications, and most of these states are currently engaged in at least one such process for a river or watershed within their borders. However, stream adjudications can take a *long* time. For example, the general stream adjudication for the Big Horn-Wind River Watershed in Wyoming was filed in 1977 and finalized in 2014,[3] a total of 37 years. The Yakima River Basin general stream adjudication in the State of Washington also started in 1977 and involved over 25,000 claimed surface water rights;[4] the Yakima County Superior Court entered the final decree on May 9, 2019, while the Washington Supreme Court decided the consolidated appeals on November 18, 2021.[5] Arizona is engaged in two general stream adjudications, one for the Gila River system (see Figure 5–1) and one for the Little Colorado system. Together, these two adjudications encompass all the surface water users in about two-thirds of the state.[6] Both began in the 1970s and are still ongoing,[7] and "[t]here are 40,000 parties involved in the Gila River adjudication and about 85,000 claims. The vast majority of claimants—around 92% of them—are asserting a right for less than 250 acre feet of water per year."[8] In turn, the Little Colorado watershed adjudication "involves

---

3 Charles Wilkinson, *Introduction to* Big Horn *General Stream Adjudication Symposium*, 15:2 WYO. L. REV. 233, 233 (2015).

4 *Water Right Adjudication Coming to a Conclusion in the Yakima Basin*, TUPPER MACK WELLS, PLLC (May 9, 2019), https://www.tmw-law.com/news-and-insights/water-right-adjudication-coming-to-a-conclusion-in-the-yakima-basin (noting that the case had lasted 42 years).

5 *Ecology v. Acquavella*, WASHINGTON DEPT. OF ECOLOGY (viewed Nov. 14, 2023), https://ecology.wa.gov/Water-Shorelines/Water-supply/Water-rights/Adjudications/Ecology-v-Acquavella.

6 Emery Cohen, "Little Colorado River fight hits home," *Arizona Daily Sun*, Feb. 19, 2016, http://azdailysun.com/news/local/little-colorado-river-fight-hits-home/article_25806405-c2da-56fb-816e-61f4c4fe0337.html.

7 *Gila River and Little Colorado River General Stream Adjudications*, ARIZONA DEPT. OF WATER RESOURCES (viewed Nov. 15, 2023), https://new.azwater.gov/adjudications/gila-river-and-little-colorado-river-general-stream-adjudications#:~:text=The%20Gila%20River%20and%20Little,%2D231%20to%2045%2D245. (as viewed June 8, 2016).

8 Sarah Porter & Susan Craig, Kyl Center for Water Policy, *Arizona's Stream Adjudications: Getting to Water Certainty*.

approximately 6,000 parties and 14,000 claims. 97% of the claims are for a water right less than 250 acre feet of water per year for domestic use, irrigation or a stock pond."[9]

Figure 5–1: The Gila River Stream Adjudication
Map courtesy of the Arizona Department of Water Resources

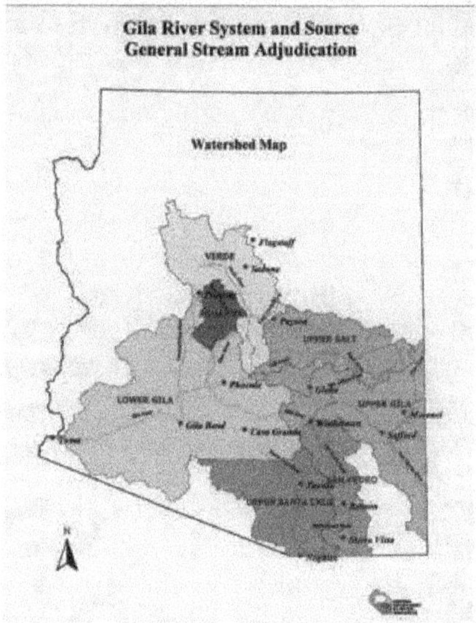

Importantly, state general stream adjudications can include *federal* water rights claims as well as state-law claims. Chapter 8 will examine what these federal water rights claims might be and how they get into *state* courts; for now, what is important is that federal water claims in the West can be numerous and significant and hence can complicate further the stream adjudication process. For example, in the Gila River and Little Colorado general stream adjudications in Arizona, the United States has filed about 15,000 claims for water rights for non-tribal federal lands. Arizona, the relevant Tribes, and the federal government settled the tribal claims to the Gila River in 2004, providing "the Gila River Indian Community with a water budget of 653,500 acre-feet of water annually."[10] In contrast, in the Little Colorado River, although the Navajo Nation and Hopi Tribe have been fighting over their respective water rights since the

---

[9] *Id.*

[10] *Gila River Indian Community Water Rights Settlement*, U.S. DEPT. OF JUSTICE (as updated June 6, 2023), https://www.justice.gov/enrd/indian-resources-section/gila-river-indian-community.

1970s,[11] as of 2024 those claims remain unresolved despite attempts at settlement.

2. Permit Conversion

In contrast to the western states, the eastern states that have adopted permit systems have tended to require existing water users to convert their existing common-law water rights into a permit. For example, when Florida adopted the Florida Water Resources Act in 1972, it required all water users (for both surface water and groundwater) to have a consumptive use permit, or CUP.[12] Existing users of water had two years to convert their existing uses into a permit, although each user was virtually guaranteed to receive a permit "if the existing use is a reasonable-beneficial use . . . and is allowable under the common law of the state."[13] However, if an existing user failed to apply for a permit within those two years, the Act created "a conclusive presumption of abandonment of the use . . . ."[14]

Other states also require permit conversion of common-law riparian rights—including some prior appropriation states. Hawai'i adopted its Water Code in 1987, based in part on the Florida Water Resources Act. However, the Hawai'i Legislature was even more stringent about converting existing water uses to permits, giving existing users only a year to apply for a permit under the new system.[15] In contrast, Maryland's water code provides that "[t]he Department shall issue a permit to a person using water prior to July 1, 1988 for agricultural purposes upon written application to the Department."[16] Oregon, as you may recall from Chapter 3, originally recognized some riparian rights but abolished future riparian rights in 1909 when it adopted its water code. The Oregon Legislature eventually provided that riparian rights being exercised in 1909 had to be registered with the Oregon Water Resources Department by December 31, 1992, so that they could be adjudicated and converted into permitted rights.[17] Failure to file creates a rebuttable presumption that the water right has been abandoned.[18]

---

[11] Ryan Heinsius, *Navajo Nation and Hopi Tribe Revive Little Colorado River Settlement Talks*, http://knau.org/post/navajo-nation-and-hopi-tribe-revive-little-colorado-river-settlement-talks#stream/0 (April 12, 2016).

[12] FLA. STAT. ANN. § 373.219(1).

[13] *Id.* § 373.226(2), (3).

[14] *Id.* § 373.226(3).

[15] HAW. REV. STAT. ANN. § 174C–50.

[16] MD. ENV'T CODE § 5–502(c)(1).

[17] OR. REV. STAT. § 539.240(1).

[18] *Id.* § 539.240(3).

Some western states also provided for permit conversion (or something close to it) of pre-code *appropriative* rights. For example, North Dakota provides for the conversion of pre-1963 appropriative rights to permits.[19] In New Mexico,

> Any person, firm or corporation claiming to be an owner of a water right which was vested prior to the passage of Chapter 49, Laws 1907, from any surface water source by the applications of water therefrom to beneficial use, may make and file in the office of the state engineer a declaration in a form to be prescribed by the state engineer setting forth the beneficial use to which said water has been applied, the date of first application to beneficial use, the continuity thereof, the location of the source of said water and if such water has been used for irrigation purposes, the description of the land upon which such water has been so used and the name of the owner thereof.[20]

Permit conversion of common-law prior appropriation water rights raises very few issues except, eventually, sufficient proof of the claimed right. However, permit conversion of riparian rights potentially raises a constitutional takings issue. At common law, remember, riparian property owners' property rights include *inchoate* rights to use water—that is, the riparian always has a right to start using water from the stream or lake, even if he or she does not do so immediately. Permit systems, however, apply only to the actual use of water. Thus, when Florida and Hawai'i deemed all existing rights abandoned after the conversion period, they effectively eliminated the riparian property owners' common-law rights to start using water at any time. (Of course, those riparian owners were free to apply for a permit, but that's not quite the same as a guaranteed right.) Moreover, this issue can also arise in "Oregon doctrine" states. For example, Oregon itself abolished unexercised riparian rights in 1909.[21]

When the takings issue arose in Florida, however, the Florida Supreme Court upheld Florida's permit system. In the 1979 case of *Village of Tequesta v. Jupiter Inlet Corporation*, it concluded that the landowners did not have a constitutionally protected right to the water itself and that the Florida Water Resource Act was the water

---

[19] "A person who used or attempted to appropriate water from any source for beneficial use over a period of twenty years prior to July 1, 1963, is deemed to have acquired a right to the use of the water without having filed or prosecuted an application to acquire a right to the beneficial use of the waters if the user shall have, by December 31, 2001, filed with the state engineer an application for a water permit." N.D. CENTURY CODE § 61–04–22.

[20] N.M. STAT. § 72–1–3.

[21] OR. REV. STAT. § 539.010(8).

law equivalent of land use regulation and zoning, with the result that "the right to the use of the water may also be limited or regulated" without requiring compensation.[22] Similarly, the Oregon Supreme Court upheld Oregon's elimination of unexercised riparian rights, concluding that "a state may change its common-law rule as to every stream within its dominion and permit the appropriation of the flowing waters for such purposes as it deems wise."[23]

C. The Adoption of Water Permitting Systems: West Versus East

Both eastern riparian states (and Hawai'i) and western prior appropriation states have enacted water use permit systems. However, the two sets of states differ regarding how early state legislatures enacted permit requirements and in how comprehensive the resulting permit system is. In general, western prior appropriation states adopted permit systems relatively early—a legislative refinement of prior appropriation to further cope with water scarcity and conflict. In contrast, about half of the eastern riparian states still do not require permits for any water use. In addition, permit programs in western states tend to be more comprehensive than in eastern states, especially in terms of the uses that require permits.[24] Specifically, in western states, pretty much all appropriations of water require a permit, subject to very limited exemptions, usually for small domestic uses. In contrast, permit programs in eastern states are often full of exemptions, or they limit their permit requirements to a very few categories of large users or to withdrawals from specific waters deemed in need of special protection. In both western and eastern states, however, a state agency oversees whatever water use permit program that exists, meaning that administrative law becomes relevant to these programs.

1. Permit Programs in Western Prior Appropriation States

All western prior appropriation states except Colorado have water permit systems, and most western states adopted their permit statutes fairly early in their histories. Wyoming, for example, was the

---

22 Village of Tequesta v. Jupiter Inlet Corp., 371 So.2d 663, 672 (Fla. 1979).

23 In re Willow Creek, 144 P. 505, 516 (Or. 1914).

24 *E.g.*, WASH. REV. CODE § 90.03.250 ("Any person, municipal corporation, firm, irrigation district, association, corporation or water users' association hereafter desiring to appropriate water for a beneficial use shall make an application to the department for a permit to make such appropriation, and shall not use or divert such waters until he or she has received a permit from the department as in this chapter provided.").

first western state to enact a permit requirement, which came into being in 1890, the same year that Wyoming became a state.

In some western states, there was a period of time when *both* the permit system and the common-law process for establishing a water right were valid ways to establish a new water right. However, in all western states, the permit process is now the *exclusive* means for establishing a new water right.[25] As one example, the Idaho Court of Appeals explained Idaho's transition from being a dual system to an exclusive permit system as follows:

> Until the law was changed in 1971, see 1971 Idaho Session Laws, ch. 177 at 843, a person desiring to appropriate the water of a stream could do so either by actually diverting the water and applying it to a beneficial use or by pursuing the statutory method, which entailed an application to the Department of Water Resources for a permit and then fulfilling the requirements of the permit. . . . Since 1971 the exclusive way to acquire a water right has been by the permit method. Nevertheless, those rights acquired by the so-called constitutional method prior to that time are still valid. [IDAHO CODE] §§ 42–103, 42–201.[26]

Finally, western permit programs are fairly comprehensive. First, they apply to all waters in the state that are subject to appropriation.[27] Second, as noted, western permit requirements apply to almost all appropriations, generally excepting only small withdrawals for domestic or other critical uses. Idaho, for example, exempts water for firefighting and forest practices from its surface water permit requirement,[28] and it exempts domestic wells from its groundwater permitting requirement.[29] Utah allows landowners to collect up to 200 gallons of rain without any regulation and to collect

---

[25] *E.g.*, ALAS. STAT. ANN. § 46–15–040(a) ("A right to appropriate water can be acquired only as provided in this chapter."); MONT. CODE § 85–2–301(1) ("After July 1, 1973, a person may not appropriate water except as provided in this chapter."); UTAH CODE § 73–3–1(1) ("A person may acquire a right to the use of the unappropriated public waters in this state only as provided for in this title.").

[26] R.T. Nahas Co. v. Hulet, 752 P.2d 625, 628 (Idaho Ct. App. 1988).

[27] *E.g.*, ALAS. STAT. ANN. § 46–15–030 ("Wherever occurring in a natural state, the water is reserved to the people for common use and is subject to appropriation and beneficial use and to reservation of instream flows and levels of water, as provided in this chapter."); VERNON'S TEX. STAT. & CODE ANN. § 11.003 ("This chapter applies to all streams or other sources of water supply lying upon or forming a part of the boundaries of this state."); UTAH CODE § 73–1–1(1) ("All waters in this state, whether above or under the ground, are hereby declared to be the property of the public, subject to all existing rights to the use thereof.").

[28] IDAHO CODE § 42–201(3).

[29] *Id.* § 42–227.

between 200 and 2500 gallons without a permit, so long as the landowner registers with the State Engineer.[30]

Colorado uses special water courts rather than permits to regulate water appropriations. However, this state system of water courts fulfills much the same function as permits, as will be discussed below in connection with permitting procedures.

2. Permit Programs in Riparian Jurisdictions

Professor Joseph W. Dellapena coined the phrase "regulated riparianism" to describe the riparian rights states (like Florida and Hawai'i) that have adopted some form of water use regulation and permitting. However, these states are far more varied than the western states in whether they have adopted water use permitting and, if so, for what uses.

In 1972, Florida became the first riparian state to adopt a permit program, through the Florida Water Resources Act. The Florida Department of Environmental Protection administers the Act at the state level and engages in state-level water resources planning, but it is the five Regional Water Management Districts that do most of the actual permitting and other water management activities, such as regional water planning.

Like western state permitting systems, Florida's permitting program is comprehensive, in terms both of the waters and the uses to which it applies. The Act provides that "[a]ll waters in the state are subject to regulation under the provisions of this chapter unless specifically exempted by general or special law."[31] Moreover, it defines "waters in the state" to include:

> any and all water on or beneath the surface of the ground or in the atmosphere, including natural or artificial watercourses, lakes, ponds, or diffused surface water and water percolating, standing, or flowing beneath the surface of the ground, as well as all coastal waters within the jurisdiction of the state.[32]

It is difficult to conceive of a water resource that *doesn't* fit into that definition!

As for uses, the Florida Water Resources Act requires a Consumptive Use Permit, or CUP, for all uses of water except domestic use.[33] In order to receive a CUP, the permit applicant must meet three requirements: (1) the propose use must be a "reasonable-

---

[30] UTAH CODE § 73–3–1.5(3), (4).

[31] FLA. STAT. ANN. § 373.023(1).

[32] *Id.* § 373.019(20).

[33] *Id.* § 373.219(1).

beneficial use"; (2) the proposed use must not interfere with "any presently existing legal use of water"; and (3) the proposed use must be "consistent with the public interest."[34] The Act does not define what it means by the "public interest," but a "reasonable-beneficial use" is "the use of water in such quantity as is necessary for economic and efficient utilization for a purpose and in a manner which is both reasonable and consistent with the public interest."[35] Once issued, the CUP specifies the allowed use, the source of the water, and any conditions on use (such as drought response measures) that the relevant Water Management District deems necessary. Most CUPs last up to 20 years, although municipalities and other government entities can receive CUPs lasting 50 years.[36] The permittee can apply to renew the CUP as it is expiring.

Since Florida's conversion to a permit system, about half of the riparian states have now adopted some form of water regulation. Professor Dellapena has found evidence of regulated riparianism in "Alabama, Arkansas, Connecticut, Delaware, Florida, Georgia, Hawaii, Iowa, Kentucky, Maryland, Massachusetts, Michigan, Minnesota, Mississippi, New Jersey, New York, North Carolina, Virginia, and Wisconsin."[37] Hawai'i, like Florida, has a comprehensive water permit system, but most other riparian states' systems are far more limited. Alabama, for example, still relies heavily on the common law.[38] Slightly more formally, under West Virginia's Water Resources Protection Act, people withdrawing large quantities of water must register their withdrawals and report their activities to the state, but they do not need a permit to withdraw and use water.[39] In turn,

> "Large-quantity user" means any person who withdraws over three hundred thousand gallons of water in any thirty-day period from the state's waters and any person who bottles water for resale regardless of quantity withdrawn. "Large-quantity user" excludes farm use, including watering livestock or poultry on a farm, though farms may voluntarily report water withdrawals to assist with the accuracy of the survey.[40]

---

[34] *Id.* § 373.223(1).

[35] *Id.* § 373.019(16).

[36] *Id.* § 373.236.

[37] Joseph W. Dellapena, *The Evolution of Riparianism in the United States*, 95 MARQ. L. REV. 53, 86 n.178 (2011).

[38] Heather Elliott, *Alabama's Water Crisis*, 63 ALA. L. REV. 383, 403 (2012).

[39] W. VA. CODE § 22–26–3(c).

[40] *Id.* § 22–26–22(10).

Arkansas regulates only groundwater withdrawals, and only in critical management areas.[41]

Among eastern riparian states that have true permit requirements, some nevertheless severely limit those requirements. In Pennsylvania, for example, the permit system applies only to public water suppliers.[42] New York requires permits only for public water supply withdrawals and withdrawals for agricultural purposes.[43] Arkansas requires surface water permits only for people constructing dams.[44]

Other regulated riparian states limit their permit requirement to withdrawals of large amounts of water. Kentucky and Virginia, for example, limit their permit requirements to withdrawals of 10,000 gallons per day or more,[45] New Jersey limits its permit requirement to diversions of over 100,000 gallons per day,[46] and Ohio requires permits only for new or increased withdrawals of two million gallons per day or more, averaged over 30 days.[47]

In addition to these limitations, many riparian states also have blanket exemptions from their water permit requirements. Kentucky, for example, exempts all withdrawals for agricultural and domestic purposes, including irrigation.[48] Maryland's water code begins with a fairly general requirement: "Every person is required to obtain a permit from the Department to appropriate or use or begin to construct any plant, building, or structure which may appropriate or use any waters of the State, whether surface water or groundwater."[49] However, it then exempts from this permit requirement: (1) "Use of water for domestic purposes other than for heating and cooling"; (2) use of less than 10,000 gallons per day (averaged over a year) for agricultural purposes; (3) "[u]se of tidal waters for oyster aquaculture purposes"; and (4) non-public-supply use of less than 5000 gallons per day (averaged over a year) of groundwater.[50]

---

41 ARK. CODE § 15–22–909.

42 32 PENN. STAT. § 593.

43 N.Y. ENVTL. CONSERV. LAW §§ 15–1501, 15–1504.

44 ARK. CODE § 15–22–210.

45 KY. ADMIN. REG. § 4:010; 9 VA. ADMIN. CODE §§ 25–210–50.A, 25–210–60.B.

46 N.J. STAT. § 58:1A–5(a).

47 OHIO REV. CODE § 1501.33(A).

48 KY. REV. STAT. § 151.140.

49 MD. ENV'T CODE § 5–502(a).

50 *Id.* § 5–502(b).

D. New Substantive Requirements Created in Water Permit Statutes

One of the interesting results of states creating permit programs is that prior appropriation jurisdictions and regulated riparian jurisdictions have begun to look very similar. This convergence of water law systems has occurred in large part because statutory permit systems give state legislatures a chance to alter the substantive law requirements for obtaining a new water right. For example, as discussed above, under the Florida Water Resources Act, proposed new uses of water must not interfere with "any presently existing legal use of water" and must be "consistent with the public interest."[51] The non-interference requirement injects a bit of priority into an eastern riparian system because earlier uses are protected from interference by later uses. The public interest requirement, in turn, is common in both prior appropriation and riparian jurisdictions and helps to ensure that the permitting agency considers the larger public impacts that a new water withdrawal might cause, such as water quality problems or problems for important species of fish.

Some of the substantive requirements that state legislatures impose reflect the unique or unusual circumstances of the state. The Hawai'i water code, for example, includes special considerations for Native Hawaiian rights and interests.[52] This section, however, surveys some of the more common substantive innovations that states have enacted as part of their permit systems.

1. Public Interest Requirements

Most states, both East and West, that have enacted permit requirements have also specified that new water rights must be in the public interest. For example, as noted above, the Florida Water Resources Act has a double public interest requirement, while in Hawai'i, all proposed new uses of water must be "consistent with the public interest."[53] The California Water Code declares "that the protection of the public interest in the development of the water resources of the State is of vital concern to the people of the State . . . ."[54] In fulfilling this state goal, the California State Water Resources Control Board issues permits "under such terms and conditions as in its judgment will best develop, conserve, and utilize in the public interest the water sought to be appropriated,"[55] and it

[51] FLA. STAT. ANN. § 373.223(1).

[52] HAW. REV. STAT. §§ 174C–3; 174C–49(a)(7); 174C–101.

[53] HAW. REV. STAT. § 174C–49(a)(4).

[54] CAL. WATER CODE § 105.

[55] *Id.* § 1253.

must deny the permit application "when in its judgment the proposed appropriation would not best conserve the public interest, guided by the California Water Plan and other applicable water resource plans (see below for a discussion of state water planning requirements).[56] Similarly, in Idaho, if an applicant's appropriation of water "will conflict with the local public interest, where the local public interest is defined as the affairs of the people in the area directly affected by the proposed use," then the Idaho Department of Water Resources "may reject such application and refuse issuance of a permit therefor, or may partially approve and grant a permit for a smaller quantity of water than applied for, or may grant a permit upon conditions."[57]

Nevertheless, surprisingly few state legislatures have defined what they mean by "the public interest." One exception is the Alaska Legislature, which enumerated the elements of the "public interest" to be:

> (1) the benefit to the applicant resulting from the proposed appropriation;
>
> (2) the effect of the economic activity resulting from the proposed appropriation;
>
> (3) the effect on fish and game resources and on public recreational opportunities;
>
> (4) the effect on public health;
>
> (5) the effect of loss of alternate uses of water that might be made within a reasonable time if not precluded or hindered by the proposed appropriation;
>
> (6) harm to other persons resulting from the proposed appropriation;
>
> (7) the intent and ability of the applicant to complete the appropriation; and
>
> (8) the effect upon access to navigable or public water.[58]

State courts in states without legislative guidance on what the "public interest" should include have sometimes found Alaska's factors to be helpful[59] but also have sometimes rejected them in favor of state-specific definitions. Thus, for example, the Nevada Supreme Court rejected the eight Alaska factors in favor of the Nevada State Engineer's 13 guidelines on the public interest, none of which include

---

56 *Id.* §§ 1255, 1256.

57 IDAHO CODE § 42–203A(5)(e).

58 ALAS. STAT. § 46.15.080(b).

59 Shokal v. Dunn, 707 P.2d 441, 449 n.3 (Idaho 1985).

economic considerations.[60] The 13 guidelines that the Nevada State Engineer gleaned from various Nevada water statutes were:

1. An appropriation must be for a beneficial use.
2. The applicant must demonstrate the amount, source and purpose of the appropriation.
3. If the appropriation is for municipal supply, the applicant must demonstrate the approximate number of persons to be served and the approximate future requirements.
4. The right to divert ceases when the necessity for the use of water does not exist.
5. The applicant must demonstrate the magnitude of the use of water, such as the number of acres irrigated, the use to which generated hydroelectric power will be applied, or the number of animals to be watered.
6. In considering extensions of time to apply water to beneficial use, the State Engineer must determine the number of parcels and commercial or residential units which are contained or planned in the area to be developed, economic conditions which affect the availability of the developer to complete application of the water to beneficial use, and the period contemplated for completion in a development project approved by local governments or in a planned unit development.
7. For large appropriations, the State Engineer must consider whether the applicant has the financial capability to develop the water and place it to beneficial use.
8. The State Engineer may also cooperate with federal authorities in monitoring the development and use of the water resources of the State.
9. [The State Engineer] may cooperate with California authorities in monitoring the future needs and uses of water in the Lake Tahoe area and to study ways of developing water supplies so that the development of the area will not be impeded.
10. Rotation in use is authorized to bring about a more economical use of supplies.

---

60 Pyramid Lake Paiute Tribe of Indians v. Washoe County, 918 P.2d 697, 700 (Nev. 1996).

11. The State Engineer may determine whether there is over pumping of groundwater and refuse to issue permits if there is no unappropriated water available.
12. [The State Engineer] may determine what is a reasonable lowering of the static water level in an area after taking into account the economics of pumping water for the general type of crops growing and the effect of water use on the economy of the area in general.
13. Within an area that has been designated, the State Engineer may monitor and regulate the water supply.[61]

Moreover, even states like Idaho that use the Alaska factors also add their own public interest considerations, such as preserving " 'minimum stream flows for the protection of fish and wildlife habitat, aquatic life, recreation, aesthetic beauty, transportation and navigation values, and water quality.' "[62] As a result, in Idaho, proposed water withdrawals that will cause water pollution or result in violations of state water quality standards violate the public interest.[63]

2. Water Availability Considerations or Protection of Minimum Flows and Levels

Many states took the opportunity in their state water codes to define when permitting of new water rights must stop because of depletion of the water resource. In prior appropriation states, these limitations generally result from an administrative determination that a river, stream, or lake is fully appropriated. For example, in New Mexico, the State Engineer must be able to determine that there is unappropriated water available in the proposed source before he or she can approve a new water right application.[64] Similarly, in California, the State Water Resources Control Board can determine that stream systems are fully appropriated, preventing new appropriative water rights in the system.[65] Even some riparian jurisdictions take a similar approach. In Hawai'i, for example, no water permit can be granted unless "the proposed use of water . . . [c]an be accommodated with the available water source . . . ."[66]

---

[61] *Id.* at 699.

[62] Shokal v. Dunn, 707 p.2d 441, 448–49 (Idaho 1985) (quoting IDAHO CODE § 42–1501 and incorporating it into water permit public interest review).

[63] *Id.* at 451–52.

[64] N.M. STAT. ANN. § 72–5–7.

[65] CAL. WATER CODE §§ 1205–1206.

[66] HAW. REV. STAT. § 174C–49(a)(1).

A different approach, more common in eastern riparian states, is for a state to decide how much water must remain in a stream or aquifer, generally referred to as "minimum flows" in streams and "minimum levels" in aquifers. For example, under the Florida Water Resources Act, Florida's regional Water Management Districts must set minimum flows for all surface watercourses and minimum levels for all aquifers and lakes.[67] "The minimum flow for a given watercourse shall be the limit at which further withdrawals would be significantly harmful to the water resources or the ecology of the area," while the minimum level shall be the level "at which further withdrawals would be significantly harmful to the water resources of the area."[68] Similarly, the Washington Department of Ecology:

> may establish minimum water flows or levels for streams, lakes or other public waters for the purposes of protecting fish, game, birds or other wildlife resources, or recreational or aesthetic values of said public waters whenever it appears to be in the public interest to establish the same. In addition, the department of ecology shall, when requested by the department of fish and wildlife to protect fish, game or other wildlife resources under the jurisdiction of the requesting state agency, or if the department of ecology finds it necessary to preserve water quality, establish such minimum flows or levels as are required to protect the resource or preserve the water quality described in the request or determination.[69]

Because Washington is a prior appropriation state, these minimum flows and levels are treated as appropriations "with priority dates as of the effective dates of their establishment."[70] Nevertheless, "[w]henever an application for a permit to make beneficial use of public waters is approved relating to a stream or other water body for which minimum flows or levels have been adopted and are in effect at the time of approval, the permit shall be conditioned to protect the levels or flows."[71]

3. Water Rights for Instream Flows

Closely related to the water availability and minimum flow requirements are statutory provisions that allow entities to secure a water right to preserve instream flow. In western prior appropriation states, instream flow permits effectively eliminate the common-law requirement of a physical diversion and often re-define beneficial use

---

67 FLA. STAT. ANN. § 373.042(1).

68 *Id.*

69 REV. CODE WASH. § 90.22.010.

70 *Id.* § 90.03.045.

71 *Id.* § 90.03.247.

to allow for instream uses like fish and wildlife protection, recreation, and aesthetics. For example, Oregon's statutes governing instream flow rights declare that "[p]ublic uses are beneficial uses"[72] and allow three other state agencies to request that the Oregon Water Resources Commission establish instream flow rights: (1) The Oregon Department of Fish and Wildlife can request instream flow rights for "the conservation, maintenance and enhancement of aquatic and fish life, wildlife and fish and wildlife habitat"; (2) the Oregon Department of Environmental Quality can request instream flow rights "to protect and maintain water quality standards"; and (3) the Oregon Parks and Recreation Department can request instream flow rights to protect public recreation and "scenic attraction."[73] In Utah, similarly, the Utah Division of Wildlife Resources and the Utah Division of Parks and Recreation can file water rights change applications to create instream flow rights for fish propagation, public recreation, or "the reasonable preservation or enhancement of the natural stream environment."[74] In 2022, moreover, the Utah Legislature amended Utah's instream flow laws to make it easier to get fresh water to the shrinking Great Salt Lake.[75]

In regulated riparian jurisdictions, instream flow rights can serve as an alternative means to minimum flows and levels for assuring protection of instream values. In Hawai'i, for instance, " '[i]nstream use' means beneficial uses of stream water for significant purposes which are located in the stream and which are achieved by leaving the water in the stream."[76] The Hawai'i Commission on Water Resources is charged with creating a program to protect instream uses of water throughout the state,[77] which encompass nine categories of uses:

(1) Maintenance of fish and wildlife habitats;

(2) Outdoor recreational activities;

(3) Maintenance of ecosystems such as estuaries, wetlands, and stream vegetation;

(4) Aesthetic values such as waterfalls and scenic waterways;

(5) Navigation;

---

72 OR. REV. STAT. § 537.334.

73 *Id.* § 537.336.

74 UTAH CODE ANN. § 73–3–30.

75 UTAH H.B. 33, § 3 (Mar. 21, 2022), *amending* UTAH CODE ANN. § 73–3–30.

76 HAW. REV. STAT. § 174C–3.

77 *Id.* § 174C–71.

(6) Instream hydropower generation;

(7) Maintenance of water quality;

(8) The conveyance of irrigation and domestic water supplies to downstream points of diversion; and

(9) The protection of traditional and customary Hawaiian rights.[78]

As part of protecting these uses, moreover, the Commission can establish minimum flow standards on a stream-by-stream basis.[79]

4. Water Resources Planning

One of the most common water-related requirements in state statutes is water resources planning. About two-thirds of the states in the United States require or encourage some form of longer-term water resources planning in their water codes. In most of these states, such planning occurs at the state level.[80] However, Florida engages in both state-level and regional water resources planning,[81] while Tennessee encourages regional water planning.[82]

States vary even more in the purposes for which they engage in water planning. Some purposes are very specific. In Alabama, for example, each water management district shall create a "plan for draining, leveeing, reclaiming, or protecting such lands and other property from overflow or damage by water or for flood prevention or for the conservation, development, utilization and disposal of water . . . ."[83] Water planning in Alaska, Delaware, Rhode Island, and Virginia concentrates on providing for current and future water supply,[84] while Illinois and Vermont emphasize water quality purposes in their water plans.[85] New Jersey and North Carolina plan for both water supply and water quality.[86] Nevada's water planning focuses on water conservation planning by water suppliers and public utilities.[87] Perhaps most unusually, Maine requires "an action plan

---

[78] *Id.* § 174C–3.

[79] *Id.* § 174C–71(1).

[80] *E.g.*, N.D. CENT. CODE § 61–02–28.

[81] FLA. STAT. ANN. § 373.036(1).

[82] TENN. CODE ANN. § 69–7–308.

[83] ALA. CODE § 9–9–23(c).

[84] ALAS. STAT. ANN. § 46.03.720(b); DEL. CODE § 1506; GEN. LAWS R.I. §§ 46–15–13 & tit. 46, c. 15.3; VA. CODE ANN. tit. 62.1.

[85] ILL. COMP. STAT. § 50/2.08; VT. STAT. ANN. § 1423(b).

[86] N.J. STAT. ANN. tit. 58, cc. 1A, 11A; N.C. GEN. STAT. §§ 130A–317, 130A–323, 143–215.8B, 143–215.73A.

[87] NEV. REV. STAT. cc. 540, 704.

to protect the State's inland waters from invasive aquatic plants and nuisance species."[88]

An increasing number of states, however, engage in comprehensive, multipurpose, and long-term water resources planning. These states include Arizona, California, Connecticut, Florida, Georgia, Hawai'i, Idaho, Indiana, Kansas, Minnesota, Mississippi, Missouri, Montana, New Mexico, New York, Oklahoma, Oregon, Pennsylvania, South Carolina, South Dakota, Texas, Utah, West Virginia, Wisconsin, and Wyoming.[89] In their planning, these states look to the availability of water in light of all demands and other considerations such as population growth, species protection, and water quality, generally over a 20- to 50-year time horizon.

E. Permitting Procedures and Administrative Law

The common-law requirements for beginning a new water use were fairly easy: Essentially, in both the East and the West, and for both surface water and groundwater, the most important step was just to start using the water, and to do so in an obvious way, especially in the West. Some early western systems had a limited registration requirement, but for the most part following formal *procedures* was not any part of creating or exercising a common-law water right.

That procedural informality changes completely when a state introduces a water right permit system. Indeed, the point of a permit system is that some state official has to give formal approval before a person or business entity can start using water. Before that approval can be granted, moreover, the proposed water user has to follow a variety of procedures. This section summarizes typical permitting procedures and the procedures used in Colorado's water courts, which result in a fairly similar process for establishing a new water right. It then identifies seven important procedural consequences resulting from the fact that administrative law requirements apply to state water agencies and their water rights decisions.

1. Typical Water Right Permitting Procedures

Most state water permit statutes begin by imposing the permit requirement and by defining the waters subject to state regulation. The first step in acquiring a new or changed water right is to file an application with the appropriate state agency and to pay any

---

[88] 38 MAINE REV. STAT. § 1872.

[89] ROBERT W. ADLER, ROBIN KUNDIS CRAIG, & NOAH D. HALL, MODERN WATER LAW: PRIVATE PROPERTY, PUBLIC RIGHTS, AND ENVIRONMENTAL PROTECTIONS, THIRD EDITION 337–347 (Foundation Press 2024).

required filing and processing fees.[90] The application will usually require the applicant to describe the proposed water use in some detail—how much water is desired, from what water source, with what point of withdrawal, for what use, and potential public interest issues or effects on other users.

Second, the agency will usually assess the application for basic completeness. If the applicant has failed to provide required information, or if the agency can determine immediately that it will need more information to assess the application, it will usually notify the applicant and give the applicant a chance to correct the defects. Applicants who fail to comply with these requests for additional information will eventually have their applications denied.

Third, in states with a water availability or minimum flow/level requirement, the agency will next check to see whether water is available from the proposed source to supply the new use. In some states, this inquiry is a first and independent way to deny the application;[91] however, in some states this criterion is part of the overall permit evaluation (Step 5). If water is not available, the agency will either deny the application outright or, sometimes, suggest a change to the application that will allow a finding of availability.

Fourth, if the application is complete, the agency will give the general public notice of the application. Members of the public generally have a window of time in which to file objections to the permit, and this window can be quite short. In New Mexico, for example, objectors have only 10 days from the last date of the notice in which to file their objections.[92] The state law may also specify that only certain kinds of members of the general public have ***standing*** to object—that is, a legal status that entitles them to participate in the permit proceeding. In New Mexico, for example: (1) the State of New Mexico itself and all of its governmental agencies always have standing to object; (2) other water rights holders can object if the proposed new water right would be detrimental to their existing water rights; and (3) members of the general public can object if they

---

[90] *E.g.*, HAW. REV. STAT. § 174C–51; N.M. STAT. ANN. § 72–5–1.

[91] N.M. STAT. ANN. § 72–5–7; Lion's Gate Water v. D-Antonio, 226 P.3d 622, 632 (N.M. 2009) ("Whether water is available for appropriation is the threshold issue that is dispositive of a permit application when water is not available for appropriation. . . . If the State Engineer makes a pre-hearing determination that water is unavailable for appropriation, secondary issues that must otherwise be considered before a permit to appropriate water can be granted become irrelevant, because the State Engineer is required to reject the application without reaching those issues."); *see also* CAL. WATER CODE §§ 1205–1206 (allowing the State Water Resources Control Board to find that a stream system is fully appropriated, after which no new permit applications will be considered for withdrawals from that system).

[92] N.M. STAT. ANN. § 72–5–5(A).

believe that the proposed new use would interfere with water conservation or otherwise be detrimental to the public welfare and "the objector will be substantially and specifically affected by the granting of the application . . . ."[93] In California, in contrast, "any person interested" may protest a permit application "for good cause."[94]

Fifth, in light of the objections filed and the requirements of state law, the permitting agency will decide whether or not to grant the application. Most water permitting agencies also have authority to modify the final water right from what the permit applicant asked for, such as by granting a water right for less water. In Michigan, for example, the Michigan Department of Environment, Great Lakes, and Energy can consider whether "preventative measures" will sufficiently mitigate the adverse environmental impacts of a proposed water withdrawal—particularly impacts on fish populations and overall stream health—and thus allow the permit to issue.[95]

Sixth, the agency will give both the applicant and the general public notice of its decision, starting the clock for any appeals of that decision. The applicant can always appeal the agency's decision if the applicant is unhappy with it, assuming that the applicant follows the rules and meets the deadlines for appealing. In addition, the State itself or other state agencies can usually appeal the water agency's decision. Members of the general public who can challenge the final agency decision are usually the same groups of people who could object to the permit application. In addition, however, many states require that a person actually have objected to the permit application in order to be able to appeal the final decision.

Seventh, if the agency grants the permit (and that decision survives any appeals), the applicant usually has a certain time in which to start using the water. In New Mexico, for example, the applicant has five years.[96] Excessive delay in using the water generally results in the permit evaporating and the water being released to other permit applicants.

2. Procedures in Colorado's Water Courts

As noted, Colorado does not use an administrative permit system. Instead, since 1879, it has determined water rights in its district courts, which have evolved into seven specialized water courts. In the Water Rights Determination and Administration Act

---

93 *Id.* § 72–5–5(B).

94 CAL. WATER CODE § 1330.

95 MICH. COMP. LAWS § 324.32723(8).

96 *Id.* § 72–5–6.

of 1969, the Colorado Legislature created the seven water divisions based on the watersheds of Colorado's major rivers. "Each water division is staffed with a division engineer, appointed by the state engineer; a water judge, appointed by the Supreme Court; a water referee, appointed by the water judge; and a water clerk, assigned by the district court."[97] Water judges and the water courts "have jurisdiction in the determination of water rights, the use and administration of water, and all other water matters within the jurisdiction of the water division."[98]

To obtain a new water right, therefore, the applicant must get a decree from the appropriate water court. The steps for obtaining this decree are:

1. Intend to divert previously unappropriated water;
2. Demonstrate this intent openly, for example, by conducting field surveys, posting notice at a diversion point, or filing for a well permit application;
3. File an application with the regional water court. The year in which the application is filed sets the date of priority;
4. Publish the application through the water division monthly water resume and by legal notice in local newspapers;
5. Allow two months for other parties to file statements of opposition;
6. Colorado Division of Water Resources engineers at the local Division Engineer's Office review the application;
7. Staff from the Division Engineer's office, generally the local water commissioners, perform field investigations to confirm the claims in the application;
8. Division Engineer submits a written report to the regional water court, with recommendations;
9 If there is no opposition, the application is reviewed by a water court referee who then issues a ruling;
10. If no protest is filed, the referee's ruling goes before the water court judge and he/she signs it in the form of a decreed water right.
11. If there is a protest, the case goes before the water court judge for trial, unless the parties can reach

[97] *Water Courts*, COLORADO JUDICIAL BRANCH (viewed Nov. 15, 2023), https://www.courts.state.co.us/Courts/Water/Index.cfm.

[98] *Id.*

> agreement. In that instance, the water court may enter an agreed-upon decree.[99]

Thus, despite relying on a court system instead of an administrative agency, the procedures in Colorado for obtaining a new water right are very similar to the permit procedures in other states—an application; public notice and opportunity to object; review by state officials; an official recommendation; and opportunity for addition public objection.

3. The Procedural Consequences of Adopting an Administrative Permit System

While it is a state's legislature that creates the state's water use permit program, the legislature will usually charge a state agency or the State Engineer's office with making permit decisions. As a result, the transition from a common-law system to a permit system also involves the addition of administrative law to the creation of water rights.

In general, administrative law is the body of law that governs the powers and limitations of government agencies, which are generally deemed part of the *executive* branch of government. Thus, federal agencies are generally subject to at least some direction from the President of the United States, while state agencies are generally subject to some direction from the state Governor. However, agencies exist only because a legislature (Congress or the state legislature) created them, and hence they are also bound by the directions and limitations contained within the statutes that they implement. Finally, for constitutional reasons of due process and separation of powers, most final agency actions are subject to judicial review in the relevant (federal or state) courts.

In water right permitting, however, the most important aspects of administrative law are the rules that govern the water agency's relationships to the regulated entities (the people and businesses seeking water permits) and the general public. Thus, for example, the water agency will be required to follow set procedures and to evaluate specific criteria when deciding whether to issue a new water right/permit, and the permit applicant will be allowed to present evidence in its favor and to challenge any denial of its application. At the same time, the permitting agency will have to make any new permit application available to the public, and members of the public will have opportunities to comment on the application and to challenge a final permit.

---

[99] COLORADO FOUNDATION FOR WATER EDUCATION, CITIZENS' GUIDE TO COLORADO WATER LAW 14 (2004 revised edition).

Thus, administrative law adds a lot of procedure to establishing a water right compared to the common law. Specifically, the creation of a permit system generally has seven important legal consequences for state water rights.

First, courts are no longer the first entities to determine whether a water right exists. Instead, a state agency has the authority to approve or disapprove an application for a new water right or a change in an existing water right in accordance with the criteria that the state legislature creates. While state courts will be able to review the agency's decision, the courts generally will be reviewing the agency's findings rather than assessing the facts for themselves.

Second, the state agency will generally have authority to specify many of the details for the permitting process (like the form of the application) and details of some of the substantive requirements through *rulemaking*—the process through which a state agency can create binding law. For example, in Kentucky and Virginia, it is the water permitting agency that specifies in regulations the sizes of water withdrawals that are exempt from the permit requirement, and the agencies can change that threshold if doing so would allow for better management of the state's water resources. In Hawai'i, the Water Resources Management Commission "shall adopt rules governing the filing of objections and the persons having standing to file objections,"[100] and it also establishes the state's instream use protection program, including instream flow standards.[101] The details of how state agencies can promulgate these regulations are generally spelled out in the state's Administrative Procedure Act or equivalent statute, but the state legislature may also impose special requirements in the water code itself. As a result, water law practitioners and their clients must pay attention to, and potentially participate in, these more general regulatory actions in addition to the proceedings that address individual water rights or disputes.

Third, a state agency's handling of a particular permit application is generally regarded as a form of *adjudication* because it will ultimately determine individual rights to water. As a result, the permit process and agency decision are subject to constitutional due process protections and statutory procedural protections. In order for the permit decision to be valid, the permit applicant will need to be notified of relevant proceedings and have an opportunity to be heard by the agency.

Fourth, although the permit applicant (and probably interested members of the general public) will have a right to appeal an adverse decision by the water agency, challengers will probably have to

---

[100] HAW. REV. STAT. § 174C–53(b).

[101] *Id.* § 174C–71.

appeal within the agency first, a requirement known as *exhaustion of administrative remedies*. Depending on the state, moreover, there may be one or two levels of administrative appeal before the challenger can go to court.

Fifth, as noted, the permit application will be subject to *public participation and comment* requirements. The agency will usually have to give public notice of the permit application and/or the agency's proposed decision and to allow for public comments. Thus, water rights holders downstream of the proposed water withdrawal may take the opportunity to object to the permit, as might members of the public who have other concerns about the proposed water use, such as effects on water quality or on fish and wildlife. The permitting agency will have to consider and respond to any public comments it receives in the process of making its decision.

Sixth, as noted above, many states now require a *public interest review* of some sort even if there are no objections from the general public. As part of a more general and holistic approach to water resources management, the public interest review allows the permitting agency to consider whether the proposed water withdrawal and use causes more harm than benefit. Public interest review requirements generally have more teeth in regulated riparian states than in western prior appropriation states, where state constitutional rights to appropriate can still significantly limit permit review requirements.

Finally, once a permit applicant or public challenger gets to court, the court will likely accord the water agency's decision some kind of *deference*. While both the exact terms that states use to describe this deference and the actual amount of deference given vary from state to state and according to the exact issue being decided, courts will generally respect the water agency's expert evaluations regarding the state of a specific water resource, the amount of water available, and the effects of a new proposed withdrawal on both existing water rights holders and the environment. In contrast, courts are less deferential to the agency's interpretation of the law itself.

Chapter 6

NAVIGABLE WATERS

Chapters 2 through 5 focus on the *state* law governing water allocation and management. However, the federal government also plays a role—sometimes quite large—in water law. This chapter examines the scope of federal regulatory authority regarding and control over certain kinds of waters—the "navigable" waters. Chapter 8 will examine federal water rights and other federal interests in water.

As a general rule, once a water is considered "navigable" from a legal perspective, the federal government will have at least some authority over that waterbody. The quintessential federal navigable water is the ocean, over which the U.S. Supreme Court gave the federal government comprehensive paramount rights in light of that government's roles in international relations and national defense.[1] Determining navigability is more complicated for freshwater and coastal waterbodies. At least four separate, but related, doctrines of "navigable waters" (or "navigability") exist for purposes of federal law, and states have also adopted varying definitions of navigability to delineate public and private rights in waterways. At the federal level, different definitions of "navigable waters" govern: (1) the geographical scope of admiralty jurisdiction under Article III of the U.S. Constitution; (2) federal authority under the Commerce Clause; (3) the federal navigational servitude; and (4) the question of title to the beds and banks of waterbodies.

A. Navigability and the U.S. Constitution

The words "navigable" and "navigability" appear nowhere in the text of the U.S. Constitution. However, the concept of navigability has been important to the scope of federal constitutional authority since the early days of the Republic. Specifically, judicial decisions have used navigability to define the scope of Article III admiralty jurisdiction and some aspects of federal power under the Commerce Clause and the related federal navigational servitude.

1. Federal Admiralty Jurisdiction

Article III, section 2 of the U.S. Constitution includes within federal judicial power "all Cases of admiralty and maritime jurisdiction." In general, admiralty and maritime law applies to ships and sailors on the navigable waters, and they operate with a strong

---

1 United States v. California, 332 U.S. 19, 34–38 (1947).

goal of achieving national uniformity in these rules, which include the rules of tort liability. Thus, what counts as "navigable waters" for admiralty jurisdiction and maritime law is critical to national-level policies.

Indeed, admiralty jurisdiction played a seminal role in defining "navigability" in early federal law. Although details of English law on the issue were complicated and confusing, admiralty jurisdiction in England was generally limited to cases involving waters influenced by the ebb and flow of the tide and cases that were not within the jurisdiction of inland counties. Given this understanding when the admiralty clause of the Constitution was adopted, early American admiralty cases similarly limited admiralty jurisdiction to coastal and tidal waters, in part to preserve the power of state courts relative to federal courts.[2] However, in *Waring v. Clark*,[3] the U.S. Supreme Court began to expand admiralty jurisdiction in the United States, reasoning that nothing in the Constitution limited admiralty jurisdiction to the scope existing in England at the time and that U.S. law should be free to evolve as was appropriate to the conditions of a new nation on a different continent. That reasoning opened the door to the more significant expansion of admiralty jurisdiction in *The Propeller Genesee Chief v. Fitzhugh*,[4] which dramatically expanded the definition of navigability under U.S. law.

The Propeller Genesee Chief involved a collision of two boats on Lake Ontario, and the issue before the U.S. Supreme Court was whether the Court had admiralty jurisdiction. Prior to this case, admiralty jurisdiction applied only to waters that were subject to the ebb and flow of the tide. *The Propeller Genesee Chief* eliminated this requirement because the United States has many large inland navigable waterways (like the Great Lakes where the case arose). Chief Justice Taney stated that admiralty jurisdiction applies to all navigable waters, defined as the public waters upon which interstate or international commerce is conducted.[5] The Court thus dropped the formalistic approach inherited from England and adopted a more functional approach to defining navigability. Although the Court did not explicitly use the term "navigability in fact" until later cases, *The Propeller Genesee Chief* decision established the concept that courts and Congress should define "navigability" in terms of waters that are physically suitable for commercial navigation and not by the artificial limitation of tidewater.

---

2 *See* The Steamboat Orleans v. Phoebus, 36 U.S. (11 Pet.) 175 (1837); Hobart v. Drogan, 35 U.S. (10 Pet.) 108 (1836); Peyroux v. Howard, 32 U.S. (7 Pet.) 324 (1833); The Steamboat Thomas Jefferson, 23 U.S. (10 Wheat.) 428 (1825).

3 46 U.S. (5 How.) 441 (1847).

4 53 U.S. (12 How.) 443 (1851).

5 *Id.* at 457.

2. Navigability Under the Commerce Clause

Article I, section 8 of the U.S. Constitution confers authority on Congress to "regulate Commerce with foreign Nations, and among the several States, and with the Indian Tribes." In the seminal case of *Gibbons v. Ogden*,[6] the U.S. Supreme Court invalidated a New York statute granting Robert Livingston and Robert Fulton the exclusive right to navigate on state waters with boats powered by fire or steam because the state statute interfered with Congress's power to regulate commerce. Responding to arguments that Commerce Clause authority was limited to regulation of commercial transactions and not navigation, Chief Justice John Marshall held that "[t]he power of Congress . . . comprehends navigation, within the limits of every State in the Union; so far as that navigation may be, in any manner, connected with 'commerce with foreign nations, or among the several States, or with the Indian tribes.' "[7] However, the Court did not directly address the scope of "navigability" for Commerce Clause purposes.

The Daniel Ball[8] presents the U.S. Supreme Court's early and still seminal answer to that question. Justice Field first reaffirmed the navigable-in-fact test provided by Chief Justice Taney in *The Propeller Genesee Chief*. The *Daniel Ball* Court then differentiated between navigable waters of the United States and navigable waters of the states. Navigable waters of the United States are those that constitute a "highway over which commerce is or may be carried on with other States or foreign countries in the customary modes in which such commerce is conducted by water."[9] The Court explained that the water body at hand, the Grand River, fit this definition because it was used to transport goods to Lake Michigan and because this "junction with the lake ... forms a continued highway for commerce, both with other States and with foreign countries, and is thus brought under the direct control of Congress in the exercise of its commercial power."[10] Therefore, according to the Court, "that power authorizes all appropriate legislation for the protection or advancement of either interstate or foreign commerce, and for that purpose such legislation as will insure the convenient and safe navigation of all the navigable waters of the United States."[11]

However, the question remained whether the federal government had authority under the Commerce Clause to enact and

6 22 U.S. (9 Wheat.) 1 (1824).

7 *Id.* at 190.

8 77 U.S. (10 Wall.) 557 (1870).

9 *Id.* at 563.

10 *Id.* at 564.

11 *Id.* at 565.

enforce a federal licensing statute against *The Daniel Ball*, a vessel that allegedly was engaged in solely *intrastate* commerce. The Court stated, however, that *The Daniel Ball* was engaged in interstate commerce, subject to federal authority under the Commerce Clause, because the goods being transported on *The Daniel Ball* were destined for other states, albeit through a chain of transport modes.

Over time, Congress sought to regulate a broader range of activities that might adversely affect various interests in navigable waters, and the U.S. Supreme Court was called on to decide whether that authority extended beyond the scope of waters covered by the "navigable in fact" test in *The Daniel Ball*. The Court answered this question in *United States v. Appalachian Electric Power Co.*[12] The *Appalachian Electric Power Co.* Court had to determine whether the federal commerce power extended to the grant of licenses required by what was then the Federal Power Commission (now the Federal Energy Regulatory Commission, or FERC) for the construction of hydroelectric dams in navigable rivers of the United States. The Rivers and Harbors Act[13] makes it unlawful to construct a dam in any navigable water of the United States without the consent of Congress. The Federal Power Commission, however, has the power to authorize construction of such dams upon specified conditions.

In *Appalachian Electric Power Co.*, the respondent applied for a license from the Federal Power Commission to construct the Radford Dam on the New River. Although the Commission initially determined that the river was not navigable, it later revised its determination and found that the New River indeed *was* navigable. As a result, Appalachian Electric Power Company could not proceed with dam construction. The Company ignored this new determination and began construction, and the Commission sought an injunction because the dam allegedly would obstruct a navigable water.

For the U.S. Supreme Court, Justice Reed concluded that the determination of a waterbody's navigability is not restricted to its purely natural conditions; rather, "[a] waterway, otherwise suitable for navigation, is not barred from that classification merely because artificial aids must make the highway suitable for use before commercial navigation may be undertaken."[14] The Court agreed with the Commission that the New River was navigable. In addition, the Court also concluded that, pursuant to the Commerce Clause, the federal government has broad powers over navigable waters, including such goals as "[f]lood protection, watershed development,

---

12 311 U.S. 377 (1940).

13 33 U.S.C. §§ 401, 403.

14 311 U.S. 377, 407 (1940).

[and] recovery of the cost of improvements through utilization of power."[15] As a result, the Commission could impose conditions on the dam that had nothing to do with protecting navigability. The Court granted the injunction until Appalachian Electric Power obtained a license from the Commission to construct the dam.

Appalachian Electric Power Co. expanded the definition of navigability from *The Daniel Ball*'s test. Under *The Daniel Ball* test, a water is navigable for Commerce Clause purposes if it is used or susceptible to use for commerce "in its natural condition." The Court in *Appalachian Electric Power* extended federal Commerce Clause power to rivers that could be navigable after improvements deemed reasonable under the circumstances, even if those improvements had not yet been made. Consider for a moment the immense changes to waterways that the U.S. Army Corps of Engineers can and has made, from channelization and dredging of rivers to improve navigation to the construction of dams to reduce flood dangers to navigation. Given this technological capacity, the *Appalachian Electric Power Co.* Court's expanded definition of "navigability" significantly extends federal Commerce Clause jurisdiction over waterways.

In addition, the Commerce Clause definition of "navigable waters" supports several federal statutes. This chapter has already mentioned the Rivers and Harbors Act and its provisions to protect navigability. The definition of navigability is also central to the application of the Clean Water Act (CWA) (the CWA is covered in more detail Chapter 11). The CWA applies to "navigable waters," which the statute itself defines as "waters of the United States, including the territorial seas"[16] The U.S. Environmental Protection Agency and Army Corps, the two agencies that implement the Act, have defined "waters of the United States" in regulations to include "all waters which are currently used, or were used in the past or may be susceptible to use in interstate or foreign commerce, including all waters which are subject to the ebb and flow of the tide,"[17] clearly drawing upon the federal government's Commerce Clause authority to protect water quality in the Nation's waters. How far that Commerce Clause authority can extend, however, remains an ongoing controversy under the Act, especially with respect to wetlands and tributaries. Thus far, the issue has been decided as a matter of statutory construction, avoiding any holding about the limits of federal authority under the Commerce Clause *per se*. In a form of "clear statement" rule, however, although the Court has indicated that Congress must be precise about legislation that approaches the "outer limits" of the Commerce Clause in regulating

---

[15] *Id.* at 426.

[16] 33 U.S.C. § 1365(7).

[17] 33 C.F.R. § 328.3(a)(1).

navigable waters.[18] The ongoing controversy over CWA jurisdiction illustrates the difficulty of determining the full geographic scope of federal regulatory power over waterbodies under the Commerce Clause.

3. The Federal Navigation (or "Navigational") Servitude

Closely related to the federal government's Commerce Clause power is a doctrine known as the federal navigation servitude (sometimes called the "navigational servitude"). Although not formally named as such by the U.S. Supreme Court until 1897,[19] the doctrine has roots in the federal government's "dominant public interest in navigation."[20] Rather than operating as a different source of federal regulatory authority over navigation and navigability, however, the navigation servitude effectively insulates the federal government from otherwise legitimate constitutional takings claims (see Chapter 14) where federal projects or operation of federal regulatory authority in navigable waters impairs private property rights in those waters. As such, the term "navigation servitude" or "navigation easement"[21] suggests either a residual federal proprietary interest in navigable waters despite other attributes of state ownership, or a significant limitation in the scope of private property rights in those waters. In *United States v. Chandler-Dunbar Water Power Co.*,[22] the U.S. Supreme Court described any private title to the beds of navigable waters as a "technical title," which is "qualified" and "subordinate to the public rights of navigation, and however helpful in protecting the owner against the right of third parties, is of no avail against the exercise of the great and absolute power of Congress over the improvement of navigable rivers."[23] As a practical matter, therefore, the navigational servitude operates as an encumbrance on riparian property ownership.

In *United States v. Twin City Power Co.*, the U.S. Supreme Court had to determine whether the navigation servitude warranted a different navigability test, *i.e.*, a different scope of waters to which it applies.[24] At issue in *Twin City Power Co.* was the Clark Hill project on the Savannah River, a navigable stream. The Clark Hill project served multiple purposes: hydroelectric power generation, flood

---

18 *See* Solid Waste Agency of No. Cook County v. U.S. Army Corps of Engineers, 531 U.S. 159, 174 (2001); *see also,* Sackett v. Environmental Protection Agency, 143 S. Ct. 1322, 1355 (2023) (Thomas, J. concurring).

19 *See* Gibson v. United States, 166 U.S. 269 (1897).

20 United States v. Willow River Power Co., 324 U.S. 499, 507 (1945).

21 *See* United States v. Grand River Dam Auth., 363 U.S. 229, 231 (1960).

22 229 U.S. 53 (1913).

23 *Id.* at 62–63.

24 United States v. Twin City Power Co., 350 U.S. 222 (1956).

control, and navigation. Specifically, the Court had to determine whether just compensation, which the United States must pay by force of the Fifth Amendment to the U.S. Constitution when it takes private property for public purposes (see Chapter 14), includes the value of the land as a site for hydroelectric power generation. Justice Douglas first stated that the federal navigation servitude applies only to projects constructed or operated specifically for navigational purposes. The Court then explained that if the Government impacts property above the ordinary high-water mark, an impacted property owner may have a valid takings claim against the government. Otherwise, however, the property is subject to the federal government's navigation servitude. The Court concluded that the Clark Hill project did not impact the landowner's property rights above the ordinary high-water mark and thus fell within the federal government's navigational servitude, eliminating the property owner's claim to compensation.

Justice Burton, joined by Justices Frankfurter, Minton, and Harlan, dissented and would have awarded compensation for the fair market value of the land. The dissent explained that to deny compensation for the land would extend the federal government's

> navigation servitude far above and beyond the high-water mark of the Savannah River. In the face of decisions uniformly limiting that servitude to the bed of the stream, the Government would take 4,700 acres of private property for a public use, substantially without compensation therefor. This would enforce the Government's right of condemnation, while repudiating its constitutional obligation to pay for the private property taken.[25]

Unlike the federal government's authority under the Commerce Clause, which encompasses non-navigable tributaries to navigable waters so long as there is a recognized impact of the regulated activity on navigability (or another recognized Commerce Clause purpose), the navigation servitude is limited to navigable waters. *United States v. Willow River Power Co.*[26] reflects this distinction, finding that a landowner was not entitled to compensation based upon a property's potential as a hydroelectric power site because hydroelectric power generation depended on the existence of the adjacent navigable stream, which is subject to the federal government's navigational servitude. In contrast, *United States v. Cress*[27] required compensation for impairment of private dam operation when a federal project on navigable water raised the level

---

25 *Id.* at 246.

26 324 U.S. 499 (1945).

27 243 U.S. 316 (1917).

of a non-navigable tributary. Thus, where property interests are impaired by federal actions not subject to the servitude, compensation may be required even for non-fee property interests. For example, the Court of Federal Claims awarded compensation for the loss of statutorily created property rights to take oysters impaired by the opening of a federal spillway.[28]

4. The Federal Navigation Servitude Versus the Commerce Clause

As noted above, the federal government's Commerce Clause authority extends to waters that can be made navigable-in-fact as well as to waters that are naturally navigable-in-fact. Thus, physical changes in waters can create interesting issues regarding the overlap—or not—of the federal government's Commerce Clause authority to act versus its insulation from constitutional takings claims pursuant to the navigation servitude. *Kaiser Aetna v. United States*, for example, involved a dispute regarding the Kai Marina in Hawai'i, which was developed by dredging and filling the Kuapa Pond.[29] Kuapa Pond originally was "a shallow lagoon separated from Maunalua Bay and the Pacific Ocean by a barrier beach" and was deemed private property under Hawai'i state law,[30] but the development project connected it to the ocean. At issue before the U.S. Supreme Court was whether, as a result of this new navigable connection to the ocean, Kuapa Pond became subject to the federal government's navigation servitude and the public had acquired a right of access to the once-private pond.

The Supreme Court answered "no." As Justice Rehnquist explained for the Court:

> [a]lthough . . . the now dredged Kuapa Pond falls within the definition of "navigable waters" as this Court has used that term in delimiting the boundaries of Congress' regulatory authority under the Commerce Clause, this Court has never held that the navigational servitude creates a blanket exception to the Takings Clause whenever Congress exercises its Commerce Clause authority to promote navigation. . . . In light of its expansive authority under the Commerce Clause, there is no question but that Congress could assure the public a free right of access to the Hawaii Kai Marina if it so chose. Whether a statute or regulation

---

[28] Campo v. United States, 157 Fed. Cl. 584 (2021).

[29] Kaiser Aetna v. United States, 444 U.S. 164 (1979).

[30] *Id.* at 164.

that went so far amounted to a "taking," however, is an entirely separate question.[31]

In addition, "the Government's attempt to create a public right of access to the improved pond goes so far beyond ordinary regulation or improvement for navigation as to amount to a taking."[32] The Court reached this decision by emphasizing "that prior to its improvement, Kuapa Pond was incapable of being used as a continuous highway for the purpose of navigation in interstate commerce."[33] Thus, according to the majority, Kuapa Pond had not been "navigable in fact" before the development, and opening the pond to public use required compensation.

However, the fact that the pond was not navigable in fact did not mean that it lost its status as a "navigable water" for all federal law purposes. Justice Blackmun, joined by Justices Brennan and Marshall, dissented first to point out that the Court had not intended, by virtue of the expansion of navigability to inland navigable-in-fact waters in *The Propeller Genesee Chief* and its progeny, to eliminate navigability based on the original test of waters subject to the ebb and flow of the tide. Kuapa Pond had always been subject to the ebb and flow of the tide and so had always been a federal "navigable water" subject to the navigation servitude. The U.S. Supreme Court later affirmed that the "ebb and flow" test remains a viable test of navigability in *Phillips Petroleum Co. v. Mississippi*.[34] The dissent also disagreed with the majority's view that the navigational servitude does not extend to all navigable waters of the United States. In the dissent's view, " 'navigational servitude' extends to the limits of interstate commerce by water; accordingly, I would hold that it is coextensive with the 'navigable waters of the United States.' "[35]

B. Navigability for State Title

The final application of the navigability doctrine under federal law relevant to water law is to determine title to the beds and banks of navigable waters. States generally have title to the beds and banks of navigable waters, which they hold in trust for the public at large. This title dates either to the time an original state won independence from England, or, for later states, the date on which the state was admitted to the Union. The Supreme Court's decision to treat later states equally to the original thirteen in this regard is known as the Equal Footing Doctrine, which the Court considers a constitutional aspect of state sovereignty. (While a state-to-be is still a federal

[31] *Id.* at 172–174.

[32] *Id.* at 178.

[33] *Id.*

[34] 484 U.S. 469 (1988).

[35] *Id.* at 186.

territory, the United States holds the title to the beds and banks of navigable waters.)

In contrast, riparian landowners possess title to the bed and banks of *non-navigable* waters (see Chapter 2)—that is, all waters that fail to meet the federal state title navigability test. As Chapter 2 discussed, a riparian's title to the bed and banks of a non-navigable water is determined by state-specific tests that divide the streambeds among property owners.

Thus, the state title navigability test is an important standard for dividing private and public rights. As Chapter 7 will discuss, for example, state public trust doctrines begin with the waters deemed to be in state ownership, and therefore public, under this test. However, the state title navigability test is also important to federalism considerations surrounding water. Despite the federal government's pervasive *regulatory authority* over the navigable waters discussed above, it is very difficult for the federal government to retain ownership of the beds and banks of waters that meet the state title navigability test. This means that states often have a direct interest in the waters that the federal government regulates. However, states, like private citizens, are subject to the federal navigation servitude.

1. The Navigability Test for Title as Between the States and the Federal Government

For a state to have title to the bed and banks of a navigable water, the waterway must meet a specific version of the navigability-in-fact test *on the date of statehood*. This is known as "navigability for title." The U.S. Supreme Court recently clarified the "navigability for title" test in the context of other navigability doctrines in *PPL Montana, LLC v. Montana.*[36]

PPL Montana involved a dispute over whether three rivers were navigable to determine whether Montana had acquired title to the riverbeds when it became a state. Notably, Montana wanted to use its title to collect rent for use of the riverbed; indeed, Montana sued seeking "compensation from PPL Montana, LLC, a power company, for its use of the riverbeds for hydroelectric projects."[37] The rivers at issue were the Missouri River, the Madison River, and the Clark Fork River. Ten of PPL Montana's hydroelectric facilities were built upon segments of these riverbeds. Montana was motivated to bring suit even though the dams had existed without paying rent for decades because in the original 2003 lawsuit, the rents would have been paid into a state trust fund for Montana public schools.

---

[36] 565 U.S. 576 (2012).

[37] *Id.* at 1222.

The U.S. Supreme Court explained that its decision was governed by the Equal Footing Doctrine and that, "[u]pon statehood, the State gains title within its borders to the beds of waters then navigable" and "[t]he United States retains any title vested in it before statehood to any land beneath waters not then navigable (and not tidally influenced)."[38] According to the Court, "[f]or state title under the equal-footing doctrine, navigability is determined at the time of statehood and based on the 'natural and ordinary condition' of the water."[39] Moreover, "[t]o determine title to a riverbed under the equal-footing doctrine, this Court considers the river on a segment-by-segment basis to assess whether the segment of the river, under which the riverbed in dispute lies, is navigable or not."[40]

Under this test, it will be difficult for Montana to demonstrate title navigability for many stretches of these rivers, although the U.S. Supreme Court left those final determinations for the remand. Nevertheless, the Court concluded that one of the segments of the Missouri River, the Great Falls reach, was not navigable because overland portage was required in the days of Lewis and Clark's explorations to travel the river because of its waterfalls. Further, the Court emphasized that the determination of navigability for title is dependent upon evidence of navigability *at the time of statehood*, not on whether a river segment is presently navigable:

> Navigability must be assessed as of the time of statehood, and it concerns the river's usefulness for "trade and travel," rather than for other purposes. Mere use by initial explorers or trappers, who may have dragged their boats in or alongside the river despite its nonnavigability in order to avoid getting lost, or to provide water for their horses and themselves, is not itself enough.[41]

The Supreme Court remanded the remaining aspects of the rivers at issue for the lower court to determine whether, on a segment-by-segment basis, any portions of the rivers met the title navigability test. For perspective on the practical ramifications of this approach, litigation on remand had only reached the summary judgment stage at the federal district court level nearly a decade after the Supreme Court's decision.[42]

---

38 *Id.* at 1228.

39 *Id.*

40 *Id.* at 1229.

41 *Id.* at 1233.

42 *See* Montana v. Talen Montana, LLC, f/k/a PPL Montana, 574 F.Supp.3d 795 (D. Mont. 2021).

2. Riparian Borders Under State Law

Whether a state has title to the submerged lands under navigable waters pursuant to the title navigability test is a question of federal law, and it governs the issue of title as between the state and federal governments. Moreover, as between those two governments, the state takes title to the high-water mark.

However, once a state *has* title to the bed and banks of a waterbody, the boundary lines on the shores and/or banks between it and private citizens is a question of state law. The U.S. Supreme Court established this distinction in *Barney v. Keokuk*,[43] which held that delineating the border between state and private ownership on a waterway's bank is a matter of individual state law. Indeed, at least one court has declined to apply the *PPL Montana* test to this issue, distinguishing between the navigability-for-title test and the test for ascertaining ordinary high-water mark.[44] In general, along the seacoast, the border is the high-water mark or mean high tide line.[45] For lakes and rivers, most states use the high-water mark or high water line.[46] However, some states (mostly in the East) use the low tide line and low watermark.[47]

In the Great Lakes, Michigan has adopted the ordinary high water mark for its 3,200 miles of shoreline.[48] The Michigan Supreme Court adopted Wisconsin's definition of the "ordinary high water mark," which is the "point on the bank or shore up to which the presence and action of the water is so continuous as to leave a distinct mark either by erosion, destruction of terrestrial vegetation, or other easily recognized characteristic."[49] Rejecting Michigan's approach, Ohio uses the "natural shoreline," defined as the line at which water usually stands when free from disturbing causes, as the boundary between privately owned uplands and the state-owned lakebed.[50] When states use the high-water mark or a similar boundary for state

[43] 94 U.S. (4 Otto) 324 (1876).

[44] *See,* Continental Resources, Inc. v. North Dakota Board of University and School Lands, 505 F.Supp.3d 908, 914–15 (D. N.D. 2020).

[45] *See, e.g.*, Tallahassee Fall Manufacturing Co. v. Alabama, 68 So. 805, 806 (Ala. 1915); State v. Ashmore, 224 S.E.2d 334, 336–41 (Ga. 1976). *But see* Boston Waterfront Development Corp. v. Commonwealth, 393 N.E.2d 356, 359–60 (Mass. 1979) (noting that Massachusetts has conveyed title to the coastal properties to private landowners down to the low tide line, although public rights to use the waters extend to the mean high tide line).

[46] *See, e.g.*, State v. Black River Phosphate Co., 13 So. 640, 643 (Fla. 1893); Revell v. People, 52 N.E. 1052, 1055 (Ill. 1898).

[47] Tallahassee Fall Manufacturing Co., 68 So. at 806 (citations omitted); Phillips v. Dep't of Natural Resources & Environmental Control, 449 A.2d 250, 252 (Del. 1982); GA. CODE ANN. § 44–8–3.

[48] *See* Glass v. Goeckel, 703 N.W.2d 58 (Mich. 2005).

[49] *Id.* at 74.

[50] *See* Merrill v. Ohio Dep't of Natural Resources, 955 N.E.2d 935 (Ohio 2011).

versus private ownership, it essentially opens up portions of the beach (above the water's edge up to the high-water mark) to the public, creating opportunities for beach walking and other land-based recreation that would not otherwise be possible.[51]

3. Pre-Statehood Conveyances and Federal, Tribal, or Private Ownership of the Banks and Banks of Navigable Waters

In much of the country, the federal government controlled vast areas of the territories that eventually became states. Moreover, the federal government sometimes actively conveyed lands and established tribal reservations before a territory became a state. In these cases, could the United States effectively convey to private parties or to Tribes the bed and banks of waters that meet the state title test of navigability?

In *Utah Division of State Lands v. United States*,[52] the U.S. Supreme Court explored the federal government's authority to circumvent the Equal Footing Doctrine in this way. The issue Court decided was "whether title to the bed of Utah Lake passed to the State of Utah under the equal footing doctrine upon Utah's admission to the Union in 1896."[53] The issue arose because the U.S. Geological Survey (USGS) had selected Utah Lake as a reservoir site in 1889 pursuant to the Sundry Appropriations Act, which authorized the USGS to identify sites "necessary for the storage and utilization of water for irrigation and the prevention of floods and overflows."[54] The Act also specified that the lands selected under the Act would thereafter be "reserved from sale as the property of the United States."[55] The 1888 Sundry Appropriations Act was later repealed and replaced with the 1890 Sundry Appropriations Act. The 1890 Act, however, maintained that "reservoir sites heretofore located or selected shall remain segregated and reserved from entry or settlement as provided by [the 1888 Act]."[56] In 1896—*after* Utah Lake had been federally reserved—Utah joined the Union.

In 1976, the Bureau of Land Management (BLM) issued oil and gas leases for lands underlying Utah Lake. Utah brought suit alleging that the BLM had violated the state's ownership and property rights, asserting that it had title to the lakebed. The U.S. Supreme Court first stated that, pursuant to *Shively v. Bowlby*,

---

51 *See Glass*, 703 N.W.2d at 74.

52 482 U.S. 193 (1987).

53 *Id.* at 195.

54 *Id.* at 198.

55 *Id.* at 199.

56 *Id.* at 193.

> Congress has the power to make grants of lands below high water mark of navigable waters in any Territory of the United States . . . . Thus . . . the Federal Government could defeat a prospective State's title to land under navigable waters by a prestatehood conveyance of the land to a private party for a public purpose appropriate to the Territory.[57]

However, although the federal government clearly had constitutional *authority* under the Property Clause of the U.S. Constitution to convey these submerged lands before statehood, the *Shively* Court had also "inferred a congressional policy (although not a constitutional obligation) to grant away land under navigable waters only 'in case of some international duty or public exigency.' "[58] Thus, the Court had created a strong presumption against such pre-statehood conveyances. In *Utah*, Justice O'Connor explained that the Court has:

> consistently acknowledged congressional policy to dispose of sovereign lands only in the most unusual circumstances. In recognition of this policy, we do not lightly infer a congressional intent to defeat a State's title to land under navigable waters. . . . We have stated that "[a] court deciding a question of title to the bed of a navigable water must begin with a strong presumption against conveyance by the United States, and must not infer such a conveyance unless the intention was definitely declared or otherwise made very plain, or was rendered in clear and especial words, or unless the claim confirmed in terms embraces the land under the waters of the stream."[59]

Furthermore, the *Utah* Court noted that it has been the federal government's longstanding policy to hold "land under navigable waters for the ultimate benefit of the States, therefore, we would not infer an intent to defeat a State's equal footing entitlement from the mere act of reservation itself."[60] Therefore, the Court concluded, "the 1888 Act fails to make sufficiently plain either a congressional intent to include the bed of Utah Lake within the reservation or an intent to defeat Utah's claim to title under the equal footing doctrine," and thus Utah had title to the lakebed.[61]

As *Utah Division of State Lands* demonstrates, the legal presumptions regarding submerged land ownership run strongly against the federal government. As a result, the presumptions also

---

[57] *Id.* at 196–197.

[58] *Id.* at 197.

[59] *Id.* at 197–198.

[60] *Id.* at 202.

[61] *Id.* at 203.

run against Tribes, who are considered trustees of the federal government—but who are *not* equivalent to states for Equal Footing Doctrine purposes. Of course, one argument is that Tribes own those submerged lands via aboriginal title, but courts have generally not recognized that argument for any kind of land ownership.

Nevertheless, Tribes do occasionally win their submerged lands title cases. For example, in *Idaho v. United States*,[62] the United States, in its own capacity and as trustee for the Coeur d'Alene Tribe, sued the State of Idaho to quiet title to the beds and banks of Coeur d'Alene Lake and the St. Joe River within the boundaries of the Coeur d'Alene Indian Reservation. Affirming the lower courts, the U.S. Supreme Court found in favor of the United States and the Tribe, emphasizing that "[t]ribal members traditionally used the lake and its related waterways for food, fiber, transportation, recreation, and cultural activities. The Tribe depended on submerged lands for everything from water potatoes harvested from the lake to fish weirs and traps anchored in riverbeds and banks."[63] Moreover, in 1888, as part of the Senate's ratification of the United States' treaty with the Tribe, the Secretary of the Interior gave Congress "a report of the Commissioner of Indian Affairs, stating that 'the reservation appears to embrace all the navigable waters of Lake Coeur d'Alene, except a very small fragment cut off by the north boundary of the reservation,' and that '[t]he St. Joseph River also flows through the reservation.' "[64] Thus, even Idaho conceded that the original Executive Order reservation included submerged lands. Although negotiations continued between the Tribe and the United States after Idaho became a state, the Court majority concluded that Congress still intended to extinguish state title.[65]

---

62 533 U.S. 262 (2001).

63 *Id.* at 265.

64 *Id.* at 268.

65 *Id.* at 280–81.

Chapter 7

STATE PUBLIC TRUST DOCTRINES

As Chapter 6 discussed, a waterway's status as a navigable water is important for at least two reasons. First, waterbodies that meet various federal-law definitions of navigability are subject to federal regulatory jurisdiction under the Commerce Clause, the federal courts' admiralty jurisdiction and application of federal maritime law, and the federal navigation servitude. Second, if a waterbody meets the federal-law test for state title navigability (natural navigability in fact at the date of statehood), the state has title to the waterbody's bed and banks. Both aspects of navigability can create public rights in those waterways.

The public trust doctrine defines a state's unique legal relationship with navigable waterways and, in some states, non-navigable waters and other natural resources. The origins of this doctrine are much debated, but courts in the United States generally trace it to ancient Rome and the *Institutes of Justinian* through English common law, and then to the United States' inheritance of that common law. There is also considerable debate in the United States about whether there is a federal constitutional aspect to the public trust doctrine. The U.S. Supreme Court has invoked and enforced the public trust doctrine, but it explicitly respects state courts' authority in defining, expanding, and applying their own versions of the doctrine. Accordingly, the importance of the public trust doctrine and the public rights it protects vary considerably from state to state. Nevertheless, in almost all states, the doctrine at least protects public rights of navigation, commerce, and fishing in navigable waters.

This chapter begins by examining what the U.S. Supreme Court has said about the public trust doctrine and its relationship to federal and state law. It then examines some of the state variations in their public trust doctrines and the various public rights that their public trust doctrines now protect.

A. The Public Trust Doctrine and the U.S. Supreme Court

As the U.S. Supreme Court noted in *PPL Montana* (discussed in Chapter 6), when a state has title to the beds and banks of a navigable river or lake, it holds those submerged lands in trust for the public.[1] The Supreme Court has been addressing what it means

1 565 U.S. 576 (2012).

for states to hold submerged lands "in trust for the public," and from where public rights in waterways derive, for well over a century. Although it had mentioned a "public trust" in earlier cases, its first lengthy discussion of that doctrine came in 1892 in *Illinois Central Railroad Co. v. Illinois*.[2]

Throughout the 1850s, the State of Illinois gave the Illinois Central Railroad Company increasing authority to develop the Chicago Harbor in Lake Michigan, including development of the submerged lands. In 1869, Illinois enacted legislation that solidified the railroad's ownership and control of the harbor by granting to the company what appeared to be absolute and perpetual title to large tracks of the harbor's submerged lands. However, in 1873, Illinois repealed that legislation. Illinois sought a decree that established and confirmed its title to the bed of Lake Michigan and an "exclusive right to develop and improve the harbor of Chicago . . . against the claim of the railroad company that it has an absolute title to such submerged lands by the act of 1869."[3] Thus, at issue in *Illinois Central* was whether the Illinois Central Railroad Company could "hold the lands and control the waters by the grant, against any future exercise of power over them by the state."[4]

The U.S. Supreme Court began its analysis by first stating the well-settled rule that:

> the ownership of and dominion and sovereignty over lands covered by tide waters, within the limits of the several states, belong to the respective states within which they are found, with the consequent right to use or dispose of any portion thereof, when that can be done without substantial impairment of the interest of the public in the waters, and subject always to the paramount right of congress to control their navigation so far as may be necessary for the regulation of commerce with foreign nations and among the states.[5]

The Court explained that this doctrine also applies to the Great Lakes, although they are fresh water and not tidally influenced, because "they are inland seas" upon which extensive interstate and foreign commerce is conducted.[6]

---

2 146 U.S. 387 (1892).

3 *Id.* at 439.

4 *Id.* at 452.

5 *Id.* at 435.

6 *Id.* In general, United States federal law continues to treat the Great Lakes as legally the same as the ocean—for example, for purposes of the Coastal Zone Management Act. 16 U.S.C. § 1453(1).

The Supreme Court thus concluded that Illinois has title to Lake Michigan's bottomlands, and "that title necessarily carries with it control over the waters above them, whenever the lands are subjected to use."[7] It explained, however, that "it is a title different in character from that which the state holds in lands intended for sale. . . . It is a title held in trust for the people of the state, that they may enjoy the navigation of the waters, carry on commerce over them, and have liberty of fishing therein, freed from the obstruction or interference of private parties."[8] Furthermore, "[t]he trust devolving upon the state for the public, and which can only be discharged by the management and control of property in which the public has an interest, cannot be relinquished by a transfer of the property."[9] Therefore, the Court concluded that because Lake Michigan is protected by the public trust, the Illinois Legislature's grant to the Illinois Central Railroad of "sovereign submerged lands"—the submerged lands to which the state received title on the basis of the state title test of navigability—was void. As a result, Illinois continues to hold title to these submerged lands in trust for the benefit of the public pursuant to the public trust doctrine.

Illinois Central established several basic principles of the public trust doctrine that most states regard as the "irreducible minimum" contours of that doctrine. First, the *Illinois Central* Court articulated three core public uses of navigable waterways that the doctrine protects—navigation, commerce, and fishing. Logically, given their shared legal history, these three public uses are also at the core of the federal government's Commerce Clause authority and navigation servitude, and so *both* the states and the federal government can act to protect them.

Second, the *Illinois Central* Court established the general principle that states cannot alienate sovereign submerged lands. Later cases, both federal and state, distinguished the *jus privatum*, generally described as bare legal title, from the *jus publicum*, generally described as the larger public and sovereign interests, in sovereign submerged lands, with the result than in many states, the state legislature *can* convey the *jus privatum* to private entities, but the submerged lands so conveyed and the water above them remains subject to the public trust doctrine—i.e., the private entity takes title subject to the public rights to use the water.

Finally, the *Illinois Central* Court recognized a limited exception to the general principle that sovereign submerged lands cannot be fully conveyed into private hands: limited grants of these submerged

---

7 *Id.* at 453.

8 *Id.*

9 *Id.*

lands *can* be legal when the conveyance furthers the purposes of the public trust. States most commonly use this exception to convey submerged lands to private parties who will develop harbor facilities, piers, docks and wharves—that is, the infrastructure and facilities necessary for navigation, commerce, and fishing to occur on the relevant waterway.

B. The Source of Law for the *Illinois Central* Decision

1. States' Interpretations of *Illinois Central*

The U.S. Supreme Court in *Illinois Central* was extremely vague regarding the public trust doctrine's legal origin in the United States. Nevertheless, the Court strongly suggested that the doctrine had a federal law and perhaps even a federal constitutional source, and most state courts deciding public trust doctrine cases after *Illinois Central* assumed that the doctrine had a federal law basis.

Arizona provides one interesting example. The Arizona Legislature has repeatedly tried to eliminate the public trust doctrine in that state. However, the Arizona Supreme Court has continually held that the public trust doctrine is required under federal law, with *Illinois Central* articulating its minimum required components.[10]

2. Later U.S. Supreme Court Interpretations on the Source of the Law in *Illinois Central*

Nevertheless, in later cases, the U.S. Supreme Court itself insisted that the public trust doctrine—and the *Illinois Central* decision itself—are based on state law. For example, in *Appleby v. City of New York*,[11] the Court decided the nature and extent of property rights that the City of New York had conveyed to two purchasers, Appleby and Latou, in 1852 and 1853 conveyances of submerged lands on the east side of the North River (now known as the Hudson River). Appleby bought Latou's property and was steadily filling in the submerged lands, creating whole new blocks of very valuable waterfront property in New York City. The City, however, wanted to dredge out the filled lands and return the river to its prior condition to promote navigability, and it argued that *Illinois Central* gave it the authority to void the grants of submerged lands. The U.S. Supreme Court, however, noted that "the conclusion reached [in *Illinois Central*] was necessarily a statement of Illinois law . . . ."[12] As a result, New York state law determined the validity

---

[10] San Carlos Apache Tribe v. County of Maricopa, 972 P.2d 179, 199 (Ariz. 1999); *see also* Defenders of Wildlife v. Hull, 18 P.3d 722, 727 (Ariz. Ct. App. 2001).

[11] 271 U.S. 364 (1926).

[12] *Id.* at 395.

of the conveyances, and the Court concluded that New York law allowed for the complete alienation of the *jus publicum*, giving Appleby full fee simple title to the submerged lands.[13]

Over 70 years later, the U.S. Supreme Court again addressed the legal status of the public trust doctrine principles from *Illinois Central* in *Idaho v. Coeur d'Alene Tribe of Idaho*.[14] This case was the Coeur d'Alene Tribe's first attempt to claim the submerged lands within its reservation (see Chapter 6), and the Supreme Court dismissed the case pursuant to Idaho's Eleventh Amendment sovereign immunity, concluding that the Tribe could not sue Idaho in federal court. In reaching that conclusion however, the Court also discussed the importance of ownership of submerged lands to a state's sovereignty:

> The principle which underlies the equal footing doctrine and the strong presumption of state ownership is that navigable waters uniquely implicate sovereign interests. The principle arises from ancient doctrines. . . .
>
> . . .
>
> Not surprisingly, American law adopted as its own much of the English law respecting navigable waters, including the principle that submerged lands are held for a public purpose. A prominent example is *Illinois Central R. Co. v. Illinois* . . . , where the Court held that the Illinois Legislature did not have authority to vest the State's right and title to a portion of the navigable waters of Lake Michigan in a private party even though a proviso in the grant declared that it did authorize obstructions to the harbor, impairment of the public right of navigation, or exemption of the private party from any act regulating rates of wharfage and dockage to be charged in the harbor. An attempted transfer was beyond the authority of the legislature since it amounted to an abdication of its obligation to regulate, improve, and secure submerged lands for the benefit of every individual. While *Illinois Central* was "necessarily a statement of Illinois law," *Appleby v. City of New York*, 271 U.S. 364, 395 . . . (1926), it invoked the principle in American law recognizing the weighty public interest in submerged lands.[15]

Thus, the *Coeur d'Alene* Court both affirmed that *Illinois Central* stated principles of Illinois state law *and* suggested again that the

---

[13] *Id.* at 395–99.

[14] 521 U.S. 261 (1997).

[15] *Id.* at 284–86.

public trust doctrine has a more general foundation in the broader principles of American law.

The U.S. Supreme Court's most recent discussion of the origins of the public trust doctrine appears in its 2012 decision in *PPL Montana, LLC v. Montana.*[16] There, the Court stated that:

> [t]he public trust doctrine is of ancient origin. Its roots trace to Roman civil law and its principles can be found in the English common law on public navigation and fishing rights over tidal lands and in the state laws of this country . . . the public trust doctrine remains a matter of state law, subject as well to the federal power to regulate vessels and navigation under the Commerce Clause and admiralty power. . . . Under accepted principles of federalism, *the States retain residual power to determine the scope of the public trust over waters within their borders, while federal law determines riverbed title under the equal-footing doctrine.*[17]

Again, therefore, the Court has left the *contours* of the public trust doctrine to state law, but it still suggested both that the *fact* of state title to those lands is grounded in the Equal Footing Doctrine and that the nature of that title includes a public trust doctrine subject to state power under constitutional principles of federalism.

3. Other Legal Sources of State Public Trust Doctrines

Although the Equal Footing Doctrine is clearly important, states' rights and responsibilities with respect to water resources can arise from other sources of law. For example, as the *Illinois Central* Court mentioned in passing, for many of the Great Lakes states—specifically, Ohio, Indiana, Illinois, Michigan, and Wisconsin—the Northwest Ordinance of 1787 remains relevant. The Ordinance was enacted by the Congress of the Confederation of the United States and created the Northwest Territory, the first territory in the United States. After the states ratified the U.S. Constitution in 1789, the newly created U.S. Congress reaffirmed the Ordinance with slight modifications. The Ordinance established several precedents for the expanding United States, including: the cession of undeveloped territories from states to the federal government (meaning that the federal government, not the original thirteen states, managed these territories); the administration of these lands by Congress until statehood; and the principle that new territories would eventually be admitted into the United States as entirely new states, rather than as expansions of existing states.

---

16 565 U.S. 576 (2012).

17 *Id.* at 1234.

With respect to water law, Article 4 of the Northwest Ordinance states that "[t]he navigable waters leading into the Mississippi and St. Lawrence, and the carrying places between the same, shall be common highways and forever free, as well to the inhabitants of the said territory as to the citizens of the United States, and those of any other States that may be admitted into the confederacy, without any tax, impost, or duty therefor." Some states continue to view this provision as an additional legal origin of the public trust doctrine and of state responsibilities to preserve public rights in navigable waterways. For example, the Wisconsin Supreme Court noted that, "[w]hile originally derived from the Northwest Ordinance, the public trust doctrine emanates from the following provision of the Wisconsin Constitution: '[T]he river Mississippi and the navigable waters leading into the Mississippi and St. Lawrence, and the carrying places between the same, shall be common highways and forever free.' "[18] Similarly, the Michigan Supreme Court relied in part on the Northwest Ordinance to support public access to the Great Lakes.[19]

C. State Versions of the Public Trust Doctrine

Regardless of the legal origins of the public trust doctrine, the U.S. Supreme Court has made it clear that states are free to change its basic contours. Because states tend to view the *Illinois Central* principles as the *minimum* requirements of the public trust doctrine, states' changes to their public trust doctrines have tended to expand the doctrine's applicability. In general, states have: (1) increased the public uses that the doctrine protects; (2) expanded the waters to which the public trust doctrine applies by changing the relevant state definition of "navigable water"; or (3) both.[20]

1. Expansions of the Public Trust Doctrine to New Waterways

The increasing importance of water for recreational use has been a driving force in the evolution and expansion of states' public trust doctrines. Indeed, the enlargement of these doctrines to encompass recreation is by far the most common expansion beyond *Illinois Central*. Depending on how a state chooses to develop its public trust doctrine, however, private landowners may view the result as an intrusion on private property rights. The potential clash between a

[18] Lake Beulah Management District v. Wisconsin Dep't of Natural Resources, 799 N.W.2d 73, 83 (Wis. 2011) (quoting WIS. CONST. art. IX, § 1.).

[19] Glass v. Goeckel, 703 N.W.2d 58, 74 (Mich. 2005).

[20] For comprehensive reviews of all 50 states' public trust doctrines, *see* Robin Kundis Craig, *A Comparative Guide to the Eastern Public Trust Doctrines: Classifications of States, Property Rights, and State Summaries*, 16 PENN. ST. ENVTL. L. REV. 1 (Fall 2007); Robin Kundis Craig, *A Comparative Guide to the Western States' Public Trust Doctrines: Public Values, Private Rights, and an Evolution Toward an Ecological Public Trust*, 37 ECOLOGY L.Q. 53 (2010).

state's evolving articulation of its public trust doctrine and existing property rights repeatedly raises the issue of how to "properly" balance public and private rights in water.

State v. McIlroy,[21] a 1980 decision by the Arkansas Supreme Court, illustrates this tension. The case started as a dispute to determine who held title to the streambeds pursuant to Arkansas' definition of "navigable water." W. L. McIlroy and his late brother's estate, owners of 230 acres of land, sought a declaration that their rights as riparian landowners on the Mulberry River were, because the stream was not a navigable river, superior to the rights of the public, allowing them to prohibit public canoeing and kayaking on the river as a trespass. McIlroy joined as defendants the Ozark Society, a conservationist group, and two companies that rented canoes for use on the Mulberry and other Ozark Mountain streams. The State of Arkansas intervened and claimed that the Mulberry River was a navigable stream and the stream bed was the state's property, not the McIlroys'.

The Arkansas Supreme Court stated first that navigability is defined "in terms of a river's potential for commercial usefulness; that is, whether the water could be used to remove the products of the surrounding land to another place."[22] The *McIlroy* Court, however, further explained that "[i]t is the policy of this state to encourage the use of its water courses for any useful or beneficial purpose. There may be other public uses than the carrying on of commerce of pecuniary value."[23] For example, the water may be necessary for agriculture, domestic uses, public supply, and/or recreation. The court concluded that "the segment of the Mulberry River that is involved in this lawsuit can be used for a substantial portion of the year for recreational purposes. Consequently, we hold that it is navigable at that place with all the incidental rights of that determination."[24]

Thus, the Arkansas Supreme Court's decision in *McIlroy* made three changes relevant to the state public trust doctrine. First, it articulated a new state-law definition of "navigable water" based on recreational use of waterways, eschewing the limited commerce-based navigable-in-fact test as a remnant of the steamboat era.[25] Second, as a result, its public trust doctrine now protects recreational use. Finally, the Arkansas Supreme Court's articulation of the navigability test appeared to change riparian property rights,

---

[21] 595 S.W.2d 659 (Ark. 1980).

[22] *Id.* at 663.

[23] *Id.* at 664.

[24] *Id.* at 665.

[25] *See also* Coleman v. Schaeffer, 126 N.E.2d 444, 445–47 (Ohio 1955) (also establishing a recreational use test of navigability).

prompting a vigorous dissent and effectively re-balancing public and private rights in water.

States use a variety of navigability tests for their state public trust doctrines, including log floatation tests (i.e., any stream that can float a log to market is "navigable")[26] and, like Arkansas, recreational boating tests. Alaska has perhaps the most idiosyncratic definition of "navigable water," reflecting the particular public values in its waters. By statute, Alaska defines a "navigable water" to be:

> any water of the state forming a river, stream, lake, pond, slough, creek, bay, sound, estuary, inlet, strait, passage, canal, sea or ocean, or any other body of water or waterway within the territorial limits of the state or subject to its jurisdiction, that is navigable in fact for any useful public purpose, including but not limited to *water suitable for commercial navigation, floating of logs, landing and takeoff of aircraft, and public boating, trapping, hunting waterfowl and aquatic animals, fishing, or other public recreational purposes* . . . .[27]

Alaska is thus the only state that explicitly identifies use of waters by seaplanes as an important public use to be protected by law.

Sometimes these state-law navigability tests change the ownership of the submerged lands, but they more often serve to open waters that are not navigable for state title to public use.[28] As a result, many states have waterways for which the beds and banks are privately owned, but where members of the public have a right to use the river, stream, or lake.[29] In these states, riparian landowners often accuse members of the public of trespass for touching the bottom or for wandering on shore, leading to some fairly technical divisions of rights. For example, in Florida, people floating such a waterway in an inner tube commit a trespass if they walk along the bottom of a river.

Many western states have reached the same result through a different route. Almost all western states declare in their state constitutions or state water codes that the state owns all the water in the state.[30] Courts in these states have often relied on this state

---

[26] *E.g.*, Felger v. Robinson, 3 Or. 455, 458 (1869).

[27] ALAS. STAT. ANN. § 38.05.965(13) (emphasis added).

[28] *E.g.*, Curry v. Hill, 460 P.2d 933, 935 (Okla. 1969).

[29] *E.g.*, The Point, Ltd. Liab. Corp., et al. v. Lake Mgmt. Ass'n, Inc., 50 S.W.3d 471, 476 (Tenn. Ct. App. 2000).

[30] ALAS. CONST., art. VIII, § 13; ALAS. STAT. § 46.15.030; ARIZ. REV. STAT. § 45–141(A); CAL. WATER CODE § 1201; COLO. CONST., art. XVI, § 5; HAW. CONST., art. XI, §§ 1, 7; KAN. STAT. ANN. § 82a–702; MONT. CONST., art. IX, § 3(3); NEB. CONST., art. XV, § 5; NEV. REV. STAT. § 533.025; N.M. CONST., art. XVI, § 2; N.M. STAT. § 72–1–1;

ownership of water to recognize public rights to use all waters within the state, even if private riparian landowners own the submerged lands. The same kinds of trespass issues can arise.

2. Expanding the Public Trust Doctrine to New Uses

Together with Arkansas, about half the states have expanded their public trust doctrines to protect public recreation on the navigable rivers.[31] This is the most common public use expansion in state public trust doctrines.

Individual states can also use their public trust doctrines to reflect the particular public values of waterways in that state. For example, in Alaska, the public has rights in "public waters," which by statute include not only navigable waters, but also "all other water, whether inland or coastal, fresh or salt, that is reasonably suitable for public use and utility, habitat for fish and wildlife in which there is a public interest, or migration and spawning of fish in which there is a public interest . . . ."[32] These definitions and public rights protections reflect Alaska's unique environmental and cultural circumstances. Alaska is a prime fishing state. Accordingly, its statutory declarations of what constitute public waters give special

N.D. CONST., art. XI, § 3; N.D. CENT. CODE § 61–01–01; OR. REV. STAT. §§ 537.010, 537.525; S.D. CODIFIED LAWS § 46–1–3; TEX. WATER CODE ANN. § 11.021(a); UTAH CODE ANN. § 73–1–1; WASH. REV. CODE § 90.03.010; WYO. STAT. ANN. § 41–3–115(a).

[31] The following states have declared public recreation to be a public use of waters that its public trust doctrine protects: Alaska, ALAS. STAT. ANN. § 38.05.965(13); California, People v. Mack, 19 Cal. App. 3d 1040, 97 Cal. Rptr. 448 (1971); Hawaii, In re Water Use Permit Applications, 9 P.3d 409, 448 (Haw. 2000); Indiana, IND. CODE 14–26–2–5(c); Iowa, Larman v. State, 553 N.W.2d 158, 161 (Iowa 1996); Kentucky, Pierson v. Coffey, 706 S.W.2d 409, 412 (Ky. Ct. App. 1985); Louisiana, LA. REV. STAT. ANN. § 14:1701; Massachusetts, Attorney General v. Woods, 108 Mass. 436, 440 (1870); Michigan, Kelley, ex. rel. MacMullan v. Hallden, 51 Mich. App. 176, 214 N.W.2d 856, 864 (1974); Minnesota, Lamprey v. State, 52 Minn. 181, 53 N.W. 1139 (1893); Mississippi, Cinque Bambini Partnership v. State, 491 So.2d 508, 512 (Miss. 1986); Montana, MONT. CODE ANN. §§ 23–2–301 to 23–2–322, 85–1–111, 85–1–112, 85–16–102, 87–2–305; New Hampshire, Opinion of the Justices, 649 A.2d 604, 609 (N.H. 1994); New Jersey, Borough of Neptune City v. Borough of Avon-by-the-Sea, 294 A.2d 47, 54 (N.J. 1972); New Mexico, New Mexico ex rel. State Game Comm'n v. Red River Valley Co., 182 P.2d 421, 429–32 (N.M. 1947); North Carolina, Fabrikant v. Currituck County, 621 S.E.2d 19, 27–28 (N.C. Ct. App. 2005); North Dakota, J.P. Furlong Enters., Inc. v. Sun Exploration & Prod. Co., 423 N.W.2d 130, 140 (N.D. 1988); Ohio, State ex rel. Brown v. Newport Concrete Co., 44 Ohio App.2d 121, 127, 336 N.E.2d 453, 457, 73 Ohio Ops.2d 124 (1975); Oklahoma, Curry v. Hill, 460 P.2d 933, 935–36 (Okla. 1969); Oregon, Luscher v. Reynolds, 153 Or. 625, 56 P.2d 1158 (1936); South Carolina, Sierra Club v. Kiawah Resort Associates, 456 S.E.2d 397, 402 (S.C. 1995); South Dakota, Hillebrand v. Knapp, 274 N.W. 821, 822 (S.D. 1937); Texas, Diversion Lake Club v. Heath, 86 S.W.2d 441, 444 (Texas 1935); Utah, J.J.N.P. Co. v. Utah, 655 P.2d 1133, 1137 (Utah 1982); Vermont, State v. Central Vermont Railway, Inc., 571 A.2d 1128, 1131 (Vt. 1990); Washington, Wilbour v. Gallagher, 462 P.2d 232, 239 &; n.7 (Wash. 1969); Wisconsin, Muench v. Public Service Commission, 53 N.W.2d 514, 519 (Wis. 1952); and Wyoming, Day v. Armstrong, 362 P.2d 137, 145–47 (Wyo. 1961).

[32] ALAS. STAT. ANN. § 38.05.965(18).

consideration to the use of waters not just for fishing, but also for spawning and migration, reflecting most obviously the peculiarities of salmon life cycles that, in Alaska, are important to commercial fishermen, recreational fishers and the recreation industry, and Native Alaskans. The public trust doctrines of Oregon[33] and Washington[34] similarly reflect the importance of salmon and shellfish, respectively, to those states' citizens.

3. Expanding Public Trust Doctrine Protections to the Environment: Ecological Public Trust Uses and Water Rights

Several states are evolving their public trust doctrines in ways that allow those doctrines to protect ecological values as well as public uses—sometimes limiting private water rights in the process. Most famously, the California Supreme Court in *National Audubon Society v. Superior Court of Alpine County*[35] ("the Mono Lake case") was faced with a dispute between the Department of Water and Power of the City of Los Angeles (DWP) and an environmental advocacy organization challenging DWP's appropriation rights to water from the tributaries to Mono Lake. Specifically, DWP possessed a permit to appropriate virtually all of the water from Mono Lake's tributaries. Consequently, Mono Lake's water level dropped dramatically, which caused significant habitat destruction and impeded recreation. The plaintiff, the National Audubon Society, sought to enjoin DWP from any further diversions from Mono Lake, "on the theory that the shores, bed and waters of Mono Lake are protected by a public trust."[36]

The California Supreme Court first began its analysis by summarizing the origins of the public trust doctrine in California. It noted that the public trust doctrine has its origin in Roman law,

---

[33] For example, Oregon's public trust responsibilities have been applied to fishing regulation. As a result, statutes purporting to convey exclusive rights to fish in navigable waters violated the Privileges and Immunities Clause in the Oregon Constitution. Hume v. Rogue River Packing Co., 92 P. 1065, 1072–73 (Or. 1907); *see also* Johnson v. Hoy, 47 P.2d 252, 252 (Or. 1935) (holding that the Legislature cannot grant an exclusive right to fish for salmon). Nevertheless, because the state has jurisdiction over navigable waters, it can regulate fishing. Oregon v. Nielsen, 95 P. 720, 722 (Or. 1908); Antony v. Veatch, 220 P.2d 493, 498–99 (Or. 1950). Specifically, fishing methods can be enjoined if they interfere with the public's common right of fishing. Radich v. Frederckson, 10 P.2d 352, 355 (Or. 1932); Johnson, 47 P.2d at 252.

[34] "[I]n Washington, the public trust doctrine does not encompass the right to gather clams on private property" because shellfish rights follow title to the submerged lands. Washington v. Longshore, 982 P.2d 1191, 1195–96 (Wash. App. 1999), *aff'd*, 5 P.3d 1256, 1259–63 (Wash. 2000) (*en banc*); *see also* Wash. State Geoduck Harvest Ass'n v. Wash. State Dept. of Natural Res., 101 P.3d 891, 895 (Wash. App. 2004) (noting that shellfish are not typical wildlife in Washington because they are considered part of the land). However, state regulation of geoducks does not violate the public trust doctrine. *Id.*

[35] 658 P.2d 709 (Cal. 1983).

[36] *Id.* at 712.

which the English common law evolved to allow the sovereign to own "all of its navigable waterways and the lands lying beneath them 'as trustee of a public trust for the benefit of the people.' "[37] Moreover, "California acquired title as trustee to such lands and waterways upon its admission to the union; from the earliest days its judicial decisions have recognized and enforced the trust obligation."[38] The court explained that the public trust doctrine's purpose traditionally was to protect navigation, commerce, and fishing. However, it expanded the public trust doctrine's objective to encompass preservation of recreation and environmental protection as well. Effectively, just as early American courts expanded the scope of the navigability doctrine to account for life on a new continent with very different geographic, economic and social realities than in England (see Chapter 6), the California Supreme Court found that the doctrine should also evolve to address changing knowledge and society's understanding and appreciation of the public values of those waters.

The *National Audubon Society* Court then discussed the scope of the public trust in California. It stated that "[e]arly English decisions generally assumed the public trust was limited to tidal waters and the lands exposed and covered by the daily tides; many American decisions, including the leading California cases, also concern tidelands. It is, however, well settled in the United States generally and in California that the public trust is not limited by the reach of the tides, but encompasses all navigable lakes and streams."[39] Therefore, it concluded "that the public trust doctrine, as recognized and developed in California decisions, protects navigable waters from harm caused by diversion of nonnavigable tributaries."[40] In addition, the court explained that the state's duty as trustee under the doctrine "is more than an affirmation of state power to use public property for public purposes. It is an affirmation of the duty of the state to protect the people's common heritage of streams, lakes, marshlands and tidelands, surrendering that right of protection only in rare cases when the abandonment of that right is consistent with the purposes of the trust."[41]

DWP's rights to use the water as a prior appropriator, however, conflicted with the state's duty as trustee pursuant to the public trust doctrine. The court established several guidelines for resolving conflicts between private water rights and public trust protections:

---

[37] *Id.* at 718.

[38] *Id.*

[39] *Id.* at 719.

[40] *Id.* at 721.

[41] *Id.* at 724.

> (a) The state as sovereign retains continuing supervisory control over its navigable waters and the lands beneath those waters. This principle, fundamental to the concept of the public trust, applies to rights in flowing waters as well as to rights in tidelands and lakeshores; it prevents any party from acquiring a vested right to appropriate water in a manner harmful to the interests protected by the public trust.
>
> (b) [T]he Legislature . . . has the power to grant usufructuary licenses that will permit an appropriator to take water from flowing streams and use that water in a distant part of the state, even though this taking does not promote, and may unavoidably harm, the trust uses at the source stream. The population and economy of this state depend upon the appropriation of vast quantities of water for uses unrelated to in-stream trust values.
>
> (c) The state has an affirmative duty to take the public trust into account in the planning and allocation of water resources, and to protect public trust uses whenever feasible. . . . As a matter of practical necessity the state may have to approve appropriations despite foreseeable harm to public trust uses. In so doing, however, the state must bear in mind its duty as trustee to consider the effect of the taking on the public trust, and to preserve, so far as consistent with the public interest, the uses protected by the trust. Once the state has approved an appropriation, the public trust imposes a duty of continuing supervision over the taking and use of the appropriated water.[42]

In accordance with these findings, the California Supreme Court determined that no responsible public official had evaluated the impact of DPW's diversions from Mono Lake or its potential impact on the public trust. As a result, DPW's diversions reflected an "apparent disregard for the resulting damage to the scenery, ecology, and human uses of Mono Lake."[43] Therefore, the court concluded that:

> [i]t is clear that some responsible body ought to reconsider the allocation of the waters of the Mono Basin. No vested rights bar such reconsideration. We recognize the substantial concerns voiced by Los Angeles—the city's need for water, its reliance upon the 1940 board decision, the cost both in terms of money and environmental impact of obtaining water elsewhere. Such concerns must enter into

---

[42] *Id.* at 727–728.

[43] *Id.* at 729.

any allocation decision. We hold only that they do not preclude a reconsideration and reallocation which also takes into account the impact of water diversion on the Mono Lake environment.[44]

California has thus determined not only that its public trust doctrine protects ecological values but also that state water rights are subject to the public trust doctrine. Some other states subsequently followed this path. Indeed, Hawaii's ecological public trust doctrine is even broader, affecting not only water rights but also environmental permits and extending to both surface water and groundwater.[45] In total, about thirteen states have some version of an ecological component to their public trust doctrines.

4. Statutes, State Natural Resources Management, and State Public Trust Doctrines

Many states have codified various aspects of their public trust doctrines through statute.[46] Other states define public rights in waters at least in part by statute.[47] Finally, as with Oregon and Washington's regulation of fishing, or Hawaii's regulation of activities around waterways, state public trust doctrines can reinforce and strengthen state regulatory authority with respect to water-related issues.

On the other hand, statutes or state constitutions may also limit state public trust doctrines. For example, in the 1980s and 1990s, the Idaho courts were judicially expanding the state public trust doctrine.[48] In 1996, however, Idaho's legislature invalidated this line

---

[44] *Id.*

[45] In re Water Use Permit Applications, 9 P.3d 409, 441–43 (Haw. 2000).

[46] For example, Georgia defines a "navigable stream" by statute to be "a stream which is capable of transporting boats loaded with freight in the regular course of trade either for the whole or part of the year. The mere rafting of timber or the transportation of wood in small boats shall not make a stream navigable." GA. CODE ANN. § 44–8–5(a). Texas defines a "navigable stream" to be "a stream which retains an average width of 30 feet from the mouth up." TEX. NAT. RES. CODE ANN. § 21.001.

[47] For example, Utah reserves to the public "the right of access to all lands owned by the state, including those lands lying below the official government meander line of navigable waters, for the purpose of hunting, trapping, or fishing." UTAH CODE ANN. § 23–21–4. More broadly, the Connecticut Environmental Policy Act recognizes "the public trust in the air, water and other natural resources of the state" and creates a broad citizen suit provision that allows any member of the public to sue to protect these resources "from unreasonable pollution, impairment, or destruction." CONN. GEN. ANN. §§ 22a–16 to 22a–17.

[48] Idaho Conservation League, Inc. v. Idaho, 911 P.2d 748, 750 (Idaho 1995); *see also* Kootenai Environmental Alliance, Inc. v. Panhandle Yacht Club, Inc., 671 P.2d 1085, 1094 (Idaho 1983) (holding that "the public trust doctrine takes precedence even over vested water rights.").

of cases, instead defining (and confining) the state's public trust doctrine by statute.[49]

In states with limited public trust doctrines, statutes may provide regulatory authority to protect waters and the public interests in them even when the public trust doctrine does not. In 2013, for example, the Wisconsin Supreme Court limited the scope of the state's public trust doctrine in *Rock-Koshkonong Lake District v. State Department of Natural Resources*.[50] The Rock-Koshkonong Lake District petitioned Wisconsin's Department of Natural Resources (DNR) for permission to increase Lake Koshkonong's water level.[51] The District alleged that the shallow water impeded recreational uses, such as boating, and harmed plants and wildlife.[52] The DNR rejected the petition.[53] An administrative law judge, the Rock County Circuit Court, and the Court of Appeals of Wisconsin all upheld the DNR's decision.[54] On appeal, the Wisconsin Supreme Court was faced with four issues: (1) what is the appropriate level of deference that should be accorded to the DNR's decision; (2) whether the DNR exceeded its authority when it rejected the District's petition under the public trust doctrine; (3) whether the DNR exceeded its authority when it considered statutory wetland water quality standards; and (4) whether the DNR must consider impacts of water levels on residential property values, commercial profits, and public revenue in its decision making.[55]

The Wisconsin Supreme Court first held that the DNR's conclusions are subject to *de novo* review. The court explained that the DNR's decision in this instance should not be afforded deference because the water level order was "heavily influenced by the DNR's interpretation of the scope of its own powers, its interpretation of the Wisconsin Constitution, its disputed interpretation of the statute it utilized, and its reliance upon [other] statutes and rules."[56]

Next, the court held that the DNR "inappropriately relied on the public trust doctrine for its authority to protect non-navigable land and non-navigable water above the ordinary high water mark."[57] The court explained that the DNR's protection of private wetlands above the ordinary high water mark exceeded its constitutional authority.

---

[49] IDAHO CODE § 58–1203.

[50] Rock-Koshkonong Lake District v. State Department of Natural Resources, 833 N.W.2d 800 (Wis. 2013).

[51] *Id.* at 803–804.

[52] *Id.* at 808.

[53] *Id.* at 804.

[54] *Id.*

[55] *Id.*

[56] *Id.*

[57] *Id.*

Rather, the DNR may regulate non-navigable wetlands pursuant to its police power to protect property. "There is no constitutional foundation for *public trust* jurisdiction over land, including non-navigable wetlands, that is not below the [ordinary high water mark (OHWM)] of a navigable lake or stream. Applying the state's police power to land above or beyond the OHWM of navigable waters—to protect the public interest *in navigable waters*—is different from asserting public trust jurisdiction over non-navigable land and water."[58]

The court also held that the DNR may consider the statutory water quality standards when making a water level determination that impacts wetlands, but it is not required to do so. Finally, the court held that the DNR "erroneously excluded most testimony on the economic impact of lower water levels in Lake Koshkonong on the residents, businesses, and tax bases adjacent to and near Lake Koshkonong," and it required the DNR to consider those factors in its decision making.[59]

Thus, in Wisconsin, the state public trust doctrine is largely limited to activities in navigable waters. The state, acting through the DNR, preserves other values and other waterways through environmental statutes and other manifestations of the state's police powers.

5. Constitutionalizing State Public Trust Doctrines

Some states have enshrined their public trust doctrines—or at least the existence of a public trust doctrine—in their state constitutions. For example, Hawaii's constitution states:

> For the benefit of present and future generations, the State and its political subdivisions shall conserve and protect Hawaii's natural beauty and all natural resources, including land, water, air, minerals and energy sources, and shall promote the development and utilization of these resources in a manner consistent with their conservation and in furtherance of the self-sufficiency of the State. All public natural resources are held in trust by the State for the benefit of the people.[60]

Similarly, Florida's constitution was amended in 1970 to provide:

> The title to lands under navigable waters, within the boundaries of the state, which have not been alienated, including beaches below mean high water lines, is held by

---

[58] *Id.* at 820–821.

[59] *Id.* at 804.

[60] HAW. CONST., art. XI, § 1.

> the state, by virtue of its sovereignty, in trust for all the people. Sale of such lands may be authorized by law, but only when in the public interest. Private use of portions of such lands may be authorized by law, but only when not contrary to the public interest.[61]

Illinois also amended its constitution in 1970 and broadly declared that "[t]he public policy of the State and duty of each person is to provide and maintain a healthful environment for the benefit of this and future generations" and that "[e]ach person has the right to a healthful environment."[62]

In contrast, Colorado has effectively had no public trust doctrine. In 1912, the Colorado Supreme Court declared almost all streams in Colorado to be non-navigable: "the natural streams of this state are, in fact, nonnavigable within its territorial limits, and practically all of them have their sources within its own boundaries, and . . . no stream of any importance whose source is without those boundaries, flows into or through this state."[63] The court then explicitly refused to follow the "modern trend" and allow public rights in non-navigable rivers based on state ownership of the water itself, concluding that the Colorado Constitution does not preserve public recreation rights in such waters.[64] Instead, "[w]ithout permission, the public cannot use such waters for recreation."[65]

However, as is true in any field of law, the state legislature can "overturn" state supreme court decisions not based on constitutional law, and in most states, the people can amend their state constitution. In 2012, several citizens of Colorado proposed to do just that with respect to the state's public trust doctrine, generating the case *In the Matter of the Title, Ballot Title, and Submission Clause for 2011–2012 #3*.[66] In this case, Richard G. Hamilton and Phillip Doe proposed Initiative 3 to enact the "Colorado public trust doctrine" by adding new subsections to the state constitution. Specifically, the respondents proposed subsections that would:

---

61 FLA. CONST., art. 10, § 11.

62 ILL. CONST., art. XI, §§ 1, 2.

63 Stockman v. Leddy, 129 P. 220, 222 (Colo. 1912), *overruled on other grounds,* Denver Ass'n for Retarded Children, Inc. v. School Dist. No. 1, 535 P.2d 200 (Colo. 1975); *see also* United States v. District Court, 458 P.2d 760, 762 (Colo. 1969) (holding that even though the Eagle River is a tributary of the Colorado River, it is non-navigable).

64 People v. Emmert, 597 P.2d 1025, 1027–28 (Colo. 1979).

65 *Id.* at 1029; *see also* Hartman v. Tresisee, 84 P. 685, 686–87 (Colo. 1905) (holding that public ownership of the water itself, as stated in the Colorado Constitution, does not create a public fishery in non-navigable streams; instead, the private landowner owns the right of fishery, and only appropriative rights can trump this common-law rule).

66 274 P.3d 562 (Colo. 2012) (*en banc*).

(a) expressly adopt a version of the public trust doctrine to "protect the public's interests in the water of natural streams and to instruct the State of Colorado to defend the public's water ownership rights of use and public enjoyment;"

(b) subordinate contract, property, and appropriative water rights to the "public estate in water;"

(c) allow public access "along, and on, the wetted natural perimeter" of any "natural stream in Colorado," and would extend this public access right to the "naturally wetted high water mark of the stream;"

(d) provide enforcement mechanisms for the new public trust doctrine; and

(e) authorize the legislature to enact laws supplemental and complementary to the new constitutional provisions.[67]

The Colorado Supreme Court, sitting *en banc*, explained that Colorado law requires:

> "that every constitutional amendment or law proposed by initiative . . . be limited to a single subject, which shall be clearly expressed in its title." A proposed initiative violates this rule if its text "relate[s] to more than one subject, and [has] at least two distinct and separate purposes not dependent upon or connected with each other." As such, the subject matter of an initiative must be "necessarily and properly connected" rather than "disconnected or incongruous."[68]

It held that the proposed ballot initiative contained a single subject because all of Initiative 3 and its titles "necessarily and properly relate to 'the public's rights in the waters of natural streams' " in compliance with Colorado law.

Justice Hobbs dissented, arguing that the Initiative and its titles contain "three separate and discrete subjects that are not dependent upon or necessarily connected with each other."[69] According to Justice Hobbs, the Initiative would:

(1) subordinate all existing water rights in Colorado created over the past 150 years to a newly created dominant water estate, the purpose of which is "to

[67] *Id.* at 564.

[68] *Id.* at 565.

[69] *Id.* at 571.

protect the natural environment and to protect the public's enjoyment and use of water;"

(2) vest in the public possessory rights to the beds and banks of the stream now owned by local public entities and private landowners in Colorado; and

(3) create a public access easement for recreation across the private property of Colorado landowners, usurping the ability of landowners to prevent trespass across their property.[70]

Justice Hobbs strongly opposed the ballot initiative and claimed, "[m]asquerading as a measure to protect the public, Initiative 2011–12 #3 contains surreptitious measures that would strip members of the public, cities, farms, and families throughout this state of their most valuable economic interests."[71]

Thus, like the dissenters in the Arkansas Supreme Court's *McIlroy* decision, Justice Hobbs in Colorado was acutely concerned about what the creation of a public trust doctrine would do to "established" private property rights in Colorado. The ballot measure at issue did not succeed in Colorado, nor have later attempts. As a result, as this text goes to press, Colorado remains without a state public trust doctrine. However, the issue is likely to recur in Colorado, and evolving public trust doctrines in other states indicate the variety of judgments possible regarding the "proper" balance between private and public rights in the nation's waterways.

---

70 *Id.* at 571–572.

71 *Id.* at 572.

Chapter 8

FEDERAL WATER INTERESTS

A. Introduction

Chapters 1 through 5 focused almost exclusively on state water law, and state law is in fact the source of most water law regarding private rights. However, as Chapters 6 (navigability) and 7 (public trust doctrine) detail, there are federal aspects to water law, especially regarding public rights. This chapter further explores the federal government's water rights and roles in water management.

This chapter covers a somewhat eclectic collection of specific topics. It begins with federal reserved water rights—that is, the collection of water rights created under federal law for federal lands, including tribal lands. As we mentioned in Chapter 5, however, state courts can now adjudicate these federal rights, and this section will also discuss the federal statute—the McCarran Amendment—that can require Tribes and the United States to defend their water rights in state court.

This chapter will then discuss federal water projects, focusing on three federal agencies that build and operate many of the federal dams and reservoirs across the United States: the U.S. Bureau of Reclamation, which operates in the West; the Tennessee Valley Authority, which operates in the Southeast; and the U.S. Army Corps of Engineers, which is responsible for a variety of kinds of projects across the country.

The third section of this chapter examines how federal law can affect water rights and water projects. It begins with a brief overview of the National Environmental Policy Act (NEPA),[1] which requires federal agencies and the entities that they permit and finance to assess the environmental impacts of major federal actions. It then explores the role of the U.S. Constitution's dormant Commerce Clause and its potential impacts on state water law.

Finally, the federal government is the level of government primarily responsible for international relations. As a result, the federal government takes the lead in any international negotiations and treaties regarding the sharing and use of waterways that cross international boundaries. The United States has entered into water treaties with both of its neighbors—Canada and Mexico—and this

1 42 U.S.C. §§ 4321–4370h.

chapter's last section will provide a brief overview of those treaties and recent developments in their implementation.

B. Federal Reserved Water Rights

1. *Winters* Water Rights for Tribes

As Chapter 6 explained, *states* generally hold title to all submerged lands beneath navigable waters. It is very difficult—although not impossible—for the federal government to reserve the ownership of these submerged lands for itself or for the benefit of Tribes. However, the federal government has a much easier time reserving rights to the *water itself* for the benefit of federal lands, including tribal reservations. Such federal water rights are called ***federal reserved water rights***.

The U.S. Supreme Court first articulated the doctrine of federal reserved water rights in 1908 in *Winters v. United States*.[2] The United States brought the case to stop settlers in Montana from taking water from the Milk River or its tributaries, arguing that the Gros Ventre and Assiniboing Tribes who were settled within the Fort Belknap Indian Reservation had first claim to that water. Congress had originally set aside the reservation on April 15, 1874, which was then settled pursuant to a May 1, 1888 treaty with the Tribes. The Milk River, a nonnavigable river, forms the reservation's northern boundary. Montana became a state on February 22, 1889, and in the same year United States military officers living on the reservation diverted 1000 miner's inches of water from the river for their domestic uses. (In Montana, a miner's inch is equal to 0.40 cubic feet per second (cfs), so the military was taking 400 cfs.) The Tribes engaged in ranching, but farming required irrigation, and eventually the Tribes diverted significant amounts of water for irrigation—namely, 10,000 miner's inches (4000 cfs) of water to irrigate about 30,000 acres.

However, at the time, settlers from the East were also migrating into Montana, and the defendants in the case included the Matheson Ditch Company, Cook's Irrigation Company, and Empire Cattle Company. Before July 5, 1898, they diverted "more than 5,000 miners' [*sic*] inches of the waters of the river and its tributaries, of 120 cubic feet per second, irrigating their lands and producing hay, grain, and other crops thereon."[3] Competition for the water came to a head in 1900, when the defendants "entered upon the river and its tributaries above the points of the diversion of the waters of the river by the United States and the Indians, built large and substantial dams and reservoirs, and, by means of canals and ditches and water

---

[2] 207 U.S. 564 (1908).

[3] *Id.* at 569.

ways, have diverted the waters of the river from its channel," expending thousands of dollars on these improvements.[4] The defendants claimed that their alleged water rights were worth $100,000 and that their lands would be worthless without the water.[5]

If principles of either pure common-law riparianism or common-law prior appropriation applied, the white settlers would have probably have won. Instead, the U.S. Supreme Court found for the Tribes and the United States, concluding that the United States *must* have reserved water for the Tribes to use:

> The case, as we view it, turns on the agreement of May, 1888, resulting in the creation of Fort Belknap Reservation. In the construction of this agreement there are certain elements to be considered that are prominent and significant. The reservation was a part of a very much larger tract which the Indians had the right to occupy and use, and which was adequate for the habits and wants of a nomadic and uncivilized people. It was the policy of the government, it was the desire of the Indians, to change those habits and to become a pastoral and civilized people. If they should become such, the original tract was too extensive; but a smaller tract would be inadequate without a change of conditions. *The lands were arid, and, without irrigation, were practically valueless.* And yet, it is contended, the means of irrigation were deliberately given up by the Indians and deliberately accepted by the government. The lands ceded were, it is true, also arid; and some argument may be urged, and is urged, that with their cession there was the cession of the waters, without which they would be valueless, and 'civilized communities could not be established thereon.' *And this, it is further contended, the Indians knew, and yet made no reservation of the waters. We realize that there is a conflict of implications, but that which makes for the retention of the waters is of greater force than that which makes for their cession. The Indians had command of the lands and the waters,—command of all their beneficial use, whether kept for hunting, 'and grazing roving herds of stock,' or turned to agriculture and the arts of civilization. Did they give up all this? Did they reduce the area of their occupation and give up the waters which made it valuable or adequate?* . . . By a rule of interpretation of agreements and treaties with the Indians, ambiguities occurring will be resolved from the standpoint of the

[4] *Id.* at 567, 569.

[5] *Id.* at 573.

> Indians. And the rule should certainly be applied to determine between two inferences, one of which would support the purpose of the agreement and the other impair or defeat it.[6]

Federal reserved water rights for Tribes have been called "*Winters* rights" ever since based on this decision.

Winters established several important principles for tribal reserved water rights. First, federal treaties with Tribes are construed to the benefit of the Tribe, as the Tribe would have understood the treaty. Second, the Tribes' water rights take as their priority date the date of the federal reservation—for the Fort Belknap Reservation, that was May 1, 1888. (Most of the large tribal reservations are in the West, so this priority date often gives Tribes very senior rights in the water systems where they live.) Third, non-exercise of the water rights does not destroy the right—the Tribes could start using water in 1898 without having forfeited their reserved right. Fourth, the federal government can reserve these rights before statehood, and the new state (here, Montana) must then implement its water law subject to those pre-existing federal reserved water rights.

However, *Winters* did not resolve all of the issues that would arise with respect to tribal reserved water rights. The U.S. Supreme Court answered many more questions regarding *Winters* rights in its 1963 decision in *Arizona v. California*,[7] a long-running and complex lawsuit involving the Colorado River and its tributaries. While *Winters* rights for the affected Tribes were just one facet of the case, the Court nevertheless made several important decisions regarding those rights that clarified the *Winters* doctrine. First, Congress can reserve federal water rights even *after* statehood, given its broad Commerce Clause authority over water and its plenary power over federal lands under the Property Clause.[8] Second, the status of the waterway as navigable or nonnavigable doesn't matter. While the Equal Footing Doctrine gives new states title to the submerged lands under navigable waters; it doesn't guarantee them complete control over the water itself.[9] Third, it does not have to be *Congress* that creates the reservation—Executive Branch reservations of federal lands also come with federal reserved water rights.[10] Finally, *Arizona v. California* created one standard for *quantifying* tribal reserved water rights, known as the ***"practicably irrigable acreage," or***

---

[6] *Id.* at 575–77 (emphasis added).

[7] 373 U.S. 546 (1963).

[8] *Id.* at 597–98.

[9] *Id.*

[10] *Id.* at 598.

PIA, standard. Under this standard, the courts determine the number of acres within the reservation that can be farmed, then award a quantity of water that allows the Tribe to irrigate those acres.[11]

Tribes have challenged the PIA standard as being too narrow, arguing that the purpose of a tribal reservation is to create a homeland and that the Tribe should be entitled to enough water for a modern homeland, not just to farm. That homeland might include, for example, a casino, schools, and modern houses. The PIA standard also raises questions about a Tribe's changing needs, including if the water resource or arable land is also changing, such as under the influence of climate change.

The U.S. Supreme Court has not squarely addressed these issues, and state and lower courts have varied in how they quantify *Winters* rights. The U.S. Court of Appeals for the Ninth Circuit, for example, has held that Tribes with treaties that reserve their pre-existing rights to fish and hunt (for example, many of the Pacific Northwest Tribes) are entitled to water rights to support those fisheries and hunting rights as well as water for agriculture.[12] Notably, the Ninth Circuit essentially invented a non-consumptive instream water right to support the Klamath Tribes, concluding that "the entitlement consists of the right to prevent other appropriators from depleting the streams waters below a protected level in any area where the non-consumptive right applies. In this respect, the water right reserved for the Tribe to hunt and fish has no corollary in the common law of prior appropriations."[13] Moreover, because the treaty recognized the continuation of an existing tribal right to hunt and fish rather than creating a federal reserved right, the hunting and fishing water rights have a priority date of "time immemorial,"[14] making them the oldest water rights in the Klamath River system. The Oregon Water Resources Department affirmed this "time immemorial" priority date in 2014 in its general stream adjudication for the Klamath Basin.[15] (Chapter 5 discusses general stream adjudications in more detail.)

In the Big Horn River System stream adjudication, the Wyoming Supreme Court acknowledged "that Congress intended to reserve water for the Wind River Indian Reservation when it was created in

---

[11] *Id.* at 600–01.

[12] United States v. Adair, 723 F.2d 1394, 1410 (9th Cir. 1983).

[13] *Id.* at 1411 (citation omitted).

[14] *Id.* at 1414.

[15] Corrected Findings of Fact and Order of Determination, *Klamath Basin General Stream Adjudication* (OWRD Feb. 28, 2014), *available at* https://www.oregon.gov/OWRD/programs/WaterRights/Adjudications/KlamathAdj/KBA_ACFFOD_00001.PDF.

1868, and we accept the proposition that the amount of water impliedly reserved is determined by the purposes for which the reservation was created."[16] However, while the Special Master concluded that the purpose of the treaty was to provide a homeland for the Shoshone and Bannack Tribes, the district court concluded that the water right was only to support agriculture.[17] Despite recognizing that it should construe treaties in the Tribes' favor, the Wyoming Supreme Court affirmed. After reviewing the treaty provisions, it had "no difficulty affirming the finding that it was the intent at the time to create a reservation with a sole agricultural purpose."[18]

In contrast, in 2001 the Arizona Supreme Court rejected reliance on the PIA standard for the Gila River Tribes.[19] As part of the Gila River general stream adjudication (also discussed in Chapter 5), the court addressed the issue of how to quantify federal reserved water rights.[20] Quoting *Winters* and *Arizona v. California*, the Arizona Supreme Court concluded that "the essential purpose of Indian reservations is to provide Native American people with a 'permanent home and abiding place,' that is, a 'livable' environment."[21] Moreover, "[s]uch a construction is necessary for tribes to achieve the twin goals of Indian self-determination and economic self-sufficiency":[22]

> Other right holders are not constrained in this, the twenty-first century, to use water in the same manner as their ancestors in the 1800s. Although over 40% of the nation's population lived and worked on farms in 1880, less than 5% do today. Likewise, agriculture has steadily decreased as a percentage of our gross domestic product. Just as the nation's economy has evolved, nothing should prevent tribes from diversifying their economies if they so choose and are reasonably able to do so. The permanent homeland concept allows for this flexibility and practicality. We therefore hold that the purpose of a federal Indian reservation is to serve as a "permanent home and abiding place" to the Native American people living there.[23]

---

16 In re General Adjudication of Big Horn River System, 753 P.2d 76, 94 (Wyo. 1988).

17 *Id.* at 94–95.

18 *Id.* at 96.

19 In re the General Adjudication of All Rights to Use Water in the Gila River System and Source, 35 P.3d 68 (Ariz. 2001) (*en banc*).

20 *Id.* at 71.

21 *Id.* at 74 (quoting *Winters*, 207 U.S. at 565, and *Arizona*, 373 U.S. at 599).

22 *Id.* at 76.

23 *Id.* (citations omitted).

As a result, the court rejected the PIA standard as a measurement of the Tribes' water rights.[24] Instead, it created a non-exclusive multi-factor analysis for the trial court to consider on remand, including the Tribe's history, tribal culture, "the tribal land's geography, topography, and natural resources, including groundwater availability," the Tribe's economic base, past water use, and the Tribe's present and projected population.[25]

Whatever test the court uses, quantification of tribal reserved water rights remains a significant issue and source of uncertainty in the West. For example, one source estimates that the tribal water rights in the Colorado River system (settled and unsettled) total over 4 million acre-feet per year, when the entire system is allocated on the assumption that there are 15 million acre-feet per year of water in the United States or 16.5 million acre-feet per year in the entire system, including Mexico's share (see below). Thus, if Tribes fully exploited their estimated and settled water rights in the system, they would claim roughly one-quarter of the water assumed to be available.

In contrast, *Winters* rights have been far less of an issue in the East, for three reasons. First, there are fewer tribal reservations in the East than in the West. Tribal reservations in the East are concentrated in Minnesota, Wisconsin, Michigan, New York, New Jersey, Connecticut, Maine, North Carolina, Florida, and the coastal areas of Alabama, Mississippi, and Louisiana. Second, what reservations exist in the East tend to be much smaller than those in the West. Finally, the East again generally has more water, reducing water conflicts generally.

Nevertheless, the second-oldest tribal water rights settlement in the U.S. occurred in the East—specifically, among Florida, the United States, and the Seminole Tribe. After Florida adopted the Florida Water Resources Act to require water rights permitting (see Chapter 5), the State of Florida and the Seminole Tribe experienced a series of conflicts over the Tribe's water rights for its six reservations, which are scattered across the southern half of Florida. The 1987 compact among the parties settled both the Tribe's water rights and its land rights claims. It also allows the Tribe to manage its water free from state control, so long as the Tribe observes several mutually-agreed-upon standards that ensure consistency with state water law and management. For example, the Tribe must ensure that its new withdrawals do not cause saltwater intrusion or interfere with the rights of other water users. In exchange, Florida

---

[24] *Id.* at 77–79.

[25] *Id.* at 79–81. *See also* State ex rel. State Engineer v. United States, 425 P.3d 723, 733–34 (N.M. App. 2018) (recognizing that the PIA standard is not the only way to quantify *Winters* rights).

guaranteed the Tribe significant consultation rights regarding any land use decisions for lands outside the Tribe's reservations that could affect the Seminole's water use and rights. The agreement also contains its own dispute resolution mechanisms, and it has virtually eliminated conflict and court battles between the Tribe and the State.

2. Federal Reserved Water Rights for Other Types of Federal Lands

Congress and the President reserve federal public lands for other purposes besides tribal reservations, such as national parks, national forests, national monuments, and so on. All these different kinds of land reservations are entitled to federal reserved water rights. For example, in its 1964 decision in *Arizona v. California,* the U.S. Supreme Court recognized water rights not only for various Tribes in the Colorado River system but also for the Lake Mead National Recreation Area in Arizona and Nevada; the Havasu Lake National Wildlife Refuge in Arizona and California; the Imperial National Wildlife Refuge in Arizona and California; and Boulder City, Nevada, which the federal government created as the management site for Hoover Dam.[26]

It was two other U.S. Supreme Court cases, however, that created the basic rules for non-tribal federal reserved water rights. The 1976 case of *Cappaert v. United States*[27] involved Devil's Hole in the Death Valley National Monument, which President Truman had created by proclamation on January 17, 1952, pursuant to the American Antiquities Preservation Act[28] (now more generally known as the Antiquities Act). This proclamation noted Devil's Hole's " 'remarkable underground pool,' " " 'a unique subsurface remnant of the prehistoric chain of lakes which in Pleistocene times formed the Death Valley Lake System' " that remains the only habitat " 'of a peculiar race of desert fish,' " the Devil's Hole pupfish.[29] This pool, the proclamation concluded, " 'is of such outstanding scientific importance that it should be given special protection . . . .' "[30]

The problem arose because, in 1968, the Cappaerts began pumping groundwater for their ranch, which was located about 2.5 miles from Devil's Hole. The water they pumped came from the same aquifer that supplied the Devil's Hole pool, and measurements of water levels at Devil's Hole since 1962 showed that they had been steady until 1969, when they began to drop. The lowered water levels exposed a rock shelf, interfering with pupfish spawning, creating a

---

26 Arizona v. California, 376 U.S. 340, 345–46 (1964).

27 426 U.S. 128 (1976).

28 16 U.S.C. § 431.

29 *Cappaert,* 426 U.S. at 132 (quoting President Truman's Proclamation).

30 *Id.* (quoting President Truman's Proclamation).

risk that the pupfish would go extinct. The Cappaerts had a valid Nevada water right that the National Park Service had protested but did not appeal, so the United States filed suit to enjoin the Cappaerts' pumping so far as it interfered with Devil's Hole and the pupfish.

The U.S. District Court for the District of Nevada found that Devil's Hole has a federal reserved water right and enjoined the Cappaerts' pumping so far as was necessary to keep the rock shelf in the pool covered with water. The U.S. Court of Appeals for the Ninth Circuit affirmed. The U.S. Supreme Court also affirmed, but it articulated a new test for determining federal reserved water rights for non-tribal federal lands.

First, the Court affirmed, Congress and the President have constitutional authority to reserve federal water rights. "Reservation of water rights is empowered by the Commerce Clause, Art. I, § 8, which permits federal regulation of navigable streams, and the Property Clause, Art. IV, § 3, which permits federal regulation of federal lands. The doctrine applies to Indian reservations and other federal enclaves, encompassing water rights in navigable and nonnavigable streams."[31] Second, the existence of federal reserved water rights does not depend on any kind of equitable balancing with state-law water rights.[32] Instead, third, the most important element in determining whether a federal reserved water right exists is congressional or presidential intent: "the issue is whether the Government intended to reserve unappropriated and thus available water. Intent is inferred if the previously unappropriated waters are necessary to accomplish the purposes for which the reservation was created."[33]

According to the Supreme Court, it was clear that President Truman's 1952 reservation of the Death Valley National Monument had intended to reserve water for the pool at Devil's Hole. The proclamation, as noted, repeatedly refers to both the pool and the pupfish as important features of the reservation.[34] The trickier question was *how much* water the President had actually reserved—the quantification issue again. According to the *Cappaert* Court:

> *The implied-reservation-of-water-rights doctrine, however, reserves only that amount of water necessary to fulfill the purpose of the reservation, no more.* Here the purpose of reserving Devil's Hole Monument is preservation of the pool. Devil's Hole was reserved "for the preservation of the unusual features of scenic, scientific, and educational

[31] *Id.* at 138 (citations omitted).

[32] *Id.*

[33] *Id.* at 139 (citations omitted).

[34] *Id.* at 139–40.

> interest." The Proclamation notes that the pool contains "a peculiar race of desert fish . . . which is found nowhere else in the world" and that the "pool is of . . . outstanding scientific importance . . . ." *The pool need only be preserved, consistent with the intention expressed in the Proclamation, to the extent necessary to preserve its scientific interest.* The fish are one of the features of scientific interest. The preamble noting the scientific interest of the pool follows the preamble describing the fish as unique; the Proclamation must be read in its entirety. Thus, as the District Court has correctly determined, the level of the pool may be permitted to drop to the extent that the drop does not impair the scientific value of the pool as the natural habitat of the species sought to be preserved. The District Court thus tailored its injunction, very appropriately, to minimal need, curtailing pumping only to the extent necessary to preserve an adequate water level at Devil's Hole, thus implementing the stated objectives of the Proclamation.[35]

Thus, after *Cappaert*, a federal reserved water right consists of the *minimum* amount of water needed to fulfill the reservation's intended purposes.

Two years after *Cappaert*, the U.S. Supreme Court again narrowed the quantity of water reserved for a non-tribal federal reserved water right in *United States v. New Mexico*.[36] This case involved the Gila National Forest in New Mexico, and the United States claimed that the reserved water right for the forest included not only water for the forest itself but also water for recreation, aesthetics, wildlife preservation, and stock watering. The New Mexico Supreme Court disagreed, concluding that the U.S. Forest Service's water rights under the federal statutes governing national forests were limited to timber preservation and improving stream flows. The U.S. Supreme Court granted *certiorari* and affirmed.

According to the U.S. Supreme Court, the federal government reserves a water right only for the *primary* purpose for which the reservation was established, not for any secondary purposes.[37] This limitation was necessary in order to avoid unduly interfering with state water law:

> Where Congress has expressly addressed the question of whether federal entities must abide by state water law, it has almost invariably deferred to the state law. Where

[35] *Id.* at 141 (emphasis added).

[36] 438 U.S. 696 (1978).

[37] *Id.* at 702.

> water is necessary to fulfill the very purposes for which a federal reservation was created, it is reasonable to conclude, even in the face of Congress' express deference to state water law in other areas, that the United States intended to reserve the necessary water. Where water is only valuable for a secondary use of the reservation, however, the arises the contrary inference that Congress intended, consistent with its other views, that the United States would acquire water in the same manner as any other public or private appropriator.[38]

The Court was also acutely aware of the harm that injecting senior federal reserved water rights into western states' prior appropriation schemes could cause: "When, as in the case of the Rio Mimbre, a river is fully appropriated, federal reserved water rights will frequently require a gallon-for-gallon reduction in the amount of water available in a water-needy state and private appropriators."[39]

Thus, only the primary purposes of the National Forests were relevant to the federal reserved water right at issue. Examining the relevant statutes, the U.S. Supreme Court concluded that:

> The legislative debates surrounding the Organic Administration Act of 1897 and its predecessor bills demonstrate that Congress intended national forests to be reserved for only two purposes—"[t]o conserve the water flows, and to furnish a continuous supply of timber for the people." National forests were not to be reserved for aesthetic, environmental, recreational, or wildlife-preservation purposes.[40]

After *Cappaert* and *New Mexico*, non-tribal federal reserved water rights depend on a two-step test. The first issue is whether the federal government intended to reserve water to fulfill the primary purpose of the federal reservation. The second issue is to determine the minimum amount of water necessary to fulfill that primary purpose. This test appears to have limited the federal government's assertions of non-tribal federal reserved water rights in some ways. For example, following these cases, the U.S. Court of Appeals for the D.C. Circuit concluded that the Federal Lands Policy and Management Act (FLPMA) did not reserve water rights for Bureau of Land Management lands in southern Utah and northern Arizona,[41] and the U.S. Forest Service has declined to assert federal

---

[38] *Id.*

[39] *Id.* at 705.

[40] *Id.* at 707–08 (citations omitted).

[41] Sierra Club v. Watt, 659 F.2d 203, 206 (D.C. Cir. 1981) (concluding that FLPMA did not "reserve" federal public lands and hence created no water rights).

reserved water rights for its wilderness areas created under the Wilderness Act.[42] Nevertheless, the federal government has continued to claim federal reserved water rights for a wide range of federal lands, including national parks, national wildlife refuges, and military installations.[43]

3. The Role of State Courts: The McCarran Amendment

As you may have noticed in the discussions above, state courts often determine federal reserved water rights, especially in the context of general stream adjudications (see Chapter 5), even though reserved water rights exist as a matter of federal law. Deciding federal water rights is often a helpful facet of general stream adjudications, allowing the state to validate and prioritize all water rights in a given system at the same time. However, doing so means that the state needs to be able to haul the United States government into state court, and it wasn't clear, initially, that Congress had waived the United States' sovereign immunity—its sovereign right to not be sued—for these lawsuits.

Congress fixed that problem in 1952 through the McCarran Water Rights Suit Act,[44] more popularly known as the McCarran Amendment. This Act provides that:

> Consent is hereby given to join the United States as a defendant in any suit (1) for the adjudication of rights to the use of water of a river system or other sources, or (2) for the administration of such rights, where it appears that the United States is the owner of or is in the process of acquiring water rights by appropriation under State law, by purchase, by exchange, or otherwise, and the United States is a necessary party to such suit.[45]

The United States also agreed to be bound by the state court judgments, although state courts cannot assess costs against the United States.[46] However, the McCarran Amendment expressly does *not* waive the United States' sovereign immunity from nonvoluntary joinder into interstate equitable apportionment lawsuits in the U.S. Supreme Court[47] (discussed in Chapter 9).

---

[42] *See* Sierra Club v. Yuetter, 911 F.2d 1405, 1408 (10th Cir. 1990) (addressing a case in which the Sierra Club sued the Forest Service to try to force it to claim water rights for 24 wilderness areas in Colorado).

[43] *See, e.g.*, Alaska v. United States, 545 U.S. 75, 101–02 (2005) (holding that the federal government had reserved the waters in Glacier Bay National Monument, later Glacier Bay National Park).

[44] 43 U.S.C. § 666.

[45] *Id.* § 666(a).

[46] *Id.*

[47] *Id.* § 666(c).

Thus, under the McCarran Amendment, the United States can be made a party to state court lawsuits about water rights, especially general stream adjudications. However, the U.S. Supreme Court had to resolve some issues about the McCarran Amendment in *Colorado River Water Conservation District v. United States*.[48] First, according to the Court, the McCarran Amendment does not give state courts *exclusive* jurisdiction over the United States' water rights; the federal district courts can still also decide these issues.[49] Second, the McCarran Amendment does extend to federal reserved water rights (as rights arising "otherwise"), so the state courts can decide *Winters* rights and other reserved water rights.[50] Finally, and most important, if both a state court proceeding and a federal court proceeding are ongoing simultaneously that involve the same water rights, the McCarran Amendment means that the federal court should generally abstain from deciding the issue in favor of state court resolution. According to the *Colorado River* Court,

> a number of factors clearly counsel against concurrent federal proceedings. The most important of these is the McCarran Amendment itself. The clear federal policy evinced by the legislation is the avoidance of piecemeal adjudication of water rights in a river system. This policy is akin to that underlying the rule requiring that jurisdiction be yielded to the court first acquiring control of property, for the concern in such instances is with avoiding the generation of additional litigation through permitting inconsistent dispositions of property. This concern is heightened with respect to water rights, the relationships among which are highly interdependent. Indeed, we have recognized that actions seeking the allocation of water essentially involve the disposition of property and are best conducted in unified proceedings. The consent to jurisdiction given by the McCarran Amendment bespeaks a policy that recognizes the availability of comprehensive state systems for adjudication of water rights as the means for achieving these goals.[51]

Thus, federal courts hearing cases about federal water rights now generally yield to concurrent state cases about the same water rights, especially if the state case is a general stream adjudication. This doctrine is known as ***Colorado River* abstention**. Moreover,

---

48 424 U.S. 800 (1976).

49 *Id.* at 808–09.

50 *Id.* at 809.

51 *Id.* at 819.

despite Tribes' frequent preference to be in federal court, *Colorado River* abstention applies even to highly contested *Winters* rights.[52]

C. Federal Water Projects

A variety of federal agencies manage water on a large scale, and federal investment in water projects across the country has been significant. This section highlights three federal agencies that play particularly prominent roles in water management: the U.S. Bureau of Reclamation, the Tennessee Valley Authority, and the U.S. Army Corps of Engineers.

1. The Reclamation Act and the U.S. Bureau of Reclamation

In 1902, Congress enacted the Reclamation Act,[53] creating what was then known as the Reclamation Service and is now known as the U.S. Bureau of Reclamation. The Act authorizes the Bureau to carry out projects to reclaim arid lands, primarily for farming, in the 17 western states, from the Pacific coast through the line of states from North Dakota to Texas.[54] Since 1910, the Secretary of the Interior, acting through the Bureau, recommends new projects to the President, who must approve them; in addition, Congress must actually appropriate the money necessary to build each reclamation project.[55] As a result, reclamation projects have long been the objects of intense lobbying in Washington, D.C.

In theory, the federal government provides the up-front money to build these large dams and reservoirs, then it makes the money back by selling water to various water users, such as irrigators and irrigation companies.[56] However, water users' persistent inability to pay the charges has repeatedly led Congress to change the repayment schedules. Many reclamation projects have never been repaid, effectively resulting in considerable federal subsidies for water in the West. Indeed, the Bureau of Reclamation describes itself as "the largest wholesale water supplier and the second largest producer of hydroelectric power in the United States, with operations and facilities in the 17 Western States."[57]

---

[52] *See* Arizona v. San Carlos Apache Tribe of Arizona, 463 U.S. 545, 567–68 (1983) (upholding *Colorado River* abstention despite the United States' and the Tribe's desire to adjudicate tribal reserved water rights in federal court).

[53] Act of June 17, 1902, ch. 1093, 32 Stat. 388, codified at 43 U.S.C. §§ 371, 372, 373, 381, 383, 391, 392, 411, 414, 419, 421, 431, 432, 434, 439, 461, 491, 498, 1457.

[54] 43 U.S.C. § 373, 373a.

[55] *Id.* §§ 413, 414.

[56] *Id.* §§ 461–475.

[57] U.S. Bureau of Reclamation, *Welcome to the Projects and Facilities Database: Reclamation's Portal for Information on Dams, Powerplants and Projects*, http://www.usbr.gov/projects/ (as viewed February 15, 2024).

The Reclamation Act's agricultural focus is still evident in its definition of "project," which is "a Federal irrigation project authorized by the reclamation law."[58] Moreover, in concert with the various Homestead Acts, the Reclamation Act and Bureau of Reclamation projects served as means to encourage people to settle the West. For example, the Act initially limited use of reclamation private water use to the 160-acre homestead parcels where people actually lived (those limits have since been expanded).[59]

Reclamation projects would seem to be perfect candidates for federal reserved water rights, but one of the most legally interesting facets of the Reclamation Act is that Congress insistently deferred to state water law. For example, the Act declares

> the policy of Congress to recognize the primary responsibilities of the States and local interests in developing water supplies for domestic, municipal, industrial, and other purposes and the Federal Government should participate and cooperate with States and local interests in developing such water supplies in connection with the construction, maintenance, and operation of Federal navigation, flood control, irrigation, or multiple purpose projects.[60]

Moreover, under Section 8 of the original Public Law (which is how everyone still refers to this provision), federal reclamation projects must get their water rights from the relevant states, pursuant to state water law.[61] In general, states were happy to give these water rights in order to get the reclamation projects and the federal money they involved. Nevertheless, the subordination of federal reclamation projects to state water law remains an important legal facet of the Bureau of Reclamation's operations. For example, in California, the Bureau of Reclamation's water rights and hence operations are subject, especially after the Mono Lake decision, to California's public trust doctrine (see Chapter 7).

2. Tennessee Valley Authority

Congress created the Tennessee Valley Authority, or TVA, in 1933[62] as part of President Franklin D. Roosevelt's "New Deal" during the Great Depression, with the goal of electrifying the rural parts of the American South. While the TVA is a federal corporation

---

58 43 U.S.C. § 371(d).

59 *Id.* § 341.

60 *Id.* § 390b(a).

61 43 U.S.C. § 383.

62 Tennessee Valley Authority Act of 1933 (Act of May 18, 1933), 48 Stat. 58, *codified as* 16 U.S.C. §§ 831 to 831dd.

(not a federal agency), it is subject to many federal agency responsibilities, such as complying with the National Environmental Policy Act (NEPA; see below) and the federal agency provisions of the federal Endangered Species Act (see Chapter 12).

The TVA operates in the southern states of the United States—Tennessee and parts of Alabama, Georgia, Kentucky, Mississippi, North Carolina, and Virginia. Water in these states is generally plentiful, and thus, unlike the Bureau of Reclamation operating in the West, the TVA does not build projects for irrigation and farming. Instead, in the 1930s, the TVA began to dam many of the South's rivers for three primary purposes: hydroelectricity generation; flood control; and navigation improvement. Watch (or watch again) the Coen Brothers' movie starring George Clooney, "O Brother, Where Art Thou?" (2000); the big dam-and-reservoir electrification project driving much of the movie's plot pays homage to the TVA's Depression-era work. Initially, the federal government funded all of the TVA's operations, but the corporation has been fully self-funded since 1999.

Providing electricity—mostly in the form of hydropower—is currently the TVA's main focus. After it built many new electricity-producing facilities during World War II to supply power for the war effort, the TVA became in the 1950s the nation's largest supplier of electricity. However, it also engages in a number of hydrological projects. Indeed, under the Tennessee Valley Authority Act, the TVA exists in part "to improve navigation in the Tennessee River and to control the destructive flood waters in the Tennessee River and Mississippi River Basins.[63] Thus, for example, it built a 650-mile navigation channel in the Tennessee River.

In the 1960s, the TVA expanded its electricity-supplying efforts by building nuclear power plants. It now has an extensive power generating network consisting of several types of electric facilities. In terms of hydroelectricity, the TVA operates "29 power-generating dams throughout the Tennessee River system, some of which date back to the TVA's early days in the 1930s [and] [a] pumped-storage plant near Chattanooga called Raccoon Mountain," plus it "[p]urchase[s] power from eight dams on the Cumberland River operated by the Army Corps of Engineers."[64] The TVA also operates three nuclear power plants, one in Alabama and two in Tennessee; ten coal-fired power plants, two in Kentucky, two in Alabama, and six in Tennessee; and "106 natural gas- and fuel oil-fired generators

---

[63] 16 U.S.C. § 831; *see also id.* § 831h–1 (directing that TVA dams should be used primarily for promoting navigation and controlling floods, while simultaneously authorizing the TVA to generate and market electricity).

[64] Tennessee Valley Authority, *Hydroelectric*, https://www.tva.gov/Energy/Our-Power-System/Hydroelectric (as viewed February 15, 2024).

at 14 sites—seven in Tennessee, five in Mississippi, one in Alabama and one in Kentucky."[65] As you'll learn in Chapter 10, all of these power plants require water to operate, and the TVA's mission now includes integrated water management.

Because the TVA operates in the South, it acquires its necessary surface water rights through principles of riparianism (unlike the Bureau of Reclamation, which operates almost entirely under prior appropriation law). Moreover, because the TVA began building its projects in the 1930s, the relevant water law for many of its projects is common-law riparianism. Assuming that the TVA owns the riparian land for most of its projects (which it usually does—the TVA also has extensive authority to purchase and condemn land), riparian law requires that its uses of the relevant rivers be reasonable. As you may recall from Chapter 2, however, riparian states view electricity generation as a reasonable use of water. Moreover, to the extent that the TVA promotes navigation, it benefits from the federal government's navigation servitude, discussed in Chapter 6.

However, the TVA can supplement its riparian rights under the Tennessee Valley Authority Act with ***flowage easements***. The Act gives the TVA authority to condemn whatever easements it needs for its various projects,[66] and flowage easements are one of the types of easements that the TVA uses. A flowage easement gives the TVA the right to flood private property, subject to the terms of the easement. Like all other appurtenant easements, flowage easements pass with the title to the flooded properties. The TVA employs these flowage easements primarily for its reservoirs.

3. U.S. Army Corps of Engineers

The U.S. Army Corps of Engineers operates a number of dam-and-reservoir systems throughout the country. Indeed, the Corps operates so many dams and reservoirs along the Missouri River, which flows through Montana, North Dakota, South Dakota, Nebraska, Iowa, and Missouri, that the U.S. Court of Appeals for the Eighth Circuit once declared the river "federalized."[67] A similar argument occurred regarding the Army Corps' authority in the Apalachicola-Chattahoochee-Flint (ACF) River system in Georgia, Alabama, and Florida in the context of whether the Army Corps had to be a party in Florida's equitable apportionment (see Chapter 9) lawsuit to divide the water in the system. As a final example, the Army Corps operates most of the large dams in the Columbia River

---

[65] Tennessee Valley Authority, *Natural Gas*, https://www.tva.gov/Energy/Our-Power-System/Natural-Gas (as viewed February 15, 2024).

[66] 16 U.S.C. § 831w.

[67] In re Operation of Missouri River System Litigation, 418 F.3d 915, 917–19 (8th Cir. 2005).

Basin in the Pacific Northwest (Oregon, Washington, and Idaho), although it is the Bonneville Power Administration that is responsible for marketing the hydropower that many of these dams produce.

Unlike the Bureau of Reclamation and the TVA, the Army Corps does not have a centralized statute that governs its water projects. Instead, Congress authorizes each project through independent legislation or in a Water Resources Development Act (WRDA, pronounced "WORD-duh")—the sporadic large pieces of legislation that Congress enacts, generally every two to three years, to authorize a variety of federal water projects simultaneously. For example, on December 23, 2022, the Water Resources Development Act of 2022 became law as Title LXXXI of Public Law 117–263.

Legally, what's important about this project-by-project approval process is that it's hard to generalize about what the Army Corps' primary responsibilities for any dam or reservoir will be—some are decidedly focused on flood control, some are for water supply, and still others are to promote navigation. In some systems, like the Missouri River, the Army Corps is supposed to be balancing so many human uses that the agency effectively has almost total discretion in how it runs the system—one reason that the Eighth Circuit decided that the Missouri River had been federalized. Anyone working with an Army Corps project, therefore, must consult the original authorizing legislation to identify the specific purposes, rules, and limitations that govern that project.

D. Federal Law Influences on Water Management

1. The National Environmental Policy Act (NEPA)

Congress enacted NEPA[68] in 1969 to "encourage productive and enjoyable harmony between man and his environment" and "to promote efforts which will prevent or eliminate damage to the environment and biosphere and stimulate the health and welfare of man . . . ."[69] NEPA's most important legal requirement is that "all agencies of the Federal Government shall—"

> include in every recommendation or report on proposals for legislation and other major Federal actions significantly affecting the quality of the human environment, a detailed statement by the responsible official on—
>
> (i) reasonably foreseeable environmental effects of the proposed agency action;

[68] 42 U.S.C. §§ 4321–4370m–12.

[69] *Id.* § 4321.

(ii) any reasonably foreseeable adverse environmental effects which cannot be avoided should the proposal be implemented;

(iii) a reasonable range of alternatives to the proposed agency action, including an analysis of any negative environmental impacts of not implementing the proposed agency action in the case of a no action alternative, that are technically and economically feasible, and meet the purpose and need of the proposal;

(iv) the relationship between local short-term uses of man's environment and the maintenance and enhancement of long-term productivity; and

(v) any irreversible and irretrievable commitments of Federal resources which would be involved in the proposed agency action should it be implemented.[70]

This "detailed statement" is now known as an ***Environmental Impact Statement, or EIS***.

Some federal agency actions related to water will clearly "significantly affect[ ] the quality of the human environment" and hence require an EIS. For example, if the Army Corps, TVA, or Bureau of Reclamation is building a build new dam with a substantial reservoir, there is no question that it will have to prepare a full EIS.[71] However, if the agency is unsure about the effects of its proposed action, it may first prepare an ***Environmental Assessment, or EA***, to determine whether those affects are reasonably foreseeable enough to be significant.[72] If it determines that there are reasonably foreseeable significant effects, it will prepare an EIS; if not, it will instead issue a ***Finding of No Significant Impact, or FONSI***.[73] An EA is limited to 75 pages and must be completed within a year; an EIS is limited to 150 pages and must be completed within two years.[74]

---

[70] *Id.* § 4332(2)(C).

[71] *See, e.g.*, Marsh v. Oregon Natural Resources Council, 490 U.S. 360, 364 (1989) (noting that the Army Corps completed an EIS for the Elk Creek Dam in Oregon, "a 238-foot-high concrete structure that will control the run-off from 132 square miles of the 135-square-mile Elk Creek watershed. When full, the artificial lake behind the dam will cover 1,290 acres of land, will have an 18-mile shoreline, and will hold 101,000 acre-feet of water."); Environmental Defense Fund v. Tennessee Valley Auth., 468 F.2d 1164, 1169, 1180–81 (6th Cir. 1972) (holding that the TVA had to complete an EIS for the Tellico Dam, "an earth embankment with a concrete spillway, and when it is operational (in 1975), it will impound the Little Tennessee and create a reservoir 33 miles long.").

[72] 42 U.S.C. § 4336(b)(1).

[73] *Id.* § 4336(b)(2).

[74] *Id.* § 4336a(e), (g).

Many federal agency activities regarding water are subject to NEPA's EIS requirement. Beside dam and reservoir building, these include: (1) the Army Corps' dredging of navigation channels;[75] (2) the Bureau of Reclamation's drawdown of lakes;[76] (3) the Bureau of Reclamation's construction of the Tucson Aqueduct as part of the Central Arizona Project;[77] and (4) the Bureau of Reclamation's management of the Colorado River.[78] Other issues are not quite as clear. For example, in April and July 2003, the United States and the State of Colorado entered into agreements that would effectively reduce the amount of and subordinate the priority of the United States' federal reserved water rights for the Black Canyon of the Gunnison National Park. The U.S. District Court for the District of Colorado concluded that "[a] permanent relinquishment of a water right with a 1933 priority date for such a scientifically, ecologically and historically important national park must be viewed as a major action requiring compliance with NEPA."[79]

A NEPA EIS forces the federal government to identify the environmental effects of its action and to consider alternatives to that action, and the EIS process is public, allowing for both public input and comments and citizen suits challenging the agency's environmental analysis. Public interest in a project can also induce a federal agency to reduce or mitigate the project's environmental effects. Nevertheless, NEPA is a procedural statute—it does not require the federal agency to choose the most environmentally benign course of action. Thus, as long as the agency correctly completes the required environmental analysis, it can go ahead and build environmentally destructive water projects if it so chooses.

2. The Dormant Commerce Clause

The Dormant Commerce Clause is the U.S. Supreme Court's interpretation of the U.S. Constitution's Commerce Clause's[80] limitations on states. Specifically, whereas the Commerce Clause itself empowers the federal government to regulate interstate commerce, the Dormant Commerce Clause restricts the states from interfering with interstate commerce.[81] The Supreme Court employs

---

[75] Delaware Dep't of Natural Resources & Envtl. Control v. U.S. Army Corps of Engineers, 685 F.3d 259, 263 (3rd Cir. 2012).

[76] Center for Envtl. Law & Pol'y v. U.S. Bureau of Reclamation, 655 F.3d 1000, 1010 (9th Cir. 2011).

[77] Animal Defense Council v. Hodel, 840 F.2d 1432, 1433–34 (9th Cir. 1988).

[78] Badoni v. Higginson, 638 F.2d 172, 180–81 (10th Cir. 1980).

[79] High Country Citizens' Alliance v. Norton, 448 F. Supp. 2d 1235, 1245 (D. Colo. 2006).

[80] U.S. CONST., art. I, § 8, cl. 3.

[81] Baldwin v. G.A.F. Seelig, Inc., 294 U.S. 511, 522 (1935).

a two-step analysis to determine whether a state law unconstitutionally discriminates against interstate commerce:

> Under the resulting protocol for dormant Commerce Clause analysis, we ask whether a challenged law discriminates against interstate commerce. A discriminatory law is "virtually per se invalid," and will survive only if it "advances a legitimate local purpose that cannot be adequately served by reasonable nondiscriminatory alternatives[.]" Absent discrimination for the forbidden purpose, however, the law "will be upheld unless the burden imposed on [interstate] commerce is clearly excessive in relation to the putative local benefits."[82]

In *Sporhase v. Nebraska ex rel. Douglas*,[83] the U.S. Supreme Court determined that groundwater (and, by implication, all fresh water) is an article of commerce[84] and that state law restrictions on taking water out-of-state can violate the Dormant Commerce Clause.[85] In reaching this conclusion, the Court expressly rejected the state's public ownership theory regarding water as "but a fiction expressive in legal shorthand of the importance to its people that a State have power to preserve and regulate the exploitation of an important resource."[86]

Nevertheless, the Court has since decided that laws restricting interstate commerce to benefit *state-owned* operations do *not* violate the Dormant Commerce Clause.[87] Many states have declared the water within their borders to be the property of the state (or the citizens of the state) and manage that water through permit systems. Moreover, the *Sporhase* Court was clearly reluctant to interfere with state water management. Thus, Supreme Court jurisprudence is currently a bit unclear regarding what aspects of a state's water law would violate the Dormant Commerce Clause, but restrictions on transporting and using the water out-of-state still may be unconstitutional.

---

[82] Department of Revenue of Kentucky v. Davis, 553 U.S. 328, 338–29 (2008) (citations omitted).

[83] 458 U.S. 941 (1982).

[84] *Id.* at 953–54.

[85] *Id.* at 957–58.

[86] *Id.* at 951 (quoting Hughes v. Oklahoma, 441 U.S. 322 (1979); Toomer v. Witsell, 334 U.S. 385, 402 (1948)). *See also* Baldwin v. Montana Fish and Game Comm'n, 436 U.S. 371, 384–387 (1978); Douglas v. Seacoast Products, Inc., 431 U.S. 265, 284–285 (1977)).

[87] United Haulers Ass'n, Inc. v. Oneida-Herkimer Solid Water Management Auth., 550 U.S. 330, 342–43 (2007).

E. International Water Relations: Treaties with Canada and Mexico

The United States shares significant transnational water resources with both Canada and Mexico. Numerous waters cross the Canada-United States border, including four of the five Great Lakes, the St. Lawrence River, and the Columbia River. Fewer waters cross the Mexico-United States border, but two of them are the critically important Colorado and Rio Grande Rivers. Resolution of international water issues is an exclusively federal prerogative in the U.S., and the federal government has entered treaties with both Canada and Mexico regarding these internationally shared water resources.

1. Canada: The Boundary Waters Treaty, the Great Lakes, and the Columbia River

In 1909, the United States and Great Britain (acting on behalf of Canada) entered into the Boundary Waters Treaty.[88] This treaty provides for the joint management and cooperation between the United States and Canada for all of their shared boundary waters, which the treaty defines as "the waters from main shore to main shore of the lakes and rivers and connecting waterways . . . along which the international boundary between the United States and Canada passes . . . ."[89] Neither country may use or divert boundary waters "affecting the natural level or flow of boundary waters on the other side of the [border]" without the authority of the International Joint Commission,[90] an adjudicative body with equal U.S. and Canadian representation.[91] In addition, the Boundary Waters Treaty forbids pollution "on either side to the injury of health or property on the other."[92]

The United States and Canada have used the pollution prevention provision of the Boundary Waters Treaty to more aggressively address water pollution issues in the Great Lakes through the Great Lakes Water Quality Agreement. "The U.S. and Canada first signed the Agreement in 1972. It was amended in 1983 and 1987. In 2012, it was updated to enhance water quality programs that ensure the 'chemical, physical, and biological integrity' of the Great Lakes."[93] More specifically, the 2012 version of the agreement

---

[88] 36 Stat. 2448 (1909).

[89] Boundary Waters Treaty, Preliminary Article, 36 Stat. at 2448–49.

[90] *Id.* art. III, 36 Stat. at 2449–50.

[91] *Id.* art. VII, 36 Stat. at 2451.

[92] *Id.* art. III, 36 Stat. 2450.

[93] U.S. Envtl. Protection Agency, *What Is the GLWQA?*, https://www.epa.gov/glwqa/what-glwqa (as viewed February 15, 2024).

addresses issues as diverse as phosphorus pollution and invasive species.

In addition, a series of agreements severely limit water withdrawals from the Great Lakes, particularly if the water is used or discharged outside of the Great Lakes Basin. These agreements include: (1) the 1985 Great Lakes Charter, a good-faith agreement among the U.S. Great Lakes states and the Canadian provinces of Ontario and Quebec on how to manage the Great Lakes water supply; (2) the 2005 Great Lakes-Saint Lawrence River Basin Sustainable Water Resources Agreement among the Governors of the U.S. states of Illinois, Indiana, Michigan, Minnesota, New York, Ohio, Pennsylvania and Wisconsin, and the Premiers of the Canadian provinces of Ontario and Quebec to further develop the Charter's principles; and (3) the 2008 Great Lakes-St. Lawrence River Basin Water Resources Compact, a legally binding interstate compact among the U.S. states of Illinois, Indiana, Michigan, Minnesota, New York, Ohio, Pennsylvania and Wisconsin and approved by Congress (see Chapter 9 for more information about interstate compacts).

The Columbia River in the Pacific Northwest is managed through the 1964 Columbia River Treaty between the United States and Canada. The treaty governs the development and operation of dams in the upper Columbia River basin for power and flood control benefits in both countries. Four dams have been constructed under this treaty: the Duncan Dam, Mica Dam, Keenleyside Dam in Canada and Libby Dam the United States. Nevertheless, while the Treaty and these dams have been quite successful in achieving their two stated goals—hydropower and flood protection—those improvements have come at significant environmental cost, particularly with regard to the many salmon species that use the river system and the Tribes and First Nations who depend on those fish. Because the Treaty can terminate in 2024 if either party gives 10 years' notice, Canada and the United States began negotiations to modernize the treaty regime in May 2018 and, as of January 2023, have completed 15 rounds of negotiations. Important aspects of the renegotiation include: (1) greatly increased participation by and benefits to affected First Nations (Canada) and Tribes (U.S.); and (2) increased attention to the environment and ecology of the Columbia River system.

2. Mexico: The U.S.-Mexico Water Treaty

The United States shares three rivers with Mexico: the Colorado River, which flows (or is supposed to flow) along the California-Arizona border into Mexico and the Gulf of California; the Rio Grande River, which forms part of the border between the United States (Texas) and Mexico as it flows toward the Gulf of Mexico; and the much smaller Tijuana River, which flows north from Mexico into California, emptying into the Pacific Ocean south of San Diego.

Historically, the United States was far less interested in negotiating water issues with Mexico than with Canada. For example, in 1898, U.S. Attorney General Harmon announced the ***Harmon Doctrine*** with respect to the Rio Grande River, claiming that the United States and its citizens could use all of the Rio Grande River and owed nothing to Mexico.[94] Thus, it wasn't until 1944—and allegedly as part of an effort to keep Mexico on the Allies' side during World War II—that the United States entered a comprehensive water treaty with Mexico.[95] The International Boundary and Water Commission implements this convention.

With respect to the Colorado River, which originates entirely in the United States, the treaty assures that the United States will deliver approximately 1.5 million acre-feet of water per year[96]—roughly 10% on average of that river's highly variable flow—to Mexico. However, the United States may reduce its deliveries of Colorado River water during "extraordinary drought" or if there is a "serious accident to the irrigation system in the United States,"[97] terms that the treaty does not define. With respect to the Rio Grande River, which originates from watersheds in both the United States and Mexico, the treaty gives the United States the right to all water from the U.S. tributaries of the river and to one-third of the water from the six major Mexican tributaries, which must average 350,000 acre-feet per year.[98] Moreover, if Mexico cannot deliver its share because of drought, it must make up the deficiency in later years. Finally, the treaty commits to the Commission the duty to investigate and make recommendations regarding the equitable distribution of the Tijuana River between the two countries.[99]

As new issues come up regarding these three rivers, the United States and Mexico address them through implementing agreements, known as ***Minutes***. For example, in 2012, the parties, acting through the Commission, negotiated Minute 319, a five-year agreement that allowed Mexico to store any surplus water from the Colorado River in Lake Mead as a hedge against drought in both countries. In 2015, the parties agreed to Minute 320 to address trash, sediment, and other water quality issues in the Tijuana River. Other ongoing

---

[94] 21 Opinions of the Attorney General 274 (1898).

[95] Treaty between the United States of America and Mexico regarding utilization of the waters of the Colorado and Tijuana Rivers and of the Rio Grande, 59 Stat. 1219 (Feb. 3, 1944).

[96] *Id.* art 10(a), 59 Stat. at 1228.

[97] *Id.* art 10(b), 59 Stat. at 1228.

[98] *Id.* art. 4, 59 Stat. at 1223.

[99] *Id.* art. 16, 59 Stat. at 1233.

negotiations include environmental protection (Minutes 319 and 323) and drought management.

Chapter 9

INTERSTATE WATER POLLUTION, APPORTIONMENT AND MANAGEMENT

Most major freshwater resources in the United States are shared by two or more states, making interstate water law a key piece of the water management puzzle. In every part of the country, the major freshwater systems cross state lines. Indeed, approximately 95% of the nation's available surface freshwater is interstate. The Great Lakes alone comprise 90% of America's surface freshwater and are shared by eight states—Illinois, Indiana, Michigan, Minnesota, Ohio, New York, Pennsylvania, and Wisconsin, as well as the Canadian provinces of Ontario and Quebec. Ten states are riparian to the Mississippi River, and after the Chicago diversion (the subject of the *Missouri v. Illinois* and *Wisconsin v. Illinois* cases discussed in this chapter), the waters (and states) of the Great Lakes are now connected with the Gulf of Mexico. New York, Pennsylvania, and Maryland share the largest river on the East coast, the Susquehanna. The Colorado River is shared by seven U.S. states, two Mexican states, and Native Americans in both nations. All these waters are often the subject of interstate disputes over management and pollution, and have been the setting for many of the legal developments in water law covered in this chapter.

This chapter is organized into the legal system's primary tools for addressing interstate water pollution and management. Our federal system provides three ways to protect, manage, and allocate interstate waters in the United States. First, the Constitution gave the U.S. Supreme Court original jurisdiction to hear cases between states, and this jurisdiction over interstate water disputes has been extended to lower courts. Under this jurisdiction, the Supreme Court has established the doctrines of interstate nuisance law and equitable apportionment of shared waters among states. Second, Congress has used its powers under the Constitution's Commerce Clause to regulate water pollution (interstate and intrastate) through the Clean Water Act and, on rare occasions, to allocate specific water resources among the states. Finally, states can enter into interstate compacts, subject to congressional approval, both to proactively address interstate pollution problems and to allocate and manage shared water resources. Such compacts now govern many interstate waters. These interstate compacts also often establish regional commissions that fill the governance gap between the state and federal levels of management.

A. Interstate Nuisance and Water Pollution

In the early 20th century, interstate water pollution and allocation disputes gave rise to the doctrines of federal interstate nuisance and equitable apportionment law. While the federal Clean Water Act of 1972 (see Chapter 11) has since displaced federal interstate nuisance law for water pollution, the key concepts and principles of the interstate nuisance doctrine are still relevant to equitable apportionment of interstate waters and may apply to new and emerging issues not yet covered by federal statute, such as the introduction of aquatic invasive species. The following discussions illustrate the rise and parallel development of interstate nuisance and equitable apportionment doctrines.

1. The Federal Common Law of Interstate Nuisance

In the early 1880s, Chicago was quickly becoming one of the nation's most populous and industrialized cities. However, the city disposed of its sewage into Lake Michigan via the Chicago River, and took its drinking water from the same source, leading to chronic outbreaks of water-borne illnesses, such as typhoid and cholera, that threatened public health. To solve this problem, Chicago built a canal to reverse the flow of the Chicago River, changing its output from Lake Michigan to the Illinois River. The reversal, however, allowed Chicago sewage to flow into the Mississippi River and ultimately into the Gulf of Mexico. The project also created a new artificial link between the waters of the Mississippi River and the Great Lakes, which previously had been hydrologically separate.

Missouri, now downstream from Chicago's sewage, brought an interstate nuisance action against Illinois in the U.S. Supreme Court, based on the Court's original jurisdiction for suits between states.[1] The two issues in *Missouri v. Illinois (I)* were: (1) whether the Court had original jurisdiction over the suit between Missouri and Illinois; and (2) whether Missouri's claims constituted an interstate nuisance action.[2] The Court exercised its original jurisdiction over the dispute because the reversal of the Chicago River significantly threatened the health and welfare of Missouri's citizens, which the Court declared was a valid state sovereign interest.[3] The Court also held that Missouri's claims satisfied the requirements for an interstate nuisance action.[4]

The Supreme Court's decision in *Missouri I* extended its jurisdiction from settling boundary disputes between states to

---

1 Missouri v. Illinois (I), 180 U.S. 208 (1901).

2 *Id.* at 218.

3 *Id.* at 241.

4 *Id.* at 248.

disputes between states over interstate pollution. In effect, the Court recognized that a state's sovereign interest in the environmental quality of its territory was as fundamental to its sovereignty as its interest in the boundaries of that territory.

Five years later, the Court was faced again with the dispute between Missouri and Illinois in *Missouri v. Illinois (II)*.[5] Missouri again brought suit against Illinois to restrain the discharge of Chicago's sewage "through an artificial channel into the Des Plaines River, in the state of Illinois."[6] The Des Plaines River empties into the Illinois River—and the Illinois River empties into the Mississippi River about 43 miles north of St. Louis. Missouri alleged that the discharge would pollute the water it relied upon for public supply, agriculture, and manufacturing purposes.[7] Specifically, Missouri asserted that the sewage discharge had caused an outbreak of typhoid fever.[8]

The Court again held that it had authority to exercise its original jurisdiction over the dispute.[9] The *Missouri II* Court established a three-part test to determine whether it should exercise its original jurisdiction over interstate pollution disputes: "Before this court ought to intervene, the case should be [1] of serious magnitude, [2] clearly and fully proved, and [3] the principle to be applied should be one which the court is prepared deliberately to maintain against all considerations on the other side."[10]

While the *Missouri II* Court had jurisdiction, it nevertheless held that there was not sufficient proof that the Chicago River diversion increased pollution in the Mississippi River, nor that it was the cause of the typhoid fever outbreaks.[11] Instead, the evidence was stronger that Missouri's own pollution of the river was the more likely cause of the increased cases of typhoid fever.[12] Thus, the Supreme Court held in favor of Illinois in light of the lack of evidence of causation.

While the *Missouri v. Illinois* cases allowed pollution from the Chicago diversion to continue, Illinois soon faced another set of challenges, led by the Great Lakes states of Wisconsin, Michigan, New York, and Ohio. These states alleged that the Chicago diversion had lowered water levels in Lake Michigan, as well as Lakes Huron,

---

5 Missouri v. Illinois (II), 200 U.S. 496 (1906).

6 *Id.* at 517.

7 *Id.* at 517.

8 *Id.* at 522–523.

9 *Id.* at 519–520.

10 *Id.* at 521.

11 *Id.* at 525.

12 *Id.* at 525.

Erie, and Ontario, by more than six inches, harming navigation and causing serious injury to their citizens and property.[13] Illinois again denied that the diversion caused any actual injury, and the U.S. Supreme Court granted jurisdiction to resolve the dispute.

As the Supreme Court typically does in its original jurisdiction interstate water cases, the Court appointed a Special Master to review the evidence and facts. Because these cases come directly to the Supreme Court, there are no lower court findings of fact for it to rely on. The Special Master in *Wisconsin v. Illinois* found that Chicago's diversion lowered the levels of Lakes Michigan and Huron by six inches and Lakes Erie and Ontario by five inches, causing damage "to navigation and commercial interests, to structures, to the convenience of summer resorts, to fishing and hunting grounds, to public parks and other enterprises, and to riparian property generally."[14] The Supreme Court adopted the Special Master's report, concluding that the reduced lake levels caused the plaintiff states and their citizens and property owners "great losses."[15]

However, while generally supporting these states' claims, the Court also acknowledged the public health problems and economic costs that would arise from immediately halting the entire Chicago diversion. The Court thus referred the matter back to the Special Master for determination of the proper relief. The Special Master's second report recommended a phased reduction in the Chicago diversion, allowing the city time to build adequate sewage treatment. The Court again adopted the Special Master's recommendations to ultimately limit the size of that diversion.

Wisconsin v. Illinois is notable because it blurs the line between equitable apportionment and interstate nuisance. The U.S. Supreme Court did not divide and allocate the waters of the Great Lakes, but it did limit one riparian state's diversion of water to a quantity that would not unreasonably injure the other riparian states. Whether this is a case of equitable apportionment or interstate nuisance is a matter of perspective, and it shows that the doctrines are inherently and fundamentally similar. Regardless of the label, the U.S. Supreme Court in *Wisconsin v. Illinois* effectively applied riparian principles of reasonable use at the interstate level, concluding that Illinois's use of Lake Michigan was unreasonable under the circumstances and needed to be reduced.

---

[13] Wisconsin v. Illinois, 278 U.S. 367, 399–400 (1929).

[14] *Id.* at 407.

[15] *Id.* at 409.

2. Modern Interstate Water Pollution Control

Interstate water pollution disputes like those presented above gave rise to a federal common law of interstate nuisance. However, with passage of the federal Clean Water Act in 1972,[16] the need for federal common law to resolve interstate water pollution disputes came into question. The Supreme Court addressed this very question in *Illinois v. Milwaukee (II)* and held that the 1972 Clean Water Act governs federal law regarding interstate water pollution.[17]

In *Illinois v. Milwaukee (I)*,[18] the Supreme Court had "recognized the existence of a federal 'common law' which could give rise to a claim for abatement of a nuisance caused by interstate water pollution. Subsequent to our decision, Congress enacted the Federal Water Pollution Control Act Amendments of 1972 [now known as the federal Clean Water Act]."[19] The Court granted certiorari in *Milwaukee II* "to consider the effect of this legislation on the previously recognized cause of action."[20] The Clean Water Act "established a new system of regulation under which it is illegal for anyone to discharge pollutants into the Nation's waters except pursuant to a permit."[21]

The petitioners "operated their sewer systems and discharged effluent under permits issued by the Wisconsin Department of Natural Resources (DNR), which had duly qualified under § 402(b) of the Act, as a permit-granting agency under the superintendence of the EPA."[22] However, they did not comply with the requirements of the permits, and therefore the state agency brought an enforcement action in state court. The state court held that the discharges from the sewer systems must conform to the effluent limitations mandated by the permit requirements.

The U.S. Supreme Court on appeal determined that the Clean Water Act displaced the federal common law of nuisance. The Court based its conclusion upon Congress' intent that the Act, rather than federal common law, was to control federal interstate water pollution disputes. *Milwaukee II* thus determined that the Clean Water Act provides the *federal* law for interstate water pollution disputes.

The Supreme Court faced the question of whether the Clean Water Act also displaced state nuisance law in interstate water

---

16 33 U.S.C. §§ 1251–1388. Chapter 11 will discuss this statute in greater detail.

17 Illinois v. Milwaukee (II), 451 U.S. 304 (1981).

18 Illinois v. Milwaukee (I), 406 U.S. 91 (1972).

19 *Milwaukee II*, 451 U.S. at 307.

20 *Id.* at 307–308.

21 *Id.* at 310–311.

22 *Id.* at 311.

pollution disputes in *International Paper Company v. Ouellette*.[23] The *International Paper* Court concluded that Congress had not preempted state tort law—indeed, Congress had explicitly preserved state tort law—when it enacted the Clean Water Act.[24] However, the Court also clarified that the state nuisance law that applies is the law of the source state: If a polluter is not a nuisance under its home state's law, it cannot be considered a nuisance under another state's law.

The *International Paper* Court offered two primary arguments to support this approach. First, the Clean Water Act specifically allows source states to adopt more stringent pollution control requirements through state nuisance law. As a result, the federal courts must respect this congressionally sanctioned state law when resolving interstate disputes, and the source state should be free to decide whether it is most appropriate to exercise that authority via common law or via statutes and regulations. Second, allowing interstate lawsuits based on the plaintiff state's nuisance laws would potentially subject facilities to numerous and at times conflicting state standards. In contrast, suits based on the source's (polluter's) own state law would require facilities to comply only with the federal Clean Water Act and their own states' common and statutory law.

B. Equitable Apportionment

1. The Origins and Principles of Equitable Apportionment

Just as pollution of shared interstate water bodies gave rise to disputes warranting the U.S. Supreme Court's jurisdiction and resolution, the diversion of water out of a shared water body presented the Court with interstate disputes beginning in the early 20th century and continuing into the present. Doctrinally, the interstate disputes over water allocation and diversion are close cousins of interstate water pollution disputes. Both involve the effects of activities in one state (discharging pollutants into or withdrawing water from a stream or lake, respectively) on the use of the water resource in the downstream state. Both involve the competing interests of one state's sovereign control over its economic activities and another state's sovereign interest in the use and integrity of its natural resources. The fundamental issues are thus the same: balancing competing state rights and sovereignty, the role of courts in our federal system, and consideration of complex facts and technical details.

---

23 International Paper Company v. Ouellette, 479 U.S. 481 (1987).

24 *Id.* at 504.

Nevertheless, the Supreme Court faced several additional issues in deciding whether it could—and should—exercise its original jurisdiction in cases involving water allocation disputes between states, and, if so, according to what principles of law. Whereas it was clear from the outset that original jurisdiction cases could address boundary disputes, the Court found it necessary to explain why it also applied to water allocation disputes. Moreover, while the Court could draw on the pre-existing law of public nuisance to address interstate air and water pollution cases, it needed to ply new waters in deciding what principles should apply to interstate water allocation disputes, particularly given differences in state water law. Not surprisingly, that challenge was most difficult in resolving a dispute between one state that (at the time) followed the law of riparian rights and another that pioneered the doctrine of prior appropriation.

The Supreme Court first addressed these interrelated issues in *Kansas v. Colorado*. In that case, Kansas alleged that Colorado diverted water from the Arkansas River that Kansas was entitled to as a riparian state.[25] Colorado, however, did not adhere to riparianism like Kansas used to, but rather already followed the system of prior appropriation for water allocation.[26] Thus, the Supreme Court was called upon to resolve the conflict that arose from the fact that Kansas was entitled to the river's natural flow pursuant to riparianism, while Colorado citizens were entitled to withdraw water under its doctrine prior appropriation.

The Court concluded that although Colorado had reduced the river's flow into Kansas somewhat, the harm to Kansas was greatly outweighed by the benefit to Colorado, which diverted the water for irrigation.[27] Therefore, the Court determined, "it would seem that equality of right and equity between the two states forbids any interference with the present withdrawal of water in Colorado for purposes of irrigation."[28] However, the Court noted that if in the future:

> the depletion of the waters of the river by Colorado continues to increase there will come a time when Kansas may justly say that there is no longer an equitable division of benefits, and may rightfully call for relief against the action of Colorado, its corporations and citizens, in

---

25 Kansas v. Colorado, 206 U.S. 46 (1907).

26 *Id.* at 85.

27 *Id.* at 113–114.

28 *Id.* at 114.

> appropriating the waters of the Arkansas for irrigation purposes.[29]

Thus, the *Kansas v. Colorado* Court indicated that interstate apportionment of shared waterways would be based on overarching equitable principles rather than each state's own water law.

In another early case, *New Jersey v. New York*, New Jersey sought to enjoin the State of New York and New York City from diverting water from the Delaware River and its tributaries.[30] New York sought to divert large quantities of water to increase New York City's water supply.[31] New Jersey alleged a strict application of riparianism and thus claimed it was entitled to an undiminished flow of the river.[32] The Supreme Court recognized, however, that "[b]oth States have real and substantial interests in the River that must be reconciled as best they may."[33]

A Special Master was appointed to the case, who first determined that the proposed diversion would not impede the river's navigability.[34] The Master also concluded that "the taking of 600 millions of gallons daily from the tributaries will not materially affect the River or its sanitary condition, or as a source of municipal water supply, or for industrial uses, or for agriculture, or for the fisheries for shad."[35]

The Master nevertheless also concluded that the diversion could impact the region's oyster fisheries.[36] He explained that this damage could be avoided if: (1) the diversion was reduced to 440 million gallons daily; (2) an efficient sewage treatment plant was constructed to reduce organic impurities in the effluent; and (3) water was released from reservoirs to restore the flow to lower reaches of the River and its tributaries.[37] The Supreme Court concurred with the Master's findings and: (1) granted an injunction to restrain the State of New York and the City of New York from diverting more than 440 million gallons of water daily from the Delaware River and its tributaries; (2) mandated that New York construct a sewage treatment plant before any diversions occurred; and (3) required that if flow fell beneath a specified threshold, water would be released

---

[29] *Id.* at 117.

[30] New Jersey v. New York, 283 U.S. 336 (1931).

[31] *Id.* at 342.

[32] *Id.* at 342.

[33] *Id.* at 342–343.

[34] *Id.* at 344.

[35] *Id.* at 345.

[36] *Id.* at 345.

[37] *Id.* at 345.

from New York City's reservoirs to restore the river's flow.[38] The Court added that "[t]he diversion herein allowed shall not constitute a prior appropriation and shall not give the State of New York and City of New York any superiority of right over the State of New Jersey and Commonwealth of Pennsylvania in the enjoyment and use of the Delaware River and its tributaries."[39]

2. Applying the Equitable Apportionment Doctrine

Over the years, the U.S. Supreme Court's equitable apportionment jurisprudence has been inconsistent. However, as shown in *Colorado v. New Mexico (I)* and more recently in *Florida v. Georgia (II)*, the Court persists in applying a range of equitable factors in deciding interstate water disputes. Arguably, equitable apportionment becomes even more difficult as long-established private uses become increasingly entrenched.

Colorado v. New Mexico (I) involved a dispute between New Mexico and Colorado over the use of the Vermejo River.[40] At the time of the dispute, the Vermejo River was fully appropriated by users in New Mexico; however, Colorado sought to divert water from its portion of the river for future uses.[41] Colorado brought suit for equitable apportionment of the Vermejo River under the Supreme Court's original jurisdiction.[42]

The Special Master appointed to the case stated that strictly following prior appropriation law would preclude any diversions from the river in Colorado because New Mexico users had previously appropriated all of the water supply.[43] However, the Master found that Colorado should be permitted a diversion of 4,000 acre-feet per year as its equitable share of this interstate waterbody.[44] New Mexico appealed this determination and alleged that the rule of prior appropriation should be strictly applied to deny Colorado's request.[45]

The Supreme Court concluded that "the criteria relied upon by the Special Master comport with the doctrine of equitable apportionment as it has evolved in our prior cases" and thus rejected "New Mexico's contention that the Special Master was required to focus exclusively on the rule of priority."[46] In reaching its conclusion,

---

38 *Id.* at 345–346.

39 *Id.* at 347.

40 Colorado v. New Mexico (I), 459 U.S. 176 (1982).

41 *Id.* at 177.

42 *Id.* at 177.

43 *Id.*at 180.

44 *Id.* at 180.

45 *Id.* at 177.

46 *Id.* at 182–183.

the Court reiterated the relevant factors that should be considered in equitably apportioning a river:

> physical and climatic conditions, the consumptive use of water in the several sections of the river, the character and rate of return flows, the extent of established uses, the availability of storage water, the practical effect of wasteful uses on downstream areas, [and] the damage to upstream areas as compared to the benefits to downstream areas if a limitation is imposed on the former.[47]

Moreover, the Court emphasized that, although both Colorado and New Mexico recognize the doctrine of prior appropriation, state law does not control apportionment of interstate waters.[48] Instead, "the just apportionment of interstate waters is a question of federal law that depends upon a consideration of the pertinent laws of the contending States and *all other relevant facts*."[49] The Court stressed that "in the determination of an equitable apportionment of the water of the Vermejo River the rule of priority is not the sole criterion."[50] It remanded the case to the Special Master to clarify the factual findings that supported apportioning 4000 acre-feet per year to Colorado.[51]

Chief Justice Burger and Justice Stevens concurred in the opinion and judgment to "emphasize that under our prior holdings these two states come to the Court on equal footing. Neither is entitled to any special priority over the other with respect to use of the water."[52] Justice O'Connor and Justice Powell also concurred in the judgment. Justice O'Connor's concurrence stressed that the Court should "exercise its original jurisdiction to alter the status quo between States only where there is *clear and convincing evidence* that one State's use is unreasonably wasteful."[53] In addition, Justice O'Connor also made two doctrinal points to guide future application of equitable apportionment in interstate water disputes. First, priority in time is properly considered, and second, the Court should be wary of considering uses not yet established when balancing equities.

Two years after *Colorado v. New Mexico I*, the Supreme Court was confronted again with the question of whether and how to equitably apportion the Vermejo River between Colorado and New

---

[47] Nebraska v. Wyoming, 325 U.S. 589, 618 (1945).

[48] Colorado v. New Mexico (I), 459 U.S. 176 (1982).

[49] *Id.* at 184 (emphasis added).

[50] *Id.* at 188.

[51] *Id.* at 190.

[52] *Id.* at 190.

[53] *Id.* at 195 (emphasis added).

Mexico. The two states went back to the Court with more detailed factual findings, and this time Justice O'Connor issued the opinion for the majority.

The Court had remanded the case to the Master in *Colorado v. New Mexico I* "to make specific findings concerning reasonable conservation measures available to the two States."[54] The Master concluded that "more careful water administration in New Mexico would alleviate shortages in New Mexico caused by Colorado's proposed diversion."[55] The Court disagreed, however, and stated that "we do not believe Colorado has produced sufficient facts to show, by clear and convincing evidence, that reasonable conservation efforts will mitigate sufficiently the injury that New Mexico successfully established last Term that it would suffer were a diversion allowed."[56]

The Court had also requested on remand that the Master analyze and compare the benefits and harms that would likely result from the proposed diversion.[57] The Master found that:

> because the diverted water would, at a minimum, alleviate existing water shortages in Colorado . . . the evidence showed considerable benefits would accrue from the diversion" and "the injury, if any, to New Mexico would be insubstantial, if only because reasonable conservation measures could . . . offset the entire impact of the diversion.[58]

The Court, however, again disagreed with the Master because in the majority's view there was inadequate evidence to approve the proposed diversion. Justice O'Connor explained:

> Colorado has not committed itself to any long-term use for which future benefits can be studied and predicted. Nor has Colorado specified how long the interim agricultural use might or might not last. All Colorado has established is that a steel corporation wants to take water for some unidentified use in the future.[59]

Moreover, "the State seeking . . . a diversion bears the burden of proving, by clear and convincing evidence, the existence of certain relevant factors. . . . This evidentiary burden cannot be met with

---

[54] Colorado v. New Mexico (II), 467 U.S. 310 (1984).

[55] *Id.* at 318.

[56] *Id.* at 321.

[57] *Id.* at 321.

[58] *Id.* at 321.

[59] *Id.* at 321–322.

generalizations about unidentified conservation measures and unstudied speculation about future uses."[60]

Justice Stevens dissented, emphasizing that New Mexico was using the Vermejo River wastefully and inefficiently. According to Justice Stevens, "[t]his fact—which is essentially undisputed—should be 'hard' enough even for the majority, and provides irrefutable support for the conclusion that there was a significant amount of waste in the District when the lawsuit began."[61] The issue of whether water waste is relevant in an equitable apportionment case remains unresolved.

The *Florida v. Georgia* saga provides the Supreme Court's most recent shaping of the equitable apportionment doctrine. The dispute between the states is over the proper apportionment of interstate rivers in the Apalachicola-Chattahoochee-Flint River Basin. In 2013, Florida (downstream) brought an original action against Georgia (upstream) alleging that Georgia consumed more than its fair share of water from the interstate river system.[62] Florida claimed that Georgia's overconsumption of Basin waters caused low flows in the Apalachicola River which seriously harmed Florida's oyster fisheries and river ecosystem. The Court referred the case to a Special Master.

After extensive discovery and a five-week trial, the Special Master in *Florida v. Georgia (I)* issued a report recommending that Florida be denied relief. On review of Florida's exceptions to the Special Master's Report, the Court disagreed with the Special Master's analysis of the threshold question of redressability and remanded for the Special Master to make definitive findings and recommendations on several issues, including: whether Florida had proved any serious injury caused by Georgia; the extent to which reducing Georgia's water consumption would increase Apalachicola River flows; and the extent to which any increased Apalachicola flows would redress Florida's injuries.

Upon remand, the Special Master agreed with Georgia, producing an 81-page report recommending that the Court deny Florida relief. The Special Master concluded that Florida failed to prove by clear and convincing evidence that Georgia's alleged over-consumption caused serious harm either to Florida's oyster fisheries or to its river wildlife and plant life. Florida filed exceptions to the Special Master's Report.[63]

---

[60] *Id.* at 323.

[61] *Id.* at 327–328 (Stevens, J., dissenting).

[62] *See* Florida v. Georgia (I), 585 U.S. 803 (2018).

[63] *See* Florida v. Georgia (II), 592 U.S. 433 (2021).

Writing for a unanimous Court in *Florida v. Georgia (II)*, Justice Barrett overruled Florida's exceptions to the Special Master's Report, and in doing so delivered a definitive statement on the prerequisites to obtaining equitable apportionment:

> Here, Florida must make two showings to obtain an equitable apportionment. First, Florida must prove a threatened or actual injury "of serious magnitude" caused by Georgia's upstream water consumption. Second, Florida must show that "the benefits of the [apportionment] substantially outweigh the harm that might result." [Colorado v. New Mexico, 459 U.S. 176, 187 (1982) (Colorado I)]. Because Florida and Georgia are both riparian States, the "guiding principle" of this analysis is that both States have "an equal right to make a reasonable use" of the Basin waters.[64]

Applying this test, the Court determined that Florida did not show that it was " 'highly probable' that Georgia's alleged overconsumption played more than a trivial role in the collapse of Florida's oyster fisheries."[65] Although the oyster population undoubtedly collapsed in 2012, the actual cause of this collapse was debatable. Georgia, having the more direct argument, claimed that Florida's mismanagement of the oyster fisheries caused the collapse with Florida overharvesting oysters and failing to replace harvested oyster shells. In turn, Florida argued that Georgia's "unreasonable agricultural water consumption caused sustained low flows in the Apalachicola River; that these low flows increased the Bay's salinity; and that higher salinity in the Bay attracted droves of saltwater oyster predators and disease, ultimately decimating the oyster population." Moreover, the Court reasoned, although Florida's evidence was sufficient to establish that increased salinity and predation contributed to the collapse, none of the witnesses or reports produced designated Georgia's overconsumption as a significant cause of the high salinity and predation. As such, the Court concluded, Florida failed to carry its heavy burden.

As a final note, the Court in this case did not need to establish a causation standard to apply in equitable apportionment cases. Because Florida failed to establish a sufficient causal connection under any of the parties' proposed standards, the Court reserved this question for future resolution.

---

64 *Id.* at 438.

65 *Id.* at 443.

3. Equitable Apportionment and Other Aquatic and Freshwater Resources

The Supreme Court has made clear that the equitable apportionment doctrine can resolve other sorts of interstate conflicts over aquatic resources. In 1983, for example, the Court determined in *Idaho* ex rel. *Evans v. Oregon and Washington*[66] that equitable apportionment was the relevant doctrine for apportioning salmon and other anadromous fish among the three Columbia River/Snake River states.[67] Following the Special Master's recommendation, the Court noted that:

> Although [equitable apportionment has its roots in water rights litigation, the natural resource of anadromous fish is sufficiently similar to make equitable apportionment an appropriate mechanism for resolving allocative disputes. The anadromous fish at issue travel through several States during their lifetime. Much as in a water dispute, a State that overfishes a run downstream deprives an upstream State of the fish it otherwise would receive. A dispute over the water flowing through the Columbia-Snake River system would be resolved by the equitable apportionment doctrine; we see no reason to accord different treatment to a controversy over a similar natural resource of that system.[68]

More recently, the Supreme Court declared that equitable apportionment was the proper doctrine to resolve original jurisdiction disputes over groundwater. In *Mississippi v. Tennessee*,[69] the state of Mississippi claimed that the city of Memphis, Tennessee was "stealing" Mississippi's groundwater by pumping the Middle Claiborne Aquifer—an interstate aquifer that eight states share—near the border between the two states.[70] Mississippi sought $615 million in damages, plus injunctive and declaratory relief.[71] Mississippi refused to ask for an equitable apportionment, instead claiming ownership of the water in the aquifer and damages for property conversion,.[72] As a result, the Court dismissed the case,[73]

66 462 U.S. 1017 (1983).

67 *Id.* at 1024.

68 *Id.*

69 595 U.S. 15 (2021).

70 *Id.* at 18.

71 *Id.*

72 *Id.* at 22.

73 *Id.* at 29.

agreeing with the Special Master that equitable apportionment was the governing doctrine.[74] It also articulated why.

"First, we have applied equitable apportionment only when transboundary resources were at issue," and "[t]he Middle Claiborne Aquifer's "multistate character" seems beyond dispute."[75] Second, "the Middle Claiborne Aquifer contains water that flows naturally between the States."[76] Moreover, "although the transboundary flow here may be a mere "one or two inches per day," that amounts to over 35 million gallons of water per day, and over ten billion gallons per year . . . . So the speed of the flow, at least in the context of this case, does not place the aquifer beyond equitable apportionment."[77] Finally, actions in one state could affect the amount (and quality) of water reaching another state.[78] *Mississippi v. Tennessee* thus clearly establishes that equitable apportionment controls interstate groundwater, but because Mississippi did not plead an equitable apportionment case, questions of how the Court would apply the doctrine to groundwater are left for a future dispute.

C. Interstate Compacts

1. Overview of the Compact Clause and Water-Related Interstate Compacts

Interstate compacts are powerful legal tools. A compact is essentially a contract between states, subject to federal legislative approval, whereupon the compact also takes on the status of federal law. The compact mechanism is provided in Article I, Section 10, Clause 3 of the U.S. Constitution, which declares that "[n]o State shall, without the Consent of Congress . . . enter into any Agreement or Compact with another State, or with a foreign Power." While this clause is phrased in the negative, it implies—and long has been held to mean—that states are free to enter into compacts with each other, so long as Congress approves.

Interstate water compacts are usually negotiated by governors and state agency officials, but a participating state can approve a compact only through state legislation. Like a contract, a compact is considered agreed to only when all parties officially sign on to that agreement—specifically, when all of the party states, through their legislatures, approve identical compact terms.

Interstate compacts increase the power of the states at the expense of the federal government. Consequently, as noted, the U.S.

---

[74] *Id.* at 26.

[75] *Id.* at 24.

[76] *Id.* at 25.

[77] *Id.*

[78] *Id.* at 25–26.

Constitution requires that Congress also approve any interstate compact through legislation (signed into law by the President or enacted by Congress over the President's veto). However, once interstate compacts become effective, they have the full force and supremacy of federal law.[79] Thus, parties (and sometimes others) can enforce the terms of a compact in federal court, preventing states from ignoring their compact duties.[80]

There are 27 interstate compacts in force in the United States governing how states allocate and manage shared water resources, plus dozens more interstate compacts that address water quality, navigation, and information exchange and coordination of research.[81] These compacts provide the legal framework for managing and allocating some of the country's most important fresh water resources, including the Great Lakes, the Colorado River, the Rio Grande, the Arkansas River, the Susquehanna River, and the Delaware River. They vary tremendously, however, in how they allocate and manage interstate waters. Some interstate compacts, especially in the West, simply divide the waters by volume among the watershed states. Other interstate compacts, especially in the Great Lakes and East, provide for more comprehensive regulation and management of water uses.

Western water compacts, such as the Colorado River Compact and the Rio Grande Compact, focus on apportioning water from a shared river or lake among the party states. However, while western compacts thus limit the total amount of water that each individual state may take from a shared resource, they usually do not provide any standards or even guidance for managing individual water withdrawals within any particular state's total allocation. They also often do not address increasingly important issues such as how states should adjust their water allocations in response to drought, population growth, or a changing climate.

When eastern states began to develop interstate compacts for water management in the 1960s and 1970s, they took a very different approach. The two major eastern water compacts are the Delaware River Basin Compact and the Susquehanna River Basin Compact. These eastern water compacts create centralized interstate management authorities comprised of the party states and federal government. These authorities, termed compact commissions, have broad regulatory powers for permitting and managing individual

---

[79] *See* Culyer v. Adams, 449 U.S. 433, 438 (1981) (stating that congressional consent "transforms an interstate compact . . . into a law of the United States").

[80] *See* Texas v. New Mexico, 482 U.S. 124, 128 (1987).

[81] For summaries of all existing interstate compacts, *see* Noah D. Hall, *Interstate Water Compacts and Climate Change Adaptation*, 5 ENVTL. & ENERGY L. & POL'Y 237 (2010).

withdrawals or diversions of all waters in the respective river basins. The commissions even set regional standards for discharges of water pollution. This centralized approach has obvious benefits for uniform management of a single resource, but it requires each party state to agree to reduce significantly its individual autonomy in managing shared water resources.

The next three sections take a closer look at three of the largest compacts governing interstate waters in the United States: The Delaware River Basin Compact; the Great Lakes-St. Lawrence River Basin Water Resources Compact; and the Colorado River Compact. Each of these compacts involves a large water system and several states, yet each takes a different approach to water allocation and management.

2. The Delaware River Basin Compact

The Delaware River headwaters are located in upstate New York, and the river empties into the Delaware Bay. In between, the river drains 13,539 square miles of land, including parts of Pennsylvania, New Jersey, New York, and Delaware. Approximately five percent of the United States' population (almost 15 million people) relies on the river for domestic and industrial water supply. This figure includes approximately seven million people who live in New York City and its suburbs, because—although it is outside the basin—the city gets half its water from the Delaware River.

The Delaware River Basin Compact[82] is an agreement among Delaware, Pennsylvania, New Jersey, New York, and the federal government to create a regional agency, the Delaware River Basin Commission, which manages the water resources of the Delaware River Basin. Each party appoints a representative to the Commission, and the Commission is authorized to act only upon the unanimous consent of all five representatives. The Compact confers on the Commission exclusive administrative authority over the Delaware River Basin. Specifically, the Commission is responsible for formulating a comprehensive water management plan for the basin and a water resources program that tracks the quantity and quality needs for water resource use within the basin. The Commission also has limited authority to allocate the waters of the basin among the signatory states and to impose conditions and obligations on the use of such waters. Along with its water management authority, the Commission may conduct and sponsor research on water resources and management and collect, analyze, and report on data related to water use, quality, and protection within the basin. The Compact also

[82] Pub. L. No. 87–328, 75 Stat. 688 (1961).

vests the Commission with the power to develop and administer water plans and projects within the basin.

Figure 9–1: The Delaware River Basin
Map courtesy of the U.S. Geological Survey

The Delaware River Basin Compact creates a rigorous water conservation and ecosystem protection regime. For example, it prohibits water development projects that substantially affect the water resources in the basin unless the Commission finds that a proposed project would "not substantially impair or conflict with the comprehensive plan."[83] Moreover, the Compact allows the Commission to develop water projects to protect "public health, stream quality control, economic development, improvement of fisheries, recreation, dilution and abatement of pollution, [and] the prevention of undue salinity."[84] The Commission can also sponsor any soil conservation, forestry, or fish and wildlife project that is related to the basin's water resources. Indeed, through the Compact, each of the signatory state agrees to enact legislation necessary to protect the utility and quality of the basin's water and ecosystem. As for enforcement, the Compact vests the Commission with the authority initiate legal action against any entity that violates the Compact's provisions.

The Commission can also control and regulate withdrawals and diversions from the basin's surface waters and groundwater. Specifically, the Commission can issue withdrawal permits to prescribe the amount of water that a user can withdraw within the

[83] Pub. L. No. 87–328, § 3.8, 75 Stat. 688 (1961).

[84] Pub. L. No. 87–328, § 4.2(a), 75 Stat. 688 (1961).

basin's protected areas. The compact allows for interbasin diversions, but only when the Commission authorizes them.

3. The Great Lakes-St. Lawrence River Basin Water Resources Compact

The Great Lakes are the largest surface fresh water system on the Earth. They contain almost 90% of North America's surface fresh water and over 20% of the world's supply. Their watershed drains almost 200,000 square miles. The United States' portion of the Great Lakes shoreline is over 4,500 miles long, longer than the United States' East and Gulf coasts combined. The Great Lakes-St. Lawrence watershed contains the cities of Chicago, Detroit, Milwaukee, Toronto, Buffalo, and Cleveland.

The Great Lakes-St. Lawrence River Basin Water Resources Compact[85] provides a comprehensive water management regime for the eight Great Lakes states: Illinois, Indiana, Michigan, Minnesota, Ohio, New York, Pennsylvania, and Wisconsin. The Canadian provinces of Ontario and Quebec are parties to a companion non-binding agreement, the Great Lakes-St. Lawrence River Basin Sustainable Water Resources Agreement. (The Boundary Waters Treaty of 1909 between the United States and Canada, discussed in Chapter 8, also applies to the waters of the Great Lakes.) The Compact's hydrologic scope is broad: The Great Lakes Compact specifically defines the "waters of the Great Lakes" to include all tributary surface waters and groundwater.[86]

The Great Lakes-St. Lawrence River Basin Water Resources Compact represents a new model for interstate water management compacts. It does not allocate specific quantities of water, nor does it give its compact commission allocation powers. Instead, it requires the party states to manage their water withdrawals according to common minimum standards for water conservation and sustainable use. It also prohibits most diversions of water out of the Great Lakes Basin to protect the total water supply. The Great Lakes compact creates a compact commission that evaluates very large consumptive uses and the few exceptions to the general prohibition on diversions. The compact commission also conducts research, collects data, and supports the water management work of the states.

---

85 Pub. L. No. 110–342, 122 Stat. 3739 (2008).

86 Section 1.2 of Pub. L. No. 110–342, 122 Stat. 3739 (2008).

Figure 9–2: The Great Lakes Watershed
Map courtesy of the Ohio Department of Natural Resources

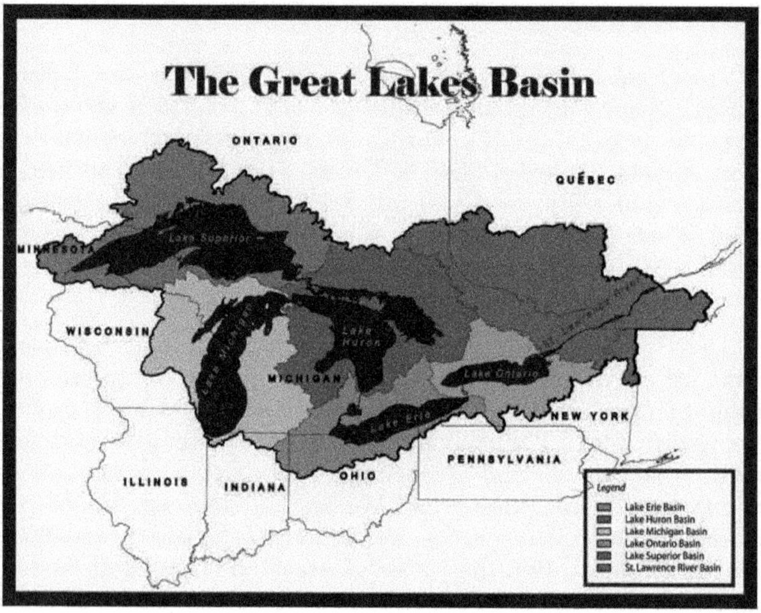

More specifically, under the Compact, withdrawals of Great Lakes water are managed pursuant to a "decision-making standard,"[87] which the individual states are primarily responsible for implementing. The decision-making standard requires that all entities withdrawing water from the system engage in water conservation, keep return flows within the watershed, prevent significant environmental impacts, and comply with riparian reasonable use principles. Further, while the standard applies only to new or increased water withdrawals in the basin, the Compact makes clear that the decision-making standard is only a minimum standard, and states may impose more restrictive standards for water withdrawals under their individual authorities.

The Compact creates two separate approaches to managing new or increased water withdrawals in the Great Lakes Basin. The differentiation is based almost entirely on whether the water is used inside or outside of the Great Lakes Basin surface watershed boundary. Water use inside of the Great Lakes Basin is managed solely by the individual states, with limited advisory input from other states for very large consumptive uses. Water withdrawals diverted

[87] Section 4.11 of Pub. L. No. 110–342, 122 Stat. 3739 (2008).

and used outside of the basin are subject to a spectrum of collective rules and approval processes, including a general prohibition on most interbasin diversions. The primary cause of interbasin diversions is the City of Chicago and it suburbs, which—despite the City's location on Lake Michigan—occupy much land that is outside the very narrow band of Great Lakes watershed to the south of the lakes (see Figure 9–2).

The Compact establishes a Council comprised of the governors of each party state (or their designated alternates). One of the most significant functions of the Council is its sole authority to approve the limited exceptions to the general prohibition on interbasin diversions. The Council can also promulgate and enforce rules to implement its duties under the Great Lakes Compact. Further, the Council has broad authority to plan, conduct research, prepare reports on water use, conduct special investigations, and forecast water levels.[88]

4. The Colorado River Compact

The law governing interstate allocation and management of the Colorado River is phenomenally complex, referred to affectionately by water law practitioners in the region as the "Law of the River." This body of "law" is comprised of a complex assembly of statutes, treaties, regulations, cases, contracts, administrative orders, and other legal documents, which the Bureau of Reclamation has recently assembled into DVD form.[89] At the heart of this body of law, however, is the Colorado River Compact, perhaps the most "famous" of all interstate water compacts.[90]

The U.S. Supreme Court in *Arizona v. California* provided background about the Colorado River and its watershed, which explains how the Colorado River Compact came about:

> The Colorado River itself rises in the mountains of Colorado and flows generally in a southwesterly direction for about 1,300 miles through Colorado, Utah, and Arizona and along the Arizona-Nevada and Arizona-California boundaries, after which it passes into Mexico and empties into the Mexican waters of the Gulf of California. On its way to the sea it receives tributary waters from Wyoming, Colorado,

---

[88] For a complete analysis of the Great Lakes Compact, *see* Noah D. Hall, *Toward a New Horizontal Federalism: Interstate Water Management in the Great Lakes Region*, 77 U. COLO. L. REV. 405 (2006).

[89] U.S. Bureau of Reclamation, *The Colorado River Documents 2008* (Sept. 2010).

[90] A more complete history of the Colorado River Compact can be found in numerous sources, including NORRIS HUNDLEY, JR., WATER AND THE WEST: THE COLORADO RIVER COMPACT AND THE POLITICS OF WATER IN THE AMERICAN WEST (2d ed. 2009).

Utah, Nevada, New Mexico, and Arizona. The river and its tributaries flow in a natural basin almost surrounded by large mountain ranges and drain 242,000 square miles, an area about 900 miles long from north to south and 300 to 500 miles wide from east to west. . . . Much of this large basin is so arid that it is, as it always has been, largely dependent upon managed use of the waters of the Colorado River System to make it productive and inhabitable. . . .

Figure 9–3: The Colorado River Basin
Map courtesy of the U.S. Bureau of Reclamation

The natural flow of the Colorado was too erratic, the river at many places in canyons too deep, and the engineering and economic hurdles too great for small farmers, larger groups, or even States to build storage dams, construct canals, and install the expensive works necessary for a dependable year-round water supply. . . .

> It is not surprising that the pressing necessity to transform the erratic and often destructive flow of the Colorado River into a controlled and dependable water supply desperately needed in so many States began to be talked about and recognized as far more than a purely local problem which could be solved on a farmer-by-farmer, group-by-group, or even state-by-state basis, desirable as this kind of solution might have been. . . . Congress passed a bill . . . directing the Secretary of the Interior to make a study and report of diversions which might be made from the Colorado River for irrigation in the Imperial Valley. The Fall-Davis Report . . . began by declaring, "[T]he control of the floods and development of the resources of the Colorado River are peculiarly national problems" and then went on to give reasons why this was so, concluding with the statement that the job was so big that only the Federal Government could do it. Quite naturally, therefore, the Report recommended that the United States construct as a government project not only an all-American canal from the Colorado River to the Imperial Valley but also a dam and reservoir at or near Boulder Canyon.
>
> The prospect that the United States would undertake to build as a national project the necessary works to control floods and store river waters for irrigation was apparently a welcome one for the basin States. But it brought to life strong fears in the northern basin States that additional waters made available by the storage and canal projects might be gobbled up in perpetuity by faster growing lower basin areas, particularly California, before the upper States could appropriate what they believed to be their fair share. . . . Hoping to prevent "conflicts" and "expensive litigation" which would hold up or prevent the tremendous benefits expected from extensive federal development of the river, the basin States requested and Congress passed an Act on August 19, 1921, giving the States consent to negotiate and enter into a compact for the "equitable division and apportionment of the water supply of the Colorado River." Pursuant to this congressional authority, the seven States appointed Commissioners who, after negotiating for the better part of a year, reached an agreement at Santa Fe, New Mexico, on November 24, 1922.[91]

And so the Colorado River Compact came into being.

---

[91] Arizona v. California, 373 U.S. 546 (1963).

Article I of the Colorado River Compact states:

> The major purposes of this compact are to provide for the equitable division and apportionment of the use of the waters of the Colorado River System; to establish the relative importance of different beneficial uses of water; to promote interstate comity; to remove causes of present and future controversies; and to secure the expeditious agricultural and industrial development of the Colorado River Basin, the storage of its waters and the protection of life and property from floods. To these ends the Colorado River Basin is divided into two basins, and an apportionment of the use of part of the water of the Colorado River System is made to each of them with the provision that further equitable apportionment may be made.[92]

Article II defines several terms, including two separate but related distinctions between the Upper Basin and Lower Basin within the larger Colorado River Basin, and between the Upper Division and the Lower Division states within the basin. The "Upper Basin" means "those parts of the States of Arizona, Colorado, New Mexico, Utah, and Wyoming within and from which waters naturally drain into the Colorado River System above Lee Ferry."[93] The "Lower Basin" means "those parts of the States of Arizona, California, Nevada, New Mexico and Utah within and from which waters naturally drain into the Colorado River System below Lee Ferry."[94] The "States of the Upper Division" are Colorado, New Mexico, Utah, and Wyoming; while the "States of the Lower Division" are Arizona, California, and Nevada.[95] The distinctions make sense because some states have land within both the Upper Basin and the Lower Basin, but for purposes of Compact governance each state is assigned to the Division in which it has the most land.

Article III of the Compact apportions 7,500,000 acre-feet of water per year for beneficial consumptive use to each of the Upper and Lower Basins of the River.[96] Article III also states that the Lower Basin states have the right to increase beneficial consumptive uses of the River by 1 million acre-feet annually.[97] Article III specifically provides that the Upper Division states shall not withhold water, and the Lower Division states "shall not require the delivery of water,

---

[92] Colorado River Compact, art. I.

[93] *Id.* art. II(f).

[94] *Id.* art. II(g).

[95] *Id.* art. II(c), (d).

[96] *Id.* art. III(a).

[97] *Id.* art. III(b).

which cannot reasonably be applied to domestic and agricultural uses."[98] Furthermore, the Compact prohibits the Upper Division states from causing the flow of the river to be depleted below 75 million acre-feet on a ten-year rolling average.[99] Thus, the Compact puts the onus on the Upper Division states to ensure that enough water is available to meet the Lower Division states' Compact rights wherever possible, arguably placing the greater risk of shortage on the Upper Division. However, this is a vast oversimplification of a much more complex system of statutes, regulations, and operating agreements for the major dams and diversion structures in the Colorado River Basin that, thus far, have avoided a major "compact call" requiring any of the Colorado River states to lose significant portions of their Compact apportionments. It remains an open question whether that lack of conflict will continue if climate change causes more significant shortages in the region.

Table 9–1: Allocations of Colorado River Water to the Upper Division States Under the Upper Basin Compact

COLORADO	51.75%
NEW MEXICO	11.25%
UTAH	23.00%
WYOMING	14.00%
TOTAL	**100.00%**

In addition to the Colorado River Compact, the Upper Division states entered into a separate compact known as the Upper Basin Compact. The Upper Basin Compact apportions water by percentage rather than by amount,[100] as shown in Table 9–1. This percentage approach to water allocation makes it relatively easy for the Upper Division states to adjust to changing water supplies. In particular, in times of continuing drought, the states essentially share any water supply shortage, much as would occur under riparianism principles. As such, the Upper Basin Compact also reflects the equitable approach to allocation of interstate waters that the U.S. Supreme Court has insisted upon in its equitable apportionment cases.

D. Congressional Apportionment of Water

Before the U.S. Supreme Court will engage in an equitable apportionment, it first asks whether Congress has enacted

---

[98] *Id.* art. III(e).

[99] *Id.* art. III(d).

[100] Upper Colorado River Basin Compact, Art. III(a)(2).

legislation to apportion waters among states, because any judicial authority to decide an allocation by reference to "interstate common law" exists only in the absence of such legislation, whether a federal statute or an interstate compact. We've discussed the constitutional authority for interstate compacts in the previous section, but Congress also has independent authority under the Commerce Clause to adopt such allocation rules with respect to navigable interstate waterways (see Chapter 6).

In practice, however, Congress has declined to exercise this authority, deferring instead to states to attempt to resolve disputes themselves by compact. Moreover, in the absence of any compact, the Supreme Court resolves interstate water disputes using equitable apportionment.

To this day, the most significant—but still hotly disputed—example of congressional apportionment occurred through Section 4 the Boulder Canyon Project Act,[101] the statute in which Congress authorized construction of the Boulder Canyon (later renamed Hoover) Dam and approved the Colorado River Compact subject to its ratification by at least six of the seven Colorado River Basin states, so long as California was one of them. As discussed above, the Upper Basin States (Colorado, New Mexico, Utah, Wyoming, and a small portion of Arizona) negotiated a separate apportionment of the Upper Basin by interstate compact. However, the Lower Basin states (California, Arizona and Nevada, plus small portions of Utah and New Mexico) were never able to successfully negotiate their own allocations of Colorado River water, largely because of ongoing disputes between California and Arizona.

Section 4 of the Boulder Canyon Project Act provides:

> The States of Arizona, California, and Nevada are authorized to enter into an agreement which shall provide (1) that of the 7,500,000 acre-feet annually apportioned to the lower basin by paragraph (a) of Article III of the Colorado River compact, there shall be apportioned to the State of Nevada 300,000 acre-feet and to the State of Arizona 2,800,000 acre-feet for exclusive beneficial consumptive use in perpetuity, and (2) that the State of Arizona may annually use one-half of the excess or surplus waters unapportioned by the Colorado River compact, and (3) that the State of Arizona shall have the exclusive beneficial consumptive use of the Gila River and its tributaries within the boundaries of said State, and (4) that the waters of the Gila River and its tributaries, except return flow after the same enters the Colorado River, shall

[101] Act of Dec. 21, 1928, c. 42, 45 Stat. 1058,

> never be subject to any diminution whatever by any allowance of water which may be made by treaty or otherwise to the United States of Mexico but if, as provided in paragraph (c) of Article III of the Colorado River compact, it shall become necessary to supply water to the United States of Mexico from waters over and above the quantities which are surplus as defined by said compact, then the State of California shall and will mutually agree with the State of Arizona to supply out of the main stream of the Colorado River, one-half of any deficiency which must be supplied to Mexico by the lower basin, and (5) that the State of California shall and will further mutually agree with the States of Arizona and Nevada that none of said three States shall withhold water and none shall require the delivery of water, which cannot reasonably be applied to domestic and agricultural uses, and (6) that all of the provisions of said tri-State agreement shall be subject in all particulars to the provisions of the Colorado River compact and (7) said agreement to take effect upon the ratification of the Colorado River compact by Arizona, California, and Nevada.[102]

On its face, Section 4 does not appear to be a congressional allocation of the 7.5 million acre-feet of Colorado River water that the Lower Basin states share each year. Instead, it reads more naturally as congressional pre-approval of a Lower Basin Compact that meets the terms of Section 4. Nevertheless, in *Arizona v. California*, the U.S. Supreme Court deemed Section 4 to be a congressional apportionment of the Lower Basin's water, concluding that:

> Congress in passing the Project Act intended to and did create its own comprehensive scheme for the apportionment among California, Arizona, and Nevada of the Lower Basin's share of the mainstream waters of the Colorado River, leaving each State its tributaries. Congress decided that a fair division of the first 7,500,000 acre-feet of such mainstream waters would give 4,400,000 acre-feet to California, 2,800,000 to Arizona, and 300,000 to Nevada; Arizona and California would each get one-half of any surplus. . . . Division of the water did not, however, depend on the States' agreeing to a compact, for Congress gave the Secretary of the Interior adequate authority to accomplish the division. Congress did this by giving the Secretary power to make contracts for the delivery of water and by

[102] Boulder Canyon Project Act, § 4, 43 U.S.C. § 617c(a).

> providing that no person could have water without a contract.[103]

Moreover, because Congress had made a statutory apportionment through the Boulder Canyon Project Act, neither equitable apportionment nor the Colorado River Compact applied to the apportionment of water among the Lower Division states.[104] The *Arizona v. California* Court concluded that "[t]he legislative history, the language of the Act, and the scheme established by the Act for the storage and delivery of water convince us . . . that Congress intended to provide its own method for a complete apportionment of the mainstream water among Arizona, California, and Nevada."[105]

Justices Harlan, Douglas, and Stewart dissented in part, objecting primarily to the amount of discretion that the majority's decision gave to the Secretary of the Interior,[106] which, they asserted, was constitutionally infirm.[107] In the dissenters' opinion, "it is the equitable principles established by the Court in interstate water-rights cases, as modified by the Colorado River Compact and the California limitation, that were intended by Congress to govern the apportionment of mainstream waters among the Lower Basin States, whether in surplus or in shortage."[108]

Nevertheless, the majority's decision means that Section 4's "allocation" among the Lower Division states has become part of the "Law of the River." Importantly, this Lower Basin allocation, unlike the Upper Basin allocation, apportions Colorado River water in terms of absolute amounts—4.4 million acre-feet per year to California, 2.8 million acre-feet to Arizona, and 300,000 acre-feet to Nevada—creating a substantial potential for conflict when drought reduces the total supply of the Colorado River. As part of the complex state and federal negotiations that finally authorized the Central Arizona Project—a long water transportation system that allows Phoenix, Tucson, Arizona Tribes, and other communities to actually use Arizona's allocation of the river—Arizona agreed to subordinate its claims to Colorado River water to California's, and in prior appropriation terms. As a result, in times of shortage, California is entitled to *all* of its Colorado River water before Arizona is entitled to *any*.

---

103 Arizona v. California, 373 U.S. 546 (1963).

104 *Id.* at 560.

105 *Id.* at 575.

106 *Id.* at 603 (Harlan, J., dissenting).

107 *Id.* at 603 (Harlan, J., dissenting).

108 *Id.* at 603 (Harlan, J., dissenting).

Chapter 10

THE WATER-ENERGY NEXUS

A. Introduction

So far in this book, we have explored water law and policy largely as if water use exists in a vacuum, independent of other considerations. The rest of the book will look at how the use of water through water law intersects with various other societal concerns—energy, water quality, species, and environmental regulation more generally.

Figure 10–1: Water and Energy Connections in the United States
Diagram courtesy of the U.S. Department of Energy

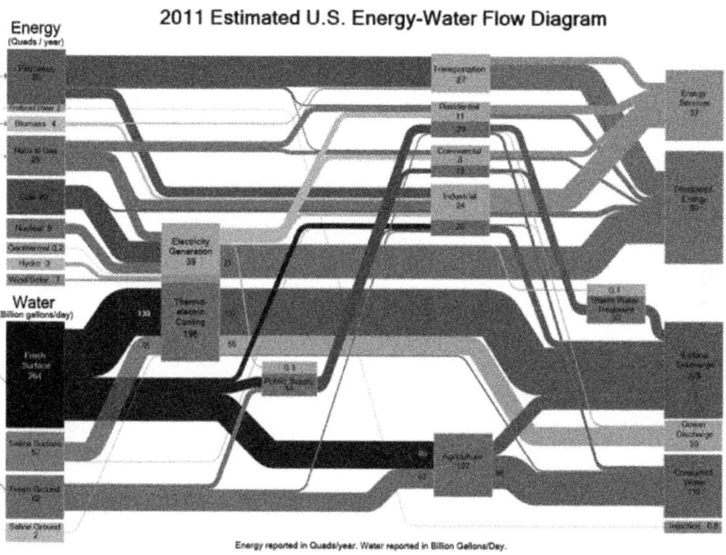

This chapter looks at the intersections between water and energy. Energy production in the United States demands a large amount of water, both in terms of primary production—the mining of coal and nuclear materials, the extraction of oil and gas, including from hydraulic fracturing ("fracking")—and in terms of converting those fuels to electricity. At the same time, it takes a lot of energy to divert, pump, treat, and distribute water. Thus, water and energy production are inextricably linked, and a shortage or problem on one side will usually cause a problem on the other. Figure 10–1 presents the U.S. Department of Energy's rather detailed illustration of these complexities, the main point being that water and energy use intersect in myriad important ways.

Paradoxically, water law and energy law have traditionally operated completely independently of each other, even at the state level. The result has been increasing conflicts between state water law and state and federal energy policies and between state water law and particular energy projects. These conflicts are likely to multiply in the future as climate change increasingly affects water supply, water demand, energy production, and energy demand.

Two important issues are emerging at the nexus of water law and energy policy: (1) how to balance water demand in the energy sector with water demand for other purposes, including recreational and ecological purposes; and (2) how to ensure sufficient energy supply to support existing and future water uses. This chapter will explore these issues through a variety of lenses. We'll first look at water use in the production of energy, which is the side of the nexus where water law is most relevant. This discussion begins by examining the basic facts about water use in energy production, particularly thermoelectric power generation, before taking a closer look at the law governing hydropower facilities. The second part of this chapter will focus on the energy demands in water use, again presenting some basic facts before looking at a particular case study of desalination for water supply. Finally, we'll look at how climate change is altering the water-energy nexus, raising new concerns for the future.

B. Water Use in the Production of Energy

Few people realize just how much water is required for energy production. A few examples are obvious: Hydropower production, for example, clearly depends on adequate water flow in rivers to generate electricity. Other examples may not be quite so obvious, such as the considerable water requirements of thermoelectric power plants—that is, power plants that rely on heat and steam to generate electricity, whether the fuel is coal, gas, or nuclear. Even forms of energy production that seem to be water-free, such as wind power and some forms of solar energy, still come with significant water demands in the manufacturing phases—an important consideration in comparing policy choices, often incorporated into what is termed a *life-cycle analysis*. Thus, for example, the production of ethanol fuel from crops like sugarcane and corn can consume significant amounts of water compared to production of conventional natural gas.

Figure 10–2: Water Withdrawals in the United States, 2015. Withdrawals for thermoelectric power generation constitute 41% of all water withdrawals in the U.S.

Graph courtesy of the U.S. Geological Survey

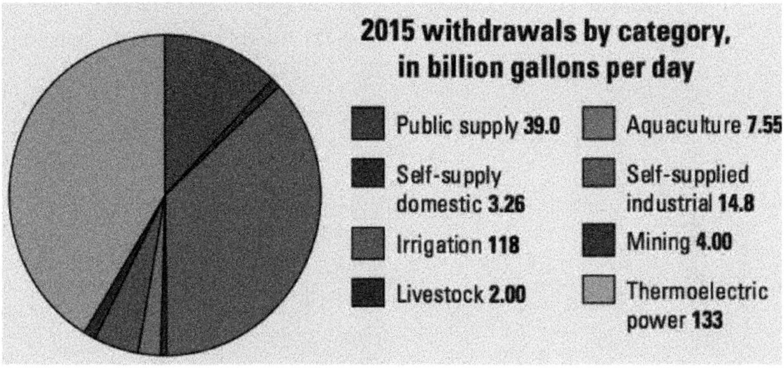

Ninety percent of the electricity generated in the United States comes from thermoelectric power plants, and thermoelectric power generation requires the largest withdrawals of water of any sector in the United States. The U.S. Geological Survey keeps track of overall U.S. water use, and it issued is latest report in 2018, based on water use in 2015. As Figure 10–2 shows, thermoelectric power generation represented 41% of water withdrawals in the U.S. in 2015—that is, almost half the water withdrawals in this country.[1] (Remember that water withdrawal is different from consumptive water use, because for power plants and many other water sectors, a percentage of the water withdrawn is later returned to the source.) In comparison, agricultural irrigation accounted for only 37% of the withdrawals (although agriculture is still the largest *consumer* of water in the United States), public water supply for 12%, and domestic use for only 1%.[2] More specifically, thermoelectric power plants withdrew 133 billion gallons per day in 2015, 72% of which came from fresh water sources.[3] However, because 28% of the water used to cool power plants is saline (think coastal power plants), thermoelectric power accounted for only 34% of the nation's total *freshwater* withdrawals,

---

[1] U.S. GEOLOGICAL SURVEY, ESTIMATED USE OF WATER IN THE UNITED STATES IN 2015, at 8 fig. 1 (2018).

[2] *Id.*

[3] *Id.* at 1.

while irrigation accounted for 42% of freshwater withdrawals.[4] Figure 10–3 shows how these withdrawals were distributed across the United States. The light states in most of the West reflect the facts both that much of the West is sparsely settled *and* that many western states depend heavily on hydropower for their electricity.

Figure 10–3: Total Water Withdrawals for Thermoelectric Power in 2015 by State
Map courtesy of the U.S. Geological Survey

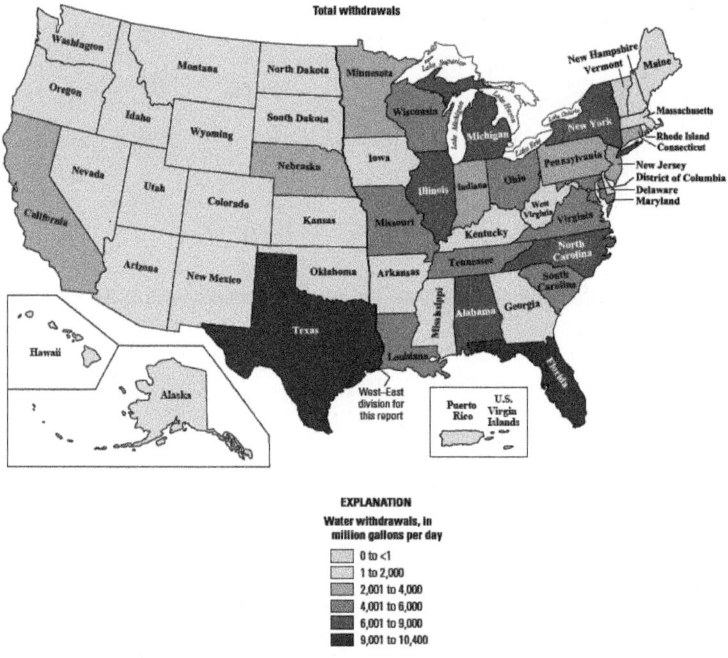

So why do thermoelectric power plants need all that water? As the Union of Concerned Scientists explains:

> Thermoelectric power plants boil water to create steam, which then spins turbines to generate electricity. The heat used to boil water can come from burning of a fuel, from nuclear reactions, or directly from the sun or geothermal heat sources underground. Once steam has passed through a turbine, it must be cooled back into water before it can be reused to produce more electricity. Colder water cools the

[4] *Id.*

steam more effectively and allows more efficient electricity generation.[5]

Power plant cooling water use raises several issues for law and policy. Power plants can vary considerably both in the amount of water that they need to withdraw on a daily basis *and* in the amount of water that they consume—*i.e.*, remove from the system entirely. The variations depend primarily on two factors: the type of fuel that the power plant uses; and the type of cooling technology that it uses.

The two basic types of water-based cooling systems are *once-through cooling* and *closed-loop cooling*. Once-though cooling systems typically withdraw large amounts of water, run that water through the power plant once to cool the system, and then discharge a lot of hot water back into the river or lake or ocean (and both those discharges and the initial withdrawals are regulated under the Clean Water Act, which Chapter 11 will discuss). As such, once-though cooling systems tend to withdraw large amounts of water but consume relatively little. About 43% of thermoelectric power plants in the United States use once-through cooling. In contrast, wet-recirculating or closed-loop cooling systems recycle their cooling water. As a result, overall withdrawals are usually lower than in once-through systems, but closed-loop systems consume most of the water that they withdraw. About 56% of thermoelectric power plants in the U.S. use closed-loop cooling systems. Some kinds of power plants in some parts of the country can also use *air or dry cooling systems*, which use almost no water, but these systems are not very efficient in hot or humid locations. They also cannot be used for nuclear power plants, nor do they work well at coal-fired power plants. As a result, less than 2% of thermoelectric power plants in the United States use dry cooling.

Table 10–1 summarizes the water used in various kinds of electricity generation. As this Table suggests, the type of fuel being used to generate electricity is the most important factor governing the power plant's use of water, but the type of cooling technology can significantly influence how much water will be consumed at that plant. These figures do not include the water required to produce the fuel in the first place, but that water cost is also important. Miners generally use between 800 and 3000 gallons of water to extract, process, and dispose of one ton of coal, but conventional natural gas extraction generally pulls significant quantities of groundwater to the surface ("produced water"), while hydraulic fracturing for natural gas both requires and produces water.

---

[5] *How It Works: Water for Power Plant Cooling*, UNION OF CONCERNED SCIENTISTS (updated July 15, 2015), https://www.ucsusa.org/resources/water-power-plant-cooling.

Table 10–1: Water Withdrawal and Consumption for Various Types of Thermoelectric Power Plants

FUEL AND PROCESS USED	COOLING SYSTEM USED	WATER WITHDRAWAL (gallons per megawatt-hour)	WATER CONSUMPTION (gallons per megawatt-hour)
Natural gas, steam turbine	Dry cooling	0–4	0–4
Natural gas, steam turbine	Once-through cooling	10,000–60,000	95–291
Natural gas, steam turbine	Closed-loop cooling	950–1450	662–1170
Natural gas or oil, combined cycle	Dry cooling	0–4	0–4
Natural gas or oil, combined cycle	Once-through cooling	7500–20,000	20–100
Natural gas or oil, combined cycle	Wet closed-loop cooling	150–2500	130–300
Natural gas, combustion turbine	ANY	0	0
Coal or petroleum residuum fueled combined cycle	Wet closed-loop cooling	~3500	~200
Coal (conventional)	Once-through cooling	20,000–51,000	100–350
Coal (conventional)	Closed-loop cooling	500–1200	480–1,100
Nuclear	Once-though cooling	25,000–61,000	100–400

Nuclear	Wet closed-loop cooling	800–12,000	400–740
Nuclear	Wet closed-loop cooling (tower)	800–2600	600–800

Of course, water use is not the only factor that policymakers consider when making decisions about generating electricity—the price and availability of the fuel are always important considerations, as are public perceptions of risk (particularly with regard to nuclear power plants). Greenhouse gas emissions, climate change impacts, and renewable portfolio standards are also increasingly important considerations, and hence we need to compare water use in traditional thermoelectric generation to water use in renewable energy sources of electricity. Table 10–2 summarizes the water use requirements of various renewable energy options for generating electricity. Again, these figures do not include the water required to produce the energy technology. Manufacturing photovoltaic cells, for example, requires significant amounts of water, as well as toxic materials.

Table 10–2: Water Use in Renewable Energy Electricity Generation

ENERGY SOURCE	**COOLING SYSTEM USED**	**WATER WITHDRAWAL (gallons per megawatt-hour)**	**WATER CONSUMPTION (gallons per megawatt-hour)**
Wind turbine	N/A	<50	0–1
Solar thermal	Dry cooling	43–79	26–79
Solar thermal	Wet cooling	725–1400	725–1400
Solar photovoltaic		~200	26–30
Geothermal, binary	Dry cooling	<25	0–1
Geothermal, binary	Hybrid cooling	~700	200
Geothermal, binary	Wet cooling	~500	~1700–4000

Biomass or waste	Once-through cooling	20,000–51,000	~300–480
Biomass or waste	Wet closed-loop cooling (pond)	~5500	~300–490
Biomass or waste	Wet closed-loop cooling (tower)	~5500	~500
Hydropower	N/A	~4500	Almost none for run-of-the river dams; significant losses to evaporation in large reservoirs

Tables 10–1 and 10–2 reveal that most forms of electricity generation—conventional or renewable—will need water rights. Thermoelectric power plants and most forms of renewable energy facilities get their water through the standard water rights law and processes of the states in which they sit. Because most of the water withdrawals for power plants come from surface water, this fact means that power plants in the East generally rely on riparian rights or regulated riparianism permits for their water rights, while power plants in the West obtain water rights through prior appropriation permits or, in Colorado, water court decrees.

However, in most states, the processes governing approval of power plants and their rate charges are independent of the processes for obtaining water rights. Indeed, almost always, different state agencies perform these two functions, and state laws generally do not require any coordination between these two kinds of regulatory activities. As a result, in most states, there is little to no coordination between energy policy and needs and water rights, use, and availability. One result, as the U.S. Department of Energy recognized in 2014, is considerable variation in how the water-electricity nexus plays out within individual states:

> Water is inherently a multi-jurisdictional management issue and is primarily a state and local responsibility. States and localities vary in philosophies regarding water rights. There is also variation across states in relevant energy policies, including renewable portfolio standards, regulation of oil and gas development activities, and regulation of thermoelectric water intake and discharge. Regulations for both oil and gas development and

> thermoelectric water use are currently undergoing substantial change. Energy for water is also the subject of policy activity at multiple scales, from appliance standards to municipal water treatment funding mechanisms. A more integrated approach to the interconnected energy and water challenges could stimulate the development and deployment of solutions that address objectives in both domains.[6]

Nevertheless, the Department also emphasized the important role that state water permitting can play in blocking new power plants or in shaping how those power plants operate:

> In states where a centralized agency looks at water use by power plants, plants might have permits denied due to a lack of sufficient water resources or the impact the plant might have on other water users in the area. The increased scrutiny allows the governing body to evaluate the effect on all water users in the network rather than one plant's needs.
>
> States in water-stressed areas such as Texas and the Southwest have more stringent water requirements for power generators. In Texas, the state's independent system operator, the Electric Reliability Council of Texas (ERCOT), has begun requiring new generators to provide proof of water rights before the council will include them in their grid planning. Plants cannot connect to the electricity transmission network if they are not included in grid planning.
>
> In Arizona, the state permitting authority reviews environmental concerns when certifying proposed plants. The authority has denied at least one power plant its Certificate of Environmental Compatibility due to the potential for groundwater depletion and the loss of habitat for an endangered species.
>
> In California, the California Energy Commission (CEC), the organization in charge of energy policy and planning, requires power plant developers to consider zero-liquid discharge technologies, such as dry cooling, unless the use of those technologies would be "environmentally undesirable or economically unsound". The agency also reviews permit applicants with regard to water needs and impacts. CEC staff members evaluate how the proposed

---

6 U.S. DEPARTMENT OF ENERGY, THE WATER-ENERGY NEXUS: CHALLENGES AND OPPORTUNITIES viii (June 2014).

> water use might affect other users in the area and the effect to the overall water supply in the state. CEC coordinates with other agencies, including the State Water Resources Control Board, and ensures that power plant developers have considered the viability of alternative cooling technologies and water sources and addressed the implications of wastewater disposal and any effect on water supply and water quality in the state.[7]

Thus, the U.S. Department of Energy is well aware of the role of state water law in national energy policy, and it is actively looking for ways to improve the relationship between the two.

C. Regulating Hydropower Production

The relationship between state water law and federal energy policy is a particularly important legal issue in hydropower production. Most electricity-producing facilities are regulated by the states, but there are two exceptions to this general rule. First, the Nuclear Regulatory Commission licenses nuclear power plants pursuant to the Atomic Energy Act of 1954.[8] Second, and most relevant to this chapter, the Federal Energy Regulatory Commission (FERC) licenses hydroelectric facilities in navigable waters pursuant to the Federal Power Act.[9]

Hydropower accounts for about 6–7% of the electricity generation in the United States, mostly in the Pacific Northwest and parts of the Southeast. The top ten hydropower generating states are, in decreasing order: Washington; Oregon; New York; California; Alabama; Tennessee; Montana; Idaho; North Carolina; and Arizona. Hydropower is by far the largest component of electricity produced by renewable resources (48%). Hydropower is also a fairly old source of electricity in the United States; the first hydroelectric power plant in the country opened on the Fox River near Appleton, Wisconsin, on September 30, 1882.

The Federal Power Act originally vested hydropower licensing authority in the Federal Power Commission,[10] which Congress later transformed into FERC. The Act gives FERC two main types of hydropower licensing authority. First, FERC has exclusive authority to license *all* hydropower facilities on federal public lands, including Indian reservations.[11] Second, FERC has the authority:

---

7 *Id.* at 74 (citations omitted).

8 42 U.S.C. §§ 2011–2297h–13.

9 16 U.S.C. §§ 791–828(c).

10 16 U.S.C. § 792.

11 *Id.* § 797(e); Federal Power Commission v. State of Oregon, 349 U.S. 435, 444–45 (1955).

> To issue licenses to citizens of the United States, or to any association of such citizens, or to any corporation organized under the laws of the United States or any State thereof, or to any State or municipality *for the purpose of constructing, operating, and maintaining dams, water conduits, reservoirs, power houses, transmission lines, or other project works necessary or convenient* for the development and improvement of navigation and *for the development, transmission, and utilization of power across, along, from, or in any of the streams or other bodies of water over which Congress has jurisdiction under its authority to regulate commerce with foreign nations and among the several States* . . . .[12]

The Federal Power Act thus clearly bases FERC's licensing jurisdiction on the federal government's Commerce Clause authority over navigable waters, as was discussed in Chapter 6. The Act emphasizes this point in its definition of "navigable waters," which are:

> those parts of streams or other bodies of water over which Congress has jurisdiction under its authority to regulate commerce with foreign nations and among the several States, and which either in their natural or improved condition notwithstanding interruptions between the navigable parts of such streams or waters by falls, shallows, or rapids compelling land carriage, are used or suitable for use for the transportation of persons or property in interstate or foreign commerce, including therein all such interrupting falls, shallows, or rapids, together with such other parts of streams as shall have been authorized by Congress for improvement by the United States or shall have been recommended to Congress for such improvement after investigation under its authority. . . .[13]

In 1940, the U.S. Supreme Court took this definition to heart, concluding that "navigable waters" for purposes of the Federal Power Act include all waters that are navigable in fact for commerce, even if that navigability comes as a result of improvements to the river.[14] Moreover, "[w]hen once found to be navigable, a waterway remains so," and waters can become navigable for purposes of the Federal

12 *Id.* § 797(e) (emphasis added).

13 *Id.* § 796(8).

14 United States v. Appalachian Electric Power Co., 311 U.S. 377, 407–09 (1940).

Power Act after statehood.[15] Finally, navigation use does not have to be continuous for a waterway to qualify as navigable.[16]

The existence of a navigable waterway gives FERC jurisdiction over the hydroelectric dam or facility. (In contrast, if the waterway is *not* navigable, the relevant state can regulate the dam or facility.) Once FERC has jurisdiction, moreover, it can regulate the facility more broadly—the conditions it imposes on licenses are not limited to navigability concerns.[17] Instead, FERC's authority is "as broad as the needs of commerce."[18]

The issue becomes more complicated, however, regarding FERC hydropower licensing and state water law. Section 27 of the Federal Power Act provides that:

> Nothing contained in this chapter shall be construed as affecting or intending to affect or in any way to interfere with the laws of the respective States relating to the control, appropriation, use, or distribution of water used in irrigation or for municipal or other uses, or any vested right acquired therein.[19]

This provision looks a lot like the deference to state water law that Congress included in Section 8 of the federal Reclamation Act, which we discussed in Chapter 8. That would seem to suggest that hydropower dams in navigable waters generally need to obey state laws regarding the use of water and that the relevant state is free to impose any conditions on the hydropower facility that do not directly contradict federal law.

However, the U.S. Supreme Court has interpreted Section 27 to give far more authority over water to FERC than the U.S. Bureau of Reclamation has under the Reclamation Act. The Court first confronted the meaning of Section 27 in 1946 in *First Iowa Hydro-Electric Cooperative v. Federal Power Commission*.[20] In this case, the First Iowa Hydro-Electric Cooperative applied to the Federal Power Commission to build a large hydroelectric dam on the Mississippi River, diverting almost all of the water from the Cedar River to the Mississippi in the process. The State of Iowa objected and sought to impose state-law requirements on the dam. Specifically, Iowa law required that all dams in navigable waters receive a permit from the state's Executive Council[21] and that all water diverted be returned to

---

15 *Id.* at 408.

16 *Id.* at 409–10.

17 *Id.* at 426–27.

18 *Id.* at 426.

19 16 U.S.C. § 821.

20 328 U.S. 152 (1946).

21 *Id.* at 164.

the stream of origin.[22] The issue for the Court was whether the dam required this Iowa permit.

The Supreme Court decided that the license from the Federal Power Commission was sufficient to authorize dam construction and operation. It concluded that the Federal Power Act separates federal and state functions with respect to hydroelectric dams:

> In the Federal Power Act there is a separation of those subjects which remain under the jurisdiction of the states from those subjects which the Constitution delegates to the United States and over which Congress vests the Federal Power Commission with authority to act. To the extent of this separation, the Act establishes a dual system of control. The duality of control consists merely of the division of the common enterprise between two cooperating agencies of Government, each with final authority in its own jurisdiction. The duality does not require two agencies to share in the final decision of the same issue. . . . A dual final authority, with a duplicate system of state permits and federal licenses required for each project, would be unworkable.[23]

As a result, in the navigable waters the Federal Power Act displaced Iowa's dam permitting requirements, and the project did *not* need a state permit as well as the federal license.[24]

As for Section 27, the *First Iowa* Court concluded that:

> The effect of § 27, in protecting state laws from supersedure, is limited to laws as to the control, appropriation, use or distribution of water in irrigation or for municipal or other uses of the same nature. It therefore has primary, if not exclusive, reference to such proprietary rights. The phrase "any vested right acquired therein" further emphasizes the application of the section to property rights. There is nothing in the paragraph to suggest a broader scope unless it be the words "other uses." Those words, however, are confined to rights of the same nature as those relating to the use of water in irrigation or for municipal purposes.[25]

Thus, to the extent that a FERC-licensed hydroelectric facility needs or interferes with actual state water rights, state water law still

---

22 *Id.* at 165–66.

23 *Id.* at 167–68.

24 *Id.* at 170.

25 *Id.* at 175–76.

applies. Moreover, FERC in its licensing process must respect existing vested state water rights.[26]

However, when the U.S. Supreme Court revisited Section 27 in 1990, in *California v. FERC*,[27] it restricted the kinds of conditions that states can impose as part of a water right permit. In that case, FERC had licensed the Rock Creek hydroelectric project on the South Fork American River in California in 1983, imposing "interim minimum flow rates of 11 cubic feet per second (cfs) during May through September and 15 cfs during the remainder of the year" in order to protect trout.[28] However, the project owner had also applied to California's State Water Resources Control Board for a state water right, and in 1987 that Board threatened to impose minimum flow requirements of 60 cfs. The issue for the Court was whether Section 27 allowed California to impose this higher minimum streamflow requirement.

The Court concluded that the Federal Power Act preempted California's requirement. Relying on *First Iowa*, it noted that "California's minimum stream flow requirements neither reflect nor establish 'proprietary rights' or 'rights of the same nature as those relating to the use of water in irrigation or for municipal purposes.' "[29] It also refused California's request to overturn *First Iowa*, concluding that "[t]here has been no sufficient intervening change in the law, or indication that *First Iowa* has proved unworkable or has fostered confusion and inconsistency in the law, that warrants our departure from established precedent."[30]

Thus, under the Supreme Court's interpretations, the Federal Power Act shifts the federalism balance at the water-energy nexus decisively toward the federal government for hydroelectric projects in the navigable waters. FERC has substantial authority to regulate these projects' water system impacts. Moreover, although it must respect vested state water rights, FERC can benefit from the federal navigation servitude that limits these rights (see Chapter 6).[31]

D. Energy Use in Water Management

Just as energy production requires water, water use requires energy. For example, on average, water treatment plants use 700 to 1800 kilowatt hours of electricity to treat 1 million gallons of water to drinking water standards; the variation depends largely on the

---

26 FPC v. Oregon, 349 U.S. at 445.

27 494 U.S. 490 (1990).

28 *Id.* at 495.

29 *Id.* at 498 (quoting *First Iowa*, 328 U.S. at 176).

30 *Id.* at 499.

31 *E.g.*, Federal Power Commission v. Niagara Mohawk Power Corp., 347 U.S. 239, 249 (1954).

initial quality of the source water. As a result, electricity accounts for about 75% of the costs of municipal water treatment and distribution, and treatment and distribution of potable drinking water accounts for about 3–4% of nation's consumption of electricity.

Of course, other factors can affect the energy costs of drinking water. In particular, western states that transport water over long distances use substantial amounts of energy in their water sectors. In 2005, for example, the California Energy Commission concluded that "water-related energy use consumes 19 percent of the state's electricity, 30 percent of its [non-power plant] natural gas, and 88 billion gallons of diesel fuel every year—and this demand is growing."[32] All by itself, California's State Water Project—one of the two systems of water canals and pipes that transport water from the San Francisco Bay Delta through the Central Valley to southern California cities like Los Angeles and San Diego—consumes about 5 billion kilowatt-hours per year, or about 2–3% of all the electricity used in the state.

California utilities also can give some sense of how much energy is required to secure a water supply from among the various options—various surface water transportation systems, groundwater pumping, desalination, or water reuse. Table 10–3 summarizes the energy cost of various water supply sources for one of southern California's large regional water and wastewater utilities, the Inland Empire Utilities Agency. These figures strongly suggest that water reuse is a significantly less energy-intensive option for water supply in southern California. However, as was discussed in Chapter 3, the prior appropriation doctrine generally prohibits new uses from interfering with existing water rights. Thus, unless a California city discharges its wastewater to the ocean (as many of them do), permits to recycle wastewater might run afoul of the "no injury" rule with respect to downstream users who rely on those return flows. Moreover, water utilities can only *recycle* wastewater after obtaining the water in the first place, so there will likely be an initially higher energy cost to obtain that water through one of the other means available.

---

[32] GARY KLEIN ET AL., CALIFORNIA ENERGY COMMISSION, CALIFORNIA'S WATER-ENERGY NEXUS 1 (Nov. 2005).

Table 10–3: The Inland Empire Utilities Agency's Water Supply Choices in Terms of Energy

SOURCE: GARY KLEIN ET AL., CALIFORNIA ENERGY COMMISSION, CALIFORNIA'S WATER-ENERGY NEXUS 23 (Nov. 2005).

SOURCE OF WATER SUPPLY	ENERGY REQUIRED (kilowatt-hours per million gallons)
Ocean desalination	13,503
California State Water Project, East Branch	9,820
California State Water Project, West Branch	7,672
Colorado River Aqueduct	6,138
Brackish water desalination	5,217
Ion exchange	3,222
Groundwater pumping	2,915
Water Reuse (wastewater recycling)	1,228

California utilities also use less energy to treat water (the water reuse option) than is true elsewhere. On average, both drinking water and wastewater treatment require 2350 to 3300 kilowatt-hours of electricity to treat 1 million gallons of water. California thus demonstrates that improvements in technology and energy efficiency can drastically lower the energy costs of water supply. Other places are also working to reduce the energy requirements of their water utilities. For example, when the Green Bay, Wisconsin, Metropolitan Sewerage District "installed new energy-efficient blowers in its first-stage aeration system [at one of its treatment plants, it] reduc[ed] electricity consumption by 50 percent and sav[ed] 2,144,000 kWh/year—enough energy to power 126 homes—and avoid[ed] nearly 1,480 metric tons of CO_2 equivalent, roughly the amount emitted annually by 290 cars."[33]

Energy efficiency in water use thus can be an important component not just of reducing water costs but also of addressing greenhouse gas emissions. More generally, one of the more important consequences of the water-energy nexus is that conservation of

[33] U.S. ENVIRONMENTAL PROTECTION AGENCY, STATE & LOCAL CLIMATE & ENERGY PROGRAM, LOCAL GOVERNMENT CLIMATE AND ENERGY STRATEGY GUIDES: ENERGY EFFICIENCY IN WATER AND WASTEWATER FACILITIES: A GUIDE TO DEVELOPING AND IMPLEMENTING GREENHOUSE GAS REDUCTION PROGRAMS 4 (2013).

energy is also conservation of water, and vice-versa. Conservation of both water and energy thus remains a first-best critical strategy for reducing the challenges emerging at their nexus.

E. Using Energy to Produce Water: Desalination

One of the most costly forms of water supply in terms of energy is desalination—that is, the use of technology to remove salts and other impurities from brackish water or seawater. However, worldwide, desalination is a rapidly increasing source of water, particularly in water-strapped but energy-rich parts of the world like the Middle East. As of early 2024, "[t]here are over 16,000 desalination plants in 177 countries. Many are micro plants, especially used to create cleaner water used for fracking in oil extraction."[34] Saudi Arabia leads the world in using seawater desalination to produce potable water supplies, generating over 1 million cubic meters per day.[35] Saudi Arabia, Kuwait, the Cayman Islands, and Algeria already have a total desalination capacity of more than 2 million cubic meters per day, followed closely by Israel (almost 1.7 million), Australia (1.62 million), and Egypt (1.4 million). The United States' total desalination capacity is almost 800,000 cubic meters per day.[36]

The energy costs of desalination vary considerably depending on the type of water being desalinated and the type of desalination technology being used. There are two main desalination technologies: ***thermal***, in which saline water is heated to distill pure water vapor; and ***reverse osmosis***, in which the saline water is forced through membranes that remove the salts. More important, however, is the salinity of the water being desalinated. Desalination of seawater, depending on the technique used, requires anywhere from 3 to 28 kilowatt-hours of electricity to produce a cubic meter of fresh water, or about 11,350 to 106,000 kilowatt-hours per million gallons—far in excess of the other energy costs shown in Table 10–3. Brackish water desalination requires far less energy, about 1000 to 8500 kilowatt-hours per million gallons, and is fairly common in states like Texas. Indeed, about two-thirds of the desalination occurring in the United States is brackish water desalination; in contrast, in the Gulf nations of the Middle East, over 61% of the desalination is seawater desalination.

While only 1% of the world's population received its water from desalination as of 2022, the United Nations projects that that number will increase to 14% by 2025. This increasing dependence on

---

[34] *Desalination by Country 2024*, WORLD POPULATION REVIEW (2024), https://worldpopulationreview.com/country-rankings/desalination-by-country.

[35] *Id.*

[36] *Id.*

desalination—especially seawater desalination—raises a number of issues for law and policy because of these technologies' energy intensity and environmental impacts. Increasing reliance on desalination plants that in turn get their electricity from fossil-fuel fired power plants would increase the supply of freshwater at the expense of increasing greenhouse gas emissions. Notably, to avoid this problem, nations like Spain and Australia have been experimenting with solar- and wind-powered desalination, respectively. Electricity typically accounts for about 44% of the costs of a reverse-osmosis desalination plant, meaning that the price of the resulting water can be acutely sensitive to increasing energy costs—a fact that can lead to difficulties for poor consumers and hence to social justice concerns. Desalination plants also produce concentrated brine that can be an environmental hazard, and they more generally raise all of the land use and environmental concerns associated with siting a large industrial facility.

Within the United States, as noted, seawater desalination plants are rare. Until late 2015, the largest seawater desalination plant in the United States was located in Tampa Bay, Florida. This $158 million facility was completed in 2008 and can produce 25 million gallons of fresh water per day. However, California has now become the seawater desalination leader. In light of its history of drought and the increasing unreliability of surface water supply systems, California began pursuing a desalination water supply strategy in 2006, although it has been scaling back the scope of this strategy ever since. As the Pacific Institute explains,

> As of May 2016, there are nine active proposals for seawater desalination plants along the California coast, as well as two additional proposed plants in Baja California, Mexico that would provide water to southern California communities. This is down from an estimated 21 proposed projects in 2006 and 19 in 2012. Since 2006, only two projects have been built: a small plant in Sand City with a capacity of 300,000 gallons of water per day and a much larger 50-million-gallon per day plant in Carlsbad.[37]

Nevertheless, in 2014 California voters approved Proposition 1, a $7.5 billion water bond measure that allocated $100 million to assist local water agencies in building desalination plants. In times of severe drought, such as occurred in 2010–2012, desalination projects can ensure a local water supply even when Central Valley Project, State Water Project, and Colorado River water deliveries falter.

---

[37] Pacific Institute, *Existing and Proposed Seawater Desalination Plants in California*, http://pacinst.org/publication/key-issues-in-seawater-desalination-proposed-facilities/.

The Carlsbad plant offers a case study of desalination as a water-supply strategy. This plant can produce 50 million gallons per day of desalinated seawater, making it the largest desalination plant in the western hemisphere. The San Diego County Water Authority and Poseidon Water, which owns the plant, have entered into a 30-year contract for the plant's entire output of water. A leading Israeli desalination company, IDE Technologies, operates the plant. The plant began delivering water to San Diego residents on December 14, 2015, and it produces enough water to serve about half a million residents, supplying roughly 7% to 10% of the Authority's water needs. The desalination facility conveys water produced at the plant via six pumps through a 10-mile pipeline to the Authority's distribution system.

However, this water is not cheap: the plant cost Poseidon about $1 billion to build, and the water the plant produces costs more than twice as much as the Water Authority pays for most of the rest of its water supply. Specifically, "San Diego has agreed to pay $2,131 to $2,367 an acre-foot for Poseidon's desalinated water, including the cost of piping the finished product to the authority's aqueduct. By comparison, . . . the authority pays just under $1,000 an acre-foot for water imported from Northern California and delivered to San Diego's doorstep by Metropolitan."[38] Those costs amount to about an extra $5.00 per month in individuals' water bills, which averaged about $80.00 per month before the plant went online.[39]

The Carlsbad Desalination Plant is a reverse-osmosis plant. It took advantage of co-locating with the Encina Power Plant to reduce both the energy costs and environmental risks associated with desalination. The power plant was already withdrawing seawater to use as cooling water; the desalination plant takes 50 million gallons of the power plant's "pre-heated" discharge water for desalination, then discharges the brine left over from desalination into the rest of the power plant's wastewater, diluting the brine before it returns to the ocean. Even so, the plant was subject to 14 lawsuits and over a decade of negotiation with state environmental agencies before it could break ground.

Poseidon Water portrays its plant as a model of environmental stewardship. Indeed, to offset its environmental impacts, Poseidon Water restored and enhanced, in partnership with the U.S. Fish & Wildlife Service, 66 acres of wetlands in the San Diego Bay National Wildlife Refuge and dedicated more than 15 acres of its lagoon- and ocean-front land to public purposes. Moreover, to offset the plant's

---

[38] Dale Kasler, "Southern California desalination plant will help ease water crunch, but price is steep," *The Sacramento Bee*, Dec. 12, 2015, http://www.sacbee.com/news/state/california/water-and-drought/article49468770.html.

[39] *Id.*

energy demands, Poseidon installed solar panels on the roof and purchased carbon emission offsets. It claims that the Carlsbad plant is the first water infrastructure project in California to have a net carbon footprint of zero.

F. Climate Change and the Water-Energy Nexus

Climate change is having a number of effects on the water-energy nexus, mostly keyed to the basic availability of water. Some of those potential effects become evident during drought, and "when severe drought affected more than a third of the United States in 2012, limited water availability constrained the operation of some power plants and other energy production activities."[40] Indeed, drought and water availability issues have already been affecting energy production:

> During the drought of 2002, lawmakers in Idaho ruled that five large coal- and gas-fired power plants should be denied water rights for cooling because they would deplete much needed freshwater for drinking and irrigation. In Nevada, the 1,580 megawatt (MW) coal-fired Mohave Generating Station was forced to close in 2005 due to lack of groundwater. A few years earlier, American National Power had to withdraw its application to build a 1,100 MW natural gas plant near Hillburn, New York, because it created a controversy concerning water rights. Far from being isolated examples, water issues have complicated power plant construction in Arizona, Georgia, California, Colorado, Massachusetts, Missouri, New Mexico, North Carolina, Pennsylvania, Rhode Island, South Dakota, Tennessee, Texas, and Wisconsin.[41]

Climate change, of course, directly affects water availability in a variety of ways. Some parts of the United States are likely to receive more precipitation as a result of climate change—although that precipitation may increasingly come in the form of flood events. However, scientists project that many parts of the United States—the Southwest, Mountain West, and Southeast in particular—will receive less precipitation overall and/or less snowpack, reducing both the total amount of water available and the timing of its availability.

> While there is significant uncertainty regarding the magnitude of effects, water availability and predictability may be altered by changing temperatures, shifting precipitation patterns, increasing variability, and more

---

40 *Id.* at v.

41 Benjamin K. Sovacool, *Running on Empty: The Electricity-Water Nexus and the U.S. Electric Utility Sector*, 30 ENERGY L.J. 11, 12–13 (2009) (citations omitted).

> extreme weather. Shifts in precipitation and temperature patterns—including changes in snowmelt—will likely lead to more regional variation in water availability for hydropower, biofeedstock production, thermoelectric generation and other energy needs. Rising temperatures have the potential to increase the demand for electricity for cooling and decrease the efficiency of thermoelectric generation, as well as increase water consumption for agricultural crops and domestic use. These changes and variations pose challenges for energy infrastructure resilience.[42]

The Department of Energy summarized its look at climate change in 2014 with five "key messages" about the implications of climate change for the water-energy nexus:

- Changing temperatures, shifting precipitation patterns, increasing climate variability, and more frequent extreme weather events can alter the availability and predictability of water and disrupt energy production and distribution.
- The future of the water-energy nexus will depend on energy and water needs, which will be shaped by climate change as well as population growth and migration patterns.
- There is both regional and seasonal variability in the effects of climate change and other future trends.
- High uncertainty underscores the importance of models because exploring interactions and identifying emergent properties enables decision making that is robust to a multitude of possible futures.
- The future of the nexus hinges on a number of things that are within the Department of Energy's long term scope of influence such as technology options, location of energy activities, and fuel source mix.[43]

Water availability, however, is only one side of the climate change implications for the water-energy nexus. The energy sector is one of the largest sources of greenhouse gas emissions, and efforts to reduce greenhouse gas emissions in energy production as part of climate change mitigation policies can have implications for water use and demand.

---

[42] U.S. DEPARTMENT OF ENERGY, THE WATER-ENERGY NEXUS: CHALLENGES AND OPPORTUNITIES vii (June 2014).

[43] *Id.* at 29.

We've already seen that the choices among fuels and cooling methods can make a significant difference in the water demands of electricity production. Similarly, some of the technologies being promoted to reduce greenhouse gas emissions from power plants also affect the water demands of those power plants—a fact that needs to be more widely acknowledged in climate change mitigation discussions.

One prominent example is carbon capture (or sequestration) and storage technologies. Proponents offer these technologies as a means of reducing greenhouse gas emissions from coal-fired power plants. Essentially, these technologies seek to capture carbon dioxide emissions from power plants and then sequester and store the carbon dioxide underground. However, sequestering all that carbon requires more energy, raising the water costs of this climate change mitigation strategy. The National Energy Technology Laboratory estimates that requiring carbon capture technology "could nearly double the amount of water a plant uses for every kilowatt of electricity it delivers," raising the electricity sector's water consumption by about 80% by 2030, assuming that additional energy needs are met through more coal-fired generation.[44] However, even if the additional energy requirements are met through non-carbon renewable sources, like wind, the water demand will still increase by 40–50%.[45] As one example, in 2022 a Louisiana power plant that considered installing carbon capture and sequestration faced a $900 million retrofit of the power plant that would reduce electricity production by 30% and increase water use by 55%.[46]

The water-energy nexus is thus a particular knotty sub-problem within the world of climate change. Nevertheless, climate change only underscores the existing need to consider water and energy law and policy together and to avoid making decisions on one side of the nexus without considering what will happen on the other side.

---

[44] Samuel K. Moore, *The Water Cost of Carbon Capture*, IEEE SPECTRUM (May 28, 2010), http://spectrum.ieee.org/energy/environment/the-water-cost-of-carbon-capture.

[45] *Id.*

[46] Sara Sneath, *The cost to capture carbon? More water and electricity*, THE GUARDIAN FLOODLIGHT (Oct. 15, 2022, 06:00 EDT), https://www.theguardian.com/environment/2022/oct/15/emissions-capture-carbon-cost-water-electricity.

Chapter 11

THE INTERSECTION OF WATER LAW AND WATER POLLUTION CONTROL LAW

A. Introduction

Thus far, we have dealt mainly with water allocation and other issues regarding water quantity. In many situations, that primary focus of water law suffices to address the relevant disputes. In other cases, however, it is impossible to address water quantity issues without considering water quality issues as well (or vice versa).

For one thing, water quality and water quantity are often integrally related from a practical perspective. Having an adequate water supply might be meaningless if the water is too contaminated to use or if the treatment necessary to make it usable is so costly that the intended use is no longer economically viable. Conversely, water withdrawals can make it difficult or impossible to achieve water quality goals if the reduced water flows concentrate pollutants or if elevated water temperatures or other physical changes cause significant ecosystem impairment. Dams, diversions, or other infrastructure built to implement a water allocation system also might pollute or cause other harm to aquatic ecosystems—for example, by blocking fish passage, altering natural stream flow patterns, or changing water quality or temperature. For all of those reasons, in a seminal case addressing the authority of a state to impose minimum flow requirements on a hydroelectric project under the federal Clean Water Act (discussed further below), Justice O'Connor labeled efforts to separate water quality and water quantity "an artificial distinction."[1]

As a matter of law, water quality and water quantity typically are the subject of separate—but overlapping—legal doctrines. Several of the common law doctrines of water law covered in earlier chapters apply to water pollution as well as water allocation. For example, we mentioned at the end of Chapter 2 that riparian rights often include a right to unaltered *quality* (and see Chapter 14), and the same can also be true for appropriative rights. Federal and state water pollution law, which is based largely on the federal Clean Water Act, the state statutes that implement and sometimes expand it, and accompanying state and federal regulatory regimes,

[1] PUD No. 1 of Jefferson County v. Washington Dept. of Ecology, 511 U.S. 700, 719 (1994).

increasingly affect or address water quantity issues as courts and regulators are faced with actual conflicts involving the intersection of water quality and water quantity. Moreover, in a very few states, like California, the same agency implements both the water quality and water quantity regimes, allowing that agency to account for both at the same time; other states, like Idaho and Florida, directly link water allocations to water quality issues through their public interest and other water right permitting requirements.

Nevertheless, in many senses water quality and water quantity law operate independently. Importantly, principles of federalism apply somewhat differently to water allocation and water quality. Generally speaking, as discussed in earlier chapters, water quantity issues are viewed as a matter of state law, because they are so integrally connected to property, land use, and state economic development. However, in Chapters 8 and 10, you also saw that various federal statutory regimes, most notably those governing the U.S. Bureau of Reclamation, the U.S. Army Corps of Engineers, and the Federal Energy Regulatory Commission (but others as well), also exert a significant influence on state water allocation from both a policy and an implementation perspective.

In many respects, water pollution law can also derive significantly from doctrines and principles of state law, especially to the remaining extent that it is governed by state common law doctrines, such as nuisance or riparian rights. To a very large extent, however, that state law system governing water quality has been supplanted by a system of cooperative federalism driven by the Clean Water Act. The Clean Water Act allows and encourages states to take over its regulatory programs, subject to federal oversight by the U.S. Environmental Protection Agency and the U.S. Army Corps of Engineers (depending on which statutory programs are at issue). Most states implement at least some aspects of the Clean Water Act through state statutes and regulations. Again, however, implementation of the federal statutory regime can also have impacts on water quantity and allocation issues, which can also generate disputes about the appropriate role of federal law in that domain.

B. Common Law Doctrines Governing Water Quality

Several common law doctrines address water quality as well as water quantity disputes. First, both of the major U.S. surface water doctrines, riparian rights and prior appropriation, govern quality as well as quantity issues. Courts can also address alleged harm from water pollution through nuisance law (public or private), because polluting activities are one of the ways in which a landowner can use their property in ways that harm another landowner or resource user.

1. Riparian Rights

Applicability of riparian rights to water quality disputes should come as no surprise: Under the original natural flow doctrine (see Chapter 2), all riparian landowners were entitled to the use and enjoyment of the natural stream unimpaired in quantity *and quality*. As was the case for water withdrawal and use, however, that somewhat absolute version of riparian rights limited development, because virtually any use of land or water can cause some diminution of water quality downstream. In cases of truly minor water pollution, a court in equity can simply decline to grant injunctive relief, and minimal pollution is also not likely to support lawsuits for damages. Despite those natural checks on unduly harsh application of the riparian rights doctrine, however, courts faced the need to balance the goal of reducing water quality degradation against a growing, industrializing economy in the 19th and early 20th centuries. As a result, the same considerations that led to the evolution of the "reasonable use" version of riparian rights for purposes of water use applied to riparian disputes involving pollution as well.

A good example of this tension was the case of *Strobel v. Kerr Salt Co.*,[2] a case in which downstream riparian landowners, owners of mills that had long relied on the natural stream flow to support their operations, sued a newer salt manufacturer whose operations caused the stream to become so salty that it impaired their businesses, killed streamside vegetation, killed fish, and made the water unfit for livestock watering. That deprivation of the flow of the stream unimpaired in *quality* would have been a clear violation of the natural flow version of riparian rights and subject to a *per se* injunction. Such an automatic rule, however, would subject any business that impaired water quality to similar treatment, including the plaintiffs themselves.

As explained by the New York Court of Appeals, the reasonable use doctrine, in contrast, allows courts to balance the uses by, and impacts on, both upper and lower riparian landowners:

> A riparian owner is entitled to a reasonable use of the water flowing by his premises in a natural stream . . . and to have it transmitted to him without sensible alteration in quality or unreasonable diminution in quantity. . . . As all other owners upon the same stream have the same right, the right of no one is absolute, but is qualified by the right of the others to have the stream substantially preserved in

2 58 N.E. 142 (N.Y. App. 1900).

> its natural size, flow, and purity, and to protection against material diversion or pollution. This is the common right of all, which must not be interfered with by any.[3]

Nevertheless, although the trial court had interpreted this principle as authorizing the defendant's use as "reasonable" when it served a legitimate economic purpose, employed a large number of workers, and reflected "ordinary care" based on the industrial practices at the time, the Court of Appeals held that the level of injury and harm to plaintiffs and others resulting from the salt manufacturing operation denied them "fair participation" in the use of the natural stream and thus justified injunctive relief to prevent a multiplicity of lawsuits for damages. Thus, the reasonable use rule for water quality under riparian rights tends to look a lot like nuisance doctrine.

In addition, however, to some extent the use of injunctive relief against defendants, even though existing "best practices" supported no better forms of pollution control, anticipated the "technology forcing" aspects of modern statutory environmental law discussed below in the context of the Clean Water Act. It forces the defendant either to curtail operations or to develop superior pollution control methods that allow the operation to continue without unreasonable harm to downstream riparian users.

The problem of multiple tortfeasors is another way in which the application of riparian rights (and other common law doctrines) is linked to water law conceptually. Even in resolving a water allocation dispute between only two users, courts and other water law administrators must consider the resulting impacts to, and influences of, a large number of other users in what is essentially a zero sum game. In *Strobel*, and in many cases like it, multiple sources of pollution may have cumulative impacts, sometimes making it difficult to trace the resulting harm to any one defendant. Acknowledging this cumulative impacts problem, the New York Court of Appeals wrote: "The fact that other salt manufacturers are doing the same thing as the defendant, instead of preventing relief, may require it."[4] Just as the difficulty of accounting for the impacts and interactions of so many actors within a given stream system supported the evolution of statutory and administrative systems of water law and management in place of individual common law actions, as discussed in Chapter 5, the challenge of dealing with multiple pollution sources led to the statutory solutions discussed in the second part of this chapter.

---

[3] *Id.* at 147. *See also* Smith v. Staso Milling Co., 18 F.2d 736, 738 (1st Cir. 1927) (upholding an injunction against pollution by upstream milling company).

[4] 58 N.E. at 148.

2. Prior Appropriation

Because the law of riparian rights was designed from the outset to protect the use and enjoyment of natural streams, riparianism's applicability to and adaptability in addressing impairment of water quality was not surprising. In contrast, states designed the prior appropriation doctrine specifically to facilitate withdrawal and off-stream use of water in ways that were virtually guaranteed to result in at least some, and often significant, impairment of natural stream flows and conditions. Nevertheless, there are aspects of prior appropriation law that also lend themselves to protecting appropriative rights against pollution, in some ways more strictly than is true under the reasonable use version of riparian rights law.

As Chapter 3 discussed in detail, prior appropriation law established that beneficial use is the "basis, the measure, and the limit" of an appropriative right. Logically, the concept of beneficial use incorporates the notion that the water appropriated is of sufficient quality to support the beneficial use, suggesting that upstream junior appropriators (and maybe others) can no more impair the *quality* of the water reaching the senior than they can deprive the senior of sufficient flow. Moreover, because of the typically absolute protection afforded to senior appropriators, under prior appropriation law courts are not free to balance the economic importance of two competing users in determining whether the senior right has been impaired, although they may be able to do so in determining whether equitable relief is appropriate as opposed to monetary damages. Thus, compared to the relative nature of riparian rights under reasonable use balancing principles, it could be argued that prior appropriation provides senior appropriators with stronger protection against upstream pollution, at least if it substantially impairs their beneficial use right.

What constitutes significant enough pollution to impair a beneficial use obviously depends on the use to which the senior is putting water and the nature and extent of the alleged pollution. According to the California Supreme Court, "So far as the rights of the prior appropriator are concerned, any use which defiles or corrupts the water so as to essentially impair its priority and usefulness for the purpose for which the water was appropriated . . . is an invasion of his private rights, for which he is entitled to a remedy both at law and in equity."[5] Relatively few prior appropriation cases have implemented this theory, perhaps because of the difficulty in making this determination, but one early case addressed this concept:

[5] Joerger v. Pacific Gas & Elec. Co., 276 P. 1017, 1026 (Cal. 1929).

> The only subordination of one water user to another is the right of the first appropriator to a sufficiency of water for his necessary uses. That includes the quality as well as the quantity. What deterioration in the quality of the water will constitute an invasion of the rights of the lower appropriator will depend upon the facts and circumstances of each case, with reference to the use to which the water is applied.[6]

As is true for riparian rights, the common law prior appropriation doctrine protects individual appropriators rather than the general public's interest in clean water, except to the extent that relief in individual cases incidentally protects other water users and the resource itself. A second, more recent concept in prior appropriation doctrine potentially useful to address water pollution, manifest more prominently in statutory provisions governing the prior appropriation system, is the public interest test discussed in Chapter 5. That test allows state engineers or others implementing a prior appropriation permit system to deny new appropriations if they would impair broader public interests (as well as the rights of senior appropriators), authority which is broad enough to encompass water pollution even if not identified expressly in the state statute.[7]

3. Nuisance Law

The only common law doctrine with the potential to protect the general public—as well as private parties—against water pollution is nuisance law. As it evolved in an industrializing society, nuisance law bears many similarities to riparian rights. A private nuisance is an unreasonable interference with a private party's use and enjoyment of their own land, and in that sense a riparian rights claim might be viewed conceptually as a specialized version of private nuisance because it alleges a violation of those benefits of private property ownership that inure to riparian landowners. Like riparian rights, nuisance law began as a relatively strict doctrine, but as conflicts with more intensive but economically valuable land uses increased, the doctrine evolved to incorporate the same kinds of balancing factors that courts apply in riparian law.[8]

---

[6] Arizona Copper v. Gillespie, 230 U.S. 46, 55 (1913) (applying Arizona territorial law in upholding an injunction against upstream copper mining operation for impairment of downstream appropriative irrigation rights); *see also* Sussex Land & Livestock Co. v. Midwest Refining Co., 294 F. 597 (8th Cir. 1923) (upholding damage award but not injunction due to water quality impairment to senior appropriator).

[7] *See, e.g.*, ARIZ. REV. STAT. § 45–153.A (authorizing denial of appropriative right "when the application or proposed use conflicts with vested rights, is a menace to public safety, or is against the interests and welfare of the public").

[8] *Compare* Restatement (2d) of Torts § 822 (compiling private nuisance balancing factors) *with id.* § 850A (factors governing application of riparian rights).

Public nuisance, by contrast, is an unreasonable interference with rights held *by the general public*, as opposed to particularized impact on a piece of private property. Water pollution that affects large bodies of water often constitutes a public nuisance. Indeed, remedying and preventing those public nuisances was one motivation for Congress to enact the Clean Water Act, discussed below. State and local government officials are presumptively entitled to bring public nuisance claims on behalf of the public at large and to seek injunctive relief to protect shared public resources like waterbodies.

A more difficult question is the extent to which private parties may bring a public nuisance claim to vindicate private interests. Because the pollution itself most often adversely affects the water in the stream and the aquatic resources it supports, rather than adjacent riparian land, a private nuisance claim may not be viable in many cases. Public nuisance envisions the kinds of harm spread among a large population, typically making the government the preferred plaintiff to seek relief that benefits the public at large. In many cases, moreover, harm from generalized water pollution is sufficiently dispersed that no individual plaintiff has sufficient incentive to bring such a case. Under the "special injury rule," however, a private plaintiff may bring a public nuisance action if he or she can allege harm that is distinct in nature or in significant degree from the harm suffered by members of the general public.

One good example of a private party bringing a public nuisance claim was *Hampton v. North Carolina Pulp. Co.*[9] In *Hampton*, the North Carolina Supreme Court reversed the dismissal of a complaint filed by a riparian landowner along the banks of the Roanoke River, a navigable waterway, seeking damages to his commercial fishing business resulting from pulp mill pollution. Earlier cases had confirmed that riparian landowners on non-navigable streams could bring such actions because, under the state rules governing fishing rights along non-navigable streams, those landowners had exclusive fishing rights to the areas harmed by the pollution (the so-called "fisherman's rule"). Thus, presumptively the harm was particularized to those plaintiffs and therefore different in kind as well as degree from the harm to the general public. The *Hampton* court, however, saw no valid distinction between the "fisherman's rule" grounds for exception to the public nuisance rule and the case of a riparian landowner with a commercial fishing business on a public, navigable stream with fishing rights shared with the general public: "The necessities of a person whose business is taking fish from a common fishery and one who, by reason of his riparian ownership and ownership of the bed of the river, has a several and exclusive

[9] 27 S.E. 2d 538 (N.C. 1943).

fishery are precisely the same, and the same principle of law must apply."[10] Thus, the North Carolina Supreme Court extended nuisance law protection to impairment of all valid fishing rights, not just those associated with private fishing access to non-navigable waters.

A more contemporary example involves litigation over "forever chemicals" that have the potential to cause significant public health and environmental harm and that persist in the environment for very long periods of time. In *Priselac v. Chemours Co.*,[11] the court dismissed a private nuisance claim because, in the court's view, plaintiff had alleged a public rather than a private nuisance. Even construing the case in the alternative as a public nuisance claim, the court held that the plaintiff had not alleged a sufficiently distinct injury from the public at large. This illustrates the difficulty of using nuisance law—at least by private parties—to address complex modern water pollution problems involving widespread contamination.[12]

When governmental plaintiffs bring public nuisance claims, they are more likely to obtain injunctive relief that reduces or prevents the pollution directly, benefitting the public at large. In contrast, even when a private plaintiff can bring a public nuisance claim, courts typically grant relief in the nature of damages rather than injunctive relief. As such, private suits for public nuisance are unlikely to stop the pollution problem, because the polluter will stop polluting only when the cost of abating the pollution is lower than the cost of paying damages to one or more successful plaintiffs. Those limitations of private remedies as a means of water pollution control led eventually to more comprehensive statutory and regulatory approaches to water pollution control, discussed next.

C. Intersection of the Clean Water Act and Water Law

1. Core Concepts of the Clean Water Act

Several core concepts distinguish statutory water pollution law, and the federal Clean Water Act (CWA)[13] in particular, from the common law doctrines governing water pollution. Although a full treatment of the CWA and other aspects of statutory and regulatory

---

[10] *Id.* at 546.

[11] 2022 WL 909406 (E.D.N.C. 2022).

[12] *See also*, Neuse River Foundation, Inc. v. Smithfield Foods, Inc., 574 S.E.2d 48, 52–54 (N.C. App. 2002) (denying, for lack of special injury, public nuisance claims brought by environmental associations and recreational fishers regarding water pollution from hog farms).

[13] 33 U.S.C. §§ 1251–1388.

water pollution control law is well beyond the scope of this chapter, a basic understanding of the Act and how it operates is necessary to understand the ways in which it intersects with other aspects of water law.

First, the concept of water "pollution" articulated in the CWA is far broader than just the discharge of chemical wastes from factories or human wastes from sewage treatment plants. The overall objective of the CWA is "to restore and maintain the chemical, physical, and biological integrity of the Nation's waters."[14] The Act defines the term "pollution" to be "the man-made or man-induced alteration of the chemical, physical, biological, and radiological integrity of water,"[15] whereas "pollutants" are defined more narrowly as a list of physical and chemical contaminants that may be released into water.[16] The term "pollution," therefore, might include activities with significant linkages to water quantity law, such as water withdrawals and conveyances; dams, diversions, or other water resources infrastructure; or stream channelization and stabilization designed to prevent or mitigate flooding. In other words, actions taken to implement the systems of water law covered in earlier chapters have significant potential to alter the chemical, physical, biological or radiological integrity of water, causing "pollution" within the meaning of the CWA. As explained below, however, discharges of pollutants are regulated far more strictly and precisely under the CWA than other kinds of water pollution.

Second, especially to accommodate the industrialization of the U.S. economy, and as other land uses intensified, the common law doctrines discussed above all operated on the principle that landowners have a right to use their land, even in ways that cause some degree of water pollution, so long as they do not cause unreasonable harm to another water user. Under the common law doctrines, therefore, the onus is on the aggrieved user to file a lawsuit, and, as is true for most civil lawsuits, the burden of proof is on the plaintiff to prove the requisite elements of his or her cause of action by a preponderance of the evidence. Absent sufficiently egregious harm, many landowners who are adversely affected by water pollution lack sufficient incentive to bear the monetary and other costs of litigation. As a result, when the harm from pollution is individually modest to each affected landowner but collectively significant, and where the sources of pollution are numerous but the cumulative impact is large, private litigation under the common law is unlikely, even when damage to the greater public interest is

---

14 *Id.* § 1251(a).

15 *Id.* § 1362(19).

16 *Id.* § 1362(6).

significant. Moreover, as noted, the remedy of monetary damages will not necessarily stop the pollution problem.

The modern version of the CWA, as amended in 1972 and thereafter,[17] sought to regulate water pollution at the source in order to keep water pollution from impairing public values. For the category of water pollution caused by "point source" discharges, in which pollutants are discharged into waters covered by the Act[18] from a "discernible, confined and discrete conveyance,"[19] no one has a "right" to discharge absent a valid permit to do so from a government agency (either the federal Environmental Protection Agency (EPA) or a state water pollution control agency operating pursuant to delegated authority from the EPA).[20] Those permits are known as National Pollutant Discharge Elimination System (NPDES) permits.[21] In the deceptively absolute language of the CWA: "Except as in compliance with [various permitting and substantive control provisions], the discharge of any pollutant by any person shall be unlawful."[22] Thus, the CWA reversed the idea that a landowner had a right to discharge unless and until another landowner or water user proved harm into a rule in which no one has a right to discharge—even for otherwise legitimate and useful economic activity—absent valid governmental permission.

A second, closely related concept that Congress changed dramatically in the CWA was the common law notion that some levels of water pollution reflect an equitable balancing of rights among competing users of a water body. That concept is reflected in the balancing factors considered in the "reasonable use" version of riparian rights and in the nuisance doctrine's basis in "unreasonable" interference with the use and enjoyment of land. Again, the common law doctrines are premised on the concept that some pollution is acceptable, with limits determined by courts on a case-by-case basis

---

17 Earlier versions of what was known as the Federal Water Pollution Control Act operated under principles that more closely resembled common law principles and focused federal attention on interstate waters, leaving most intrastate water quality problems to the states. While the 1972 amendments to the Act created the CWA's contemporary structure, the name "Clean Water Act" actually comes from the 1977 amendments.

18 The scope of the relevant term "navigable waters" for purposes of this statute, *see* 33 U.S.C. § 1362(12), is complicated and discussed briefly below.

19 *Id.* § 1362(14). Pollution from other sources, so-called "nonpoint sources," including more dispersed runoff of pollutants from various land uses, is subject to a much less prescriptive set of controls designed and implemented mainly by individual states.

20 CWA permits are also issued by the U.S. Army Corps of Engineers for the discharge of dredged and fill material, often to fill and build in wetlands. *See id.* § 1344. Only two states have received authority to issue these "dredge and fill" permits, so the Corps issues almost all Section 404 permits.

21 *See id.* § 1342(a).

22 *Id.* § 1311(a).

depending on the competing interests of the parties. Although courts applying common law principles have the authority to consider public interests in making those determinations, public welfare is not the dominant consideration.

The CWA, in contrast, is based on the somewhat controversial, absolutist concept that all water pollution is presumptively bad, to be tolerated only where justified by necessity and only until control methods improve sufficiently to eliminate it. Thus, in the 1972 CWA, Congress established an ambitious—and as yet elusive—"national goal that the discharge of pollutants into the navigable waters be eliminated by 1985."[23] That statutory goal is manifested in several operative provisions of the statute designed to force technology steadily in the direction of eliminating all point source pollutant discharges. However, the "zero discharge" goal is also tempered by pragmatism in ways that more closely mirror the common law origins of water pollution control. As a practical matter, CWA NPDES permits establish prescriptive limits on the kinds and amounts of pollution the covered facility may release, using two basic sets of rules, both of which have some heritage in analogous common law doctrines.

One of the factors common law courts have used in determining whether water pollution unlawfully violates the rights of another user is that dischargers should be held to some standard of technological sufficiency in their conduct. In other words, in determining whether the challenged pollution is "unreasonable" relative to the competing rights of other parties, courts will inquire whether the operation is being conducted in accordance with some reasonable standard of care or practice common to similarly situated businesses or activities. This inquiry is similar to the "ordinary standard of care in the community" analysis that courts have used to determine whether an appropriator is guilty of waste in the prior appropriation system. Courts also may ask whether economically viable superior technology or methods exist to control the pollution to guard against the possibility that all existing operators are uniformly using (usually because it is cheaper) inadequate control technology or practices.

The authors of the CWA translated this concept of "best practices" into a more rigorous system in which the EPA and state officials determine by rule or in individual permits the "best technology" for controlling pollution from particular pollutant sources. Specifically, the EPA and the states use that analysis to calculate and impose legally enforceable, technology-based effluent limitations for each discharger. The level of stringency (or the precise

---

[23] *Id.* § 1251(a)(1).

definition of "best") varies depending on the type of discharger, whether the source is existing or new, the kinds of pollutants released (e.g., toxic pollutants are treated more stringently than the so-called "conventional" pollutants like grease and pH), whether the pollutants are discharged directly into waterbodies or through a public sewage treatment plant, and other factors. The basic concept, however, is to require all similarly situated dischargers throughout the nation to reduce their pollution to roughly the same standards based on a uniform model best technology. At least in theory, those technology-based limits should become stricter over time as technology improves, with the ultimate aim of achieving the zero discharge goal for each kind of facility.[24] By implementing technology-based control requirements across the board rather than waiting for individual plaintiffs to file lawsuits, the CWA abates water pollution immediately and pervasively, rather than just in response to harm to individual riparian owners or other water users.

A second factor judges consider in determining whether pollution is actionable under the various common law doctrines discussed above is the nature and severity of harm caused to individual plaintiffs. In nuisance and riparian rights, for example, courts will balance the resulting harm to the plaintiffs against the harm to the defendants by imposing higher control costs. In a prior appropriation pollution case, the court will determine whether the pollution is severe enough to impair the plaintiff's more senior beneficial use of water. Nether analysis focuses on the resource itself or on harm to the general public, although courts may consider that issue in determining whether to grant injunctive relief, or in deciding public nuisance cases.

The CWA also adopts a harm-based approach to water pollution control, but like the technology-based approach, does so in a more public and comprehensive way than is true under common law doctrines. Rather than focusing on harm to individual landowners or water resource users, the CWA requires individual states to adopt water quality standards (WQS) at levels necessary to protect the various water resources within their borders and their various uses of those waters. Thus, WQS consist of two major components: (1) designated uses of each water body (such as protection of fish and aquatic life, water-based recreation, or public water supply); and (2) specific water quality criteria[25] that specify the water quality deemed

---

[24] Note that technology-*based* effluent standards do not actually mandate the use of a particular technology, but rather the *level* of pollution control achievable by using that technology, leaving individual pollution sources to innovate to develop cheaper or more efficient pollution controls.

[25] Water quality criteria come in various forms, such as narrative, numeric, chemical, and biological, as well as "anti-degradation" requirements designed to guard

sufficient to protect those uses. This system of state-specific WQS but with nationwide coverage both was a carryover from federal law before 1972 and was designed to meet an interim federal goal of "fishable and swimmable waters"[26] before the more ambitious zero discharge goal could be met. Moreover, while the EPA adopts technology-based standards for each category of industry on a nationwide basis, state-set WQS reflect differences in regional ecology, hydrology, climate, and other factors but are still subject to EPA oversight to ensure that the nation attains the CWA's basic goals.

Notably, state WQS for a particular waterbody—say, a pristine mountain lake or headwater stream—can require regulatory controls on dischargers that are more stringent than what the national technology-based effluent limitations can achieve. In such situations, the second step in the WQS process is to translate WQS into control requirements for individual dischargers, known as water quality-based effluent limitations, or WQBELs. This translation is often a challenging task, given variability in flow and other conditions in waterbodies and the often difficult-to-assess cumulative nature of multiple pollution sources within a watershed. WQBELs also may require the discharger to come up with some novel means of controlling pollutant discharges, if the discharger was already using the best control technology available. Finally, as discussed in more detail below, WQBELs can implicate the law governing water allocation because water withdrawals reduce stream flow, which in turn reduces the amount of water available to dilute pollutants from dischargers individually and collectively.

Compared to the largely case-by-case process through which the common law governed water quality, the CWA's nationwide statutory system has been quite effective in reducing discharges of pollutants across the board. Nevertheless, significant water quality problems remain around the nation as a result the sheer magnitude of the problem and other factors, such as the emerging importance of pollutants like hormone mimickers or "forever chemicals" like those at issue in the *Priselac* case discussed above. The CWA has been comparatively less effective in addressing other forms of water pollution—that is, damaging activities that fit within the broad statutory definition of "pollution" but that do not involve discharges of pollutants to the waters of the United States from point sources. For example, "nonpoint source pollution"—the runoff or other dispersed addition of pollutants to waterbodies from a range of land

---

against backsliding in overall water quality due to new discharges and cumulative impacts from multiple pollution sources, details that are beyond the scope of this explanation.

[26] *See* 33 U.S.C. § 1251(a)(2).

uses and other activities—remains a significant water quality problem, as are other human structures (like dams) and activities (like agriculture) located in and adjacent to waterbodies and that impair their physical, chemical or biological integrity. The CWA provides for state-specific programs to control those kinds of pollution, along with federal grant funding and other incentives. In deference to principles of federalism, Congress views land use, economic activity, and the other factors that govern the nature of nonpoint source pollution and appropriate control strategies as more state-specific pollution issues, with control of land use and water resources being traditionally—if not constitutionally—left to state and local governments.

2. Connections Between the CWA and Water Law

Under the basic conceptual structure described above, the CWA was designed as a federal environmental statute to establish a comprehensive, nationwide approach to water pollution control and restoration and protection of the health of the nation's waters. Nevertheless, it suggests several important connections between that statutory regime and principles and implementation of state water law. This is not surprising, given the natural linkages between water quality and water quantity as discussed at the beginning of this chapter. Some of the more important examples are explained below, but this is just a partial list of the many possible connections.

a. CWA Regulation of Water Use Infrastructure

Both the riparian rights and prior appropriation systems dictate who has the legal right to use particular amounts of water for specified purposes. Those legal rules, however, often require infrastructure to effectuate that sanctioned water use, to prevent flooding, or for other water resource management purposes, in the form of dams, withdrawal structures, water conveyance systems like canals, and stream channelization and stabilization structures. That infrastructure can range from relatively modest facilities that cause little or no harm aside from the water use itself, to structures that can alter aquatic ecosystems quite significantly.

Clearly those kinds of structures alter the chemical, physical, and biological integrity of waterbodies, creating "pollution" within the CWA's general ambit. However, unless those structures result in the "discharge of a pollutant," they are subject only to whatever controls an individual state may impose under a nonpoint source pollution management program.[27] If they *do* involve such a discharge, they require either a NPDES permit or a Section 404 "dredge and fill" permit and may be subject to more stringent

[27] *See id.* § 1329.

technology-based or water quality-based pollution control requirements.

The application of the CWA's permitting schemes to water infrastructure has generated a significant amount of controversy, litigation and more recently, regulation. The fundamental question for either scheme is whether those facilities cause a "discharge of a pollutant," which the CWA defines as "any addition of any pollutant to navigable waters from any point source."[28] This chapter, however, will focus on the NPDES permit program, while Chapter 13 will address in more detail the Section 404 permit program.

Two relatively early CWA cases addressed whether dams and other water storage and use facilities required NPDES permits. In *National Wildlife Federal v. Gorsuch*,[29] the U.S. Court of Appeals for the D.C. Circuit held that a dam does not require a NPDES permit because, even though the dam changed the water temperature and changed levels of dissolved oxygen and nutrients flowing into the downstream river, those pollutants would have reached the downstream stream segment even absent the dam. According to the D.C. Circuit, therefore, the dam did not "add" any pollutants to the waterway. Likewise, in *National Wildlife Federal v. Consumers Power Co.*,[30] the U.S. Court of Appeals for the Sixth Circuit found that material from fish chopped up by the turbines in a pumped storage electric power generation facility did not result in the addition of pollutants, because the fish came from the same water body (Lake Michigan) into which they were released. More recently, however, the U.S. Court of Appeals for the Second Circuit has questioned the logic of these two prior cases,[31] and it may eventually create a circuit split on the issue of dams, requiring U.S. Supreme Court resolution or a new EPA rulemaking.

An issue that has generated even more controversy is whether NPDES permits are required for the vast system of water conveyances around the country, which often result in the transfer of pollutants from one body of water into another. That can occur either when waterbodies themselves are used as water conveyances or when water is transferred by artificial means from one watershed to another where demand is greater as a result of urbanization or for other uses.

---

[28] *Id.* § 1262(12).

[29] 693 F.2d 156, 174–83 (D.C. Cir. 1982).

[30] 862 F.2d 580, 581–82 (6th Cir. 1988).

[31] Catskill Mountains Chapter of Trout Unlimited, Inc. v. City of New York, 273 F.3d 481, 489–92 (2d Cir. 2001) (technically distinguishing the D.C. Circuit's and Sixth Circuit's decisions but also refusing to defer to the EPA's view of dams).

Again, the legal issue in these cases is whether conveying water, with any pollutants accumulated in that water body from other sources, constitutes an "addition of any pollutant *to navigable waters* from any point source." In such cases, it is usually clear that pollutants are present and that they are released through a point source. What courts have found more ambiguous in the statutory text is whether the term "addition . . . to navigable waters" means addition those to waters as a whole, or an addition to each individual navigable water. Under the former reading, which the EPA and various defendants have characterized as the "unitary waters" concept, there is no "addition" of pollutants to the navigable waters as a whole, but rather simply a transfer of pollutants from one portion of the navigable waters to another. Under the latter reading, the conveyance adds pollutants from one navigable water body into another, thus requiring a permit.

Conceptually, which approach makes the most sense depends on perspective about the goals and control mechanisms in the Act. Through the water quality standards program, one of the goals of the Act is to protect each water body for its designated uses. From that perspective, it matters where pollutants are in the navigable waters. If water conveyances transfer pollutants from heavily polluted waters to clean ones, the clean receiving waters may no longer meet water quality standards or support their previous uses. On the other hand, the main focus of the NPDES permit program is to control pollutants at their source, that is, when they are first disposed into navigable waters. From that perspective, it is not likely that Congress intended that NPDES permits be issued for the vast system of water conveyances around the country and to require the operators of those conveyances to treat pollutants that had been generated by previous sources.

Legally, the playing field on which this issue was addressed shifted when it moved from the courts to the EPA. A number of courts rejected the unitary waters theory and required permits for water conveyances from one waterbody into another.[32] The only time the U.S. Supreme Court considered the issue, in a case involving pumping of water for flood control and water resource management in the Florida Everglades,[33] it remanded for a determination of whether the receiving water was really a "meaningfully distinct body of water" before it would pass on the validity of the unitary waters

---

[32] *E.g.*, Catskill Mountains Ch. of Trout Unlimited, Inc. v. City of New York, 451 F.3d 77 (2d Cir. 2006); Miccosukee Tribe of Indians of Fla. v. South Fla. Water Management Dist., 280 F.3d 1364 (11th Cir. 2002), *vacated on other grounds*, South Fla. Water Management Dist. v. Miccosukee Tribe, 541 U.S. 95 (2004).

[33] South Fla. Water Management Dist. v. Miccosukee Tribe, 541 U.S. 95, 112–15 (2004).

theory. In essence, the Court suggested that the pumping of pollutants from one portion of a waterbody to another portion of the same waterbody, even if separated by artificial dikes, would not constitute an "addition" of pollutants to navigable waters. If the lowers courts found that the transfer was to a meaningfully distinct waterbody (which the U.S. District Court for the Southern District of Florida actually did[34]), then the Supreme Court would have to rule on the unitary waters concept.

Before the Supreme Court could revisit that issue, however, the EPA promulgated a regulation governing water transfers, known as the Water Transfers Rule, to:

> [c]larify that water transfers are not subject to regulation under the National Pollutant Discharge Elimination System (NPDES) permitting program. Th[e] rule defines water transfers as an activity that conveys or connects waters of the United States without subjecting the transferred water to intervening industrial, municipal, or commercial use.[35]

Conceptually, this interpretation of the statute falls somewhere in between the two perspectives outlined above—that is, a water transfer from one water body to another does constitute an addition of pollutants to navigable waters, but only if an intervening industrial, municipal or commercial use adds pollutants to that water. In *Friends of the Everglades v. South Florida Water Management District*,[36] the U.S. Court of Appeals for the Eleventh Circuit upheld the EPA's interpretation as reasonable and entitled to deference under *Chevron U.S.A. Inc. v. Natural Resources Defense Council, Inc.*,[37] even though that court had indicated earlier that it would have rejected the unitary waters theory under a *de novo* standard of review.[38]

b. *Water Law and Water Quality Standards*

The CWA's water quality standards (WQS) program can intersect with water allocation law in at least two major ways. First,

---

[34] *See* Miccosukee Tribe of Indians v. South Fla. Water Management District, 2007 WL 7377465, at *2 (S.D. Fla. 2007) (noting the district court's 2006 decision to this effect).

[35] NPDES Water Transfers Rule, 73 Fed. Reg. 33697 (June 13, 2008) (codified at 40 C.F.R. § 122.3(i)).

[36] 570 F.3d 1210 (11th Cir. 2009).

[37] 467 U.S. 837 (1984).

[38] *Friends of the Everglades*, 570 F.3d at 1218; *see also* Catskill Mountains Chapter of Trout Unlimited, Inc. v. EPA, 846 F.3d 492, 501 (2d Cir. 2017) ("While we might prefer an interpretation more consistent with what appear to us to be the most prominent goals of the Clean Water Act, *Chevron* tells us that so long as the agency's statutory interpretation is reasonable, what we might prefer is irrelevant.").

because WQSs consist of both designated uses of all surface waters in each state and water quality criteria (WQC) that dictate the water conditions necessary and sufficient to protect and support those uses, minimum stream flows or other water quantity requirements can—at least in concept—be one component of those WQC. Second, even with respect to other forms of WQC, including criteria specifying maximum levels of particular pollutants, implementation requires consideration of how much water is present in different portions of the waterbody to dilute those pollutants.

The U.S. Supreme Court has ruled definitively that states may include water quantity requirements as part of their WQS program. In *PUD No. 1 of Jefferson County v. Washington Department of Ecology*,[39] the Court upheld a minimum stream flow requirement that the State of Washington imposed on a hydroelectric project in a water quality certification under Section 401 of the CWA.[40] Although most of the opinion construed the scope of state water quality certification authority for federally licensed or permitted projects under Section 401, the Court also flatly rejected the contention that the CWA in general, and the WQS program in particular, could not address water quantity issues:

> Petitioners also assert more generally that the Clean Water Act is only concerned with water "quality", and does not allow the regulation of water "quantity". This is an artificial distinction. In many cases, water quantity is closely related to water quality; a sufficient lowering of the water quantity in a body of water could destroy all of its designated uses, be it for drinking water, recreation, navigation or, as here, as a fishery. In any event, there is recognition in the Clean Water Act itself that reduced stream flow, *i.e.*, diminishment of water quantity, can constitute pollution. First, the Act's definition of pollution as "the man-made or man-induced alteration of the chemical, physical, biological, and radiological integrity of water" encompasses the effects of reduced water quantity. This broad conception of pollution—one which expressly evinces Congress' concern with the physical and biological integrity of water—refutes petitioners' assertion that the Act draws a sharp distinction between the regulation of water "quantity" and water "quality". Moreover, § 304 of the

---

[39] 511 U.S. 700 (1994).

[40] Section 401 requires any applicant for a federal license or permit involving any discharge into the navigable waters to obtain certification from the state in which the discharge originates that the discharge will meet WQS, other applicable requirements of the CWA, and "any other appropriate requirement of state law." 33 U.S.C. § 1341(a), (d).

Act expressly recognizes that water "pollution" may result from "changes in the movement, flow, or circulation of any navigable waters . . ., including changes caused by the construction of dams."[41]

The Court also upheld Washington's use of its anti-degradation program authority and authority to protect designated uses independent of specific WQC to assert minimum flow requirements to protect the fishery threatened by the dam project.

Thus, states clearly are *authorized* to impose minimum flow conditions, or water quantity requirements, through the WQS program of the CWA. A more challenging issue, not yet addressed judicially, is whether states are *required* to do so—and whether the EPA may impose water quantity-based requirements for a state that has failed to do so. Although Congress clearly delegated to states the primary responsibility to promulgate WQS for waters within its borders, it also subjected those standards to the EPA's oversight, including giving the EPA authority to adopt WQS for states that fail to do so or whose standards to not meet all applicable statutory requirements.[42] Although the EPA has, on rare occasions, adopted WQS for states deemed out of compliance with WQS requirements, it has never done so for water quantity provisions, and most states have not used their WQS programs in this way despite the broad authority to do so that the Supreme Court recognized in *PUD No. 1*. To date, no party has challenged the failure of states to adopt minimum flow requirements where necessary to protect designated uses of waters, but the CWA's WQS requirements could provide an additional untapped strategy to force states to protect minimum stream flows, in addition to the authority discussed in earlier chapters under more traditional principles of water law.

Other provisions of the CWA, however, seek to preserve state authority over water quantity issues. The Act's first section, for example, states that "[i]t is the policy of Congress that the authority of each State to allocate quantities of water within its jurisdiction shall not be superseded, abrogated, or otherwise impaired by" the Act.[43] Section 510, moreover, states that the CWA shall not "be construed as impairing or in any manner affecting any right or jurisdiction of the States with respect to the waters (including boundary waters) of such States."[44] These provisions have received limited attention in the courts, and thus it remains an open question

---

41 511 U.S. at 719–20.

42 33 U.S.C. § 1313(c)(3), (4).

43 33 U.S.C. § 1251(g).

44 33 U.S.C. § 1370.

whether the EPA can impose minimum stream flow and other water quantity provisions on states in order to meeting water quality goals.

The second significant way in which the WQS program intersects with water quantity law is in the implementation of WQC through NPDES permits. Recall that the permitting authority must impose WQBELs when technology-based controls are insufficient to attain WQS. There is an obvious connection between water quality and water quantity in this regard because the more water that is available to dilute all of the pollutants released into a particular stream or stream segment, the more likely it is that the WQS will be met, or the less stringent the WQBELs will need to be. Thus, in adopting WQBELs, permit writers must consider flow as well as pollution.

In one case in Colorado, an industrial discharger tried unsuccessfully to assert that a requested water exchange agreement violated the "no injury" rule in Colorado's prior appropriation system because it would reduce stream flows in ways that would require it to incur more expensive pollution control costs.[45] The Colorado Supreme Court rejected this claim because the proposed exchange affected only the amount of *excess* water in the stream and did not diminish any valid appropriative rights held by the discharger:

> We are not unaware of the interrelationship between water quantity and water quality concerns. . . . However, exchanges . . . are innovative methods of increasing the beneficial use of the state's waters. Under the current legislative scheme, the impact [of the exchange] is tolerated as a consequence of the policy of maximum beneficial use. The decision whether further to integrate the consideration and administration of water quality concerns into the prior appropriation system is the province of the General Assembly or the electorate.[46]

The CWA regulatory regime, by contrast, does recognize the intersection of water quantity and water quality goals represented by the WQS. Under Section 303(d), states must calculate "total maximum daily loads" (TMDLs) for waters that do not meet their WQS and use those calculations to impose appropriate permit requirements. The EPA's TMDL regulation provides that "[d]eterminations of TMDLs shall take into account critical conditions for stream flow, loading, and water quality parameters."[47] Most courts have limited new discharges to water body segments that

---

[45] City of Thornton v. Bijou Irrigation Co., 926 P.2d 1 (Colo. 1996).

[46] *Id.* at 94–95.

[47] 40 C.F.R. § 131.7(c)(1).

already violate WQS,[48] although the statute is somewhat ambiguous about whether WQS can be met by increasing stream flows rather than reducing pollution. Clearly, stream flow augmentation cannot be used to reduce technology-based treatment obligations, reflecting the oft-cited concept that "dilution is not the solution to pollution."[49] Congress did suggest, however, that stream flow augmentation might be considered to "control pollution not susceptible to other means of prevention, reduction or elimination."[50] Thus, when the national technology-based effluent limitations are not sufficient to meet WQS in a particular waterbody and the relevant industrial dischargers with NPDES permits have few options to reduce the concentration of pollutants in their discharges other than reducing production or shutting down completely, states might consider increasing the amount of water to address the pollution problem. Again, however, it remains an open question whether *the EPA* can impose such a requirement on states.

c. *Water Law and Technology-Based Pollution Control*

Technology-based effluent limitations, which set the default NPDES permit limitations, have a less direct connection to water resources management because they do not depend on the volume or quality of the receiving water. However, Congress intended the CWA's ultimate zero-discharge goal to be implemented primarily through increasingly strict technology-based standards. As a result, there are several indirect connections between the manner in which those standards are written and implemented and water quantity issues.

For example, the best way to achieve the zero-discharge goal for particular point sources is to eliminate those discharges altogether, through process changes that might include manufacturing techniques that minimize or eliminate water use. In fact, the U.S. Geological Survey has found that technology-based water pollution controls required under the CWA encouraged greater water use efficiency in U.S. industry.[51] Congress sought even more specifically to promote zero discharge of municipal sewage wastes by providing grants and other incentives for wastewater reuse and recycling, in

---

48 *E.g.*, Friends of Pinto Creek v. U.S. E.P.A., 504 F.3d 1007 (9th Cir. 2007). *But see*, Assateague Coastkeeper v. Maryland Dept. of Environment, 28 A.3d 178, 205–06 (Md. App. 2011) (disagreeing that section 303(d) prohibits all new discharges to impaired waters).

49 33 U.S.C. § 1252(b) (prohibiting federal agencies from considering reservoir storage to augment streamflow "as a substitute for adequate treatment or other methods of controlling waste at the source.")

50 *Id.* § 1254(d).

51 U.S. GEOLOGICAL SURVEY, CIRCULAR 1441, ESTIMATED USE OF WATER USE IN THE UNITED STATES IN 2015, at 55 (2018).

which adequately treated municipal wastewater is used for irrigation and other secondary uses.[52] Although that concept has not been implemented widely from a national perspective, water reuse has been increasing significantly in areas that are short on overall water supply.[53] In 2020, EPA and a range of partners released a collaborative plan to stimulate further adoption and implementation of reuse programs.[54]

Ironically, however, achieving zero discharge by eliminating discharges altogether potentially can conflict with other water resource policy goals, especially in arid regions where stream flow has been diminished substantially by water withdrawals. In those areas, municipal sewage effluent can be a significant source of downstream water supply and a source of water to maintain otherwise dewatered aquatic ecosystems.[55] Whether zero discharge is the best policy under those conditions remains the subject of significant discussion. Indeed, achieving the zero-discharge goal, particularly in arid parts of the country, may eventually turn on whether eliminating discharges *of pollutants* also requires eliminating discharges *of water*.

D. Federalism and the Intersection of Water Quality and Water Quantity

As discussed in many of the earlier chapters, water law involves frequent questions about the appropriate roles of the state and federal governments in regulating and managing water resources. Earlier chapters explained that water allocation law basically is within the province of the states. It is not entirely clear whether that result is required under the Tenth Amendment or other constitutional provisions, or whether it simply reflects a congressional policy determination, particularly in western states where, pursuant to the Desert Lands Act, Congress segregated water rights from the land and left water allocation to the policy discretion of the individual states.[56] On the other hand, earlier chapters also explained the powerful *influence* of federal law on state water law and water resources policy. Those influences include the construction of a massive nationwide system of dams and other water resources

---

[52] *See* 33 U.S.C. §§ 1254(*o*), 1255(d).

[53] *See* NATIONAL RESEARCH COUNCIL, WATER REUSE: EXPANDING THE NATION'S WATER SUPPLY THROUGH REUSE OF MUNICIPAL WASTEWATER (2012).

[54] U.S. EPA, National Water Reuse Action Plan, Improving the Security, Sustainability, and Resilience of Our Nation's Water Resources (Feb. 2020).

[55] *See, e.g.*, Arizona Public Service Co. v. Long, 160 Ariz. 429, 773 P.2d 988 (1989) (discussing dispute over right to use treated sewage effluent discharged into the Salt River).

[56] *See* California Oregon Power Co. v. Beaver Portland Cement Co., 295 U.S. 142 (1935) (discussed in Chapter 3).

infrastructure, and the resulting federal operation of water projects and possession and sale of water rights, as well as the impact of federal regulatory statutes on the operation of state water law.

In an effort to constrain the impacts of federal law on state water rights, in statutes such as the Reclamation Act[57] (discussed in Chapter 8) and the Federal Power Act[58] (discussed in Chapter 10), Congress has adopted savings provisions seeking to clarify its intent to recognize and preserve the integrity of state water law and state control of its water resources. As noted above, virtually identical language appears in the CWA. In full, this provision state that:

> It is the policy of Congress that the authority of each State to allocate quantities of water within its jurisdiction shall not be superseded, abrogated or otherwise impaired by [the CWA]. It is the further policy of Congress that nothing in this [Act] shall be construed to supersede rights to quantities of water which have been established by any State. Federal agencies shall co-operate with State and local agencies to develop comprehensive solutions to prevent, reduce and eliminate pollution in concert with programs for managing water resources.[59]

Also as noted above, this expression of congressional reluctance to interfere with state water rights affects some of the issues discussed above. For example, the EPA cited this section in its justification for the Water Transfers Rule, which limits the extent to which water transfers are subject to NPDES permits:

> While section 101(g) does not prohibit the EPA from taking actions under the CWA that it determines are needed to protect water quality, it nonetheless establishes in the text of the Act Congress's general direction against unnecessary Federal interference with State allocation of water rights.
>
> Water transfers are an essential component of the nation's infrastructure for delivering water that users are entitled to receive under State law. Because subjecting water transfers to a federal permitting scheme could unnecessarily interfere with State decisions on allocations of water rights, this section provides additional support for the Agency's interpretation that, absent a clear

---

57 *See* California v. United States, 438 U.S. 645 (1978).

58 *See* California v. FERC, 495 U.S. 490 (1990).

59 33 U.S.C. § 1251(g); *see also id.* § 1370 ("Except as expressly provided in this Act, nothing in this Act shall . . . be construed as impairing or in any manner affecting any right or jurisdiction of the States with respect to the waters (including boundary waters) of such States.").

Congressional intent to the contrary, it is reasonable to read the statute as not requiring NPDES permits for water transfers.[60]

Sensitivity to states' rights also influenced the manner in which Congress distinguished regulation of point source pollution, in which the EPA has a dominant role, with management of nonpoint source pollution, in which the federal role is far more muted. For point sources, particularly in the NPDES permitting regime and in the system of nationally applicable technology-based effluent limitations that it effectuates, Congress wanted to ensure minimum levels of across-the-board pollution control for all similarly situated dischargers. This strategy prevents states from engaging in a "race to the bottom" to protect their industries and to attract more development relative to other states. Moreover, because particular kinds of industrial facilities and municipal waste treatment plants are not likely to vary greatly based on geography, a relatively uniform system of point source control requirements is feasible. Nonpoint source pollution control, by contrast, implicates land use and economic development policies that Congress believed were more appropriately left to state discretion.[61] Thus, the Clean Water Act includes state planning programs to address nonpoint source pollution generally.[62] Unlike NPDES permits, however, those provisions do not automatically impose enforceable obligations on individual pollution sources.[63] That federalism-based decision has resulted in generally weaker and much less consistent control of nonpoint source pollution around the country, but Congress remains reluctant to adopt a more intrusive approach to issues affecting state land and local use policy.

Similarly, federalism concerns affect the manner in which the WQS program is interpreted and administered, including in particular its ability to address minimum flow standards and other water quantity issues. Generally speaking, Congress assigned to the states the primary task of defining the designated uses of waterbodies in their states, at least beyond the minimum "fishable and swimmable" goals established in the CWA.[64] Congress assigned a more significant oversight role to the EPA with respect to the water

---

[60] NPDES Water Transfers Rule, 73 Fed. Reg. 33697, 33697 (June 13, 2008) (codified at 40 C.F.R. § 122.3(i)).

[61] *See* 33 U.S.C. § 1251(b) (establishing Congressional policy "to recognize, preserve, and protect the primary responsibilities and rights of States to prevent, reduce, and eliminate pollution, [and] to plan the development and use (including restoration, preservation, and enhancement) of land and water resources . . . .").

[62] 33 U.S.C. §§ 1288, 1329.

[63] *See* Central Sierra Environmental Resource Center v. Stanislaus National Forest, 30 F.4th 929, 942–43 (9th Cir. 2022).

[64] 33 U.S.C. § 1251(a)(2).

quality criteria designed to protect those uses.[65] With respect to the water quantity issue addressed above, in *PUD No. 1* the Supreme Court cited the statutory provisions reserving water resource management authority to the states, but noted that "[t]his language gives the States authority to allocate water rights; we therefore find it peculiar that petitioners argue that it prevents the State from regulating stream flow."[66]

That language alone might suggest a greater reluctance to interpret the statute as requiring states to adopt minimum flow standards where necessary to authorize protection for designated uses, or especially to authorize the EPA to adopt such requirements if a state failed to so do. The Court read the CWA savings provisions more narrowly, however, writing that they "preserve the authority of each State to allocate water quantity as between users; they do not limit the scope of water pollution controls that may be imposed on users who have obtained, pursuant to state law, a water allocation."[67] The Court also cited legislative history indicating that while Congress intended to preserve state authority in the area of water rights to the greatest extent possible, it did not intend to subvert incidental effects on state water law where necessary to effectuate the water quality goals of the Act.[68]

Perhaps the most significant and contentious federalism issue regarding the scope of the CWA and its implications for state water resources management is the longstanding controversy over the waters to which the Act, and particularly its point source permitting requirements, applies. As discussed above, the CWA prohibits the "discharge of a pollutant" absent a permit from the EPA, a delegated state, or for certain kinds of discharges, from the U.S. Army Corps of Engineers.[69] The Act defines "discharge of a pollutant" as "any addition of any pollutant to *navigable waters* from any point source."[70] The Act also defines "navigable waters" to be "the waters of the United States, including the territorial seas."[71]

Controversy has swirled for decades over applicability of these terms to waters such as wetlands, intermittent and ephemeral streams, non-navigable tributaries of traditional navigable waters (see Chapter 6), and purely intrastate water bodies. Conceptually, advocates for a more limited scope of federal authority argue that, in

---

[65] *See* Mississippi Commission on Natural Resources v. Costle, 625 F.2d 1269 (5th Cir. 1980); *compare* 33 U.S.C. § 1313(c) *with id.* § 1314(a).

[66] 511 U.S. at 720.

[67] *Id.*

[68] *Id.* at 721.

[69] 33 U.S.C. §§ 1311(a), 1342, 1344.

[70] *Id.* § 1362(12) (emphasis added).

[71] *Id.* § 1362(7).

using the term "navigable waters," Congress intended to use its traditional Commerce Clause power over navigable waters to address pollution as it affects the national economy. Extending that authority to smaller, isolated waters is closer to the land use and water management issues that Congress intended to leave to state and local governments, and possibly exceeds federal constitutional authority. Those who suggest a broader reach point to legislative history in which Congress made clear that it intended to invoke the broadest scope of authority constitutionally permissible and the fact that hydrological connections between all water bodies make it difficult to protect and restore traditional navigable waters if unregulated discharges continue to upstream waters. As such, since at least 1977, the EPA's and Army Corps' joint CWA regulations sought to link CWA jurisdiction to "[a]ll other waters. . . the use, degradation, or destruction of which could affect interstate or foreign commerce . . . ."[72]

Chapter 6 discussed the meaning of the term "navigable waters" in various contexts, including the broad permissible scope of federal regulatory authority under the Commerce Clause under cases such as *United States v. Appalachian Electric Power Co.*[73] Given this breadth of authority over traditional navigable waters, the U.S. Supreme Court held relatively early in the CWA's history that the Act at least applied to wetlands adjacent to navigable waters, for which a hydrological connection is clear.[74] However, further clarity has been elusive in the three decades since that decision. The scope of the term "navigable waters" for CWA purposes is complicated and arguably broadened by reference to the term "waters of the United States," a phrase with no similar long history of judicial interpretation. Nevertheless, in 2001 the Supreme Court held that the fact that Congress retained its reference to "navigable waters" in the Act indicates its intent to retain that concept as a limit on the scope of the Act's jurisdiction.[75] A 2006 Supreme Court effort to address the issue produced a fractured 4–1–4 decision. The dispositive concurring opinion by Justice Kennedy found that CWA jurisdiction over waterbodies that do not fall clearly within the Commerce Clause test for navigability "depends upon the existence of a significant nexus between the [waters] in question and navigable waters in the traditional sense."[76] The four-justice plurality opinion written by Justice Scalia would have adopted a far narrower test for

---

[72] 33 C.F.R.

[73] 311 U.S. 377 (1940).

[74] U.S. v. Riverside Bayview Homes, 474 U.S. 121 (1985).

[75] *See* Solid Waste Agency of Northern Cook County v. U.S. Army Corps of Engineers, 531 U.S. 159 (2001).

[76] Rapanos v. United States, 547 U.S. 715, 779–80 (2006) (Kennedy, J., concurring).

CWA jurisdiction, limited to "relatively permanent, standing or flowing bodies of water."[77]

The Obama Administration (2015), Trump Administration (2020), and Biden Administration (2023) all issued regulations attempting to refine the definition of "waters of the United States," but none have yet survived litigation and/or changes in administration. Most recently, the Supreme Court rejected Justice Kennedy's "significant nexus" test from *Rapanos*, despite nearly universal adoption among the federal Courts of Appeals. Instead, the Court unanimously concluded in *Sackett v. EPA* that the *Rapanos* plurality was correct: the CWA's use of "waters" encompasses "only those relatively permanent, standing or continuously flowing bodies of water 'forming geographic[al] features' that are described in ordinary parlance as 'streams, oceans, rivers, and lakes.' "[78] Justice Alito's five-Justice majority opinion cited federalism concerns as part of its rationale for this limitation on CWA jurisdiction. In response, the Biden Administration adopted yet another set of regulations curtailing the geographic scope of the CWA.

---

[77] *Id.* at 732.

[78] Sackett v. EPA, 143 S. Ct. 1322, 1336 (2023). NOTE: The dissenters disagreed about the definition of "adjacent" for adjacent wetlands, not about which basic *Rapanos* test was the correct one.

Chapter 12

HUMAN USE OF WATER AND ENDANGERED SPECIES

A. Introduction

As Chapters 11 and 13 make clear, streams, rivers, and lakes are not just sterile sources of water for human uses—they are fundamental components of larger and complex aquatic ecosystems. As a result, when humans take large amounts of water from these systems, or when they change the hydrology of these systems by building dams, reservoirs, and canals, human water use can put other species in peril.

The most prominent national legal manifestation of how profoundly human water use can affect other species—and even entire aquatic ecosystems—is the federal Endangered Species Act (ESA).[1] Many states also have state endangered species laws, some of which are arguably more protective than the federal ESA. Implementation of these state species statutes can provide good clues regarding aquatic conflicts at the state level. For example, when New York and Vermont embarked on an eight-year program to remove sea lampreys, a nuisance species, from Lake Champlain, they decided to use poisons in the streams and rivers that flow into Lake Champlain in order to kill sea lamp larvae, a plan that was (unsuccessfully) challenged under the Vermont Endangered Species Act.[2] However, this chapter will focus on the federal ESA, both to provide a national picture of conflicts between species protection and water use and because most state species protection laws are structured similarly to the ESA, so understanding the ESA provides a good start to evaluating state laws later.

ESA issues have become pervasive in water law. Although, as you might expect, ESA conflicts are more common in the West, where water supplies are already limited and prior appropriation doctrines have (at least historically) allowed users to drain water sources dry, species issues related to water are also becoming common in the East. You can get some sense of the breadth of water-species conflicts from

[1] 16 U.S.C. §§ 1531–1544.

[2] Elliott v. U.S. Fish & Wildlife Service, 747 F. Supp. 1094, 1100 (D. Vt. 1990).

the fact that that human use of all of the following rivers, lakes, aquifers, and water systems has generated ESA litigation:

- All American Canal (California near the Mexico border)
- Apalachicola-Chattahoochee-Flint River Basin (Alabama, Florida, and Georgia)
- Big Bear Lake (California)
- Big Timber Creek (Idaho)
- Central Valley Project (California)
- Chewuch River (Washington)
- Colorado River (Arizona, California, Colorado, Nevada, New Mexico, Utah, and Wyoming)
- Columbia River (Oregon and Washington)
- Comel Spring (Texas)
- Coosa River (Alabama)
- Delaware River (Delaware and Pennsylvania)
- Devil's Hole (Nevada)
- Edwards Aquifer (Texas)
- Eel River (California)
- Everglades (Florida)
- Grassy Lake and Little River (Arkansas)
- Huzzah River (Missouri)
- Klamath River (California and Oregon)
- Little Tennessee River (Tennessee)
- Little Truckee River (Nevada)
- Mahogany Creek (Idaho)
- Meramec River (Missouri)
- Missouri River (Iowa, Kansas, Missouri, Montana, Nebraska, North Dakota, and South Dakota)
- Neversink Dam and Reservoir (New York)
- Otter Creek (Idaho)
- Pahsimeroi River (Idaho)
- Pascagoula River (Mississippi)
- Piru Creek (California)

- Platte River (Nebraska)
- Pyramid Lake (Nevada)
- Quoddy Bay (Maine)
- Rio Grande River (New Mexico)
- Rock Creek (Montana)
- Salt Basin Aquifer (New Mexico)
- Salt River (Arizona)
- San Carlos Reservoir (Arizona)
- San Joaquin River (California)
- San Marcos Spring (Texas)
- San Pedro River (Arizona)
- Skokomish River (Washington)
- Snake River (Idaho and Wyoming)
- South Platte River (Colorado)
- Trinity River (California)
- Tulare Lake (California)
- Upper Salmon River (Idaho)
- Ventura River (California)
- Yaak River (Montana)
- Yuba River (California)

This chapter surveys the ways in which the federal ESA and water law interact. It begins by examining the ESA's purposes, then focuses on the issue of how aquatic species can become listed for protection under the Act. Finally, it examines how water use and management can trigger federal agencies' duties under Section 7 of the Act and the more general "take" prohibition in Section 9.

B. The ESA's Purposes and Goals

When Congress enacted the contemporary ESA in 1973, it recognized that many species of fish, wildlife, and plants had already become extinct; that "other species of fish, wildlife, and plants have been so depleted in numbers that they are in danger of or threatened with extinction;" and that these endangered and threatened species "are of esthetic, ecological, educational, historical, recreational, and scientific value to the Nation and its people. . . ."[3] Importantly, therefore, the ESA is *anthropocentric* in perspective: it seeks to

[3] ESA § 2(a), 16 U.S.C. § 1531(a).

protect species primarily because of their importance to human beings. While some may find that anthropocentrism offensive, it has been critically important when courts have had to place financial or commercial value on species protection, as we'll see.

Congress declared three purposes for the Act. First, the ESA is "to provide a means whereby the ecosystems upon which endangered species and threatened species depend may be conserved . . . ."[4] Thus, the ESA has an ecosystem perspective on species conservation even though it operates by protecting individual species. This ecosystem perspective can become particularly important in the context of aquatic ecosystems.

Second, the ESA is "to provide a program for the conservation of such endangered species and threatened species . . . ."[5] "Conservation" and "conserve" are important words in the ESA, and they underscore Congress's recovery and restoration goals for species. Specifically, Congress defined "conserve," "conserving," and "conservation" to mean:

> to use and the use of all methods and procedures which are necessary to bring any endangered species or threatened species to the point at which the measures provided pursuant to this chapter [the ESA] are no longer necessary. Such methods and procedures include, but are not limited to, all activities associated with scientific resources management such as research, census, law enforcement, habitat acquisition and maintenance, propagation, live trapping, and transplantation, and, in the extraordinary case where population pressures within a given ecosystem cannot be otherwise relieved, may include regulated taking.[6]

Thus, the ESA's ultimate goal is to rehabilitate species and ecosystems to the point where its provisions are no longer needed. In the water context, therefore, the ESA can promote a more holistic approach to aquatic ecosystem management.

Third, the ESA has an international law component and functions as the domestic U.S. law through which the United States fulfills its various species-related treaty obligations, particularly its migratory bird treaties with several nations and its international trade obligations under the multilateral Convention on International Trade in Endangered Species of Flora and Fauna, or CITES.[7] Many

---

4 ESA § 2(b), 16 U.S.C. § 1531(b).

5 *Id.*

6 ESA § 3(3), 16 U.S.C. § 1532(3).

7 ESA § 2(b), 16 U.S.C. § 1531(b); *see also* ESA § 3(4), 16 U.S.C. § 1532(4) (defining "Convention" to refer to CITES).

of the trade-related provisions of the Act, especially in Section 9, operate to fulfill these international obligations.

With respect to water law, the ESA has been most important, quite naturally, with regard to species that depend on fresh water habitat: fish, aquatic plants, waterfowl, aquatic invertebrates, and migratory birds. Notably, when the U.S. Supreme Court first interpreted the ESA in 1978—a mere five years after Congress enacted it—the case involved a water project. *Tennessee Valley Authority v. Hill*[8] asked the Court to decide whether the completion of the Tennessee Valley Authority's (see Chapter 8) almost-finished Tellico Dam project was still legal under the ESA. The Tellico Dam would block the Little Tennessee River that runs through Georgia, North Carolina, and Tennessee, destroying farms, fisheries, and Native American archaeological sites, which were among the reasons that residents opposed the dam. Legally, however, the most effective challenges came through federal environmental laws, first through the National Environmental Policy Act (NEPA, see Chapter 8) and, once that litigation was finished, through the ESA. Hill and his fellow litigants petitioned the U.S. Fish & Wildlife Service in January 1975 to list the three-inch snail darter (see Figure 12–1) for protection under the ESA, and the Service officially listed the fish as an endangered species in October 1975. The Tellico Dam would destroy all of the snail darter's known critical habitat, threatening it with extinction.

The U.S. Supreme Court determined that the ESA required it to enjoin completion of the Tellico Dam. According to the Court:

> It may seem curious to some that the survival of a relatively small number of three-inch fish among all the countless millions of species extant would require the permanent halting of a virtually completed dam for which Congress has expended more than $100 million. The paradox is not minimized by the fact that Congress continued to appropriate large sums of public money for the project, even after congressional Appropriations Committees were apprised of its apparent impact upon the survival of the snail darter. We conclude, however, that the explicit provisions of the Endangered Species Act require precisely that result.
>
> * * *
>
> Concededly, this view of the Act will produce results requiring the sacrifice of the anticipated benefits of the project and of many millions of dollars in public funds. But

[8] 437 U.S. 153 (1978).

examination of the language, history, and structure of the legislation under review here indicates beyond doubt that Congress intended endangered species to be afforded the highest of priorities.[9]

Figure 12–1: The Snail Darter
Photograph courtesy of the U.S. Fish & Wildlife Service

Congress's view of the anthropocentric value of species also became important to the case, particularly regarding the remedy. As the Court detailed:

> The legislative proceedings in 1973 are . . . replete with expressions of concern over the risk that might lie in the loss of any endangered species. Typifying these sentiments is the Report of the House Committee on Merchant Marine and Fisheries on H.R. 37, a bill which contained the essential features of the subsequently enacted Act of 1973; in explaining the need for the legislation, the Report stated:
>
> > "As we homogenize the habitats in which these plants and animals evolved, and as we increase the pressure for products that they are in a position to supply (usually unwillingly) we threaten their—and our own—genetic heritage.
> >
> > "The value of this genetic heritage is, quite literally, incalculable.

[9] *Id.* at 172–74.

> "From the most narrow possible point of view, *it is in the best interests of mankind to minimize the losses of genetic variations*. The reason is simple: they are potential resources. They are keys to puzzles which we cannot solve, and may provide answers to questions which we have not yet learned to ask.
>
> "To take a homely, but apt, example: one of the critical chemicals in the regulation of ovulations in humans was found in a common plant. Once discovered, and analyzed, humans could duplicate it synthetically, but had it never existed—or had it been driven out of existence before we knew its potentialities—we would never have tried to synthesize it in the first place.
>
> "Who knows, or can say, what potential cures for cancer or other scourges, present or future, may lie locked up in the structures of plants which may yet be undiscovered, much less analyzed? . . . Sheer self-interest impels us to be cautious.
>
> "*The institutionalization of that caution* lies at the heart of H.R. 37 . . . ."
>
> H.R. Rep. No.93–412, pp. 4–5 (1973). (Emphasis added.)
>
> As the examples cited here demonstrate, Congress was concerned about the unknown uses that endangered species might have and about the unforeseeable place such creatures may have in the chain of life on this planet.[10]

As a result of this congressionally mandated valuing of listed species and precautionary approach, the Court concluded that courts had to enjoin projects or actions that violate the ESA. Injunctions are equitable remedies at law, and normally courts will balance the harms imposed against the value of the activity when deciding whether to impose an injunction. For the ESA, however, the Supreme Court concluded that Congress had already completed this balancing legislatively:

> Here we are urged to view the Endangered Species Act "reasonably," and hence shape a remedy "that accords with some modicum of common sense and the public weal." But is that our function? We have no expert knowledge on the subject of endangered species, much less do we have a mandate from the people to strike a balance of equities on the side of the Tellico Dam. Congress has spoken in the plainest of words, making it abundantly clear that the

---

[10] *Id.* at 177–79.

> balance has been struck in favor of affording endangered species the highest of priorities, thereby adopting a policy which it described as "institutionalized caution."[11]

Thus, according to the U.S. Supreme Court, Congress has effectively cabined judges' discretion when it comes to ESA remedies.

Figure 12–2: The Completed Tellico Dam
Photograph courtesy of the Tennessee Valley Authority

TVA v. Hill was a very powerful first U.S. Supreme Court case for the ESA. However, the Court's decision triggered a significant political reaction, which has become another important reality of ESA implementation. Congress amended the ESA to add a "safety valve" provision by creating the seven-member Endangered Species Committee, which can, by a supermajority vote of 5–2, allow a federal project to proceed even when the project might destroy a listed species.[12] Because this Committee holds the fate of species in its hands, it is often referred to as the "God Squad." Congress also ordered the Committee to review the Tellico Dam project, but the Committee decided, 7–0, that the dam was not worth completing (and in fact probably should not even have been started on economic grounds). Undaunted, Congress enacted special legislation that allowed the Tellico Dam to be completed despite the ESA (a legislative exemption), and the dam was completed in 1979 (see Figure 12–2).

---

[11] *Id.* at 194.

[12] ESA § 7(e)–(n), 16 U.S.C. § 1536(e)–(n).

Fortunately, biologists found several other populations of the snail darter, and in 1984 the species was considered healthy enough that the U.S. Fish & Wildlife Service reclassified it to being a threatened species. (Tennessee also lists the snail darter as a threatened species under state law.) However, according to the Service's most recent evaluation of the darter in 2013, the darter remains subject to a number of threats, including: poor habitat; water quality impairments and industrial and municipal wastewater discharges (see Chapter 11); operation of towboats in the Tennessee River; releases of cool or cold water from various dams, which can cause thermal shock or dislodge the darters; runoff from riverfront development; agricultural runoff; and mercury contamination leading to bioaccumulation of mercury in fish tissues.[13]

C. Listing Species for Protection Under Section 4

No species receives *any* protection under the ESA until it is formally listed as an endangered or threatened species. Section 4[14] governs the listing process. The Secretary of the Interior, acting through the U.S. Fish & Wildlife Service, has jurisdiction over terrestrial and fresh water species, while the Secretary of Commerce, acting through the National Marine Fisheries Service (NMFS, pronounced "nymphs") of the National Oceanic and Atmospheric Administration (NOAA), has jurisdiction over marine species and anadromous species—that is, species like salmon that start life in fresh water, migrate out to sea for a while, and then return to fresh water to spawn. (NOTE: NOAA subdivisions have undergone some name changes over time, so sometimes NMFS is referred to as "NOAA Fisheries.")

Procedurally, the appropriate Service lists a species under the ESA by promulgating a federal regulation,[15] generally following the informal rulemaking procedures of the federal Administrative Procedure Act.[16] These procedures are called "notice and comment rulemaking" because the relevant agency must publish notice of the proposed listing in the Federal Register, allow for public comment on the proposal, and then publish a final decision in the Federal Register. The ESA specifies that the relevant agency must publish notice of any final listing decision at least 90 days before it takes

---

13 U.S. FISH & WILDLIFE SERVICE, SNAIL DARTER (*PERCINA TANASI*) FIVE-YEAR REVIEW: SUMMARY AND EVALUATION 15–19 (March 2013).

14 There are two ways to refer to sections of the ESA: by their citation in the United States Code, which is the most formal and legally correct reference; and by their section numbers from the original Public Law that Congress enacted, which is how practitioners usually still refer to these provisions. Citations in this chapter give both formats. Thus, Section 4 of the ESA is also 16 U.S.C. § 1533.

15 ESA § 4(a)(1), (b)(4), 16 U.S.C. § 1533(a)(1), (b)(4).

16 5 U.S.C. § 553(b).

effect, and the agency can allow no more than a year to elapse between the proposed listing and its final decision.[17]

As was shown in *TVA v. Hill*, the ESA also allows citizens to petition the Services to list a species (or, later, to de-list or change the status of a species). The citizen must submit the petition with scientific evidence supporting the requested listing decision. The appropriate Service then has 90 days to decide whether the petition "presents substantial scientific evidence or commercial information indicating that the petitioned action may be warranted."[18] If not, the petition process ends (subject to judicial review in court), but if further review is warranted, the Service has an additional 12 months to conduct a status review of the species and publish its finding.[19] The agency has three choices at this point. First, it can conclude that the petitioned action is not warranted, in which case the petition process is complete (subject to judicial review). Second, it can conclude that the petitioned action, like listing a species, *is* warranted, in which case the 12-month finding will also usually function as the proposed rulemaking for the listing decision. Finally, the agency can conclude that listing of the species is warranted, but that actual listing is currently precluded by other, higher priority species. If the agency makes this third finding, it must re-visit the status of the petitioned species every year until the agency decides either to list the species or to remove it from consideration.

So, when is the listing of a species warranted? First, species listings are based "solely . . . on the best scientific and commercial data available"[20]—that is, the U.S. Fish & Wildlife Service and NMFS are *not* supposed to consider economic impacts in their listing decisions. Second, in its evaluation of a species, the relevant Service must consider five factors:

(A) the present or threatened destruction, modification, or curtailment of its habitat or range;

(B) overutilization for commercial, recreational, scientific, or educational purposes;

(C) disease or predation;

(D) the inadequacy of existing regulatory mechanisms; or

(E) other natural or manmade factors affecting its continued existence.[21]

---

17 ESA § 4(b)(5), 16 U.S.C. § 1533(b)(5).

18 ESA § 4(b)(3), 16 U.S.C. § 1533(b)(3).

19 *Id.*

20 ESA § 4(b)(1)(A), 16 U.S.C. § 1533(b)(1)(A).

21 ESA § 4(a)(1), 15 U.S.C. § 1533(a)(1).

This list of factors is disjunctive—*i.e.*, joined by an "or" at the end—so any one of the factors can be sufficient to list a species. At the time Congress adopted species protection statutes, hunting and habitat destruction were the biggest threats to species. Now, however, habitat destruction and impairment are the primary reasons that the Services list species under the ESA, although climate change impacts are becoming more prominent.

If a species warrants listing, the relevant Service has two more decisions to make. First, it must decide whether the species' status under the Act should be endangered or threatened. An endangered species is "in danger of extinction throughout all or a significant portion of its range. . . ."[22] A threatened species, in turn, "is likely to become an endangered species within the foreseeable future throughout all or a significant portion of its range."[23] The most important legal and practical difference between the two statuses is that endangered species automatically receive all of the Act's Section 9 "take" and trade protections (discussed below),[24] while the two agencies can enact regulations providing lesser protections to threatened species, known as "Section 4(d) rules" after the ESA provision that authorizes them.[25]

The second decision that the relevant Service is supposed to make as part of the species' listing is the designation of the species' critical habitat.[26] "Critical habitat" is:

> (i) the specific areas within the geographical area occupied by the species, at the time it is listed . . . , on which are found those physical or biological features (I) essential to the conservation of the species and (II) which may require special management considerations or protection; and
>
> (ii) specific areas outside the geographical area occupied by the species at the time it is listed . . . , upon a determination by the [relevant agency] that such areas are essential for the conservation of the species.[27]

Thus, critical habitat designations most importantly help to conserve listed species—that is, to allow those species to recover to the point where they no longer need the Act's protections. However, the agencies can consider several more factors when designating critical habitat than they can when deciding to list a species. These factors

---

22 ESA § 3(6), 16 U.S.C. § 1532(6).

23 ESA § 3(20), 16 U.S.C. § 1532(20).

24 ESA § 9(a), 16 U.S.C. § 1538(a).

25 ESA § 4(d), 16 U.S.C. § 1533(d).

26 ESA § 4(a)(3), 16 U.S.C. § 1533(a)(3).

27 ESA § 3(5)(A), 16 U.S.C. § 1532(5)(A).

include economic impacts and national security interests.[28] Moreover, unless the exclusion of an area of critical habitat will lead to the species' extinction, the agency can decide *not* to include critical habitat if the benefits of exclusion outweigh benefits of the designation.[29]

The listing of an aquatic species—especially when the listing arises because of human use of water—tends to raise political controversies and generate legal battles. However, the listing of one aquatic species in a system also tends to signal that the entire system is in trouble. As a result, ESA listings in that aquatic system often begin to multiply, and recovery efforts can quickly escalate to the ecosystem scale.

Consider the Bruneau Hot Springsnail (see Figure 12–3), a tiny fresh water snail first identified in the 1950s and found only in the thermal pools along a 5.28-mile stretch of the Bruneau River and Hot Creek in southwest Idaho. Groundwater pumping by farmers in the area reduced the water table, which in turn reduced the springs' flow to less than 10% of what it had been in 1954, reducing the snails' habitat and threatening the species with extinction.

In August 1985, the U.S. Fish & Wildlife Service proposed to list the Bruneau Hot Springsnail as an endangered species, touching off a political and legal controversy that lasted until June 1998. Idaho's U.S. Senators asked the Service to delay the listing, citing "devastating effects" on the local agricultural community and providing funding for two scientific studies to prove (or, they hoped, disprove) the connection between groundwater pumping and threats to the species. However, although the researchers conducting the two studies found additional populations of the snail, all of the pools were hydrologically connected and the studies essentially proved that groundwater pumping was the cause of the snail's decline. As a result, the Service issued its final rule listing the snail as an endangered species in January 1993. Unfortunately, it neglected to make the U.S. Geological Survey's study public, which is a procedural violation of the listing process, and the U.S. Court of Appeals for the Ninth Circuit ordered the Service to go through another notice and comment period with the study made public—although it left the listing in place in the meantime.[30]

---

[28] ESA § 4(b)(2), 16 U.S.C. § 1533(b)(2).

[29] *Id.*

[30] *See generally* Idaho Farm Bureau Federation v. Babbitt, 58 F.3d 1392 (9th Cir. 1995).

Figure 12–3: Bruneau Hot Springsnail
Photograph courtesy of the U.S. Fish & Wildlife Service

The Service complied, re-noticing the listing and allowing comment through December 1995. At that point, however, the Bruneau Hot Springsnail got caught up in Congress's 1995–1996 ESA listing moratoria, during which Congress eliminated all funding for ESA listings. In April 1996, Congress finally allowed the president to waive the last moratorium, which President Bill Clinton did immediately, giving the U.S. Fish & Wildlife Service $4 million for listing and critical habitat decisions for the rest of Fiscal Year 1996. The Service, however, emerged from the moratoria with a long list of petitions and court orders to address, so it finally returned to the Bruneau Hot Springsnail in 1997, opening another comment period and finally affirming its original listing of the snail as endangered on June 17, 1998.

The Bruneau Hot Springsnail continues to affect water users in southwestern Idaho. In September 2002, Region 1 of the U.S. Fish & Wildlife Service finalized the snail's recovery plan. Under this plan, the Service will consider downlisting the snail to threatened status only when "groundwater management activities have been implemented and monitoring indicates an increasing trend in water levels in the geothermal aquifer and occupied geothermal springs for a period of 10 years."[31] Thus, effectuating the federal ESA's goal of recovering listed species requires, as a practical matter, that the State of Idaho regulate groundwater use. Moreover, before the Service will completely de-list the Bruneau Hot Springsnail, water levels in the hot springs must stabilize at levels significantly higher than in 1998, stable populations of Bruneau Hot Springsnail must occupy about 131 springs in the recovery area, and "groundwater levels [must be] permanently protected against further reductions through implementation of groundwater management activities."[32] Again, therefore, the snail's recovery requires Idaho to regulate groundwater use and to legally guard against groundwater depletion.

However, the snail's story has grown even more complex. The Bruneau River is a 153-mile-long tributary of the Snake River. Water developments in the Snake River, especially large hydroelectric power dams (see Chapter 10), combined with overfishing, led NMFS to begin listing Snake River salmonid species (salmon, remember, are anadromous species) for protection under the ESA beginning in the early 1990s. By 1997, NMFS had listed four such species for protection—Snake River sockeye salmon (endangered, 1991), Snake River spring/summer Chinook salmon (threatened, 1992), Snake River fall-run Chinook salmon (threatened, 1992), and Snake River Basin steelhead (threatened, 1997). Moreover, NMFS retained these listings after reviews in 2005 and 2006. In the meantime, the U.S. Fish & Wildlife Service was also listing a number of other species in the Snake River watershed for protection, such as the bull trout (threatened, 1999) and the Snake River Physa snail (endangered, 1992). Eventually, over a dozen species had been affected enough by water management in this ecosystem to warrant the ESA's protections.

These comprehensive watershed and ecosystem issues stretch throughout Idaho and into southeast Washington and northeast Oregon (see Figure 12–4); they also involve the migration of the salmon and steelhead to the Pacific Ocean through the Columbia River that forms the Washington-Oregon border. In recognition that the species' issues must be addressed on a larger scale, NMFS has taken the lead on a more comprehensive recovery plan strategy, working in cooperation with the U.S. Fish & Wildlife Service, the affected states, and Tribes in the region.

---

[31] REGION 1, U.S. FISH & WILDLIFE SERVICE, RECOVERY PLAN FOR THE BRUNEAU HOT SPRINGSNAIL iii (Sept. 2002).

[32] *Id.* at iii–iv.

Figure 12–4: The Snake River Recovery Plan Management Boundaries
Map courtesy of NOAA Fisheries West Coast Region

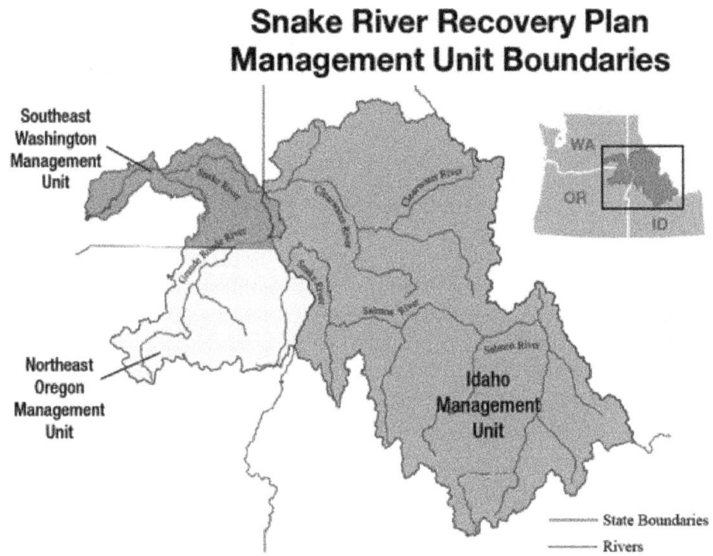

In November 2017, NOAA Fisheries issued a new recovery plan for the Snake River.[33] The plan concluded that the anadromous fishes' habitat and fish passage had improved, but that much more remains to be done.[34] The plan also addresses the federal government's trust responsibility to Pacific Northwest Tribes and their treaty rights to salmon.[35] However, the large hydropower dams in the Snake and Columbia Rivers remain the primary threats to the endangered fish, and as of 2022 and 2023, discussions about removing some of the Snake River dams grew increasingly serious.[36] In December 2023, the federal government announced a new agreement to partner with tribes and states to restore wild salmon populations in the upper Columbia River Basin, including $1 billion

---

[33] WEST COAST REGION, NOAA FISHERIES, ESA RECOVERY PLAN FOR SNAKE RIVER SPRING/SUMMER CHINOOK SALMON (*ONCORHYNCHUS TSHAWYTSCHA*) & SNAKE RIVER BASINSTEELHEAD (*ONCORHYNCHUS MYKISS*) (Nov. 2017), *available at* https://media.fisheries.noaa.gov/dam-migration/final-snake-river-spring-summer-chinook-salmon-and-snake-river-steelhead-recovery-plan-2017.pdf.

[34] *Id.* at 30–31.

[35] *Id.* at 42–44.

[36] *E.g.*, Alex Baumhardt, *Feds consider removing Snake River dams in leaked agreement with plaintiffs in lawsuit*, WASHINGTON STATE STANDARD (Nov. 30, 2023, 8:00 am), https://washingtonstatestandard.com/2023/11/30/feds-consider-removing-snake-river-dams-in-leaked-agreement-with-plaintiffs-in-lawsuit/.

in new federal salmon restoration investments, and a 10-year accompanying pause to litigation over ESA and other claims.[37]

D. Section 7: Protection of Species from Federal Activities

Once the U.S. Fish & Wildlife Service or NMFS has listed a species under Section 4, two sets of legal protections apply: Section 7, which applies only to federal agencies; and Section 9, which applies to everyone. This part will discuss the application of Section 7 in the context of federal water management decisions. (Chapter 8 discussed the federal government's involvement in water management in more detail.)

1. Section 7's Two Requirements for Federal Agencies

Section 7 has two principal requirements. First, under Section 7(a)(1), all federal agencies "shall, in consultation with and with the assistance of the [appropriate expert agency], utilize their authorities in furtherance of the purposes of [the ESA] by carrying out programs for the conservation of endangered species and threatened species listed pursuant to section 1533. . . ."[38] Section 7(a)(1) can be used in two ways. Federal agencies themselves can use Section 7(a)(1) to justify actions to conserve listed species even when members of the public would prefer that the agency do something else. In the context of water management, for example, agencies like the U.S. Bureau of Reclamation or Army Corps of Engineers might choose to keep water in a system to help listed species rather than deliver it to human water users, or they might release water from a dam at certain times and rates to simulate natural river flow conditions for downstream species.

One good example is what happened in *Carson-Truckee Water Conservancy District v. Clark*.[39] The Secretary of the Interior operates the Stampede Dam and Reservoir on the Little Truckee River in California, part of the complex water management system for Pyramid Lake and Lake Tahoe, pursuant to the Washoe Project Act.[40] That Act does not require the Secretary to sell all the water from the project, so the Secretary kept some water in the system to protect two ESA-listed fish species, the cui-ui ("quee-wee") and the Lahontan cutthroat trout. The Carson-Truckee Water Conservancy

---

[37] *See*, Office of the White House, Press Release, Dec. 14, 2023, *Biden-Harris Administration Announces Ten-Year Partnership with Tribes and States to Restore Wild Salmon, Expand Clean Energy Production, Increase Resilience, and Provide Energy Stability in the Columbia River Basin*.

[38] ESA § 7(a)(1), 16 U.S.C. § 1536(a)(1).

[39] 741 F.2d 257 (9th Cir. 1984).

[40] 43 U.S.C.A. §§ 614–614d.

District sued to try to force the Secretary to sell more water to it, but the U.S. Court of Appeals for the Ninth Circuit upheld the Secretary's actions under Section 7(a)(1), concluding that "the ESA supports the Secretary's decision to give priority to the fish until such time as they no longer need ESA's protection."[41]

However, the language of Section 7(a)(1)—"shall"—also creates a mandatory duty for federal agencies to act to conserve listed species. As a result, other parties can use Section 7(a)(1) to sue federal agencies to force them to do more to protect listed species. For example, the Sierra Club sued the U.S. Department of Agriculture, arguing essentially that the Department was encouraging farmers in the Edwards Aquifer region of eastern Texas to pump groundwater, harming several ESA-listed species that depend on regular flows from the aquifer in violation of Section 7(a)(1). Both the federal district court and the U.S. Court of Appeals for the Fifth Circuit found for the Sierra Club, with the Fifth Circuit concluding that "Congress intended to impose an affirmative duty on each federal agency to conserve each of the species listed pursuant to § 1533. In order to achieve this objective, the agencies must consult with FWS as to each of the listed species, not just undertake a generalized consultation."[42] As a result, it upheld the district court's injunction ordering the Department "to develop, in consultation with [the U.S. Fish & Wildlife Service], 'an organized program for utilizing USDA's authorities for the conservation of the Edwards-dependent endangered and threatened species as contemplated by the ESA.' "[43]

Second, the far more important requirement of Section 7 is found in Section 7(a)(2). This was the requirement, for example, at issue in *TVA v. Hill*. Section 7(a)(2) prohibits federal agencies from engaging in activities, funding actions, or permitting private actions that are "likely to jeopardize the continued existence of any endangered species or threatened species or result in the destruction or adverse modification of habitat of such species which is determined by the [relevant expert agency] to be critical. . . ."[44] Under the U.S. Fish & Wildlife Service's and NMFS's joint ESA regulations, "jeopardize the continued existence of" "means to engage in an action that reasonably would be expected, directly or indirectly, to reduce appreciably the likelihood of both the survival and recovery of a listed species in the wild by reducing the reproduction, numbers, or distribution of that species."[45] (NOTE: Many of the ESA regulations were amended in

---

41 *Carson-Truckee*, 741 F.2d at 262.

42 Sierra Club v. Glicksman, 156 F.3d 606, 616 (5th Cir. 1998).

43 *Id.* at 618 (quoting the district court).

44 ESA § 7(a)(2), 16 U.S.C. § 1536(a)(2).

45 50 C.F.R. § 402.02.

2019 and then changed again in April 2024. The definition of "jeopardize," however, has not changed.)

What counts as "destruction or adverse modification," however, did change. Under the old regulations, "destruction or adverse modification" of critical habitat "means a direct or indirect alteration that appreciably diminishes the value of critical habitat for the conservation of a listed species. Such alterations may include, but are not limited to, those that alter the physical or biological features essential to the conservation of a species or that preclude or significantly delay development of such features."[46] Under the 2019 amendments, "Destruction or adverse modification means a direct or indirect alteration that appreciably diminishes the value of critical habitat as a whole for the conservation of a listed species."[47] Can you see why the change in definition matters?

2. Section 7(a)(2)'s Consultation Process

Federal agencies taking actions that might trigger Section 7(a)(2) are called "action agencies," and to comply with this provision's requirements, they must engage in a potentially long consultation process with the relevant "expert agency"—that is, the U.S. Fish & Wildlife Service or NMFS (or maybe both, if species relevant to both are present). The process begins with ***informal consultation***, where the action agency identifies an action that it proposes to take, fund, or permit that might affect ESA-listed species. It then asks the expert agencies whether listed species exist in the geographical area where the action will occur. If no ESA-listed species are present, the Section 7(a)(2) consultation is complete. If ESA-listed species exist in the area, the action agency evaluates whether the proposed action is likely to affect the listed species or their critical habitat. If the action agency concludes that there is no likely effect and the relevant expert agency concurs, Section 7(a)(2) consultation ends. If there is a likely effect, however, the agencies proceed to ***formal consultation***.

In formal consultation, the action agency first assesses whether its proposed action is likely to jeopardize a listed species or damage or destroy its critical habitat. The document that the action agency produces is called a ***Biological Assessment***, or **BA**. The relevant expert agency then reviews this assessment and performs its own impact analysis, producing a ***Biological Opinion***, or **BiOp**. The

---

[46] *Id.* (2018).

[47] *Id.* (2023). NOTE: The Services jointly proposed new changes to the Section 7 regulatory definitions in June 2023, Endangered and Threatened Wildlife and Plants; Revision of Regulations for Interagency Cooperation, 88 Fed. Reg. 40753 (June 22, 2023), which were finalized in April 2024. 89 Fed. Reg 24,268 (April 5, 2024). However, the proposed rules would leave the 2019 definition in place.

Biological Opinion might conclude that no jeopardy, damage, or destruction is likely, in which case the action agency can proceed with confidence that its proposed action will not violate Section 7(a)(2). In such a case, moreover, the expert agency might also provide the action agency with an ***Incidental Take Statement*** **(ITS)** in the Biological Opinion, which insulates the action agency and any private permittee from "take" liability under Section 9, discussed below.

Alternatively, the expert agency might conclude in its Biological Opinion that jeopardy, damage, or destruction are likely—*i.e.*, that the action agency is likely to violate Section 7(a)(2). If so, the expert agency may suggest ***reasonable and prudent alternatives*** **(RPAs)** to the proposed action that will allow the action agency to avoid jeopardizing the species or damaging or destroying the species' critical habitat—assuming, of course, that such alternatives exist. Again, the expert agency might also include an ITS to go with the RPAs.

Legally, the Biological Opinion is technically just advice to the action agency; the decision on whether to go forward with the proposed action, and how, remains with the action agency. That said, an action agency is foolish to ignore the Biological Opinion: courts take Biological Opinions very seriously, and if the action agency takes an action that the expert agency concludes will violate Section 7(a)(2), courts will likely agree that the action agency has violated the ESA and, pursuant to *TVA v. Hill*, enjoin the action or project. Nevertheless, to make things even more complicated, both the action agency and citizens can challenge the Biological Opinion itself.

Section 7(a)(2) thus creates multiple bases for lawsuits—failure to consult; procedural violations of the consultation process; substantive violations of Section 7(a)(2); and arbitrary and capricious conclusions throughout the consultation process, including in the Biological Opinion. Section 7(a)(2) thus rivals Section 4 as a source of ESA litigation, and most ESA litigation is either about the listing process and conclusions (including critical habitat determinations) or about Section 7(a)(2) consultations and conclusions.

3. The Requirement of Agency Discretion

The U.S. Fish & Wildlife Service and NMFS have issued a joint regulation that limits Section 7(a)(2)'s application to federal agency actions over which the agency has some discretion: "Section 7 [of the ESA] and the requirements of this part apply to all actions in which there is discretionary Federal involvement or control."[48] In *National*

[48] 50 C.F.R. § 402.03. This regulation remains unchanged.

Association of Home Builders v. Defenders of Wildlife,[49] the U.S. Supreme Court applied this interpretation of the ESA to hold that Section 7 does not apply to the Environmental Protection Agency's (EPA's) decision whether to approve Arizona's state permitting program under the Clean Water Act (see Chapter 11), because the Clean Water Act states that the EPA *must* approve the state program if it meets all of the specified criteria.[50]

The regulation and especially the *NAHB* decision have inspired new legal arguments in water-related Section 7 cases, and several federal agencies have tried to assert that they lack discretion to change particular water management activities and hence do not have to comply with Section 7. For example, the U.S. Bureau of Reclamation successfully argued that it does *not* have discretion to change the implementation of its Annual Operating Plans for the Glen Canyon Dam on the Colorado River,[51] and hence it does not have to consult under Section 7 regarding those changes. Similarly, the Bureau successfully argued that it had no discretion regarding the renewal of long-term water service contracts for water from California's Central Valley Project,[52] meaning that the Bureau could not use those contract renewals to aid ESA-listed species affected by the Project (see below). However, Section 7 *does* apply to the Bonneville Power Administration's and U.S. Army Corps of Engineers' operation of the many federal hydropower dams in the Columbia River,[53] and hence those operations have been subject to repeated ESA consultations under Section 7(a)(2).

4. Applying Section 7(a)(2) to Federal Water Management

With respect to water law, Section 7(a)(2) controversies again tend to center on large systems where federal agencies manage water supplies with sufficient discretion so that Section 7 applies. Because federally operated water projects tend to be large and to affect entire watersheds, moreover, these controversies tend to be long running. We will take quick looks at three of these controversies.

The Central Valley Project in California is the federal water project, operated in conjunction with the State Water Project, that sends water from the San Francisco Bay Delta south, reaching as far as San Diego. The U.S. Bureau of Reclamation (see Chapter 8)

---

[49] 551 U.S. 664 (2007).

[50] *Id.* at 664–69.

[51] Grand Canyon Trust v. U.S. Bureau of Reclamation, 691 F.3d 1008 (9th Cir. 2012).

[52] Natural Resources Defense Council v. Salazar, 686 F.3d 1092 (9th Cir. 2012);

[53] National Wildlife Federation v. National Marine Fisheries Service, 524 F.3d 917, 928–29 (9th Cir. 2008).

operates the Central Valley Project, and those operations can jeopardize a number of ESA-listed species. The most famous of these is the Delta smelt (see Figure 12–5), another small fish like the snail darter that has generated considerable litigation under Section 7(a)(2). Delta smelt can be killed outright in the huge pumps that power water deliveries from the project, but they are also sensitive to changes in salinity that occur as the pumps draw seawater farther inland than is natural. As a result, the U.S. Fish & Wildlife Service listed the fish as a threatened species in March 1993.

Figure 12–5: The Delta Smelt
Photograph courtesy of the U.S. Fish & Wildlife Service

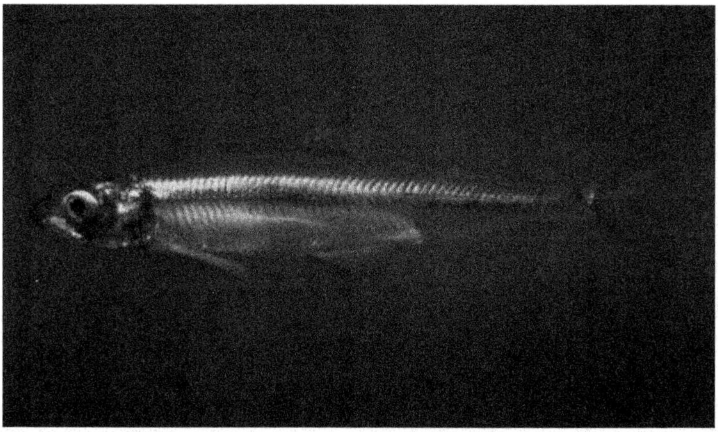

Nevertheless, conflict over the Central Valley Project's operations did not reach a crisis point until 2007. In May 2007, Judge Oliver W. Wanger of the U.S. District Court for the Eastern District of California invalidated the Biological Opinion governing the project's ongoing operations, holding that the BiOp improperly concluded that those operations would not jeopardize the delta smelt.[54] After a later seven-day evidentiary hearing, Judge Wanger issued a decision in December 2007 imposing flow restrictions on water withdrawals from the Bay Delta that could reduce the amount of water withdrawn by up to 35%. The U.S. Court of Appeals for the Ninth Circuit eventually upheld the new 2008 Biological Opinion in 2014, after Judge Wanger had again invalidated it.[55] However, by that point drought exacerbated legal restrictions under the ESA on

---

[54] Natural Resources Defense Council v. Kempthorne, 306 F. Supp. 2d 322, 387–88 (E.D. Cal. 2007).

[55] San Luis & Delta-Mendota Water Authority v. Jewell, 747 F.3d 581 (9th Cir. 2014).

Central Valley Project water deliveries for much of the period between 2011 and 2015, and farmers and other water customers received *no* water from the project in 2014 and 2015. Some water deliveries resumed in 2016, but many farmers in the San Joaquin Valley still received only 5% of their normal allocations.

The delta smelt, unfortunately, may come to represent a failure of the ESA to protect aquatic species from large-scale human water use. In spring 2015, after surveyors found only six Delta smelt in the system, biologists at the University of California, Davis, and within the U.S. Fish & Wildlife Service announced that the Delta smelt is in critical danger of extinction. This announcement and the drought-driven water crises in California have led to several popular demands that California and the Bureau of Reclamation invoke the Endangered Species Committee procedures to allow water deliveries to resume despite the Delta smelt. Indeed, in March 2016, U.S. Fish & Wildlife Director Dan Ashe told the U.S. House of Representatives' Interior, Environment and Related Agencies Appropriations Subcommittee that it was reasonable for the Administration to consider convening the Endangered Species Committee to debate the Delta smelt's future in light of California's drought problems. Of course, as the Tellico Dam illustrates, Congress can also just exempt specific projects or situations from the ESA, and in 2015 the U.S. House of Representatives debated a bill to relieve some of California's drought problems, H.R. 2898, that proposed to reduce ESA protections for the Delta smelt and other species affected by reduced water supplies. While none of these proposals became law, by 2022 biologists considered the Delta smelt extinct in the wild, with populations dependent on releases of lab-raised fish.

North of the San Francisco Bay Delta, straddling southern Oregon and northern California, is the Klamath River Basin, which has evolved into a more cautiously optimistic example of how major water supply projects and ESA-listed species might be able to co-exist. The U.S. Bureau of Reclamation controls water deliveries in the Klamath reclamation project, which was built in 1905 and operates through a number of hydroelectric dams that used to be owned by PacifiCorp. The Klamath project delivers irrigation water to about 240,000 acres of cropland in both states; it also provides water to several National Wildlife Refuges. However, the project's dams and reservoirs also changed water quality and reduced flows in the system, with the result that the Klamath River Basin is now home to three ESA-listed species of fish: the Lost River sucker (endangered, 1988), the short-nosed sucker (endangered, 1988), and the Southern Oregon/Northern California Coast (SONCC) coho salmon (threatened, 1997) (see Figure 12–6). The two suckers are now largely confined to lakes in the upper Klamath Basin, but the

SONCC coho used to migrate throughout the system to and from the Pacific Ocean until the dams blocked many parts of its habitat. In addition, several Tribes depend on water remaining in the system, and the coho and other salmon in the system are important both to the Tribes and to commercial fishermen who fish for the salmon in coastal waters.

Figure 12–6: Coho Salmon

Photograph courtesy of the National Marine Fisheries Service

The coho's need for cool water flows precipitated the ESA crisis in the Klamath River Basin. On April 6, 2001, severe drought in the region prompted the Bureau of Reclamation to terminate water deliveries to farmers and ranchers in order to avoid violating Section 7(a)(2) with respect to the coho, touching off a more-than-decade long series of lawsuits and then negotiations. The Bureau was able to deliver some water again in July 2001, and the farmers received about $40 million in federal and state disaster aid. Nevertheless, the irrigators sued the Bureau for breach of contract and an unconstitutional taking of water rights. (We'll discuss that litigation in Chapter 14.)

NMFS prepared a Biological Opinion in 2002 that concluded that the Bureau's operation of the project would jeopardize the SONCC coho. It proposed instead a 10-year RPA to supposedly increase water flows through the system. However, the U.S. Court of Appeals for the Ninth Circuit invalidated the BiOp and its RPA in

2005.[56] On remand, the U.S. District Court for the Northern District of California enjoined the Bureau of Reclamation "from making irrigation diversions at the Klamath Project unless flows in the Klamath River below Iron Gate Dam meet 100% of the . . . flow levels specifically identified by NMFS in the Biological Opinion as necessary to prevent jeopardy."[57] The Ninth Circuit affirmed the injunction 10 months later, requiring the Bureau of Reclamation to re-initiate the Section 7(a)(2) formal consultation process.[58]

However, as a result of a confluence of factors, the Klamath River Basin transitioned—albeit fitfully—to a cooperative solution that will both help water users and better protect the fish. First, the FERC licenses for four of the five hydroelectric dams on the Klamath River expired in 2006. Because FERC is a federal agency, the re-licensing process would require ESA consultation, as well as an environmental impact analysis pursuant to NEPA (see Chapters 8 and 10). PacifiCorp, the operator of the dams, concluded that future operations under the new environmental conditions would not be economically viable. Second, 2010 was another severe drought year, cutting off irrigators from water supplies and creating another political uproar. Third, federal politics had changed. President George W. Bush and his advisor Karl Rove favored operating the Klamath Project for the irrigators; indeed, many accuse them of influencing the BiOp at issue in the 2005 case. However, when President Obama entered office, this pressure ceased. After intense negotiation and compromise, in February 2010, the relevant parties signed the Klamath Hydroelectric Settlement Agreement, which set out the terms for initiating the decommissioning and removal of the four dams. About two weeks later, the parties signed the Klamath Basin Restoration Agreement, which provided, among other things, for reduced withdrawals for irrigation and increased water flows. Nevertheless, while the irrigators would receive greater security and predictability under the agreement, they could still be cut off in extreme drought years.

The negotiated agreements required Congress's approval and financing to remove the dams. Congress, however, let the agreements expire in December 2015 without acting. In the meantime, the State of Oregon completed its general stream adjudication (see Chapter 5) for the Klamath River and awarded large and early water rights to the Klamath Basin Tribes, some of them dating "to time immemorial"

---

[56] Pacific Coast Federation of Fishermen's Associations v. United States Bureau of Reclamation, 426 F.3d 1082 (9th Cir. 2005).

[57] Pacific Coast Federation of Fishermen's Associations v. U.S. Bureau of Reclamation, 2006 WL 798920, at *7 (N.D. Cal. 2006).

[58] Pacific Coast Federation of Fishermen's Associations v. U.S. Bureau of Reclamation, 226 Fed. Appx. 715 (9th Cir. 2007).

(see Chapter 8), so that the Tribes now have large water rights that are senior to the Bureau of Reclamation's rights for the Klamath reclamation project. The Tribes has repeatedly called the river (see Chapter 3) based on these rights. As a result of continuing water issues and the Tribes' new authority, the U.S. Department of the Interior (for the Bureau of Reclamation, the Bureau of Indian Affairs, and the U.S. Fish & Wildlife Service), the U.S. Department of Commerce (for NMFS), the Tribes, PacifiCorp, and the states of Oregon and California negotiated a new agreement in early April 2016. After a few more delays (including because of the COVID-19 pandemic), the dams started coming out in 2023, and the last of the four dams was breached in January 2024. Prior dam removals suggest that the fish may recover quickly.

Finally, in the middle of the country, the U.S. Army Corps' management of several dams in the Missouri River illustrates the challenges that federal managers face in trying to balance multiple demands for water—including for ESA-listed species—in a system that can change dramatically from year to year. The Missouri River main stem reservoir system spans 1770 miles and includes six dams and reservoirs that the U.S. Army Corps of Engineers operates. Under the Flood Control Act of 1944,[59] the dominant purposes of the Army Corps' management are to avoid flooding and to maintain downstream navigation. However, the Army Corps can also manage the system for a number of other purposes, including irrigation, hydroelectric power generation, water supply, water quality, recreation, and fish and wildlife enhancement.[60] There are three ESA-listed species in the river: the pallid sturgeon (endangered, 1990); the least tern (endangered, 1985); and the piping plover (threatened, 1985).

Complicating the Army Corps' task still further are increasing numbers of extreme weather events that affect the Missouri River. For example, a particularly severe regional drought lasting from 1988 to 1990 in the plains regions was the first major drought that the modern Missouri River dam system had ever experienced, and the Army Corps revised its Master Manual for operating the system in response. The process took 14 years and comprehensively evaluated the demands on the river system, culminating in the 2004 revised Master Manual. This manual incorporated ongoing suggestions from the U.S. Fish & Wildlife Service regarding the Missouri River's flow regimes and avoidance of ESA jeopardy, as presented in 2000 and 2003 Biological Opinions, and the U.S. Court of Appeals for the Eighth Circuit upheld both the 2003 BiOp and the

---

59 16 U.S.C. § 460d.

60 South Dakota v. Ubbeholde, 330 F.3d 1014, 1019–20 (8th Cir 2003).

2004 Master Manual in 2005 against multiple challenges from a variety of litigants.[61] The U.S. Supreme Court denied *certiorari* in April 2006.[62] Thereafter, the Army Corps again amended its Master Manual in 2006 to incorporate the U.S. Fish & Wildlife Service's RPA suggestions for modifying releases from the reservoirs. Each year, the Army Corps continues to forecast conditions on the river and to come up with an Annual Operating Plan for the next year, which is typically finalized in December.

In 2011, the Missouri River flooded severely. The flooding caused significant property damage and loss of life but was expected to be a net benefit for the river's ESA-listed species, at least after the waters receded again. While the Army Corps remains committed to flood control, it also attributes some of the 2011 flooding on the Missouri River to its inexperience with the more historical flow regime that it put in place to comply with Section 7, starting with the 2004 Master Manual. Indeed, in October 2011, senators from most of the Missouri River states called on the Army Corps to amend the Master Manual yet again, to prioritize flood control over both recreation and ESA concerns. However, in December 2011, an expert panel cleared the Army Corps of any wrongdoing, concluding that the flood conditions exceeded anything that the Army Corps could have anticipated. However, it also recommended that the Master Manual be amended to include the possibility of such severe flood conditions in the future.

The next year, however, the Missouri River system was once again coping with severe drought—the conditions that inspired ESA-based amendments to the Master Manual. In May 2012, the environmental group American Rivers listed the Missouri River as the fourth most-endangered river in the nation, citing outdated flood management practices.

The Missouri River thus raised—and continues to raise—the issue of how to satisfy human water management and ESA goals simultaneous in wildly fluctuating conditions. In contrast, the Klamath River Basin and Bay Delta underscore the complications that severe drought can add to achieving both of these goals. Climate change is expected to exacerbate both conditions. Increasing stress on water systems and aquatic species is likely to prompt recurring evaluations of the "proper" role of Section 7 in federal water management, and these three systems model three possible legal and policy responses: (1) increased flexibility and adaptability on the part of the federal manager (Missouri River); (2) broad community-based reorganization of system operations (Klamath River); or (3) removal

---

[61] In re Operation of the Missouri River System Litigation, 421 F.3d 618, 638 (8th Cir. 2005).

[62] North Dakota v. U.S. Army Corps of Engineers, 547 U.S. 1097 (2006).

of ESA-based species protections from the equation, either through conscious exemption or species extinction (Bay Delta).

E. Section 9: Protection Against "Takes"

Section 9 of the ESA[63] is entitled "Prohibited Acts," but it is most commonly known as the Act's "take" provision. Specifically, Section 9 states that, "with respect to any endangered species of fish or wildlife" listed for protection under the ESA, "it is unlawful for any person subject to the jurisdiction of the United States to—"

> (A) import any such species into or export any such species from the United States;
>
> (B) take any such species within the United States or the territorial sea of the United States;
>
> (C) take any such species on the high seas;
>
> (D) possess, sell, deliver, carry, transport, or ship, by any means whatsoever, any such species taken in violation of paragraphs (B) and (C);
>
> (E) deliver, receive, carry, transport, or ship in any interstate or foreign commerce, by any means whatsoever and in the course of a commercial activity, any such species;
>
> (F) sell or offer for sale in interstate or foreign commerce any such species; or
>
> (G) violate any regulation pertaining to such species or to any threatened species of fish or wildlife listed pursuant to section 1533 of this [Act] and promulgated by the Secretary pursuant to the authority provided by this [Act].[64]

In addition, "[i]t is unlawful for any person subject to the jurisdiction of the United States to attempt to commit, solicit another to commit or cause to be committed, any offense defined in this section."[65] Thus, the ESA prohibits third-party as well as direct takes of endangered species, a fact that could have implications for states issuing water rights and agencies delivering water in ESA-constrained water systems.

Several things are worth noting about this "take" prohibition. First, it applies beyond the mere taking of listed species to prohibit all trade and commerce in endangered fish and wildlife, part of the ESA's implementation of the CITES treaty. Second, the prohibition

---

63 16 U.S.C. § 1538.

64 ESA § 9(a)(1), 16 U.S.C. § 1538(a)(1).

65 ESA § 9(g), 16 U.S.C. § 1538(g).

on take applies in the oceans as well as on land, meaning that anadromous species like salmon are protected everywhere. Third, these provisions apply only to fish and wildlife; endangered plants receive a different set of protections.[66] Finally, Section 9 applies primarily to *endangered* species; its prohibition for threatened species is against violating the regulations for threatened species.[67] As was mentioned in connection with the Section 4 listing process, the U.S. Fish & Wildlife Service and NMFS have authority to promulgate tailored requirements for the protection of threatened species,[68] and for some species they have used this authority to promulgate what are known as "Section 4(d)" rules.[69] For example, the threatened polar bear's 4(d) rule specifies that emission of greenhouse gases does not constitute a "take."

Until 2019, the Services relied on a joint default regulation that gave threatened species all of the protections to which endangered species are entitled *unless* the Services promulgated a special "4(d)" rule for the species.[70] Under that rule, threatened species were generally treated the same as endangered species under Section 9. However, as part of the 2019 ESA regulation amendments, the Trump Administration ended this regulation's application, applying it only to species listed "on or prior to September 26, 2019, unless the Secretary has promulgated species-specific provisions."[71] Nevertheless, in April 2024 the Services finalized new amendments that restore the default protections for threatened species, effective May 6, 2024.[72]

The ESA defines "take" to mean "to harass, harm, pursue, hunt, shoot, wound, kill, trap, capture, or collect, or to attempt to engage in any such conduct."[73] According to the agencies' joint regulations:

> Harass in the definition of "take" in the Act means an intentional or negligent act or omission which creates the likelihood of injury to wildlife by annoying it to such an extent as to significantly disrupt normal behavioral patterns which include, but are not limited to, breeding,

---

66 *See* ESA § 9(a)(2), 16 U.S.C. § 1538(a)(2).

67 ESA § 9(a)(1)(G), 16 U.S.C. § 1538(a)(1)(G).

68 ESA § 4(d), 16 U.S.C. § 1533(d).

69 *See* 50 C.F.R. §§ 17.40–17.48 (the collection of 4(d) regulations).

70 50 C.F.R. § 17.31 (2018) (cross-referencing 50 C.F.R. § 17.21 (prohibitions for endangered species)).

71 *Id.* § 17.31(a) (2023).

72 Endangered and Threatened Wildlife and Plants; Regulations Pertaining to Endangered and Threatened Wildlife and Plants, 89 Fed. Reg. 23,919, 23,921 (April 5, 2024).

73 ESA § 3(19), 16 U.S.C. § 1532(19).

feeding, or sheltering. This definition, when applied to captive wildlife, does not include generally accepted:

(1) Animal husbandry practices that meet or exceed the minimum standards for facilities and care under the Animal Welfare Act,

(2) Breeding procedures, or

(3) Provisions of veterinary care for confining, tranquilizing, or anesthetizing, when such practices, procedures, or provisions are not likely to result in injury to the wildlife.[74]

"Harm," in turn, "means an act which actually kills or injures wildlife. Such act may include significant habitat modification or degradation where it actually kills or injures wildlife by significantly impairing essential behavioral patterns, including breeding, feeding or sheltering."[75] The U.S. Supreme Court upheld this definition of "harm" in 1995.[76]

Whereas federal agencies can be protected from "take" liability through a Section 7 Incidental Take Statement (ITS), private entities and states need to acquire an ***incidental take permit*** **(ITP)** pursuant to Section 10 in order to receive the same kind of exemption. Section 10 allows the expert agencies to authorize takes of listed species in a variety of circumstances: (1) "for scientific purposes or to enhance the propagation or survival of the affected species;" (2) for undue economic hardship if a species listing affects a contract; (3) for subsistence takes by Alaska Natives; and (4) for takes that are "incidental to, and not the purpose of, the carrying out of an otherwise lawful activity."[77] ITPs are the fourth category, and they require that the permittee implement a ***habitat conservation plan*** **(HCP)**.[78] Several rivers and other aquatic habitats are the subjects of completed or developing HCPs, such as the Etowah River in Georgia, the Lower Colorado River in Arizona, the Cedar River Watershed in Seattle, Washington, and the Walton County seashore in Florida.

Individual water users can certainly violate Section 9 by taking ESA-listed aquatic species through their diversions. For example, a user's diversion pump might kill an endangered or threatened species, or ESA-listed species might be carried into irrigation ditches and canals, where they become stranded and die—a not-infrequent

---

[74] 50 C.F.R. § 17.3. This definition did not change in either the 2019 or 2024 amendments.

[75] *Id.* This definition did not change in either the 2019 or 2024 amendments.

[76] Babbitt v. Sweet Home Chapter of Communities for a Great Oregon, 515 U.S. 687, 696–701 (1995).

[77] ESA § 10(a)(1), (b), (e), 16 U.S.C. § 1539(a)(1), (b), (e).

[78] ESA § 10(a)(2), 16 U.S.C. § 1539(a)(2).

occurrence at hydropower dams and on irrigated fields. These kinds of events pose little difficulty in terms of proving an ESA violation.

However, it is far more difficult to prove that a water user's withdrawal of water "takes" an ESA-listed aquatic species just by reducing the total water available at that moment. As we have seen, natural flows can vary considerably, and an individual withdrawal might not change environmental conditions or habitat all that much, particularly if the individual water user is taking a relatively small amount of water compared to the total flow.

As a result, litigation over ESA "take" liability has tended to focus on the managing agencies, whether federal or state, that control enough water to make a difference to the species involved. For example, Florida, with help from Alabama, fought with Georgia over water in the Apalachicola-Chattahoochee-Flint River Basin for decades (see Chapter 9). The U.S. Army Corps of Engineers operates several dams in the system. Georgia needs the water primarily as water supply for Atlanta, which lacks sufficient water for its growing size. Florida, in contrast, wants the water to flow down the Chattahoochee River into the Apalachicola River in Florida, which in turns flows into Apalachicola Bay and supports several lucrative fisheries, including an oyster fishery that is highly dependent on fresh water inflows.

After the three states tried but failed to negotiate an interstate compact that would equitably apportion the system's water, litigation began in earnest, primarily against the Army Corps of Engineers. This litigation over the Corps' operation of its ACF Basin dams proceeded in two basic thrusts. One set of lawsuits challenged the Army Corps' allocation of water from the Lake Lanier Reservoir at the top of the system, near Atlanta, with the challengers claiming that the allocations for Atlanta's water supply violated Congress's purposes in establishing the reservoir and hence required Congress's permission. This set of lawsuits was initially successful, if convoluted, with the U.S. Court of Appeals for the D.C. Circuit declaring that the Army Corps needed to go to Congress to get permission to give water to Atlanta.[79] However, the many cases were ultimately consolidated through multi-district litigation into the U.S. District Court for the District of Florida,[80] which concluded that the D.C. Circuit was correct and that the Army Corps did indeed have to go to Congress before it could allocate water from Lake Lanier for

79 Southeastern Federal Power Customers, Inc. v. Geren, 514 F.3d 1316, 1323–25 (D.C. Cir. 2008); *see also* Alabama v. U.S. Army Corps of Engineers, 424 F.3d 1117 (11th Cir. 2005); Georgia v. U.S. Army Corps of Engineers, 302 F.3d 1242 (11th Cir. 2002) (all discussing the Army Corps' allocation of water from Lake Lanier).

80 In re Tri-State Water Rights Litigation, 481 F. Supp. 2d 1351, 1352–53 (Jud. Panel Mult. Lit. 2007).

Atlanta's water supply.[81] On appeal, however, the U.S. Court of Appeals for the Eleventh Circuit reversed,[82] and the U.S. Supreme Court denied *certiorari* to review the decision in June 2012.[83]

The second set of cases challenged the flow regime at the Jim Woodruff Dam at the border of Georgia and Florida on a number of environmental grounds, including the ESA. The Apalachicola River contains four ESA-listed species: the Gulf sturgeon (threatened, 1991), the fat threeridge mussel (endangered, 1998), the purple bankclimber mussel (threatened, 1998), and the Chipola slabshell mussel (threatened, 1998). Alabama and Florida sued the U.S. Army Corps of Engineers, alleging that its operation of the Jim Woodruff dam violated the ESA. The problems became especially acute during the drought of 2006:

> The mussels in the Apalachicola River are slow moving, and, while capable of moving to deeper water refuges for short distances, they generally cannot escape the adverse conditions they currently are experiencing in side channels and sloughs along the river. Particularly dramatic flow reductions, as have been previously experienced in the Apalachicola River, quickly sever the connection between the main river channel and occupied mussel habitats outside the main channel before mussels can relocate, resulting in stranding and death due to heat, predation, and dessication [*sic*]. As a result, hundreds, if not thousands of dead and dying mussels were observed in the Apalachicola River during field visits between June 12 and 14, 2006. Among the dead and dying mussels were members of two species protected under the ESA: the threatened purple bankclimber and the endangered fat threeridge.[84]

Florida asked the U.S. District Court for the Northern District of Alabama to maintain water releases from the dam at 6300 cubic feet per second through September 2006, arguing that the Army Corps was causing a "take" of listed species in violation of Section 9.[85] Judge Bowdre disagreed, however, concluding that, while "[n]o one disputes that protected mussels are dying by the hundreds, that more will die at 5,000 cfs, and that their habitat is being modified by the decreased

---

81 In re Tri-State Water Rights Litigation, 639 F. Supp. 2d 1308, 1350–54 (M.D. Fla. 2009).

82 In re: MDL-1824 Tri-State Water Rights Litigation, 644 F.3d 1160, 1186–92 (11th Cir. 2011).

83 Florida v. Georgia, 567 U.S. 946 (2012); Alabama v. Georgia, 567 U.S. 946 (2012); Southeastern Federal Power Customers, Inc. v. Georgia, 567 U.S. 946 (2012).

84 Alabama v. United States Army Corps of Engineers, 441 F. Supp. 2d 1123, 1125 (N.D. Ala. 2006).

85 *Id.* at 1124.

flows so that they are facing death, harm and harassment,"[86] "but-for" causation was absent: "The court cannot hold the Corps responsible for the absence of rain."[87]

By 2008, the U.S. Fish & Wildlife Service had issued a Biological Opinion that protected the Army Corps from "take" liability through an ITS. As a result, the Middle District of Florida ruled against the ESA claims in 2010,[88] and no party appealed.

Another example of Section 9 litigation focusing on government agencies occurred in Texas. In March 2010, The Aransas Project, a non-profit corporation, sued the Texas Commission on Environmental Quality ("TCEQ"), alleging that it and its officials had violated Section 9 by allowing water rights holders to use water in the winter of 2008–2009, resulting in a "taking" of ESA-listed Whooping Cranes. The U.S. District Court for the Southern District of Texas allowed several water users to intervene in the litigation because it recognized that the defendants' potential liability under Section 9 threatened the intervenors' ability to exercise their state-law water rights.[89] Nevertheless, in 2013, the district court found that TCEQ *had* caused a "take" of the Whooping Cranes, based on an extended chain of "but for" causation:

> During the 2008–2009 winter, there was a severe drought. As the winter progressed, the AWB cranes began to demonstrate unusual behavior. For example, parents would deny their juveniles food, and the birds began venturing out of their specific territories in search of food and fresh water. . . . Such behavior indicates that the parent was under food stress. . . . [In addition,] the lack of freshwater inflows had increased salinities across the Refuge. These hyper-saline conditions, verified by field measurements, led to a decrease in blue crabs and wolfberries, the staple diet of the AWB flock. This food shortage led to bird emaciation, stress behavior, and an over-all decline in bird health. That is, without proper freshwater inflows, the [Whooping Crane's] critical habitat had been thrown out of balance, with ramifications up and down the food chain. That winter, at least 23 . . . cranes, or 8.5% of the . . . flock, died at the

---

[86] *Id.* at 1132.

[87] *Id.* at 1134.

[88] In re Tri-State Water Rights Litigation, Case No. 3:07–md–01 (PAM/JRK), *Memorandum and Order* (M.D. Fla. July 21, 2010), *available at* http://www.sam.usace.army.mil/Portals/46/docs/planning_environmental/acf/docs/072110court_ruling.pdf.

[89] The Aransas Project v. Shaw, 2010 WL 1644645, at *4–*5 (S.D. Tex. April 23, 2010).

Refuge. Another 34 birds that left Texas in spring, failed to return in fall.[90]

In December 2014, however, the U.S. Court of Appeals for the Fifth Circuit reversed, finding that the district court had not properly evaluated proximate cause under the correct legal standard: "Nowhere does the court explain why the remote connection between water licensing, decisions to draw river water by hundreds of users, whooping crane habitat, and crane deaths that occurred during a year of extraordinary drought compels ESA liability."[91] In 2015, the U.S. Supreme Court denied *certiorari* to review the decision.[92]

Both the Army Corps and the TCEQ cases indicate that courts are reluctant to find agencies liable for ESA "takes" in connection with water management during a drought. Clearly, drought combined with water use complicates the issue of ESA "take" causation, in part because the confluence of the two factors raises the issue of what should be considered the normal baseline for evaluating the "take" claim: Does "normal" mean the river under natural conditions (including drought), so that any water use is a potential "take," or is "normal" instead the river under conditions of human use, so that species deaths should be blamed on the drought? Again, as with Section 7(a)(2), these issues will become even more complicated as climate change increasingly affects water systems, suggesting that ESA litigation over water management will become even more prominent into the future.

---

[90] The Aransas Project v. Shaw, 930 F. Supp. 2d 716, 724 (S.D. Tex. 2013).

[91] The Aransas Project v. Shaw, 775 F.3d 641, 658–59 (5th Cir. 2014).

[92] The Aransas Project v. Shaw, 576 U.S. 1035 (2015).

Chapter 13

COMPREHENSIVE WATER RESOURCES MANAGEMENT AND WATERSHED PLANNING

A. Introduction: Imperatives for Comprehensive Approaches

In several earlier chapters, we highlighted the fact that many aspects of water law are unduly fragmented. Water quantity law is distinct from water quality law. Surface water and groundwater rights usually are governed by different, if often connected, bodies of law. When water bodies and water systems cut across geographic boundaries, they can be subject to multiple and conflicting bodies of law and management regimes, in addition to competition for water resources between jurisdictions. Numerous agencies and other decisionmakers often govern or influence water resources policy for single bodies of water, with some in charge of water quality, others water quantity, others fish and wildlife protection and management, and others related land use, dam construction and hydroelectric power generation or flood control.

Indeed, a useful exercise for students of water law to underscore this point is to brainstorm one list of all of the statutes, regulations, policies, bodies of case law, and other sources of law and policy that govern a single watershed and then to compile a similar list of all of the "players" within a given watershed—all of the agencies and officials responsible for implementing water law and policy, all of those whose activities may impair or otherwise affect water resources, and all users or beneficiaries of water and other watershed resources. Those lists necessarily will vary depending on watershed size, location around the country, and other factors, but they will all be quite long and diverse.[1]

Watersheds and aquatic ecosystems themselves, by contrast, are highly integrated, although they are comprised of multiple individual components.[2] They flow from narrow, steep mountain headwaters to

---

[1] For an example of how complex regulatory fragmentation of water basins can become, *see* Robin Kundis Craig, *Climate Change, Regulatory Fragmentation, and Water Triage*, 79 U. COLO. L. REV. 825 (Summer 2008).

[2] For a somewhat dated but still accurate analysis of these and other imperatives for watershed-based restoration and protection programs, *see* Robert W. Adler, *Addressing Barriers to Watershed Protection*, 25 ENVTL. L. 973 (1995). Similar analyses include SOCIETY FOR ECOLOGICAL RESTORATION INTERNATIONAL, LARGE-SCALE ECOSYSTEM RESTORATION, FIVE CASE STUDIES FROM THE UNITED STATES (Mary

broader, flatter downstream segments with wide floodplains. They include hydrological and physically connected systems of streams, lakes, wetlands and groundwater components. They reflect a mosaic of connected aquatic and terrestrial habitats, in which land use and water resource use can be difficult to separate. From an ecological and hydrologic perspective, natural water systems reflect four dimensions: longitudinal (upstream to downstream), lateral (open waters to wetlands and other transition zones to uplands), vertical (surface water to groundwater) and temporal (all of these systems change over time).

Moreover, also as highlighted in other chapters, there is an ongoing tension among those aspects of water law and water resources policy that focuses on utility for traditional economic uses and those laws and institutions designed to restore and protect the resource itself—that is, between laws and policies that focus on discrete components of water systems as opposed to those that seek to protect and manage the watershed as an aquatic ecosystem and for broader ecosystem values. In earlier chapters, we highlighted those aspects of water law that seek to promote private uses through property law and similar legal mechanisms and those that seek to preserve and protect public uses and values. A wide range of other laws and regulations also govern the use and management of water, aquatic resources, and aquatic ecosystems, the full scope of which cannot be addressed here.[3]

Doyle & Cynthia A. Drew, eds. 2008) (discussing case studies of the Everglades, Platte River, California Bay-Delta, Chesapeake Bay and Upper Mississippi River restoration programs); NATIONAL RESEARCH COUNCIL, NEW STRATEGIES FOR AMERICA'S WATERSHEDS (1999); WATERSHED MANAGEMENT: BALANCING SUSTAINABILITY AND ENVIRONMENTAL CHANGE (Robert L. Naiman, ed. 1992); NATIONAL RESEARCH COUNCIL, RESTORATION OF AQUATIC ECOSYSTEMS (1990); Keith H. Hirokawa, *Driving Local Governments to Watershed* Governance, 42 ENVTL. L. 157 (2012); Ann E. Drobot, *Transitioning to a Sustainable Energy Economy: The Call for National Cooperative Watershed Planning*, 41 ENVTL. L. 707 (2011); Craig Anthony (Tony) Arnold, *Adaptive Watershed Planning and Climate Change*, 5 ENVT'L & ENERGY L. & POL'Y J. 417 (2010); A. Dan Tarlock, *Putting Rivers Back in the Landscape: The Revival of Watershed Management in the United* States, 14 HASTINGS W.-N.W. J. ENVTL. L. & Pol'y 1059 (2008); Noah D. Hall. *Toward a New Horizontal Federalism: Interstate Water Management in the Great Lakes Region*, 77 U. COLO. L. REV. 405 (2006); Ludwik A. Teclaff, *Evolution of the River Basin Concept in National and International Water Law*, 36 NAT. RESOURCES J. 359 (1996). For a more tempered view, *see* James L. Huffman, *Comprehensive River Basin Management: The Limits of Collaborative, Stakeholder-Based, Water Governance*, 49 NAT. RESOURCES J. 117 (2009).

[3] Just a few major examples include the Endangered Species Act, 15 U.S.C. §§ 1531–1544 (see Chapter 12); the Coastal Zone Management Act, 15 U.S.C. §§ 1451–1466; the Oil Pollution Act, 33 U.S.C. §§ 2701–2762; the National Environmental Policy Act, 42 U.S.C. §§ 4321–4370h (see Chapter 8); the Solid Waste Disposal Act (often known, as amended, as the Resource Conservation and Recovery Act), 42 U.S.C. §§ 6901–6992k; and the Comprehensive Environmental Response, Compensation, and Liability Act (CERCLA, or "Superfund"), 42 U.S.C. §§ 9601–9675. For an analysis of the potential use of some of these existing legal tools to protect fresh water and

Yet there are many ways in which aquatic ecosystems and aquatic resources face serious challenges from pollution, habitat loss and fragmentation, overuse, and other sources, and a disturbing percentage of aquatic ecosystems are impaired according to a range of chemical, physical and ecological measures. The causes of that impairment are also diverse, making these problems difficult to address through any single statute or other body of law.

A number of institutional, economic and sociological imperatives also suggest the wisdom of more integrated approaches to water resources planning and watershed protection and management. From a political perspective, tens of thousands of distinct public entities are involved in water resources planning, regulation, and management in the United States, making coordination among those entities a major challenge, both within and across watershed boundaries. The fragmentation of water resource issues (quality versus quantity, surface versus groundwater, etc.) between different sources of law and management compounds this challenge. Coordination makes sense from an economic perspective to ensure the most efficient use of scarce fiscal and other resources to address the most important water resource problems, with an equitable distribution of costs. Sociologically, the concept of "bioregionalism" suggests that attachment to place—including key watersheds such as the Chesapeake Bay Region or the Columbia River drainage—helps to increase public support for, and involvement in, water resources protection and restoration efforts.

As such, a key challenge for water law, and for the aggregate collection of water resources and watershed managers, users, and other constituents, is how to manage and protect watersheds and integrated water resources in ways that reconcile the many competing and sometimes conflicting sources of law and policy; that facilitate cooperation and conflict resolution between the numerous institutional managers of water resources law and policy; and that appropriately balance public and private interests and values and take into account all legitimate stakeholders within watersheds.

This chapter explores various legal doctrines and institutional mechanisms that have been used to accomplish those goals. First, we explore some of the many discrete legal tools available to protect instream flows and other public water resource values. (The full scope of such mechanisms is far too large to address in a single chapter, but this brief survey will highlight the challenges of protecting water resources in the face of increasing economic demand, and the opportunities to modify existing sources of law to do

---

freshwater ecosystems, *see* Sandra B. Zellmer, *Charting a Course to Conserve 30% of Freshwaters by 2030*, 64 WM. & MARY L. REV. 169 (2022).

so.) Second, we describe a range of more comprehensive and collaborative approaches to water law and management, including comprehensive watershed management programs, adaptive management, and, at the international level, integrated water resources management (IWRM).

B. Existing Legal Tools to Protect Aquatic Ecosystem Values

The first important concept in efforts to integrate water resources law and management is that many of the legal doctrines discussed in earlier chapters can, and often are, called upon to do double duty. Specifically, a law or body of law that is apparently designed to serve one purpose can be adapted for a related one. Indeed, all students of law recognize eventually that flexibility is one of law's greatest strengths generally, and such flexibility is essential to the proper functioning of legal systems. Several examples will illustrate the point.

1. Using Traditional Water Law to Protect Instream Flows and Ecosystems

As discussed in Chapters 2 and 3, some components of both riparian rights and prior appropriation doctrine can be used to keep water in aquatic ecosystems. As such, the perception that traditional water law is designed mainly to allocate property rights to water among human economic uses is overly simplistic.

Ironically, riparian rights were initially more protective of instream flows under the traditional "natural flow" doctrine, but riparianism has evolved more in the direction of promoting consumptive uses through the "reasonable use" doctrine. Riparian rights law sometimes can be used successfully to maintain water levels in natural water bodies,[4] but in other cases municipal water supply needs or other realities of the modern economy require balancing of development and conservation.[5] Conceptually, there is no reason why the reasonable use doctrine of riparian rights, or its statutory or administrative versions, cannot accommodate reasonable uses while protecting instream flows and aquatic ecosystem uses and values. Instream uses are simply one factor to balance in the process, and it is predictable that some decisions will favor human off-stream use while others may be more protective of instream flows as judges and administrators strike those difficult

---

[4] *See generally, e.g.*, Glen Lake-Crystal River Watershed Riparians v. Glen Lake Assn., 695 N.W.2d 508 (Mich. App. 2004) (upholding trial court order to protect downstream riparian uses and values).

[5] *See, e.g.*, Hudson River Fisherman's Assn. v. Williams, 139 A.D.2d 234, 241 (N.Y. Ct. App. 1988) (holding that a "trout stream must unfortunately give way to the predictable and unrelenting growth in human water demands).

balances. Indeed, as Chapter 5 discussed, "regulated riparian" jurisdictions like Florida and Hawai'i provide for these protections in minimum flow requirements.

Traditional prior appropriation doctrine, by contrast, did not even recognize instream flow as a legally cognizable "beneficial use." Nevertheless, prior appropriation has evolved in most states to do so, as we discussed in Chapters 3, 5, and 11. Conceptually, however, nothing about prior appropriation theory is inherently or fundamentally inconsistent with the goal of protecting instream flows and aquatic ecosystems; regulators just have to decide that rivers and other waterbodies cannot be appropriated below the needs of the larger system. Indeed, some states have enacted legislation to promote the transfer of water rights to support instream flows,[6] and recent cases have upheld the rights of states and tribes to protect instream flows under existing systems of water law.[7] In addition, some states like California are beginning to recognize that diversions that imperil fish and wildlife are unreasonable appropriations that can be curtailed, especially during drought.[8]

It is true that some aspects of prior appropriation law, as implemented, had the *effect* of dewatering western streams and other aquatic ecosystem components. Because so much land in the West is geographically distant from water sources, for example, prior appropriation allowed water to be transported to wherever it could be put to a valid beneficial use, even outside the watershed of origin. This practice had the effect of removing water from watersheds, and even where water remained within a watershed, return flows from land that is geographically remote from the source were not likely to return in sufficient amounts, or sufficiently quickly, to recharge the surface water system. Likewise, the "use it or lose it" doctrine of prior appropriation law encourages those with appropriative rights to use as much water as could be justified. Although the prohibition against waste purports to check this tendency, as Chapter 3 discussed, judges and water rights administrators have been reluctant to strip users of

---

[6] *E.g.,* change meets several lists of statutory requirements. MONT. CODE ANN. § 85–2–408(1); UT. CODE ANN. §§ 65A–16–201, 73–3–30.

[7] *See, e.g.*, Center for Environmental Law and Policy v. Dept. of Ecology, 468 P.3d 1064 (Wash. 2020); Stanford Vina Ranch Irrigation Co. v. State, 50 Cal. App. 5th 976 (Cal. Ct. App. 2020); In Re: CSRBA Case No. 49576 Subcase No. 91-7755, 448 P.3d 322 (Idaho 2019); Fox v. Skagit Cty., 372 P.3d 784 (Wash. Ct. App. 2016).

[8] *E.g.*, Santa Barbara Channelkeeper v. City of San Buenaventura, 19 Cal. App. 5th 1176, 1180–81 (2018) (alleging that the City's diversions from the Ventura River are unreasonable during the summer months because of impacts on the endangered Southern California steelhead trout); Stanford Vina Ranch Irrigation Co. v. State, 50 Cal. App. 5th 976, 1002–07 (2020) (upholding emerging drought restrictions on Stanford Vina Ranch's diversions from Deer Creek to protect salmon and steelhead trout).

water rights that are so critical to economic stability in an arid region.

The only barrier to turning those principles in the other direction to protect instream flows and both human instream uses (like fishing, swimming and boating) and ecosystem values was the initial failure of western states to recognize instream uses as "beneficial" for purposes of the issuance of appropriative rights. Once states began to change that limitation, those who sought to protect instream uses were able to apply for, or purchase, instream flow appropriative rights. Those rights, in principle, enjoy the same benefits and legal protections as other appropriative water rights, and significant progress has been made in doing so around the West.[9]

Nevertheless, the most basic principle of prior appropriation, "first in time, first in right," can still significantly limit the applicability and potential benefit of recent trend toward recognition of instream flow rights. Because so many western stream systems have been fully appropriated, many instream flow rights tend to be very junior in the priority scheme, and in some over-appropriated systems no rights remain available for appropriation. Instream flow rights are most important to the natural environment and for other instream uses during droughts and other times of scarcity, meaning that they may not be exercisable when most needed. Of course, people and agencies seeking to better protect instream flows can try to purchase more secure senior rights that will be honored even in times of shortage, but those are usually expensive. Moreover, the "no harm" doctrine might prevent full use and enjoyment of an instream flow right purchased from a senior whose previous return flows were relied on by junior appropriators, and who are thus entitled to continue to use part of the purchased water right off stream.

Given the public nature and public ownership or control of water, however, one might ask why anyone should have to pay for, or otherwise secure, a private property right for public instream uses and values. If protection of instream flows is designed to protect particular private interests, such as a sufficient flow rate to support a guided kayaking business, it makes sense that private parties should have to secure a private right for that flow. Of course, other users who benefit from that flow will be "free riders" (in this case, perhaps both literally and figuratively) on the private water right. However, if an instream flow right is designed to protect a purely public good, such as an endangered species or public recreation, it is less likely that private parties will devote private financial or other resources to secure that right. Likewise, it makes less sense to

---

[9] *See* Lawrence J. MacDonnell, *Environmental Flows in the Rocky Mountain West: A Progress Report*, 9 WYO. L. REV. 335 (2009).

require a special "right" to protect what should logically be part of the baseline public ownership and control of water.

Two doctrines discussed in Chapters 3, 5, and 7 are designed to address this apparent conceptual anomaly in water law. The "public interest test" embodied in the prior appropriation doctrine of many western states, usually by statute although occasionally through judicial application, is designed to ensure that new water rights do not impair important public uses and values in water bodies. The public trust doctrine similarly can be invoked to protect public uses and values against excessive water withdrawal and use—at least in states like California that are willing to apply the doctrine to curb water rights. Both of those doctrines, however, also have attributes that have limited their utility in providing effective protection for instream uses and values. The public interest test applies to *new* water rights claims, but not to existing rights, and any effort to do so would be subject to a takings analysis (discussed in Chapter 14). Similarly, the few state courts[10] that have allowed the public trust doctrine to affect prior appropriation law have determined that the two must be reconciled in an effort to effectuate both[11] rather than ruling that the public trust doctrine trumps prior appropriation law. Most westerns states, however, have either explicitly deemed the public trust doctrine irrelevant to water allocations or effectively ignored it when issuing water rights.[12]

Thus, the conceptual breadth of water law and its potential to manage and protect water resources and aquatic ecosystems more comprehensively belies the *reality* that, for the most part, water law remains devoted to allocation of property rights among competing users. Efforts to use water law more broadly are infrequent and constrained in their impact. This resistance to a system-based approach may reflect the fact that the primary mission of those responsible for implementing the statutory and administrative forms of water law in most states, certainly in the West where water quantity has the greatest potential to impair ecosystem and other public values, is to administer and enforce private water rights fairly and efficiently, and not to manage larger aquatic systems for a wider range of values.

---

10 As Chapter 7 discussed, the U.S. Supreme Court has made clear that the scope and application of the public trust doctrine is a matter of state law. *See* PPL Montana, LLC v. Montana, 565 U.S. 576 (2012).

11 *See* National Audubon Soc. v. Superior Court of Alpine County, 658 P.2d 709 (Cal. 1983) (*en banc*) (discussed in Chapter 7). Idaho courts were heading in the same direction as California, but the Idaho Legislature enacted statutes that limited the state public trust doctrine to its traditional role of protecting public navigation, commerce, and fishing in the navigable waters.

12 *See* People v. Emmert, 597 P.2d 1025 (Colo. 1979).

2. Using Water Pollution Law to Address Water Quantity Problems

As was discussed in Chapter 11, it is a mistake to envision the Clean Water Act (CWA) and other aspects of water pollution law as entirely distinct from water quantity law.[13] To begin, the underlying objective of the CWA is to "restore and maintain the chemical, physical, and biological integrity of the Nation's waters."[14] Similarly, the statutory definition of water "pollution" is the "man-made or man-induced alteration of the chemical, physical, biological, and radiological integrity of water,"[15] and diminution of water quantity can have impacts on all of those attributes of water bodies. Thus, conceptually, it should not seem strange that the CWA might be used in ways that protect water quantity as well as water quality.

Indeed, as explained in Chapter 11, the U.S. Supreme Court found that a sharp divide between water quality and water quantity is an "artificial distinction"[16] and upheld a state water quality certification based on minimum stream flows. Moreover, at least some states have incorporated minimum flow requirements into their system of water quality standards. Likewise, there are cases in which plaintiffs have used nuisance law, the traditional common law remedy to address water pollution, to protect water quantity as well as water quality, just as riparian rights and prior appropriation doctrines have been used to redress water pollution. Thus, the apparent legal distinction between water quality and water quantity is not entirely accurate.

Again, however, this conceptual potential in the CWA to address broader watershed and ecosystem management and protection goals and other aspects of water pollution law reflects considerable unfulfilled promise. Few states have adopted stream flow or other water quantity-based water quality standards, notwithstanding the authority to do so recognized in *PUD No. 1 of Jefferson County*. Most provisions of the CWA remain focused largely on controlling discharges of pollutants from factories, sewage treatment plants, and other sources.

Nevertheless, several of the CWA's provisions focus specifically on watershed protection, and others have been implemented in ways that serve those purposes. The most prominent example is Section 404 of the Act,[17] which authorizes permits from the U.S. Army Corps of Engineers (Army Corps), or from states with delegated authority,

---

13 *See* 33 U.S.C. § 1331(a).

14 *Id.* § 1251(a).

15 *Id.* § 1362(19).

16 PUD No. 1 of Jefferson County v. Wash. Dept. of Ecology, 511 U.S. 700 (1994).

17 33 U.S.C. § 1344.

for any discharge of "dredge and fill material" into the waters of the United States. Section 402,[18] by contrast, authorizes National Discharge Elimination System (NPDES) permits from either the U.S. Environmental Protection Agency (EPA) or a delegated state for discharges of all other kinds of pollutants into the nation's waters. This dual permitting system, which has caused some degree of legal uncertainty about which discharges fit into which category,[19] resulted in part from Army Corps' historic authority to protect waters from pollution and other impairments that might adversely affect navigability (and thereby national defense and other important functions of shipping channels) under the Rivers and Harbors Act of 1899,[20] and in part from a disagreement between the Senate and the House of Representatives when they enacted the 1972 CWA about whether water pollution permitting authority should remain with the Army Corps (as favored by the House Committee) or move to the relatively new EPA (as proposed by the Senate).

A large percentage of discharges of dredged and fill material are to fill wetlands and other aquatic areas to support development. As a result, after the courts first held that at least some wetlands are part of the "waters of the United States" and therefore subject to the CWA's permitting requirements,[21] the Section 404 permitting program evolved in part into a wetlands protection program (among other functions of the program). For example, the Army Corps is required to deny Section 404 permits if there are "practicable alternatives" that will be less damaging to aquatic ecosystems and not result in other significant environmental effects,[22] and the EPA has the authority to veto permits if they have "an unacceptable adverse effect on municipal water supplies, shellfish beds and fishery areas (including spawning and breeding areas), wildlife, or recreational areas."[23] The wetland protection aspect of the Section 404 permit program is extremely complex and is reviewed more

---

[18] *Id.* § 1342.

[19] *See* Coeur Alaska, Inc. v. Southeast Alaska Conservation Council, 557 U.S. 261 (2009) (deciding whether discharges of a mine waste slurry that would fill a lake required an NPDES or Section 404 permit under the CWA).

[20] 33 U.S.C. §§ 401–466n; U.S. v. Republic Steel Corp., 362 U.S. 482 (1960) (upholding the applicability of the Rivers and Harbors Act to discharges of industrial waste).

[21] NRDC v. Callaway, 392 F. Supp. 685 (D.D.C. 1975). The U.S. Supreme Court later confirmed this result in United States v. Riverside Bayview Homes, 474 U.S. 121 (1986). As discussed in Chapter 11, however, the exact geographic scope of this authority has been narrowed and remains hotly disputed.

[22] 40 C.F.R. § 230.10(a).

[23] 33 U.S.C. § 1344(c); *see* James City County, Va. v. E.P.A., 12 F.3d 1330 (4th Cir. 1993) (upholding EPA veto of Army Corps permit pursuant to section 404(c) of the CWA).

extensively in other sources,[24] but it illustrates the potential to use a statute whose operative provisions focus primarily on discharges of pollutants to serve broader watershed management and ecosystem protection goals.

Other provisions of the CWA similarly focus on—or have the potential to focus more comprehensively on—watershed and ecosystem goals. For example, Section 403 of the CWA[25] established ocean discharge criteria that aspire to similar kinds of ecosystem protection for coastal waters as Section 404 does for coastal and inland wetlands. More broadly, in addition to chemical-specific water quality criteria that assess aquatic ecosystem health solely by reference to individual parameters, biological water quality criteria (or "biocriteria") adopted by states pursuant to Section 303(c) of the CWA[26] define aquatic ecosystem integrity by virtue of a much more holistic assessment of species richness and diversity relative to unimpaired reference ecosystems.[27]

Some CWA programs and provisions are also designed specifically to integrate various components of water pollution control and other aspects of aquatic ecosystem restoration and protection within watersheds. Some provisions orchestrate or fund programs designed to implement comprehensive, water body-specific aquatic ecosystem restoration and management programs of the kind discussed later in this chapter.[28] Others are generic planning provisions that seek to address multiple pollution sources within a watershed,[29] or that provide for comprehensive planning programs that encourage or require water pollution control agencies and officials to address water pollution in a more integrated way.[30]

Despite these integrative CWA provisions, however, the statute and its implementation by EPA, states, and Tribes remains focused rather than comprehensive. Despite the CWA's potential breadth,

---

[24] *See, e.g.*, ROYAL C. GARDNER, LAWYERS, SWAMPS, AND MONEY: U.S. WETLAND LAW, POLICY, AND POLITICS (2011).

[25] 33 U.S.C. § 1343.

[26] 33 U.S.C. § 1313(c).

[27] *See generally* WAYNE S. DAVIS & THOMAS P. SIMON, EDS. BIOLOGICAL ASSESSMENT AND CRITERIA: TOOLS FOR WATER RESOURCE PLANNING AND DECISIONMAKING (1995); Robert W. Adler, *The Two Lost Books in the Water Quality Trilogy: The Elusive Objectives of Physical and Biological Integrity*, 33 ENVTL. L. 30, 70–75 (2003).

[28] *See* 33 U.S.C. §§ 1267 (Chesapeake Bay), 1268 (Great Lakes), 1269 (Long Island Sound), 1270 (Lake Champlain), 1330 (National Estuary Program).

[29] *See id.* § 1313(d) (requiring states to calculate "total maximum daily loads" (TMDLs) of pollutants in waters that violate water quality standards, and to develop control strategies from aggregate sources such that the standards are met).

[30] *See, e.g., id.* §§ 1288 (calling for area wide waste treatment management plans), 1329 (calling for statewide nonpoint source pollution control plans with a watershed focus).

implementation and most of its provisions are directed largely at water quality rather than quantity and apply mainly to surface water rather than groundwater. Moreover, despite best intentions, many of the CWA's comprehensive planning provisions have a checkered history of implementation and effectiveness. The following section describes other efforts to address multiple aspects of water resources management and watershed restoration and protection in a more integrated way.

C. Institutional Mechanisms to Promote Comprehensive Watershed Management

Even given the cross-cutting sources of law described above and others like them, discrete laws and legal regimes are not sufficient to address the wide range of conflicts and contradictions inherent in application of so many different legal principles, by so many managers and affecting so many stakeholders, within watersheds and aquatic ecosystems. Various institutional mechanisms have been designed and implemented in different regions in efforts to better plan and coordinate comprehensive water systems management. Although the kinds of processes described below overlap to a significant degree, and individual programs may have components of each mixed together, the following discussion lays out some of the basic concepts and provides one major example of each.

1. Comprehensive Watershed Programs

There are literally thousands of watershed-based management, restoration and protection programs around the country. Those programs have many components in common, but equally often they vary depending on physical, biological, economic, political and sociological factors. In some cases, watershed institutions vary based simply on history: when, where, why, and by whom they were designed and how they evolved over time. They also vary in size, from small urban stream systems to major interstate or international river basins, and in focus, from a single focused objective (such as restoring a particular lost, threatened or endangered species) to comprehensive water resources management and protection. Although a huge amount has been written about the breadth and diversity of those efforts,[31] and it is impossible to address them comprehensively here, the basic concepts can be summarized briefly.

Regardless of program size and focus, one common component of watershed programs—shared with the analogous international concept of Integrated Water Resource Management—is integration of multiple factors rather than more discrete decisions about

---

[31] *See supra* note 2.

individual legal or other issues and disputes. Such programs ensure that all of the legal, scientific, political or governance, and other factors that affect particular water resource decisions are considered in tandem rather than in isolation. They adopt a process in which all affected stakeholders have a robust opportunity for input, although the exact roles of different stakeholders vary depending on program design and philosophy, or, in some cases, on the legal parameters established for the program by legislative or other sources.

Increasingly, watershed programs also incorporate iterative approaches or to guide their efforts. As one of us has suggested, an evolving model of comprehensive watershed programs includes the following components:

1) Comprehensive watershed-wide resource inventories and evaluations form the basis for program design. Before making final decisions or committing resources, program implementers catalogue and evaluate the status of the resource, its potential health, existing sources of impairment, and potential solutions. Scientific tools such as GIS, biocriteria, and satellite imagery are useful in this process, and are most cost-effective at larger watershed scales. Smaller-scale inventories and assessments require more localized, on-the-ground techniques.

2) Planners establish specific goals and objectives using numeric or other objective performance standards where possible. The standards can change over time, but specificity is critical to ensure program accountability and appropriate revisions. Goals and objectives should focus on environmental rather than bureaucratic terms. For example, performance ratings should value biological conditions and environmental results rather than the number of BMPs [best management practices] installed or the number of permits issued.

3) Careful targeting should help select solutions and allocate resources. In a perfect world with unlimited resources, program planners could implement all viable solutions. In the real world, and one of increasingly scarce public means, this is not possible. For example, after setting goals for habitat restoration, planners can then order projects based on potential watershed benefits, cost, likelihood of success, and other factors, to implement the best projects first. As

the highest priority projects end, others can then follow until the program meets its goals. . . .

4) Participants make decisions collectively and wherever possible by consensus, but ultimate program goals and objectives remain paramount. Binding, enforceable commitments to implementation are essential. All affected interest groups should retain full involvement, using consensus decision methods wherever possible and Alternative Dispute Resolution methods when necessary. Ultimately, however, accountability to national, regional, and local goals requires the existence of some process to resolve impasses and to mandate decisions and implementation when necessary.

5) The process must be iterative rather than static. Watershed programs must be dynamic to account for changing environmental and artificial factors, including shifting goals and values, and to modify programs as needed. This process requires ongoing evaluation of program implementation and results, so that implementers can modify or retain programs and strategies when necessary.[32]

Pursuing these goals often requires changes in governance structures, particularly in light of the ongoing alterations to many systems that climate change is driving. Increasingly, researchers are recognizing that both the ecological and economic goals for the system may have to be able to evolve,[33] and governance structures may have to do so as well. This new vision of watershed governance is often referred to as Adaptive Water Governance. It seeks to promote the ecological resilience of key features of the watershed or, when necessary, to guide the transformation of the water system into a new but productive configuration.[34]

---

[32] Adler, *supra* note 2, at 1105–1106. For a more current summery of "best practices" in watershed programs, *see* U.S. ENVIRONMENTAL PROTECTION AGENCY, IDENTIFYING AND PROTECTING HEALTHY WATERSHEDS, CONCEPTS, ASSESSMENTS AND MANAGEMENT APPROACHES (Feb. 2012), *available at* https://www.epa.gov/sites/production/files/2015-10/documents/hwi-watersheds-complete.pdf.

[33] *See generally, e.g.*, Robin Kundis Craig, *The Clean Water Act, Climate Change, and Energy Production: A Call for Principled Flexibility Regarding "Existing Uses,"* 4:2 GEO. WASH. J. ENERGY & ENVTL. L. 27 (Summer 2013) (discussing the need to revise the Clean Water Act's "existing use" protections in light of climate change impacts on waterways).

[34] For a collection of articles addressing Adaptive Water Governance and resilience in six river basins across the United States, see Volume 51:1 of the *Idaho Law Review*, *available at* http://www.uidaho.edu/law/law-review/articles/volume-51.

The Chesapeake Bay Program[35] is a good example of the more traditional kind of comprehensive, collaborative watershed program on a very large scale.[36] To give some sense of the complexity and magnitude of the effort, the Chesapeake Bay is the largest estuary in the United States, encompassing a watershed of some 64,000 square miles that covers portions of six states plus the District of Columbia, with a population of more than 17 million people (and growing by more than a million every decade). More than 100,000 rivers, streams, and creeks drain into the Bay, all of which carry pollution from cities, industries, and large amounts of agricultural land. This contamination has resulted in significant pollution of the Bay and its tributaries, as well as habitat loss and impairment and declining fisheries and other resources. Efforts to control that pollution and to restore the Bay affect a large number of diverse stakeholders in a complex, multi-jurisdictional setting. Pollution control efforts are complicated by the fact that much of the pollution comes from upstream states such as Pennsylvania that have extensive agricultural areas that generate significant amounts of nutrient runoff (especially phosphorus and nitrogen), while much of the economic harm from Bay pollution is in downstream states such as Maryland and Virginia. Until 2010, however, each state largely controlled its own water pollution goals, with the authority to establish instate water quality standards subject to oversight from the EPA.[37] This division of authority resulted in a problem of interstate externalities—i.e., the upstream polluting state has less incentive to impose pollution control costs on its population when the resulting harms are external to the state.

To address this problem, the Chesapeake Bay States, with funding and legislative authority from Congress and cooperation from EPA,[38] have established a complex but comprehensive and collaborative program to restore and maintain the health of the Chesapeake Bay ecosystem, overseen by the interstate Chesapeake Bay Commission. The two Bay States most affected by pollution of the estuary (Maryland and Virginia) first established the Commission in 1980, but the program has grown to include all of the states with land in the watershed, plus the District of Columbia. The Commission is supported by a large and complex set of committees and institutions that set goals and strategies for the program, monitor the Bay's health to assess progress, and seek input from all

---

35 *See* Chesapeake Bay Program, *available at* http://www.chesapeakebay.net/.

36 Other efforts of this nature include the Great Lakes Program, *see* https://www.epa.gov/greatlakes, and the Delta Stewardship Council, an effort to restore and protect the San Francisco Bay Delta region, *see* http://deltacouncil.ca.gov/.

37 33 U.S.C. § 1313(c).

38 *Id.* § 1267.

of the relevant stakeholders.[39] Those collaborative efforts resulted in adoption of the 2014 Chesapeake Bay Watershed Agreement, which sets forth a program vision, a set of principles to guide the program, a detailed and specific set of intended program goals and outcomes, and a commitment to develop comprehensive management strategies to achieve those goals.[40]

Despite all of this effort, however, progress toward restoration and protection of the Bay has been slow and inconsistent, although there has been promising improvement according to some ecological measures.[41] In an effort to speed progress, in 2010 EPA adopted a Bay-wide TMDL under the CWA,[42] unprecedented in scope as a comprehensive "pollution diet" covering such a massive watershed, backed up by a series of increasingly detailed Watershed Implementation Plans (WIPs) (last adopted in 2019) to achieve the identified pollution goals within specific portions of the whole watershed. Agricultural groups challenged EPA's authority to adopt such a comprehensive pollution control plan for the Bay states. A federal district court and the U.S. Court of Appeals for the Third Circuit upheld the action,[43] but interest groups on all sides continue to challenge various aspects of TMDL and WIP implementation.[44] Whether this latest effort to implement a comprehensive, watershed-based pollution control plan for the Chesapeake Bay will succeed is yet to be seen, particularly because scientists expect that there will a significant lag time (roughly 20 to 50 years) before the Chesapeake Bay's ecological systems can respond to these pollution controls.

---

[39] For a full program history, *see* Chesapeake Bay Program, *Chesapeake Bay Program History*, available at http://www.chesapeakebay.net/about/how/history.

[40] The Agreement can be found at https://d18lev1ok5leia.cloudfront.net/chesapeakebay/Chesapeake-Bay-Watershed-Agreement-Amended.pdf (as amended in 2022).

[41] *See* Chesapeake Bay Program 2017–18 Bay Barometer, available at https://d18lev1ok5leia.cloudfront.net/chesapeakebay/documents/2017-2018_rack_card.pdf.

[42] U.S. Environmental Protection Agency, Region 3, Chesapeake Bay Program Office, *Chesapeake Bay Total Maximum Daily Load for Nitrogen, Phosphorous and Sediment* (Dec. 29, 2010), *available at* https://www.epa.gov/chesapeake-bay-tmdl.

[43] American Farm Bureau Federation v. EPA, 792 F.3d 281 (3d Cir. 2015), *cert. denied*, 577 U.S. 1138 (2016).

[44] *See, e.g.*, Maryland Small MS4 Coalition v. Maryland Dept. of the Envt., 276 A.3d 573 (Md. Ct. App. 2022) (upholding stormwater general permits against challenge by municipalities); Potomac Riverkeeper, Inv. v. Maryland Dept. of the Envt., 189 A.3d 819 (Md. Ct. Sp. App. 2018) (upholding permits limits designed to implement Chesapeake Bay TMDL allocations); Maryland Dept. of the Envt. v. Anacostia Riverkeeper, 134 A.3d 892 (Md. Ct. App. 2016) (upholding municipal stormwater general permit as sufficient to comply with TMDL and WQS); Natural Resources Defense Council, Inc. v. Environmental Protection Agency, 301 F. Supp. 3d 133 (D.D.C. 2018) (rejecting TMDL based on minimum amount of trash removed from river rather than maximum amount of trash permissibly discharged).

2. Adaptive Management

Although some use the term "adaptive management" somewhat loosely to describe the kind of iterative process discussed above, in a stricter scientific sense it has a more precise meaning. Adaptive management uses a "learning by doing" approach similar to an iterative watershed or other ecosystem management program. It does so, however, through a series of intentionally designed experiments using the ecosystem—in our case aquatic ecosystem of watershed—being managed or restored. Aquatic and other ecosystems are so complex, and affected by so many variables, that it is often difficult to know in advance how a particular management action will affect an ecosystem. To test that response, adaptive managers design a considered experiment in which they take a particular action, develop a hypothesis about the expected response, and monitor the results scientifically to determine the extent to which the hypothesis was correct. If the outcome moves the system toward established program goals, that set of management actions can be continued. If the response pushes the system in the wrong direction or is not as positive as expected, a new experiment can be designed to improve program performance by modifying or replacing restoration or other management strategies.[45]

For example, in the Chesapeake Bay Program discussed above, it became clear that chemical pollution alone was not responsible for the decline in the populations of crab, oyster, and other valuable aquatic species. Another likely cause was declining aquatic habitat, such as loss of areas with submerged aquatic vegetation (SAV), which absorb nutrient pollution and provide food and shelter for crabs and other aquatic species. An example of an adaptive management experiment might be to hypothesize that crab populations would rebound better in areas that benefit from restored SAV in addition to reduced pollution loads. Then, program managers could implement habitat restoration efforts in some areas but not in others (control areas) and measure the difference in response. If the results verify the hypothesis, then more resource expenditures in SAV habitat restoration would be warranted. A more sophisticated version might be to try multiple habitat restoration methods to determine which produced the greatest benefit relative to the cost and other factors and to use that as a basis for future program design.

A good example of a program that employs adaptive management systematically at a large scale is the Glen Canyon Dam

---

[45] *See* C.S. Holling, *Large-Scale Management Experiments and Learning by Doing*, 71 ECOLOGY 2060 (1990).

Adaptive Management Program (GCDAMP).[46] The GCDAMP is a stakeholder-driven collaborative process designed to help restore the aquatic resources of the Colorado River from Glen Canyon Dam through Marble Canyon and the Grand Canyon and down to Lake Mead. An adaptive management approach is particularly useful in efforts to restore and manage the Colorado River for several reasons.

First, the Colorado River drains a large, complex, and inter-jurisdictional river basin, covering portions of seven U.S. states and two states in Mexico. Water from the river is the lifeblood of much of the arid southwest, including a vast agricultural economy and large metropolitan areas outside the basin itself (including Denver and other Front Range cities in Colorado and large portions of Southern California). The watershed is highly varied in terrain and hydrology, flowing from headwaters high in the Rocky Mountains and Wind River Mountains through erosional desert canyons and into the Sea of Cortez in Mexico. Compared to the Chesapeake Bay, given the Colorado River region's aridity and fierce competition for scarce water resources, water quantity issues predominate over water quality, although the latter is also an issue along with significant problems of habitat loss, impairment, and fragmentation.[47] Among other problems, overuse of the Colorado River and other human-caused sources of ecosystem impairment has resulted in the significant decline in a number of fish species indigenous to the system, several of which have been listed as endangered under the federal Endangered Species Act.

Second, the legal and management regime governing the Colorado River is varied, complex, and the subject of significant ongoing disputes, as Chapters 8 and 9 discussed. Within the United States, allocation of the river is governed by the Colorado River Compact of 1922,[48] the U.S. Supreme Court decision in *Arizona v. California*,[49] and a series of later decrees, another interstate compact among the states in the upper Colorado River Basin,[50] a body of federal statutes and regulations specific to the Colorado River,[51] and

---

[46] *See* U.S. Dept. of the Interior, Bureau of Reclamation, *Glen Canyon Dam Adaptive Management Program*, available at https://www.usbr.gov/uc/progact/amp/index.html.

[47] *See generally,* ROBERT W. ADLER, RESTORING COLORADO RIVER ECOSYSTEMS: A TROUBLED SENSE OF IMMENSITY (2007).

[48] The Compact is codified at multiple locations, *e.g.*, UTAH CODE ANN. § 73–12a–2; COLO. REV. STAT. § 37–61–101; also available at https://www.usbr.gov/lc/region/pao/pdfiles/crcompct.pdf.

[49] 373 U.S. 546 (1963).

[50] *See* Upper Colorado River Basin Compact of 1948, available at https://www.usbr.gov/lc/region/pao/pdfiles/ucbsnact.pdf.

[51] *E.g.*, Boulder Canyon Project Act, Dec. 21, 1928, c. 42, 45 Stat. 1058; the Colorado River Storage Project Act, Act of Apr. 11, 1956, Pub. L. No. 485–203, 70 Stat.

the usual array of federal and states laws and regulations that affect river use and management (NEPA, the Endangered Species Act, the Clean Water Act, etc.).[52] Internationally, the U.S.-Mexico Water Treaty[53] also governs allocation of the river, further complicating management decisions.

Third, and perhaps most significant from the perspective of adaptive management, decisions about use and management of the river and its large and intricate system of dams, diversions, hydroelectric works and other modifications generate significant conflicts among users. Yet the ecosystem's response to particular management choices, such as increasing flow from a dam during a particular season in an effort to restore a particular ecosystem component, may have uncertain effects on other resources. For example, the manner in which the Bureau of Reclamation operates the large dams along the river and their associated hydroelectric facilities affects the temperature, flow rate, and chemical and physical properties of the water that flows downstream. That action, in turn, may either favor or disfavor different species of fish. One flow regime might benefit endangered species of Colorado River fish that evolved in warmer, more turbid conditions and are protected by federal law relative to trout and other recreational game fish that are prized by anglers and have more direct economic benefit. Similarly, downstream flow regimes that help to restore endangered fish might have different consequences for rafters and kayakers who use the Grand Canyon for recreation and a major tourism industry. To some extent, choices among management options reflect value decisions about which resources are most important.[54] Those choices, however, must be guided by valid and evolving scientific information about the effects of particular management choices on different river resources.

To address those difficult choices, Congress established the GCDAMP, in which the Bureau of Reclamation's decisions regarding operation of the Glen Canyon Dam are guided by a stakeholder process and a series of defined "experiments" to assess the impact of different river flow regimes, restoration efforts, and other management choices. Since the program began, the Bureau has

---

105 (codified as amended at 43 U.S.C. §§ 620–620o); Colorado River Basin Project Act, Pub. L. No. 90–537, 82 Stat. 885 (1968) (codified as amended at 43 U.S.C. §§ 1501–1556).

[52] For a full compilation of "the Law of the River," *see* U.S. BUREAU OF RECLAMATION, THE COLORADO RIVER DOCUMENTS 2008 (Sept. 2010) (CD compilation of documents), and for a more complete history, *see* NORRIS HUNDLEY, JR., WATER AND THE WEST, THE COLORADO RIVER COMPACT AND THE POLITICS OF WATER IN THE AMERICAN WEST (2d ed. 2009).

[53] Treaty for the Utilization of the Waters of the Colorado, Tijuana and Rio Grande Rivers, Feb. 13, 1944, U.S.-Mex., Art. 10, 59 Stat. 1219.

[54] *See* John C. Schmidt et al., *Science and Values in River Restoration in the Grand Canyon*, 48 BIOSCIENCE 9:735 (1998).

implemented a series of experimental flow releases coupled with extensive scientific monitoring of how the system responded to those flows in the context of a range of river resources.[55] In October 2016, the Bureau issued the final Environmental Impact Statement exploring options for the future of the program,[56] putting into place a Long-Term Experimental and Management Plan (LTEMP) that will govern adaptive management of Glen Canyon Dam operations for 20 years, until 2036.

Notably, despite longstanding calls for a basin-wide management program similar to what exists in the Chesapeake Bay and the Great Lakes watersheds,[57] the Colorado River is subject to three distinct large adaptive management programs covering different stretches of the river,[58] as well as a separate collaborative program involving the United States and Mexico regarding trans-boundary management choices. As with other watershed programs of this magnitude, long-term success or failure is difficult to measure relative to what conditions would be absent the programs. Moreover, just as the Chesapeake Bay Program prompted litigation despite the effort's intended collaborative approach,[59] the GCDAMP has generated controversy and resulting litigation over legal implementation and program design and effectiveness.[60]

Climate change further justifies—and poses additional challenges for—adaptive management approaches to aquatic ecosystem restoration and protection. The Colorado River Basin states and the Bureau of Reclamation continue to negotiate agreements on how to manage the river in the face of severely declining flows resulting from climate change. In 2019, Congress enacted the Colorado River Drought Contingency Plan Authorization Act,[61] directing implementation of a series of negotiated drought

---

55 *See* U.S. Geological Survey, *Grand Canyon Research and Monitoring Center, Three Experimental High-Flow Releases from Glen Canyon Dam, Arizona—Effects on the Downstream Colorado River Ecosystem* (Fact Sheet 2011-3012) (Feb. 2011).

56 U.S. DEPT. OF THE INTERIOR, BUREAU OF RECLAMATION, GLEN CANYON DAM: LONG TERM EXPERIMENTAL AND MANAGEMENT PLAN ENVIRONMENTAL IMPACT STATEMENT (2016), *available at* https://ltempeis.anl.gov/documents/final-eis/.

57 *See* David Getches, *Colorado River Governance: Sharing Federal Authority as an Incentive to Create a New Institution*, 68 U. COLO. L. REV. 573 (1997).

58 In addition to the GCDAMP for the river segment between Glen Canyon and Hoover Dams, river management is governed by the Upper Colorado River Endangered Fish Recovery Program for the upper river, *see* http://www.coloradoriver recovery.org/, and the Lower Colorado River Multispecies Conservation Program for the lower portions of the river within the United States, *see* http://www.lcrmscp.gov/.

59 *See supra* notes 41–42.

60 *See* Grand Canyon Trust v. U.S. Bureau of Reclamation, 691 F.3d 1008 (9th Cir. 2012) (upholding adaptive management plan against multiple challenges.

61 Pub. L. No. 116–14, 133 Stat. 850.

contingency measures in the Basin.[62] As discussed at the end of Chapter 9, in early 2023 the Lower Basin States entered another agreement to collectively conserve at least 3 million acre-feet of water through 2026. That agreement supports a 7-state and federal plan to manage drought shortages in the Basin through that period, thus avoiding litigation or other means of resolving conflicts related to basin-wide water shortages. One of us has argued, however, that the basic Compact regime lacks sufficient attention to environmental needs and fails to include all affected interest groups in negotiations, and therefore that the Compact itself should be amended to require sufficient attention to environmental protection and restoration.[63]

3. An International Perspective: Integrated Water Resources Management

The Global Water Partnership (GWP)[64] is an international collaboration based in Stockholm but involving partners in 85 nations, which is designed to foster Integrated Water Resources Management (IWRM), a concept that overlaps the watershed management ideas implemented in the United States. GWP defines IWRM as "a process [that] promotes the coordinated development and management of water, land and related resources in order to [maximize] the resultant economic and social welfare in an equitable manner without compromising the sustainability of vital ecosystems."[65] Like watershed management in the United States, it shuns disaggregated or fragmented decisionmaking in favor of a coordinated, collaborative approach, but it is driven substantively by concepts of sustainable development.[66]

In the United States, some organizations have endorsed the concept of IRWM as a guiding set of principles. For example, the American Water Resources Association (AWRA) has endorsed IWRM, but defined slightly differently as "the coordinated planning, development, protection, and management of water, land, and related resources in a manner that fosters sustainable economic activity, improves or sustains environmental quality, ensures public health and safety, and provides for the sustainability of communities

---

[62] *See* Agreement Concerning Colorado River Drought Contingency Management and Operations (2019), available at https://www.usbr.gov/dcp/docs/final/Companion-Agreement-Final.pdf.

[63] *See* Robert W. Adler, *Toward Environmental Amendments to the Colorado River Compact, in* Cornerstone at the Confluence, Navigating the Colorado River Compact's Next Century (Jason Anthony Robison, ed. 2022).

[64] *See* Global Water Partnership, *Toward a Water Secure World*, at http://www.gwp.org/.

[65] *See* Global Water Partnership, *What is IWRM?*, at http://www.gwp.org/en/ToolBox/ABOUT/IWRM-Plans/.

[66] *See* The Dublin Statement on Water and Sustainable Development, available at: http://www.wmo.ch/pages/prog/hwrp/documents/english/icwedece.html.

and ecosystems."[67] The U.S. Army Corps of Engineers has similarly endorsed IWRM in principle.[68]

Nevertheless, IWRM *per* se has not taken root in the United States in the same way it has in other countries, and the United States is not one of the nations that has formed a partner program with the GWP. The lack of adoption *might* be explained by the fact that the United States has a large set of watershed-based institutions that have evolved around the country for decades that at least appear to be pursuing similar goals as IWRM. Thus, the distinction may be largely semantic, but that hypothesis warrants further analysis. The lack of *national* adoption might further be explained by the federal government's traditional deference to states in many aspects of water management, as Chapters 3, 8, and 11 have explored.

Nevertheless, the United States might benefit from national leadership in IWRM. As one commentator has noted, despite the fact that, unlike some other nations, the United States has a "wealth of collaborative watershed management efforts that reflect a high degree of technical cooperation," "there is a desperate need for national leadership and guidance from the political and legal/ institutional pillars to ensure the long-term sustainability of these efforts."[69]

---

[67] *See* AMERICAN WATER RESOURCES ASSN., INTEGRATED WATER RESOURCES MANAGEMENT IN THE UNITED STATES (adopted January 21, 2011), *available at* http://aquadoc.typepad.com/files/2011_iwrm_position_statement_final.pdf.

[68] *See* U.S. ARMY CORPS OF ENGINEERS, NATIONAL REPORT: RESPONDING TO NATIONAL WATER RESOURCES CHALLENGES, BUILDING STRONG COLLABORATIVE RELATIONSHIPS FOR A SUSTAINABLE WATER RESOURCES FUTURE (2010), *available at* https://www.mvp.usace.army.mil/Portals/57/docs/Civil%20Works/nationalreport_final.pdf.

[69] Jefferey A. Ballweber, *A Comparison of IWRM Frameworks: The United States and South Africa*, 135 J. CONTEMP. WATER RESEARCH AND EDUCATION 74 (2006).

Chapter 14

PUBLIC INTERESTS, PRIVATE RIGHTS IN WATER, AND CONSTITUTIONAL TAKING CLAIMS

Throughout this book, you have seen moments when private water rights, water use, or water management conflict with public needs or desires or ecological requirements for the same water. This chapter examines the private water right holder's classic legal response—to sue for an unconstitutional taking of private property.

This chapter begins with an overview of the U.S. Supreme Court's taking jurisprudence under the U.S. Constitution. It will then examine in detail the two critical issues for taking litigation in the water rights context. First, courts should determine exactly what the nature of the property right in water actually is in order to evaluate whether the government took that private property right. Second, given the character of the government action, courts must determine whether there was: (a) a ***physical taking*** of the water right, which automatically requires the government to compensate the water rights holder; (b) a ***regulatory taking*** of the water right, in which case courts will balance public interests and private rights to determine whether compensation is owed; or (c) ***no taking*** at all, either because the water right holder did not have the right claimed or because government regulation did not amount to a taking.

A. Overview of Taking Law

1. Taking Under the U.S. Constitution

The Fifth and Fourteenth Amendments to the U.S. Constitution prohibit the taking of private property for public use without compensation by, respectively, the federal and state or local governments. The Fifth Amendment states that "[n]o person shall be . . . deprived of life, liberty, or property, without due process of law; nor shall private property be taken for public use, without just compensation."[1] Similarly, the Fourteenth Amendment states that "[n]o State shall . . . deprive any person of life, liberty, or property, without due process of law. . . ."[2] The U.S. Supreme Court has confirmed numerous times that the Fifth Amendment's taking prohibition applies to state and local governments through the

1 U.S. CONST., amend. V.

2 U.S. CONST., amend. XIV, § 1.

Fourteenth Amendment's due process clause,[3] a constitutional doctrine known as *incorporation*.

Importantly, the U.S. Constitution does not forbid federal, state, and local governments from taking private property; thus, eminent domain remains constitutionally permissible for all levels of government, including to acquire water rights. Instead, the Constitution prohibits governments from taking private property *without paying a fair price for it* (just compensation) and *without observing fair procedures in doing so* (due process of law). As a result, the fight in water rights taking litigation is rarely over whether the government can do whatever it did.[4] Instead, the legal fights focus on whether the government owes compensation to the water rights holder and, if so, how much.

The U.S. Supreme Court recognizes three categories of taking. First, the government can physically take private property by taking title, by actually occupying that property, or by forcing the private landowner to endure some physical invasion by the government or by the general public. In a classic physical taking, for example, a government condemns private land for a public road or a government building. According to the U.S. Supreme Court, "When the government physically takes possession of an interest in property for some public purpose, it has a categorical duty to compensate the former owner, regardless of whether the interest that is taken constitutes an entire parcel or merely a part thereof."[5] Thus, classifying a water rights taking as a ***physical taking*** can make the private property owner's case for compensation against the government much easier.

Until 1922, the prohibition on uncompensated governmental taking of private property was limited to physical taking. In 1922, however, in *Pennsylvania Coal Co. v. Mahon*,[6] the U.S. Supreme Court recognized that a second category of unconstitutional taking exists—specifically, that federal, state, and local *regulation* might also amount to an unconstitutional taking of private property. As Justice Oliver Wendell Holmes articulated in that decision, "while

[3] *See, e.g.*, Dolan v. City of Tigard, 512 U.S. 374, 383–84 (1994); Keystone Bituminous Coal Association v. DeBenedictis, 480 U.S. 470, 481 n.10 (1987).

[4] *But see generally* Kelo v. City of New London, Connecticut, 545 U.S. 469 (2005) (challenging whether the government's use of eminent domain for redevelopment served a "public use," as the Fifth Amendment requires; the U.S. Supreme Court concluded that it did).

[5] Tahoe-Sierra Preservation Council, Inc. v. Tahoe Regional Planning Agency, 535 U.S. 302, 322 (2002) (citing United States v. Pewee Coal Co., 341 U.S. 114, 115 (1951)).

[6] 260 U.S. 393 (1922).

property may be regulated to a certain extent, if regulation goes too far it will be recognized as a taking."[7]

The "too far" language from *Pennsylvania Coal* means that most ***regulatory takings*** are evaluated through a balancing test. Courts now evaluate the need for compensation through the three-factor balancing test that the Supreme Court established in *Penn Central Transportation Co. v. New York City*.[8] Under the *Penn Central* test, courts examine: (1) "[t]he economic impact of the regulation on the claimant," (2) "the extent to which the regulation has interfered with distinct investment-backed expectations," and (3) "the character of the governmental action."[9] Governments tend to win regulatory taking cases evaluated through the *Penn Central* analysis, an acknowledgement that most government regulation is both even-handed (i.e., does not single out particular property owners) and serves important public purposes, like protecting public health and safety.

Finally, in *Lucas v. South Carolina Coastal Council*,[10] the U.S. Supreme Court recognized a small set of ***categorical takings***. In *Lucas*-type taking claims, a government regulation deprives the property owner of *all* economic use of the property.[11] Like physical takings, these categorical regulatory takings automatically require compensation to the private property owner.[12] However, "all" means "*all*." If the landowner retains some use of the property, however small, courts will use the *Penn Central* balancing test instead of the *Lucas* categorical rule. Thus, according to the Supreme Court, *Lucas* created "a narrow exception to the rules governing regulatory takings for the 'extraordinary circumstance' of a permanent deprivation of all beneficial use," and, as a result, *Lucas* categorical takings are "relatively rare."[13]

2. Taking Claims Under State Constitutions

The U.S. Constitution is not the only legal basis for taking claims: State constitutions also usually prohibit taking of private property without compensation. Moreover, in some states, the state constitution might be *more* protective of private property rights than the federal constitution. The Virginia Constitution, for example, prohibits the Virginia General Assembly from enacting "any law whereby private property shall be taken *or damaged* for public uses,

---

[7] *Id.* at 415.

[8] 438 U.S. 104 (1978).

[9] *Id.* at 124.

[10] 505 U.S. 1003 (1992).

[11] *Id.* at 1017, 1019.

[12] *Id.* at 1019, 1029, 1031–32.

[13] Tahoe-Sierra Preservation Council, 535 U.S. at 524 n.19.

without just compensation. . . ."[14] Kentucky, similarly, requires compensation "for property taken, injured or destroyed by" government entities.[15]

Of course, private property owners cannot always rely on state constitutions, even if they are more favorable. For example, although the U.S. Constitution's taking prohibitions apply to state governments, state constitutional taking prohibitions do *not* apply to the federal government. Thus, if a private water rights holder is asserting a taking claim against the U.S. Bureau of Reclamation, the U.S. Army Corps of Engineers, the U.S. Fish & Wildlife Service, or any other federal agency involved in the management of water, the water rights holder does not have a state-law claim.

3. The U.S. Court of Federal Claims and the U.S. Court of Appeals for the Federal Circuit

Taking claims in the federal courts require litigants to sue in the United States Court of Federal Claims instead of the normal federal district courts. Congress created this court in 1855, when it was known as the U.S. Court of Claims. In 1887, Congress enacted the Tucker Act, which gave this court jurisdiction over all claims against the federal government except tort, equitable, and admiralty claims. Under current statutes:

> The United States Court of Federal Claims shall have jurisdiction to render judgment upon any claim against the United States founded either upon the Constitution, or any Act of Congress or any regulation of an executive department, or upon any express or implied contract with the United States, or for liquidated or unliquidated damages in cases not sounding in tort.[16]

Appeals of decisions from the Court of Federal Claims go to the U.S. Court of Appeals for the Federal Circuit, a specialized, non-geographically defined federal court of appeals. Congress created the Federal Circuit in 1982, and it has nationwide jurisdiction to hear appeals in a variety of subject areas, "including international trade, government contracts, patents, trademarks, certain money claims against the United States, federal personnel, veterans' benefits, and public safety officers' benefits claims."[17]

---

[14] VA. CONST., art. I, § 11 (emphasis added); *see also* CA. CONST., art. I, § 19 ("Private property may be taken *or damaged* for a public use and only when just compensation, ascertained by a jury unless waived, has first been paid to, or into court for, the owner." (emphasis added)).

[15] KY. CONST. § 242.

[16] 28 U.S.C. § 1491(a)(1).

[17] United States Court of Appeals for the Federal Circuit, *Court Jurisdiction*, http://www.cafc.uscourts.gov/the-court/court-jurisdiction.

B. Defining the Property Right: What Exactly *Is* a Water Right?

The first step in analyzing a claim of an unconstitutional taking is to define the property right at issue. For cases involving standard real property, this step generally poses little difficulty. Water rights, however, pose several definitional problems. First, almost all states define water rights as a "right to use" or usufructuary right, rather than as a right to particular water molecules. Second, as you learned in Chapters 2, 3, and 4, riparian rights to use surface water differ significantly from water rights created under a prior appropriation scheme, and both types of rights can differ significantly from how a particular state defines a right to use groundwater. Thus, to a far greater degree than is true for land, water rights depend intensely on state law, requiring courts to closely examine state law to define the right.

1. Inherent Limitations on Water Rights

In *Lucas*, the U.S. Supreme Court indicated that if the state or federal government acts within the traditional limitations on private property rights, no unconstitutional taking occurs. Specifically, the Court stated that:

> [O]ur "takings" jurisprudence . . . has traditionally been guided by the understandings of our citizens regarding the content of, and the State's power over, the "bundle of rights" that they acquire when they obtain title to property. It seems to us that the property owner necessarily expects the uses of his property to be restricted, from time to time, by various measures newly enacted by the State in legitimate exercise of its police powers; "[a]s long recognized, some values are enjoyed under an implied limitation and must yield to the police power." *Pennsylvania Coal Co. v. Mahon,* 260 U.S., at 413. And in the case of personal property, by reason of the State's traditionally high degree of control over commercial dealings, he ought to be aware of the possibility that new regulation might even render his property economically worthless (at least if the property's only economically productive use is sale or manufacture for sale).[18]

Thus, even if a regulation destroys all economic value of the private property, the government will not owe compensation if "the nature of the owner's estate shows that the proscribed use interests were not part of his title to begin with."[19] The *Lucas* Court explicitly identified

---

[18] *Lucas,* 505 U.S. at 1027–28.

[19] *Id.* at 1027.

the common-law public nuisance and public necessity doctrines as inherent limitations on real property.[20]

Water rights are subject to many more legal limitations. For example, as we saw in Chapter 6, the federal navigation servitude "trumps" private water rights, including some riparian property rights, for federal actions taken within the geographic scope and the purpose of the servitude. Chapter 6 also noted that the federal navigation servitude thus serves as a defense to constitutional taking claims. Chapter 7 explored how, in some states like California and New Jersey, the state public trust doctrine can limit the exercise of private water rights, raising the possibility of the public trust defense to a taking claims. Prior appropriation states require that the water rights holder put water to a beneficial use and not waste it; common-law riparian states require that the water use be a "reasonable use." As such, water uses that violate any of these principles cannot be constitutionally "taken" because the claimant had no property right in the use to begin with. And, of course, no property owner, including water rights holders, can cause a public or private nuisance.

Thus, if a water right holder is trying to do something outside the scope of the water right, like a wasteful or unreasonable use, or if the water right already allows what the government is doing, like maintaining and improving navigation, there can be no constitutional taking. Given the complexity of water rights and some states' "background principles," defining the exact scope of a state water right under the relevant state's law is a critical first step in any water right taking case.

2. Defining Riparian Rights in Federal Taking Litigation: An Example from Florida

Most taking claims involving water rights focus on governmental actions that directly or incidentally affect the exercise of those rights. In such cases, the court must focus on the legal scope of the water right as created under state law. These problems of definition can arise with respect to both riparian and appropriative rights.

The problem of defining riparian water rights for taking claim purposes arose in *Mildenberger v. United States*,[21] which involved the U.S. Army Corps of Engineers' flood control project in and around Lake Okeechobee, near Orlando, Florida. Congress authorized this Central and South Florida Project ("C & SF Project") in 1948 to aid flood control, conserve water, prevent saltwater intrusion, preserve fish and wildlife, and aid navigation. However, the project also

---

[20] *Id.* at 1029 & 1029 n.16.

[21] 643 F.3d 938 (Fed. Cir. 2011).

degraded the water quality in the St. Lucie River.[22] In November 2006, after two particularly bad years of declining water quality, species' deaths, and algal blooms, 22 riparian landowners along the St. Lucie River and St. Lucie Canal sued the federal government in the Court of Federal Claims, arguing that the Army Corps had taken their riparian rights to enjoy a pollution-free river, including their rights to swim, boat, fish, and use the water for recreation. They sought $50 million in compensation.

The Court of Federal Claims granted the federal government's motion to dismiss, ruling that the riparian landowners' suit was filed outside the six-year statute of limitations applicable to claims for compensation under the Tucker Act.[23] However, that court also held that the landowners' alleged riparian rights of fishing, swimming, boating, and recreation were not compensable rights because, under Florida water law, those rights are held in common with the public. Additionally, the court rejected the riparian landowners' asserted right to observe wildlife as unsupported by any legal authority. Noting that the riparian landowners had not identified any cases applying Florida law to hold that the pollution of a navigable waterway effected a compensable taking of property, the Court of Federal Claims also again found that any right of riparian owners to pollution-free water is not a vested, compensable right because it is held in common with the public. Finally, the court found that the federal navigation servitude insulated the Corps' operation of the C & SF Project and the discharge of water into the St. Lucie River from taking claims.[24]

On appeal, the Federal Circuit affirmed, mainly on the ground that the statute of limitations had run.[25] However, the Federal Circuit also held that the landowners "failed to establish that Florida law recognizes compensable property interests in the riparian rights they allege were injured by the Government."[26] "Florida law recognizes 'several special or exclusive common-law littoral rights: (1) the right to have access to the water; (2) the right to reasonably use the water; (3) the right to accretion and reliction; and (4) the right to the unobstructed view of the water.' "[27] However, while " 'a riparian owner may use the navigable waters and the lands thereunder opposite his land for purposes of navigation and of conducting commerce or business thereon, . . . such right is only

---

22 *Id.* at 941–42 (citations omitted).

23 28 U.S.C. § 1491.

24 *Mildenberger*, 643 F.3d at 943–44.

25 *Id.* at 946.

26 *Id.* at 948.

27 *Id.* (quoting Walton Cty. v. Stop the Beach Renourishment, Inc., 998 So.2d 1102, 1111 (Fla. 2008)).

concurrent with that of other inhabitants of the state, and must be exercised subject to the rights of others.' "[28] According to the Federal Circuit, the landowners' claimed riparian rights all fell into the second category, rights that they shared with the general public, or simply were not recognized under Florida law.[29] As a result, even if the statute of limitations had not run, the federal government would not owe compensation.

3. Defining Prior Appropriation Rights in Federal Taking Litigation: An Example from California

The Court of Federal Claims and the Federal Circuit can also face some interesting issues in defining the scope of water rights created under prior appropriation law. For example, in the case of *Casitas Municipal Water District v. United States*,[30] the Casitas Municipal Water District (CMWD) operated the U.S. Bureau of Reclamation's Ventura River Project by controlling the Robles Diversion Dam, a structure used to divert water from the Ventura River into the Robles-Casitas Canal, a 4.5-mile canal that transports the water to a manmade reservoir known as Lake Casitas, where water is held for delivery to the CMWD's customers. The CMWD had a water right from California's State Water Resources Control Board. In 1997, the National Marine Fisheries Service (NMFS) listed the west coast steelhead trout as an endangered species under the federal Endangered Species Act (see Chapter 12), eventually requiring the CMWD and the Bureau to install fish passage at the dam and to send more water through the dam ("bypass") at certain times of year, reducing the amount of water that the CMWD could divert and sell. The CMWD sued the United States in January 2005, alleging that application of the Endangered Species Act had resulted in a constitutional "taking" of the CMWD's water right.

The Court of Federal Claims initially classified the taking as a regulatory taking and found in favor of the United States, but the Federal Circuit reversed on appeal, concluding that the case involved a physical taking (see below).[31] On remand, the Court of Federal Claims had to define the scope of the CMWD's property right. The CMWD claimed that it had to be compensated for all that water that it could not divert because of the need to comply with the Endangered Species Act. The United States argued that the CMWD could be compensated only for the water that it could not put to actual beneficial use, *after* considering any limitations that California had

---

[28] *Id.* (quoting Ferry Pass Inspectors' & Shippers' Ass'n v. White's River Inspectors' & Shippers' Ass'n, 57 Fla. 399, 48 So. 643, 645 (1909)).

[29] *Id.* at 948–49.

[30] 102 Fed. Cl. 443 (Fed. Cl. 2011).

[31] *Id.* at 450–51.

the right to impose on the water right to protect fish and wildlife, such as through California's public trust doctrine (see Chapter 7). In effect, the United States was arguing that the CMWD's water right was already inherently limited by requirements that its use of water "must not violate California's public trust doctrine, its reasonable use doctrine, or that portion of the California Fish and Game Code—Section 5937—that requires dam owners to operate their projects in such a way as to keep downstream fish in good condition."[32]

The Court of Federal Claims found for each party on one issue. First, it agreed with the United States that a water right in California is limited to the beneficial use of that water.[33] However, the court agreed with the CMWD that the government had not proven that inherent limitations to protect fish and wildlife would have reduced the amount of water that Casitas could use. It noted that harm to fish is not a *per se* violation of state law; instead, under the public trust and reasonable use doctrines, "[t]he fundamental premise . . . is that water is a tremendously valuable resource in California and that it is the continuing duty of the state to ensure that the water is best used to meet the needs of the state and of the people as a whole."[34] The United States had not shown that conserving the steelhead trout met California's public interest balancing.[35] As for the California Fish & Game Code, the United States:

> assumes that the operating criteria set forth in the biological opinion impose the same limitations on Casitas as does Section 5937. But Section 5937 provides no quantifiable standard that would allow this court to determine whether requirements of the biological opinion and Section 5937 are one and the same. Section 5937 does not define "good condition," nor does it indicate how far below the dam fish must be kept in good condition. Given such a lack of specificity, we have no way to assess whether the requirements set forth in the biological opinion are indeed requirements to which Casitas was already subject under either Section 5937 or its streambed alteration agreement. We thus conclude that this defense too must fail.[36]

---

[32] *Id.* at 451.

[33] *Id.* at 453–55.

[34] *Id.* at 459.

[35] *Id.* at 461 (citations omitted).

[36] *Id.* at 462.

Nevertheless, the federal government's victory regarding beneficial use proved critical because Casitas could not prove that it had (yet) lost any beneficial use of the water:

> While the government has interfered with plaintiff's ability to divert water—and has done so since the opening of the fish passage facility necessitated by the steelheads' ESA listing—it remains to be seen whether the government's actions will subsequently interfere with Casitas's beneficial use of its water. Absent such a present, compensable injury, Casitas's takings claim is simply not ripe.[37]

As a result, the court dismissed the case and the Federal Circuit affirmed,[38] making *Casitas* is thus one of the very few cases where a physical taking classification did not result in compensation.

4. Is State Certification a Better Procedure for Defining State Water Rights in Federal Courts?

Notably, the federal courts in *Mildenberger* and *Casitas Municipal Water District* found themselves in the unenviable position of trying to determine, respectively, Florida and California water law and property rights on their own, from published cases and statutes. However, there is a good argument that both these courts got state law wrong. For *Mildenberger*, the riparian property right to water of a certain quality has a solid foundation in the common law of many eastern states, as Chapter 11 discussed. Indeed, in Florida, a series of cases supported the plaintiffs' claims to a riparian property right to water of a certain quality—although it is true, as the Federal Circuit emphasized, that these cases were not taking cases *per se* but rather litigation among riparians.[39] North Carolina also appears ripe to recognize a compensable riparian property right to water of a certain quality,[40] and several other states have cases indicating that

---

[37] *Id.* at 472.

[38] Casitas Mun. Water Dist. v. U.S., 708 F. 3d 1340, 1358–60 (Fed. Cir. 2013).

[39] *See, e.g.*, Harrell v. Hess Oil & Chem. Corp., 287 So.2d 291, 295 (Fla. 1973) (holding that pollution of waterways can injure landowners' riparian rights, giving rise to a private cause of action distinct from the public management aspects of those waterways); Deltona Corp. v. Adamczyk, 492 So.2d 463, 463–64 (Fla. Dist. Ct. App. 1986) (affirming both damages and an injunction when the defendant's actions in pumping water from Evans Lake were "interfering with the natural quantity and quality of water in Evans Lake to any extent or degree that causes damage to appellee's lands or otherwise injures appellee." (emphasis added)); N. Dade Water Co. v. Adken Land Co., 130 So. 2d 894, 897–99 (Fla. Dist. Ct. App. 1961) (enjoining a sewage treatment plant's operation when it polluted non-navigable lakes).

[40] *See* L & S Water Power, Inc. v. Piedmont Triad Reg'l Water Auth., 712 S.E.2d 146, 150 (N.C. Ct. App. 2011) (holding that a diversion of water by a municipal water authority unconstitutionally took a downstream hydroelectric dam's riparian rights because "[u]nder North Carolina's "reasonable use" rule, a riparian owner is entitled to the natural flow of a stream running through or along his land, undiminished and

riparian property rights include rights to water of a certain quality.[41] Thus, the Court of Federal Claims and the Federal Circuit were probably a bit too dismissive of the landowners' characterization of their riparian rights in *Mildenberger*.

As for the *Casitas* case, it is possible that the California courts would have also evaluated the claim as a physical taking claim.[42] How the California courts would have handled the public trust doctrine issue, however, is a far more open question. Specifically, the different California Courts of Appeals appear to differ in their

---

unimpaired in quality, except as may be caused by the reasonable use of water by other riparian owners" (emphasis added; citation omitted); Coastal Plains Utils., Inc. v. New Hanover Cnty., 601 S.E.2d 915, 927 (N.C. Ct. App. 2004) (emphasizing that " '[A] riparian proprietor is entitled to the natural flow of a stream running through or along his land in its accustomed channel, undiminished in quantity and unimpaired in quality, except as may be occasioned by the reasonable use of the water by other like proprietors.' " (quoting Smith v. Town of Morganton, 187 N.C. 801, 803, 123 S.E. 88, 89 (1924) (emphasis added)). However, North Carolina's reasonable use doctrine also allows for "diminution in the quantity and quality of a watercourse that is consistent with the beneficial use of the land." Biddix v. Henredon Furniture Indus., Inc., 331 S.E.2d 717, 721 (N.C. Ct. App. 1985). Thus, a showing of unreasonable use would probably still be necessary before a taking claim could succeed.

[41] *See, e.g.*, Collens v. New Canaan Water Co., 234 A.2d 825, 831 (Conn. 1967); Montelious v. Elsea, 161 N.E.2d 675, 678 (Ohio Ct. Com. Pl. 1959); Harrell v. City of Conway, 271 S.W.2d 924, 926 (Ark. 1954); Jessup & Moore Paper Co. v. Zeitler, 24 A.2d 788, 790 (Md. 1942); Hite v. Town of Luray, 8 S.E.2d 369, 371–72 (Va. 1940); Fackler v. Cincinnati N.O. & T.P. Co., 17 S.W.2d 194, 195 (Ky. Ct. App. 1929); Smith v. Town of Morganton, 123 S.E. 88, 89 (N.C. 1924); Johns v. City of Platteville, 157 N.W. 761, 761 (Wis. 1916) (quoting Winchell v. City of Waukesha, 85 N.W. 668, 670 (Wis. 1901)); Mills Power Co. v. Mohawk Hydro-Electric Co., 140 N.Y.S. 655, 656 (N.Y. App. Div. 1913).

[42] For example, the California Court of Appeals, Fourth District, has noted:

> In the context of water rights, our highest court has found a physical taking where the government diverted water for its own consumptive use or decreased the amount of water accessible by the owner of the water rights. (Washoe County v. United States (2003) 319 F.3d 1320, 1326, citing Dugan v. Rank (1963) 372 U.S. 609, 614, 625–626, 83 S. Ct. 999, 10 L. Ed.2d 15 [government's upstream impounding of water at a dam constitutes a taking of water rights from downstream owners, analogizing government action to taking of airspace over land]; Int'l Paper Co. v. United States (1931) 282 U.S. 399, 407–408, 51 S. Ct. 176, 75 L. Ed. 410 [taking found where the Secretary of War ordered a private power company to withdraw water from the petitioner's mill to increase power production for government uses].)
>
> County's action with respect to Allegretti in the present case—imposition of a permit condition limiting the total quantity of groundwater available for Allegretti's use—cannot be characterized as or analogized to the kinds of permanent physical occupancies or invasions sufficient to constitute a categorical physical taking. The County did not physically encroach on Allegretti's property or aquifer and did not require or authorize any encroachment (*e.g.* Yee v. City of Escondido, *supra*, 503 U.S. 519, 527, 112 S. Ct. 1522); it did not appropriate, impound or divert any water. The County's permit decision does not effect a *per se* physical taking under any reasonable analysis.

Allegretti & Company v. County of Imperial, 138 Cal. App. 4th 1261, 1273 (4th Dist. 2006). This case thus suggests that California follows federal law regarding what qualifies as a physical taking.

interpretations. For example, while the Third District has emphasized the same "public interest" balancing test that the *Casitas* court relied on,[43] the California Court of Appeals First District has emphasized instead that the public trust doctrine "prevents any party from acquiring a vested right to appropriated water in a manner harmful to the interests protected by the public trust."[44] Given that the California Supreme Court has not further explored the mechanics of how the state public trust doctrine does or can affect water rights, the Court of Federal Claims and the Federal Circuit were acting without much guidance, and it is not clear that the California courts would have reached the same conclusions. In particular, the Court of Federal Claims assumed that it was the *United States'* burden to prove the public interest balancing, an assignment of the burden of proof that is at least debatable.

The main point here is that water rights taking claims in the Court of Federal Claims often force that court to make what is at best an educated guess about the property rights contours of state water rights. Instead, the best authority regarding the scope of state water rights as property rights is the relevant state's supreme court. Under the Federal Rules of Civil Procedure, a party in a federal lawsuit can ask a federal court, or the court can *sua sponte* decide, to certify a question of state law to the relevant state courts. The procedure is doubly discretionary: both the federal court and the state court can deny the request. However, when federal courts certify such questions and state courts answer them, the certification process provides the federal courts which much more certain grounds for assessing state law. Increased use of certification also prevents federal court decisions that are inconsistent with state property rights rulings in state courts.

The Court of Federal Claims and the Federal Circuit have been showing an increasing willingness to use the federal court certification procedure to ask the state courts directly about state water rights law—perhaps a sign that these courts are learning just how complex state water rights can be. For example, in a series of cases involving New Mexico state water rights related to federal grazing permits, the Court of Federal Claims certified the questions of state water law and the scope of state water rights to the New Mexico Supreme Court, then used that state court's answers to

---

[43] State Water Resources Control Board Cases, 136 Cal. App. 4th 674, 778 (3rd Dist. 2006).

[44] Light v. State Water Resources Control Bd., 226 Cal. App. 4th 1463, 1481 (1st Dist. 2014).

conclude that no taking of the state water rights had occurred as a result of the curtailment of cattle grazing on federal lands.[45]

Certification to the state supreme court had a significant effect on the Klamath Basin water rights taking claims. As you may recall from Chapter 12, the listing of several species of fish under the federal Endangered Species Act reduced the water available out of the Klamath River and the Klamath Basin for irrigation, especially in drought years. The Klamath River Basin water users filed their taking lawsuit in the Court of Federal Claims in October 2001, claiming that when the U.S. Bureau of Reclamation stopped delivery of water during the drought of 2001, it unconstitutionally took their contractual water rights without compensation. The Court of Federal Claims issued summary judgment in favor of the federal government, claiming that the plaintiff water users had not lost compensable water rights under Oregon law. On appeal, however, the Federal Circuit certified the property rights questions to the Oregon Supreme Court, which accepted the certification. In March 2010, the Oregon Supreme Court issued its decision, determining that, under Oregon law, it was possible for the private plaintiffs to have acquired an equitable or beneficial property right in the irrigation water, despite the fact that the federal government held the actual state water rights for the Klamath Project.[46] In light of this decision, the Federal Circuit remanded the federal case to the Court of Federal Claims for further analysis of the plaintiffs' property rights under Oregon law.[47] The Court of Federal Claims denied class certification in 2014.

At close to the same time, as noted in Chapter 12, the Oregon courts finished the Klamath Basin general stream adjudication and awarded the Klamath Tribes very large and very senior water rights. Moreover, downstream in California, the Yurok Tribe and Hoopa Valley Tribe also have large instream flow rights that date to "time immemorial." In light of these senior tribal water rights, the Court of Federal Claims concluded in September 2017 that there had been no taking because, on the basis of priority, the farmers and ranchers would not have been entitled to any water in 2001 (despite the fact that the Klamath Tribes' water rights had not been quantified in 2001).[48] The Federal Circuit affirmed in 2019,[49] and the U.S.

---

[45] Walker v. United States, 66 Fed. Cl. 57 (Fed. Cl. 2005); Walker v. United States, 69 Fed. Cl. 222, 232–33 (Fed. Cl. 2005); Walker v. United States, 162 P.3d 882 (N.M. 2007); Walker v. United States, 79 Fed. Cl. 685, 694–95 (Fed. Cl. 2008).

[46] Klamath Irrigation District v. United States, 227 P.3d 1145, 1169 (Or. 2010) (*en banc*).

[47] Klamath Irrigation District v. United States, 635 F.3d 505, 519–20 (Fed. Cir. 2011).

[48] Baley v. United States, 134 Fed. Cl. 619, 670–74 (2017).

[49] Baley v. United States, 942 F.3d 1312, 1336–37 (Fed. Cir. 2019).

Supreme Court denied *certiorari* in 2020.[50] Thus, after 19 years of litigation, the courts declared that there had been no taking on the basis of the most basic property rights limitation in prior appropriation law: first in time, first in right.

C. Physical Versus Regulatory Takings of Water Rights

One of the most difficult issues in water rights constitutional taking litigation is whether the physical taking analysis or the regulatory taking analysis applies. The court's choice has significant consequences for the litigation's outcome. If the court decides that a physical taking analysis applies and that the government has physically interfered with a water right, compensation is automatic. In contrast, if the court decides that a regulatory taking analysis applies, the government will get the benefit of the *Penn Central* balancing test and a court will probably find no compensable taking. This section examines these two analyses in more detail.

1. Physical Takings of Water Rights

In the *Casitas* litigation, the Federal Circuit, as noted, determined that the case involved a physical taking. In reaching that conclusion, the Federal Circuit summarized the prior U.S. Supreme Court case law on physical takings of water rights as follows:

> A trilogy of Supreme Court cases involving water rights provides guidance on the demarcation between regulatory and physical takings analysis with respect to these rights. In *International Paper Co. v. United States*, 282 U.S. 399 (1931), the United States, during World War I, issued a requisition order for all of the hydroelectric power of the Niagara Falls Power Company (Niagara Power). *Id.* at 405. At the time that the United States' order was issued, Niagara Power leased a portion of its water to International Paper Company (International Paper), which diverted the water via a canal to its mill. *Id.* at 404–05. In response to the United States' direction to "cut off the water being taken" by International Paper to increase power production, Niagara Power terminated the diversion of water to International Paper. *Id.* at 405–06. This termination resulted in International Paper being unable to operate its mill for nearly nine months. *Id.* The United States did not take over the operations of either Niagara Power or International Paper, nor did it physically direct the flow of the water. Instead, the United States caused

---

50 Baley v. United States, ___ U.S. ___, 141 S. Ct. 133 (2020).

Niagara Power to stop International Paper from diverting water to its mill so that the water would instead be available for third party use—"private companies for work deemed more useful [by the government] than the manufacture of paper." *Id.* at 404. This third-party use served a public purpose of supplying power for the war effort. The Supreme Court found that the government directly appropriated water that International Paper had a right to use.

In *United States v. Gerlach Live Stock Co.*, 339 U.S. 725 (1950), the claimants held riparian water rights for irrigation of their grasslands by natural seasonal overflow of the San Joaquin River, *id.* at 729–30. The [Bureau of Reclamation] built Friant Dam, a part of the Central Valley Project, upstream from the claimants' land. *Id.* at 730, 734. The Friant Dam was built to store high stage river flows which then were "diverted . . . through a system of canals and sold to irrigate more than a million acres of land." *Id.* at 729. As a result, "a dry river bed" was left downstream of the dam, and the overflow irrigation of the claimants' lands virtually ceased. *Id.* at 729–30. Thus, the United States caused water to be physically diverted away from the claimants for third party use—delivery under water contracts. The Friant Dam served a public purpose of "mak[ing] water available where it would be of the greatest service." *Id.* at 728. The Supreme Court analyzed the government's action as a physical taking.

Dugan v. Rank, 372 U.S. 609 (1963), similarly involved claims arising out of the United States' physical diversion of water for third party use, by the Friant Dam. In *Dugan*, landowners along the San Joaquin River, owning riparian and other water rights in the river, alleged that the BOR's storage of water upstream behind Friant Dam left insufficient water in the river to supply their water rights. *Id.* at 614, 616. The Supreme Court agreed and analyzed the government's physical appropriation of water as a physical taking.

We agree with both parties that, in each of these cases, the United States physically diverted the water, or caused water to be diverted away from the plaintiffs' property. We also agree that in each of these cases the diverted water was dedicated to government use or third-party use which served a public purpose. Additionally, we agree that the Supreme Court analyzed the government action in each of these cases as a *per se* taking. Finally, we concur with the

> government that our focus should primarily be on the character of the government action when determining whether a physical or regulatory taking has occurred.[51]

The Federal Circuit then concluded that the physical taking analysis was appropriate for evaluating the *Casitas* claims, because:

> When the government forces Casitas to divert water away from the Robles-Casitas Canal to the fish ladder for the public purpose of protecting the West Coast Steelhead trout, this is a governmental use of the water. The fact that the government did not itself divert the water is of no import. The government admits that Casitas was forced by the [Bureau of Reclamation's] adoption of the [Endangered Species Act Biological Opinion] to build the fish ladder and divert the water.[52]

Thus, the Federal Circuit concluded that the federal government had directly and physically interfered with the CMWD's water right because of the forced diversion.

The Federal Circuit's opinion in *Casitas* is one of the two most important contemporary physical taking cases involving water rights. *Tulare Lake Basin Water Storage District v. United States*[53] is the other—and the two decisions are not necessarily completely consistent. *Tulare Lake* involved another clash between the federal Endangered Species Act and state water rights—specifically, between California's Central Valley Project and State Water Project, which deliver water to much of California, and the delta smelt and winter run Chinook salmon, two species of fish listed for protection under the Act. In 1992, to protect the salmon, NMFS imposed restrictions on how much water could be pumped out of the Bay Delta, reducing the amount of water available to the Tulare Lake District, Kern County Water Agency, and their water users. The District and the Agency sued the United States, claiming that the pumping restrictions had deprived the District "of at least 9,770 acre-feet of water in 1992; at least 26,000 acre-feet of water in 1993, and at least 23,050 acre-feet of water in 1994. Kern County Water Agency, by contrast, is alleged to have lost a minimum of 319,420 acre-feet over that same period."[54]

The Court of Federal Claims determined that these were physical taking claims, even though the federal government had not required that the water be physically diverted elsewhere. Unlike the

---

[51] Casitas Municipal Water District v. United States, 543 F.3d 1276, 1289–90 (Fed. Cir. 2008).

[52] *Id.* at 1292–93.

[53] 49 Fed. Cl. 313 (Fed. Cl. 2001).

[54] *Id.* at 316.

Federal Circuit in *Casitas*, the Court of Federal Claims relied on land-based taking cases to conclude that "[c]ase law reveals that the distinction between a physical invasion and a governmental activity that merely impairs the use of that property turns on whether the intrusion is 'so immediate and direct as to subtract from the owner's full enjoyment of the property and to limit his exploitation of it.' "[55] It then characterized the government's action in *Tulare Lake* as a restriction on use—the classic conception of a *regulatory* taking—but concluded that the situation still qualified as a physical taking because of the very nature of a water right:

> In the context of water rights, a mere restriction on use—the hallmark of a regulatory action—completely eviscerates the right itself since plaintiffs' sole entitlement is to the use of the water. Unlike other species of property where use restrictions may limit some, but not all of the incidents of ownership, the denial of a right to the use of water accomplishes a complete extinction of all value. Thus, by limiting plaintiffs' ability to use an amount of water to which they would otherwise be entitled, the government has essentially substituted itself as the beneficiary of the contract rights with regard to that water and totally displaced the contract holder. That complete occupation of property—an exclusive possession of plaintiffs' water-use rights for preservation of the fish—mirrors the invasion present in [land-based invasions]. To the extent, then, that the federal government, by preventing plaintiffs from using the water to which they would otherwise have been entitled, have rendered the usufructuary right to that water valueless, they have thus effected a physical taking.[56]

Together, *Tulare Lake* and *Casitas* suggest that any government action that diminishes the amount of water available to a water right holder should be evaluated as a physical taking, automatically requiring compensation for any diminishment in the amount of water that the right holder could put to beneficial use. However, reasonable minds can (and do) differ on how exactly to describe a physical taking in the water rights context, especially in the difficult cases. It is therefore probably more helpful to think about government interference with water rights as a spectrum. At one end of the spectrum are cases where a government physically diverts water away from private users or physically prevents private users from accessing their water rights, such as when private diversion ditches cross public lands and a federal agency cuts off access to those

---

[55] *Id.* at 319 (quoting United States v. Causby, 328 U.S. 256, 265 (1946)).

[56] *Id.*

ditches. These cases most clearly require a physical taking analysis. At the other end of the spectrum are cases in which a government regulation affects exactly *how* a water rights holder uses the water but in no way reduces the quantity of water that rights holder can use—for example, federal and state requirements that municipal water suppliers treat drinking water to reduce impurities and prevent water-borne disease. Such regulations should be subject to a regulatory taking analysis (and the taking claim would almost certainly fail under *Penn Central*).

Endangered Species Act requirements affecting water rights tend to fall in-between these two extremes. Imposed as a statutory regulation, these requirements often leave the water rights holders some discretion in how to proceed and generally leave most or all of their water rights intact. However, they also tend to demand that the water rights holders leave more water in the aquatic system at key times (such as under drought conditions or during spawning or migration) and therefore sometimes reduce the total amount of water available for physical diversion and use, as was the case in both *Casitas* and *Tulare Lake*. For these borderline situations, case law examining alleged constitutional takings of easements—another kind of right to use—might provide courts with better guidance about how to deal with water rights. These cases, while also complex, generally engage in a more nuanced analysis that is intensely focused on the exact property right at issue and the exact nature of the government action.[57]

2. The Regulatory Taking Analysis and Water Rights

As noted above, federal constitutional regulatory taking claims, and many state constitution-based regulatory taking claims, are evaluated through the *Penn Central* balancing test of three factors: (1) "[t]he economic impact of the regulation on the claimant," (2) "the extent to which the regulation has interfered with distinct investment-backed expectations," and (3) "the character of the governmental action."[58] In *Edwards Aquifer Authority v. Bragg*,[59] the Texas Court of Appeals evaluated regulatory taking claims to groundwater. The case was based on the Texas Constitution, which states that "[n]o person's property shall be taken, damaged or destroyed or applied to public use without adequate compensation being made . . . ."[60] Nevertheless, Texas is one of the states that uses

---

[57] Robin Kundis Craig, *Defining Riparian Rights as "Property" through Takings Litigation: Is There A Property Right to Environmental Quality?*, 42 ENVTL L. 115, 122–25 (Winter 2012).

[58] *Id.* at 124.

[59] 421 S.W.3d 118 (Tex. App. (San Antonio) 2013).

[60] TEX. CONST. art. I, § 17.

the *Penn Central* analysis even for regulatory taking claims under its state constitution.

Bragg involved the Edwards Aquifer Authority's regulation of groundwater use from the Edwards Aquifer. In 1994, Texas enacted legislation to regulate use of the Edwards Aquifer in response to Endangered Species Act litigation, attempting to protect several federally listed species that depend on flows from the aquifer into springs near San Antonio. The legislation caps the total amount of groundwater that can be withdrawn from the aquifer and then assigns individual withdrawal permits on the basis of the permittee's historic use of the aquifer.

The Braggs owned two properties that are located over the Edwards Aquifer. They purchased the sixty-acre Home Place Orchard in 1979 for $60,000.00 to use as their home and as a commercial pecan orchard, and in 1980, they drilled a well into the Edwards Aquifer and began using aquifer water for irrigation. The Braggs purchased the forty-two-acre D'Hanis Orchard, another pecan orchard, in 1983 for $210,800.00, which was originally irrigated with water from sources other than the Edwards Aquifer. When this water proved insufficient, however, the Braggs drilled a well into the Edwards Aquifer, but they did not complete this well until 1995, after the Edwards Aquifer legislation and permitting program were enacted. However, lawsuits kept the legislation from going into effect until 1996.

The Braggs applied for Edwards Aquifer permits, seeking 228.85 acre-feet per year for the Home Place Orchard and 193.12 acre-feet per year for the D'Hanis Orchard. However, based on historic use, the Edwards Aquifer Authority awarded the Braggs only 120.2 acre-feet per year for the Home Place Orchard and denied them any water rights for the D'Hanis Orchard. The Braggs sued in November 2006, alleged a constitutional taking of their water rights and seeking $134,918.40 in compensation for the D'Hanis Orchard and $597,575.00 in compensation for the Home Place Orchard.

The Texas Court of Appeals fairly quickly concluded that the regulatory taking analysis applied. In its view, physical taking are a "relatively narrow" category of taking claims that arise only when the government effectuates a physical invasion of the property at issue.[61] As a result, it applied the *Penn Central* regulatory taking analysis.

The Braggs' regulatory taking claims were aided by the Texas Supreme Court's 2012 ruling that landowners overlying aquifers own the groundwater *in the ground*, just like they own oil.[62] This ruling

---

61 *Id.* at 139.

62 Edwards Aquifer Authority v. Day, 369 S.W.3d 814, 831 (Tex.2012).

changed Texas's traditional rule of capture for groundwater, where property rights do not attach until the groundwater is pumped, strengthening the Braggs' claim to property rights in the unpumped groundwater.

In evaluating the first *Penn Central* factor, economic impact on the claimant, courts generally look at the diminution in value to the property as a whole—not just the economic loss from the affected property interest. In *Bragg*, the Edwards Aquifer Authority argued that the regulations actually increased the value of the Braggs' two properties.[63] The Court of Appeals disagreed, however, emphasizing the Braggs' "absolute title" to the water beneath their land and concluding that the relevant use of water at issue "is the Braggs' ability to operate and irrigate a pecan orchard, which the trial court found to be the highest and best use of the properties, for the purpose of producing a sustainable commercial pecan crop in Medina County."[64] Moreover, after the Braggs "could no longer use the water from the Edwards Aquifer well, the cost to lease water for one year in 2007 was $4,200.00; in 2008, water cost $6,000.00; in 2009, water cost $6,000.00, and in 2010, water cost $3,450.00"[65]—an increase in irrigation costs of about 10%. However, the Texas Court of Appeals also emphasized the more extensive impacts on the Braggs' commercial pecan farms:

> To reduce their water consumption, the Braggs reduced the number of trees by thirty to fifty percent and reduced the watering of the remaining trees. This, in turn, resulted in the Braggs' inability to raise a commercially viable crop on their properties, unless they purchased or leased water under the permit scheme. Despite what might amount to only a ten percent increase in their irrigation expense, we do not consider this merely an incidental diminution in value. The result of the regulation forces the Braggs to purchase or lease what they had prior to the regulation-an unrestricted right to the use of the water beneath their land. Thus, we conclude this factor weighs heavily in favor of a finding of a compensable taking of both orchards.[66]

Courts' evaluation of the second *Penn Central* factor, the extent of interference with the property owner's reasonable investment-backed expectations, is supposed to be an objective evaluation based on what a reasonable person would have thought about the property. As the *Bragg* court summarized, "The purpose of the investment-

63 *Bragg*, 421 S.W.3d at 137.

64 *Id.* at 138.

65 *Id.* at 140.

66 *Id.* at 141 (citation omitted).

backed expectation requirement is to assess whether the landowner has taken legitimate risks with the reasonable expectation of being able to use the property, which, in fairness and justice, would entitle him or her to compensation."[67] Moreover, "[t]he existing and permitted uses of the property constitute the 'primary expectation' of the landowner that is affected by the regulation."[68] Timing vis-à-vis the regulatory regime can be important, and:

> When the Braggs purchased the orchards, the water underlying their properties was not regulated by the Act. Although the Braggs had no reasonable investment-backed expectation that there would never be a regulatory scheme in place that might govern their use of the water beneath their land, the lack of such regulations when they purchased both orchards shaped their expectation that they would have unrestricted use of their water to supply the needs of their pecan trees.[69]

As such, the Braggs' investment-backed expectations for both properties—continued and commercially profitable use as pecan orchards—were reasonable, and "we conclude this factor weighs heavily in favor of a finding of a compensable taking of both orchards."[70]

The third *Penn Central* factor, the character of the government's action, is often the fuzziest. However, the purpose of this factor is to evaluate the reasonableness of the government regulation at issue in light of the changes it made to the existing property rights. Hence, retroactive regulation, which changes the legality of or liability for something the plaintiff has already done, is more suspect than prospective regulation, to which the plaintiff can adjust. The importance of the public value being protected is also important; for example, courts tend to give more weight to regulations that demonstrably protect public health than to regulations that improve aesthetic or recreational values. As noted, the Edwards Aquifer Authority characterized the groundwater regulation as a measure that enhances property values by increasing the sustained use of the aquifer. The Texas Court of Appeals in *Bragg* conceded the importance of state regulation of groundwater, quoting the legislation's purposes to conclude that, "[g]iven the importance of 'protect[ing] terrestrial and aquatic life, domestic and municipal water supplies, the operation of existing industries, and the economic

---

67 *Id.* at 142.

68 *Id.* (citation omitted).

69 *Id.* at 143.

70 *Id.* at 144.

development of the state,' . . . this factor weighs heavily against a finding of a compensable taking."[71]

Two *Penn Central* factors thus counted in favor of a taking and one against. The Texas Court of Appeals then took a broader look at the "surrounding circumstances" of the case, emphasizing the importance of dependable irrigation to agriculture in Texas:

> We believe courts may also consider the nature of the plaintiff's business beyond the financial considerations analyzed under the economic impact factor. In this case, the Braggs' business is agricultural and therefore heavily dependent on water. The particular crop cultivated by the Braggs, pecans, needs water year-round. The Braggs' source of water is either sub-surface or rain. Rain, at least in drought-ridden Texas, is inconsistent and unpredictable. This is especially so in semi-arid Medina County, Texas. Mr. Bragg's testimony established that a lack of sufficient water not only effects the yield of the current crop but also the quality and size of the pecans in a future crop. No expert disputed that rain alone could not provide a sufficient source of water. Therefore, we conclude the Act's restrictions on the amount of water the Braggs could draw from their own wells weighs in favor of a compensable taking.[72]

Pursuant to this conclusion, moreover, the court remanded the case to the trial court for a proper calculation of the compensation owed.[73]

Like all regulatory taking litigation, the *Bragg* case identifies a conflict between public values—the value of the Edwards Aquifer for water supply and for habitat—and private property interests—the Braggs' desires for the groundwater to irrigate their real property. This conflict came to a head because a legislature acted to protect public values—namely, the Texas Legislature enacted the Edwards Aquifer Authority Act (EAAA). The EAAA is an example of how water law can evolve because, for the Edwards Aquifer, it replaced the common-law rule of capture with a permit requirement grounded in some form of correlative rights. Groundwater management through groundwater management districts had already existed in Texas before the state legislature enacted the EAAA, but the EAAA was unique in imposing a statutory cap on water withdrawals. As we have seen throughout this book, evolving water law—and especially new rules—are often the occasions for sparking taking litigation. Generally, however, the public values and purposes that the change

---

[71] *Id.* at 145.

[72] *Id.* at 146.

[73] *Id.* at 152.

promotes prompt courts to find that no taking has occurred. The *Bragg* court thus reached an unusual regulatory taking result.

D. Calculating the Compensation Owed When a Constitutional Taking of a Water Right Has Occurred

Once a court has found, under any of the three analyses, that an unconstitutional taking has occurred, the government owes the property owner compensation. The basic rule for compensation in a taking case is the same as in an eminent domain case: the person whose property has been taken is entitled to the fair market value of the property for its highest and best use (but not counting any increase in value from the government's intended improvements) as of the date of the taking. For real property, this assessment usually involves appraisals based on comparative sales and what uses would have been allowed under the applicable zoning regulations, and "battles of the experts" regarding valuation occur frequently.

Valuing water rights can be even more complicated. A proper evaluation of the value of a water right, for example, should consider how much water the right holder could have used absent the government action. Thus, the existence of drought during the alleged taking should be relevant everywhere, and priority can be important in the West, as the Klamath River taking litigation demonstrated. At the height at the California drought in 2015, for example, water use was curtailed for all water rights with a priority date of or after 1858. Logically, therefore, nothing the government did to reallocate water could have resulted in a constitutional taking of any water right more junior than 1858, because priority and curtailment are inherent limitations on those rights.

The aftermath of the *Tulare Lake* physical taking decision provides a good example of how water right compensation calculations occur. The Court of Federal Claims held its trial regarding compensation in July 2002.[74] In an opinion issued on December 31, 2003, the court concluded that the plaintiffs were entitled to $13,915,364.78 in compensation, plus interest.[75]

The Court of Federal Claims used a three-step process to calculate compensation. First, it "determine[d] the amount of water not available to plaintiffs as a result of ESA restrictions, a concept the experts refer to as 'water impact.' "[76] The water impact calculation, "in turn, depends on three factors: the overall amount of

---

[74] Tulare Lake Basin Water Storage District v. United States, 59 Fed. Cl. 246, 247 (Fed. Cl. 2003).

[75] *Id.*

[76] *Id.* at 250.

pumping foregone, the portion of that loss properly attributable to ESA restrictions, and the method by which that quantity would otherwise have been distributed."[77] After a complex examination of water losses on particular dates and their relationships to the Endangered Species Act requirements, California water quality standard requirements, and contractual delivery discretion, the court concluded that the plaintiffs had suffered regulatory "water losses in the amounts of 114,635 acre-feet for the period April 3–27, 1992 and 120,892 acre-feet for 1994, and [contractual] water losses in the amounts of 34,400 acre-feet for 1993 and 59,967 acre-feet for 1994."[78]

Second, "we must then assess the appropriate method to value that loss."[79] Like any property taken by the government, the water had to be valued at its fair market value at the time of the taking. The court heard both the plaintiffs' and the defendant's experts' arguments regarding how to value the water but was unconvinced by any of them. Instead, for the regulatory losses:

> A much better indication of value, we believe, are the prices set by the Drought Water Bank sales—arm's-length transactions that most closely approximate an open market for water at the precise time when plaintiffs would, as the result of ESA-imposed pumping curtailments, have entered such a market. Indeed, the use of the Drought Water Bank as a replacement market for water was more than theoretical: in the face of the ESA cutbacks, plaintiffs purchased some 110,000 acre-feet of water over the three-year period. Among the replacement options plaintiffs faced, in fact, the Drought Water Bank alone provided a substitute that was available to all plaintiffs.[80]

Using this valuation, the court concluded that the value of the regulatory losses "was $68.38 per acre-foot for 1992 and $66.34 per acre-foot for 1994."[81] However, the contractual water supplies were made available during exceptionally wet years, making the Drought Bank prices inappropriate. Instead, the court based the value of the contractual water on the cost of delivery plus a reasonable profit, or $3.00 an acre-foot.[82] As a result, the regulatory losses in times of drought because of the Endangered Species Act were worth

---

[77] *Id.*

[78] *Id.* at 259–60.

[79] *Id.* at 250.

[80] *Id.* at 263.

[81] *Id.* at 264.

[82] *Id.* at 264–66.

considerably more than the contractual losses—in fact, they made up most of the total award.[83]

"Finally, we must determine the appropriate rate of interest to be applied to plaintiffs' award . . . ."[84] The Court of Federal Claims originally used the federal government's fairly conservative interest rate for Treasury bills—which, notably, still netted the plaintiffs about $10 million in interest.[85] However, in response to the plaintiffs' motion for reconsideration, the Court of Federal Claims acknowledged that "[j]ust compensation . . . requires that the owner of the property be compensated not only for the value of the property on the date of the taking, but also for any delay in payment of that amount."[86] As a result, it applied the "prudent investor rule," under which "the appropriate interest rate is calculated based not on an assessment of how a particular plaintiff would have invested any recovery, but rather on how 'a reasonably prudent person' would have invested the funds to 'produce a reasonable return while maintaining safety of principal.' "[87] Under this rule, moreover, the Treasury bill interest rate was inappropriate,[88] and the plaintiffs' interest award increased to an amount reflecting more normal investment strategies, an amount to be determined in later filings.[89]

E. Conclusion

Casitas, *Tulare Lake*, *Bragg*, and water rights taking litigation in general raise important questions about the governmental and public costs of reallocating water to conservation purposes—water that is fundamentally public to begin with, and for which the original individual water rights holders paid relatively little to acquire the right to use. In this context, it is worth noting that although property owners actually win very few constitutional taking claims, the litigation itself is expensive for governments. Given these public expenses, governments seeking to promote water conservation and public uses of water through changes in water law might be well advised to provide some compensation up front to affected water rights holders, regardless of the constitutional status of the new law.

---

83 *See id.* at 266 (valuing regulatory losses in April 1992 at over $5.6 million and regulatory losses in 1994 at over $8 million).

84 *Id.* at 250.

85 *Id.* at 266.

86 Tulare Lake Basin Water Storage District v. United States, 61 Fed. Cl. 624, 627 (Fed. Cl. 2004).

87 *Id.* (citing and quoting United States v. 429.59 Acres of Land, 612 F.2d 459, 464–65 (9th Cir.1980)).

88 *Id.* at 630.

89 *Id.* at 631.

TABLE OF CASES

INDEX

References are to Pages